Memory Construction
and the Politics of Time in
Neoliberal South Korea

Memory Construction and the Politics of Time in Neoliberal South Korea

Namhee Lee

Duke University Press   *Durham and London*   2022

© 2022 Duke University Press
This work is licensed under a Creative Commons Attribution-
NonCommercial 4.0 International License, available at https://
creativecommons.org/licenses/by-nc-nd/4.0/.
Designed by Courtney Leigh Richardson
Typeset in Portrait and Univers by Westchester Publishing Services

Library of Congress Cataloging-in-Publication Data
Names: Lee, Namhee, author.
Title: Memory construction and the politics of time in neoliberal South Korea / Namhee Lee.
Description: Durham : Duke University Press, 2022. | Includes bibliographical references and index.
Identifiers: LCCN 2022020081 (print)
LCCN 2022020082 (ebook)
ISBN 9781478016342 (hardcover)
ISBN 9781478018988 (paperback)
ISBN 9781478023616 (ebook)
Subjects: LSCH: Social movements—Korea (South)—History. | Democratization—Korea (South)—History. | Political culture—Korea (South)—History. | Korea (South)—Politics and government—1988–2002. | Korea (South)—Politics and government—2002– | Korea (South)—Social conditions—1988– | Korea (South)—History. | BISAC: HISTORY / Asia / Korea Classification: LCC DS 922.4635 L44 2022 (print) | LCC DS 922.4635 (ebook) DDC 951.95—dc23/eng/20220706
LC record available at https://lccn.loc.gov/2022020081
LC ebook record available at https://lccn.loc.gov/2022020082

ISBN 978-1-4780-9279-7 (ebook other)

Cover art: Participants of the commemorative ceremony of Park Chung-hee bowing before his statue, Kumi, North Kyŏngsang Province, November 14, 2016. © Ohmynews. Unauthorized reproduction and redistribution prohibited.

This book is freely available in an open access edition thanks to TOME (Toward an Open Monograph Ecosystem)—a collaboration of the Association of American Universities, the Association of University Presses, and the Association of Research Libraries—and the generous support of Arcadia, a charitable fund of Lisbet Rausing and Peter Baldwin, and the UCLA Library. Learn more at the TOME website, available at https://openmonographs.org.

This work was supported by the Academy of Korean Studies Grant (AKS-2014-R-28).

Contents

Acknowledgments   vii
Notes on Romanization and Translations   xi

Introduction: The Politics of Time and Neoliberal Disavowal   1

1 The Paradigm Shift from Minjung (People) to Simin (Citizen) and Neoliberal Governance   23

2 The Paradigm Shift from the Political to the Cultural and Huildam Literature   45

3 The Park Chung-hee Syndrome, Mass Media, and "Culture War"   71

4 The Rise of New Right Historiography and Its Triumphalist Discourse   95

Epilogue: The Politics of Time and the Poetics of Remembrance   121

Notes   137   *Bibliography*   177   *Index*   207

Acknowledgments

It is now difficult to appreciate the sense of urgency that initially prompted this project, given the long delay in finishing it. At the time, the beckoning of the need to comprehend and to engage in the debates that I discuss in this book overwhelmed all other research projects and writings. Along the way, the task that I set out seemed too daunting, that I was not equipped to engage fully with all the relevant historiographical, theoretical, as well as ethical issues. The book manuscript languished for a number of years. I took it up again only with help of friends and colleagues, and I hope the current shape of the book is still considered worthwhile an endeavor, if only to share what Korean scholars commonly call *munje ŭisik* (awareness of the issues) in place of a comprehensive and in-depth treatment of all the relevant issues that the topic deserves.

I am grateful to colleagues and friends who have invited me over the years to their lecture series, workshops, and conferences, including Im Chi-hyŏn [Jiehyun Lim], Andre Schmid, Clark Sorenson, Hyaeweol Choi, Ruth Barraclough, Robert Oppenheim, Im Chong-myong, Nojin Kwak, Narayanan Ganesan, Sung Chull Kim, John Lie, Kyong-Ae Park, Paula Im, Chin Chae-kyo, Alain Delissen, Valérie Gelézeau, Marie-Orange Rivé-Lasan, Nayoung Aimee Kwon, Ji-Yeon Jo, Theodore Hughes, Jennifer J. Chun, Kim T'aek-hyŏn, Chanhaeng Lee, Youngju Ryu, Nojin Kwak, Jeffrey Guarneri, Charles Kim, Laura Nelson, Yumi Moon, Leighanne Yuh, Jiyoung Song, Sunyoung Park, Youjeong Oh, Jia-Ching Chen, Eli Friedman, Park Myŏng-nim, Yonson Ahn, Yvonne Schulz Zinda, Kang Chŏng-in, Pak T'ae-gyun, Jong Chol An, You Jae Lee, Hwansoo Kim, and Russell Burge.

Sunyoung Park deserves special thanks for organizing the 2015 workshop, "New Perspectives on the Cultural History of 1980s South Korea"; this book is an extension of the discussion that started from the workshop. My friend and colleague Thu-Huong Nguyen-Vo urged me to move on with this project when it lay dormant. Her support and her prodding to do the book manuscript at the Center for the Study of Women (CSW) and our many conversations that helped me to formulate and sharpen my ideas have been crucial to finishing the project. Thanks must also go to Grace Hong at the CSW for organizing the workshop and for her support, Jennifer J. Chun for her sharp, probing questions, and Todd Henry, Marie Kennedy, and Wang Chaohua for their valuable comments and suggestions. The ever-resourceful Sanghun Cho at UCLA's East Asian Library has been indispensable with his always positive and quick response to all of my numerous inquiries and requests, big and small. Jenny Gavacs's probing questions and the demand for clarity helped shape this book into what it is now. Lisa Kim-Davis has been a critical interlocutor and a wise counselor when the going got tough and helped to improve the book considerably. During the final revision process of the manuscript, Sharon L. Allerson helped not only with editing but also with her kind and encouraging words.

Lisa Yoneyama generously provided critical comments and suggestions on the first draft of this book, and two anonymous reviewers provided invaluable suggestions and comments. It is only due to my shortcomings that I was not able to incorporate all of their excellent suggestions.

It has been truly a privilege to work with Ken Wissoker, whose support of this project, astute judgment, and expert stewardship at every stage of the publishing process has been a gratifying and enlightening experience. My thanks also go to Joshua Gutterman Tranen, Kimberly Giambattisto, and John Donohue for their great care and celerity in overseeing the book's production process.

Michael has been a pillar of wisdom and strength through all the travails one goes through in life, and he never ceases to amaze me with his voracious appetite for wonder in life and his many talents, including sewing hats for the Women's March and masks during the pandemic. I am also grateful to have spent several months during the pandemic with Hanyu and Hana at home. My sister Kyunghee has been my friend, confidante, and ally; I thank her for all the years of love and support and for seeing me through the frantic months in the final stage of book making.

My research for this project received generous support of the Korean Studies Grant of the Academy of Korean Studies and UCLA'S Faculty Research Grants Program.

Some of the materials in the following publications have been incorporated into various chapters: "From Minjung to Simin: The Discursive Shift in Korean

Democratic Movements," in *South Korean Social Movements: From Democracy to Civil Society*, ed. Gi-Wook Shin and Paul Y. Chang (New York: Routledge, 2011), 41–57; "Social Memory of the 1980s and Unpacking the Regime of Discontinuity," in *Revisiting Minjung: New Perspectives on the Cultural History of 1980s South Korea*, ed. Sunyoung Park (Ann Arbor: University of Michigan Press, 2019), 17–45.

Notes on Romanization and Translations

This book employs the McCune-Reischauer romanization; exceptions are those Korean authors who have published in English using a different spelling and the names of well-known historical figures and places, such as Syngman Rhee and Seoul. In the case of Korean authors with different spellings in their English publications, the McCune-Reischauer romanization is provided in square brackets at the first occurrence of the name in the main text and in the bibliography. East Asian names are written according to the standard usage in East Asia, with surnames preceding given names. English translations of the titles of cited works are provided in the bibliography.

Unless otherwise noted, all translations in the book are by the author.

Introduction
The Politics of Time and Neoliberal Disavowal

In March 1997, ten years into South Korea's transition to liberal democracy and as the news of Dolly, the world's first cloned sheep, went out globally, the Korea University student publication asked its students who among historical figures they most wished to clone. Six out of 180 respondents selected Park Chung-hee, South Korea's dictator for nearly two decades. In a country where university students waged a tenacious and vociferous protest and brought down an authoritarian regime more than once, that their successors would even consider cloning Park—even as a mischievous way to express their disapproval against sitting president Kim Young-sam, whom they selected as the least desirable figure to clone in the same survey—caught the attention of the mass media. What would have been unthinkable even a year or two before was soon emerging: politicians, public figures, and ordinary Koreans were professing their admiration for the former dictator, which the mass media promptly dubbed the "Park Chung-hee syndrome."[1] Heated debates on Park's legacies followed in newspapers, online forums, and academic conferences.

The syndrome was the first of a series of paradigmatic shifts in the collective memory of recent history in post-1987 South Korea. In 2004, a presidential committee to investigate "pro-Japanese collaborators" of the colonial period (1910–1945) again reignited public debate on the colonial period. There has always existed the view that the country could move forward only by dealing with the issue of collaboration, even if only symbolically by publishing a list of collaborators some sixty years after liberation from Japan. By the beginning of a new century, however, the country's attainment of democracy and global economic standing gave rise to a view that it had overcome any pernicious colonial influences, that it was time to move on, rather than dwell on the painful past.

The latest transformation in historical judgment has been the New Right revisionist scholarship. Emerging in the early twenty-first century, the New Right history, as in the case of the Park Chung-hee syndrome and the debates on the colonial period, centers on the notion that "times have changed." Not only did the previous era's "leftist nationalist" perspective of the *minjung* historiography no longer serve the present moment, but it also got in the way of country's future progress. Offering a positive and celebratory view of Korean history better accommodated the needs of contemporary society. Through these debates, the paradigm of minjung, the central conceptual framework under which the three-decade-long democratization movement was carried out and that also generated one of the most profound social, academic, religious, and artistic movements the country has seen, had been declared anachronistic and consigned to the past.

This book examines what might be called the minjung project's "afterlives," its changing meanings and its representation over the last three decades, and the ways in which the discourse of the end of the minjung paradigm operates to make its emancipatory and egalitarian aspirations illegible or obscure in the present. With the retreat of authoritarianism by the 1990s and the explosion of previously neglected and unvoiced identities and desires, academics, social commentators, and some of the erstwhile minjung practitioners effectively announced the end of the minjung project, that there had been paradigm shifts from minjung (people) to *simin* (citizen), from the political to the cultural, and from the collective to the individual. Minjung had become a grand narrative whose time had passed, its vision of politics as "a practice of conflict and as a horizon of emancipation" considered no longer suitable in the new era.[2] Not only was the minjung project judged as too partisan and no longer appropriate for the democratic society, but, simultaneously, violence and oppression were construed as perpetrated not only by the authoritarian state but also by self-righteous and militant radical leftists. The rise of the Park Chung-hee syndrome and New Right scholarship also functioned to discursively allocate to the past or deem outmoded all the events and development that do not conform to contemporary South Korea's dominant liberal democratic ideal. I call this the politics of time. Arising from the profound and wide-ranging transformations both in and out of South Korea, the politics of time has largely worked to disavow the revolutionary politics of the twentieth century in general, and in particular the 1980s minjung project, and to discharge contemporaries from both to injustices that happened in the past as well as to the present that has not dealt with the past historical injustices.

My discussion of the politics of time is indebted to Jacques Rancière's suggestion that a notion of time that separates the present from the past acts as "a principle of impossibility" and to Walter Benjamin's critical view on the notion of history as progressive. In the era of post–grand narratives, Rancière notes, a seeming innocuous statement such as "times have changed" is effortlessly recast into "a statement of impossibility." That is, to say that the times have changed does not simply denote an actual passage of time and the disappearance of things that had been present in that time period. It also denotes that the possibilities that had been imbued with the idea of time have become impossible, no longer belonging to the present and in the realm of what is possible.[3] Benjamin's well-known "Theses on the Philosophy of History" offers a similar understanding of time and a view of history where history does not progress according to a prescribed linear trajectory, where there is a deep and abiding connection between the past and the present, especially a connection between the injustice committed in the past and the emancipatory possibility of the present. For Benjamin, the view of history as progress presents twofold dangers: first, a reconfiguration of the history of the past entailing an erasure, distortion, or toning down of subversive dimensions, and second, the danger of historical writings falling into complicity with the tendency of the present, aligning with the dominant of contemporary society. A critical view of history is obtained when the view of history as continuous progress is rendered void and when the historian—and society—sharpen the awareness of the past injustice and engage with the struggles of those who suffered defeat, their aspirations and dreams unfulfilled.[4]

For sure, the discourse of the paradigm shifts in recent South Korean history is first and foremost grounded in the wide-ranging societal transformation. Political liberalization following the democratic transition gave rise to the "liberalization" of culture and "massification" of popular culture, with the outpouring of a dizzying array of cultural outlets. This period also saw the emergence of a new generation who was no longer "obsessed" with ideology and politics and instead sought self-expression, leisure, and entertainment as active creators and critics of popular culture.[5] The paradigm shift from minjung to simin and from the political and cultural also marks the profusion of creative energy in all spheres of society.

At the same time, the much-celebrated transition to democracy was immediately followed by a set of global transformations: the collapse of the Soviet Union and the "actually existing socialism" of Eastern Europe, the extensive economic restructuring ushered in by globalization and neoliberalism, and the emergence of "free market democracy" in former authoritarian regimes. Even as the country was undergoing an exhilarating and swift political liberalization, a series of economic downturns and financial crises in 1997 known as the "International Monetary Fund (IMF) crisis" drove the country toward a path of all-out neoliberal restructuring, giving priority and acquiescing to the demands of the market.

The politics of time that operates in the revisionist history cannot be considered without the twin development of political liberalization and neoliberalism injecting the ferocity and alacrity in the process of the paradigm shifts. As scholars from Michel Foucault to Wendy Brown have observed, neoliberalism is much more than economic or trade policies, or change in the relationship between the state and economy; it has become a governing rationality that "extend[s] specific formulation of economic values, practices, and metrics to every dimension of human life."[6] In the process of disseminating the model of the market to all domains and activities, human beings are reconfigured "exhaustively as market actors . . . as *homo oeconomicus*."[7] American studies scholars in particular have observed how neoliberal development globally was both a response to emerging decolonization and new social movements, as well as a way to obscure unequal and racially hierarchical structures of global capitalism by promoting multicultural neutrality.[8] In this context, neoliberalism is viewed as an "epistemological structure of disavowal," mobilized to respond to the emancipatory post–World War II social movements. The structure of disavowal transfigures the previously liberatory movements and ideas into a new mode of power through the process of selective and uneven affirmation and incorporation of previously marginalized subjects, ideas, and practices.[9]

Public discussions of the legacies of Japanese colonial rule and the Park Chung-hee regime, and the revision of textbooks initiated by the New Right, have shown the extent of neoliberal rationality, the economization of human life in all of its aspects, including "the most basic cultural and ethical values" that inform one's view of the past.[10] Scholars writing about the historiographical debates have so far been mostly informed, understandably so, by the binary ideological framework that focuses exclusively on the historical experience of Korea's twentieth century and do not take into account the neoliberal development. Scholarly discussion of neoliberal rationality in South Korea has also so far been focused on institutional reorganization and management of power resources propelled by neoliberal restructuring—the domain of political economy.[11] Neoliberal governance in the domain of culture and society at large so far has been discussed mainly in the context of how neoliberalism has pushed certain institutional changes. Until recently, even this kind of critique aimed to expose how neoliberal institutional changes were not in sync with their professed ideology.[12]

My discussion of the memory reconstruction and history rewriting extends analyses of neoliberalism to the domains of both political economy and culture, showing that alongside paradigm shifts in political and economic spheres, contestation over history and memory—the domain of knowledge production—has emerged as one of the more distinctive features of the byproducts of neoliberal rationality in South Korea. As Park Chung-hee's brand of developmentalism—South Korean-style capitalism, as it were—is considered universal and a model to be emulated by other developing countries, and as Park Chung-hee is revived as a nationalist hero singularly responsible for South Korea's "Miracle on the Han River," not only is his authoritarian rule whitewashed, but also the minjung project is disavowed as inherently authoritarian and destructive. New Right scholars also reconfigure the individual first and foremost as Homo economicus, constructing a form of "neoliberal historiography."[13] In particular, they argue that the colonial subjects who were conscripted forcibly to provide sexual service for soldiers and other forms of industrial labor were merely performing their jobs for which they received wages commensurate with their labor, eschewing the colonial context in which threat and violence were used for mobilization of their labor along with the other historical and ethical considerations.

This book also expands the current theoretical understanding of social memory by highlighting the central role of mass media, especially the conservative mass media, in constituting the Park Chung-hee syndrome and later in the emergence and articulation of the revisionist views of New Right scholarship. Scholars have emphasized how social memory, rather than fixed and immutable, is culturally reconstructed, with the decisive roles played by the trinity of agents of memory, collective practices of recollection, and the creation of spaces through which such memory is expressed and conveyed.[14] South Korea's democratic transition gave the conservative mass media an unprecedented opening to become a powerbroker and an arbiter of social issues. As such, conservative mass media plays a central role in aiding the vested interests to retain their hegemonic position, playing off deeply entrenched Cold War anticommunism.[15] Yet, there has been scant attention paid in scholarly work to the rapidly expanding role of mass media in collective memory making and rewriting history. I analyze how the conservative mass media has become the agent and venue of the trinity of social memory, as well as a "historiographical apparatus," setting the agenda and the parameters and terms of public discourse.[16]

The Regime of Discontinuity

The organizing framework of disparate developments and phenomena analyzed in this book is the regime of discontinuity, around which each chapter revolves and through which chapters interact with one another. I characterize articulations or narratives that not only enunciate a radical break from the past but that which function to modulate, distort, or silence a certain kind of memory or history of the past as constituting the regime of discontinuity, following historian Pierre Nora's formulation in a different context.[17] Nora's well-known project in the 1970s was initiated by what he perceived to be an overall decline in the capacity of French national culture to sustain what he called realms of memory—the array of rituals, sites, ideas, and traditions that had long been considered part of the nation's collective past. Faced with revelations of atrocities of the Stalinist era and failure of the Soviet Union, French intellectuals at the time also attempted to recast the memory of their previous leftist political engagements. The French Revolution, a lived tradition that had animated French politics until then, was also consigned to a relic of the past. Memory stepped in to offer a way out of the traditional left-right dichotomy and the revolutionary republic tradition.[18] Nora's notion of the regime of discontinuity was therefore a case of nostalgia for a unitary nation that was no longer a "convincing or operative unit of study,"[19] as well as a case of retreat from politics.

The regime of discontinuity in South Korea that I examine in this book shares much the same political orientation and ethos as Nora's in its overall effect—it engages in the politics of time, making certain experiences of the past illegible or concealed in the present. It has manifested in a variety of forms and with varying degrees of articulation and cohesiveness. It also has a number of different historical references. The first such historical reference is South Korea's transition to parliamentary democracy in the late 1980s, which was clearly a break from the previous authoritarian system and was welcomed as the dawn of a new era. Revision of the constitution with the consequent direct presidential election of 1987, and the subsequent political liberalization were some of the most obvious cases of such a break.

The second reference is the 1990s, when the claim by academics, commentators, and cultural gatekeepers that South Korea had entered a new era and was in the midst of a break with the past became all the more vigorous. With the emergence of the aforementioned series of discourses of paradigm shifts, from minjung (people) to simin (citizen), from the political to the cultural, from the collective to the individual, the regime of discontinuity became a defining ethos of the 1990s. The rise of New Right historiography in the 2000s, with its attempt to reassess the colonial period and the Syngman Rhee and Park Chung-hee periods, constitutes another kind of regime of discontinuity. This discourse is also celebratory, à la Francis Fukuyama's end of history which anticipated the new millennium to be free from limitations of the past and considered capitalism as universally beneficial, with only democracy now remaining as the "final form of all human government."[20]

Democratic Transition in the Late 1980s and the Minjung Movement

Every decade of post-1945 South Korea began with a major historical event,[21] but the decade of the 1980s remains singularly significant in the history of South Korea. That decade witnessed the most explosive and remarkably vociferous emancipatory project, known as the minjung movement, whose goal was to build a new society based on more expansive ideas that went beyond the principles and values of Western-style liberal democracy. The minjung movement was a civil and human rights movement, a democracy movement, an anti-government movement, a labor movement, a farmers' movement, a women's movement, a student and youth movement, an environmental movement, and a decolonization project. Building on previous anti-colonial and post-1945 social movements in South Korea and with "a striking commonality of purpose, so many people in so many settings devoted themselves so ardently to the work of transformation."[22] Tackling everything from South Korea's real and perceived dependent status vis-à-vis the United States and Japan to the government legitimacy, to collusion between the state and the *chaebŏl* (family-owned large conglomerates), to equitable distribution of wealth, to revaluating preexisting values and meanings, and experimenting with new forms and content in art, literature, music, and theater, the minjung movement was "an epic contest," as Robert Darnton characterized the French Revolution, of "possibili[ty] against the givenness of things."[23] After nearly three decades of persistent challenges and with much sacrifice,[24] 1987 saw the peaceful transfer of government through direct presidential election and the establishment of parliamentary democracy.

The magnitude of post-1987 changes led scholars to designate the term *1987ch'eje* (1987 regime or 1987 system) to denote their significance, as they continue to shape today's political landscape.[25] Even the names of the post-1987 governments—such as the Civilian Government of Kim Young-sam (1993–1998), the Government of the People of Kim Dae-jung (1998–2003), and the Participatory Government of Roh Moo-hyun (2003–2008)—suggested the hopefulness of this era and optimism about the progress of history.[26] It is safe to say that ordinary Koreans by and large shared the sense of an irreversible path toward historical progress.

Yet, post-1987 democratic consolidations have been less than satisfactory in their overall outcome, leading many to cast doubt on the real achievements of the democratization movement. The much celebrated reforms of the early phase of the Kim Young-sam administration ended with widely shared disappointment over the corruption of Kim's inner circles and family members; the politically progressive governments of Kim Dae-jung and Roh Moo-hyun adopted further neoliberal measures that gave rise to further polarization of society, among other discouraging developments.[27] The experience of the IMF crisis in the late 1990s was so devastating that many South Koreans considered it their second toughest experience after the Korean War. Despite high-level political liberalization, the overall quality of life declined as real income was reduced, and the gap between the haves and have-nots intensified virtually in all aspects of society; by 2011, the "phenomenon of polarization" (*yanggŭkhwa hyŏnsang*) had entered the *Encyclopedia of Korean Culture*.[28] The sense of increasing insecurity about the future in the post-1997 years was in sharp contrast to the earlier authoritarian period. Notwithstanding that Chun Doo-hwan was the scourge of the nation in the 1980s, the country was reveling in spectacular economic development—"the first of its kind since the time of Tan'gun."[29] The concomitant rise of confidence of Koreans in their ability to bring about such development also drove them to the streets in June 1987 to demand political reform and democratization of society.

Over the course of the radically transformed post-1987 era, the previous era's emancipatory movement, as encapsulated in the slogans of *minjok, minju,* and *minjung* (nation, democracy, and people), lost much of its theoretical purchase and sociopolitical relevance. To invoke minjung in the 1990s was to be charged with invoking platitudes and being anachronistic. The 1980s came to be mostly remembered as an era of antagonism, with ubiquitous images of streets strewn with broken stones and Molotov cocktail bottles, riot police with their Darth Vader–like gear, and the strident shouts of "Down with military dictatorship!"

and "Liberation of labor" (*nodong haebang*). The subsequent paradigm shift in discourse from minjung (people) to simin (citizen) effectively announced the end of the minjung project—the end of the "politics of antagonism"—and the inauguration of a new era.[30] Some well-known former *undongkwŏn*—an epithet referring to either the South Korean democratization movement of the 1980s as a whole or its individual participant, or both[31]—have also become not only a part of the establishment but also agents of neoliberalism, if only unwittingly, as I discuss in chapter 1.

Post-minjung South Korea became not only post-authoritarian and postmodern but post-ideological as well. The postmodern critique of modern subjectivity as the core constituting element of modernity also meant the privileged ontological place of minjung as the cohesive and unitary subjectivity of minjung discourse became no longer ideal or tenable. As historian Im Tae-sik puts it, "Anyone who still talks of minjok, minjung or revolution became as rare as a state-designated national monument . . . and became a [target of] mockery by the public."[32] Those who seemed unable to move on were admonished to be "flexible," "cool," and "commonsensical."[33]

Even as post-1987 South Korea became increasingly disenchanted with the minjung project, the 1980s and its minjung movement not only continue to define Korean society but also remain crucially alive. The decade has served as a primary reference point for current debates as well as for the political identity of not only the "386 generation" but also for later generations.[34] One's relation to and perspective on the 1980s and its minjung movement were considered to be a key barometer of one's position on the political spectrum in South Korea until recently. The 1980s minjung project has also remained a source of both inspiration and refutation for contemporary Korea and particularly its social movements, even as it has been scrutinized as yet another form of a will to power and its ethos—its communal spirit, self-effacement, and self-righteousness—seem to offer steady fodder for both nostalgia and ridicule in popular culture.[35]

Neoliberal Restructuring

Only a decade had passed since the democratic transition before South Korea was hit by the wave of global neoliberalism and its extensive restructuring. Many of the recently democratized countries in Latin America, Asia, and Southern and Eastern Europe have undergone extensive restructuring ushered in by globalization and neoliberalism that is geared to establishing the free market on a world-economic scale. More specifically, *restructuring* here refers to a set of structural reforms "designed to seek the deeper integration of the economy of developing countries into the capitalist world-system through trade liberalization and the removal of all barriers to the cross-border flow of capital, goods and services, with the extended role of the market and the re-oriented role of the state."[36] The consequences of this restructuring are not only that these countries have often been without corresponding democratic practices or institutions but also, more insidiously, that the democracy they avow has become a specific type of democracy, a "free market democracy."[37]

Needless to say, the neoliberalism that brought about the devastating restructuring is much more than economic or trade policies, or an ideology or reorientation of the nexus between the state and the economy. Earlier neoliberal development was also in part a response to a series of crises of legitimacy in the wake of decolonization and desegregation movements and fights for civil rights that occurred globally following World War II. The culmination of key anti-colonial and new social movements occurred in the same decades as the collapse of the Bretton Woods Agreement and election of neoconservatives such as Ronald Reagan and Margaret Thatcher in the United States and in the United Kingdom, respectively. These new social movements challenged the legitimating frameworks of existing liberal governance with their social differences, alternative social worlds, and potential alternative projects.[38]

In the United States, neoliberalism has worked to obscure racist and classist structures of global capitalism by promoting multicultural neutrality; capitalism appears as a natural process isolated from politics and culture, as argued by scholars such as Lisa Duggan.[39] The neoliberal turn in the United States incorporated the language of identity from Black, Chicano, and Asian American nationalist movements, as well as a celebratory version of the discourse of freedom and equality coming out of the civil rights era, exploiting the call for more equitable redistribution of resources.[40] In *Death beyond Disavowal*, transnational feminist studies scholar Grace Hong extends these arguments further and argues that neoliberalism is first and foremost an "epistemological structure of disavowal," as previously discussed. Through the structure of disavowal, the previous social movements' ethos, ideas, and practices have been selectively appropriated to serve the contemporary capitalistic order.[41]

As many scholars have noted and political theorist Wendy Brown aptly sums up, neoliberalism represents the "'economization' of political life and of other heretofore noneconomic spheres and activities, a process of remaking the knowledge, form, content, and conduct appropriate to these spheres and practices." To say such is "not to claim that neoliberalism literally *marketizes* all spheres, even as such marketization is certainly one important effect of neoliberalism. Rather, the point is that neoliberal rationality disseminates the model of the market to all domains and activities—even where money is not at issue—and configures human beings exhaustively as market actors, always, only, and everywhere."[42] Sociologist Hyun Ok Park characterizes the logic of the contemporary neoliberal economic order as "capitalist unconscious" in her compelling analyses of how this capitalist logic manifests in seemingly disparate pursuits of various peoples and states, cutting across political spectrums and across the borders of South Korea, North Korea, and China.[43]

It was therefore not only the democratic transition but also the neoliberal turn following the transition that propelled the paradigm shift from minjung to simin in South Korea. The shift ushered in primacy of the notions of "citizen" and "liberal democracy" in both public discourse and social movements. "Citizen" here ultimately meant "middle class," the discourse of which swept the globe in the 1990s.[44] The primacy of citizen signaled that the individuals construct their emancipatory narrative—following the liberal principles of individual freedom, formal equality, and political rights—as rights-bearing and rights-claiming citizens. With the neoliberal turn, the widely circulated discourse of liberal democracy during the 1990s and early 2000s became transposed into a discourse of neoliberalism. That is, democracy is invoked not only to "rescue the social" eroded by the market but also to defend "the liberty of the market."[45]

Post-1997 South Korea has experienced neoliberalism not only as the structural and institutional reorganization of society but also as a reconstitution of the "moral economy of the society, a whole way of life, a mode of social being—and becoming—in the world."[46] Indeed, South Korea has become a Thatcherian place where there is no "such thing as society; only individual men and women and family."[47] This book illustrates how the neoliberal rationality has also permeated contestation over history and memory in South Korea.

Contestation over History and Memory

The 1990s were celebrated as an era freed from the shackles of a surfeit of ideologies—both state-led Cold War anti-communism and minjung-focused leftist ideology. Political liberalization that followed the democratic transition also brought about new interpretations and new perspectives concerning the most critical moments of Korean history. Literature and popular culture, such as films and TV dramas, proliferated, giving new and varied voices to the past. The emergence of blockbuster films that became a part of the "Korean wave" (*hallyu*) also pointed to the pervasiveness of memory and history in society; many of these films dealt with major historical events such as the division of the country, the Korean War, and the conflicted legacy of Park Chung-hee's regime.⁴⁸ The advent of blockbuster films, as well as the general boom in film and TV dramas, also indicated that cinematic images increasingly reconfigure not only narratives of the past but also how one acquires knowledge about the past; these narratives involve a diverse array of social and cultural processes far beyond the walls of academia or the printed word.

President Kim Young-sam, the first civilian president in over thirty years, called for the "rectification of history" (*yŏksa parojapki*) as a way to establish legitimacy of his own government and to show his administration's willingness to "deal with the past."⁴⁹ Related actions included the demolition of the building that had housed the former Japanese governor-general and the trial of the two former presidents, Chun Doo-hwan and Roh Tae-woo, held responsible for the 1980s Kwangju massacre.⁵⁰ State-initiated projects were soon phased out, but the mantle of the rectification of history was taken up by a large number of individuals and grassroots groups, becoming a veritable social movement.⁵¹ Individuals in this movement had disparate goals and different projects but shared an intense and personal engagement with history. History became pervasive in public consciousness.

Individual and social memories of the 1980s are deeply intertwined with the above development and some of the more iconic literary, filmic, and dramatic representations of the period. The immensely popular television drama *Sandglass* broadcast in 1995, for example, brought to the Korean public for the first time actual footage of state troops indiscriminately killing citizens during the Kwangju uprising, at a time when many people were still in the dark about what had happened in Kwangju.⁵² It is possible to think of the proliferation of memory culture as a case of an "excess" of memory, where the historical consciousness of the public exceeds the capacity of the received framework or interpretation, thus resisting incorporation into institutional history.⁵³ What is relevant here is that all of the above developments indicate Korean society's tremendous need or desire for "truths" to live by, a sense of participating in a national story, and meanings that sustain its variegated identities. It also indicates that professional historians have a more limited impact on public discussions than do literary, filmic, or cultural works, public memorial sites, and claims by politicians.⁵⁴ The case of the Park Chung-hee syndrome suggests, for example, that "real" histories of the Park Chung-hee period exist outside academia.

Even as history has become a major site over which various groups make divergent and often diametrically opposing claims and where they negotiate and contest the meanings of the past and visions for the future of Korea, there is also an equally powerful sense that history is no longer a stabilizing force, a sense of uncertainty about whether history will be able to guide the country and chart its future. This is so even as history is present everywhere—in films, television dramas, novels, museum exhibits, literature, and theme parks. Although this predicament is a global phenomenon,[55] contentious debates about history in Korean society of recent decades have only heightened this sense of uncertainty.

One of the most consequential developments of the post-1987 era has been a series of debates about how to evaluate colonial and authoritarian legacies: from the Park Chung-hee syndrome, to the Roh Moo-hyun government's attempt to legislate resolution of the issue of "pro-Japanese collaborators,"[56] to the New Right's claim that the history textbooks used by middle and high schools were too critical of South Korea. Inordinately contentious and protracted, these debates have been called a civil war, *tout court*.

These debates reveal a deep division within Korean society over how central a role their country's overcoming the colonial and authoritarian past should play in undergirding current political development and visions for the future. Should the country's commitment to democracy and its future vision require that it continue to remind itself of its colonial and authoritarian legacies? Or are these legacies—seven decades after the liberation of the country from Japanese colonial rule, four decades after the death of Park Chung-hee, and three decades after the historic 1987 triumph of democracy—by now secondary matters for contemporary and future South Korea? Should not "truth" about the past and any unresolved historical issues be left for future historical judgment? Might not repeated and public retelling of the "shameful" stories of Korea's past, as some on the right have insisted, actually get in the way of standing tall as a modern democracy and a global economic power? Is it not time to move on?

These questions, though raised not only by the New Right,[57] constitute the core underlying intellectual and political grounds of New Right scholarship, the emergence of which marked the most dramatic and contentious turn to the right in Korean historiography to date. The New Right's regime of discontinuity includes revisionist scholarship on the colonial period and on the authoritarian presidencies of Syngman Rhee and Park Chung-hee. Immediate political context aside, one might say that the revisionist views stem from conflicting perspectives on the relationship between modernization and democracy, the two main tasks Koreans designated as national goals as early as the late nineteenth century—and achievements for which South Korea has deservedly been recognized. Efforts to resolve contradictions and social conflicts arising from modernization and capitalism and to seek alternative forms to capitalism consumed much of the intellectual struggle and revolutionary politics globally in the twentieth century, and Korea was certainly no exception. The emergence of New Right scholarship with its triumphalist narrative of the victory of capitalism over other alternative ideologies signaled a declaration to abandon this historical struggle and to reconfigure the meaning and practice of politics.

The discourse of the victory of capitalism over socialism at the end of the last millennium has made capitalism appear as "the only valid social horizon, granting it a sacralized sense of finality."[58] For those aligned with the New Right in South Korea, celebration of such achievement seemed further justified by not only South Korea's meteoric rise economically but also by the dismal conditions in North Korea from the early 1990s. In the neoliberal age, economic development has become "cultural dominant."[59] As such, North Korea deserves its subalternity vis-à-vis South Korea, if not globally. Indeed, the New Right's triumphalist discourse would have been unlikely without the demise of socialist regimes worldwide and the economic deterioration in North Korea.[60]

Persistence of the Cold War Regime and Mass Media

It is the ultimate irony of history that one of the most valuable forms of social capital of the New Right is the continuing Cold War system in the Korean Peninsula. In fact, one might say that the only thing that has not changed in the Koreas since the division is the Cold War system. Even though the Cold War was effectively over in 1989 everywhere else, it is still very much alive in the Korean Peninsula. Not only has North Korea been an archenemy of South Korea, but anti-communism has become the south's "emotional infrastructure"; South Korea's "ideological chastity" had to be protected at all costs.[61] The generation who did not directly experience the war also inherited bipolar allegiances that the war required.[62] At the same time, anti-communism as state ideology and state policy was part and parcel of the Park Chung-hee developmental state's pursuit of high economic growth. A large percentage of the population, beneficiaries of the unprecedented economic growth, became ardent supporters of Park's regime. Even though Park's type of developmental state faced bankruptcy in the financial crisis of 1997, the support base remained more or less intact until recently.[63]

High-profile political liberalization in South Korea often belies the still-pervasive Cold War structure on the Korean Peninsula. Despite claims of a total break from the past in the post-1987 era, South Korea still maintains the National Security Law (NSL),[64] for example, a most draconian body of law that restricts freedom of thought and whose indiscriminate application has been one of the principal mechanisms used by previous authoritarian regimes to control and discipline society.[65] The NSL has functioned as a "ventilator" for the Cold War system that should have been a historical relic.[66] Even during the presidency of Kim Dae-jung, who remains one of the most notable victims of this law, the application of the NSL was not reduced.[67]

Given the interlocking relationship between anti-communism, economic development, and continuing Cold War infrastructure on the Korean Peninsula, South Korea's ideological topography cannot be adequately explained along received notions of left and right that pivot on the issue of class as based on European historical experience. The axis on which the left and right is divided in South Korea is generally considered anti-communism. But, more precisely, it is anti–North Korean sentiment. If the earlier politics of anti-communism was born out of unrelenting competition with North Korea and the state-building process of eliminating dissent, the rise of the politics of *chongbuk chwap'a* (leftists who follow the North Korean state ideology of self-reliance) in the late 1990s and early 2000s has functioned more specifically to discredit groups or individuals who advocate a reconciliatory approach to North Korea and also those who are associated with or sympathetic to the governments of Kim Dae-jung and Roh Moo-hyun.[68] The two governments' Sunshine Policy of engaging North Korea through economic assistance and cooperation has been an object of scathing criticism from the conservatives.[69] In fact, by the 2000s, one's attitude toward and support of the Sunshine Policy became a major criterion by which to judge and categorize one's political identity, whether one was on the left or right, progressive or conservative.[70]

Along with the continuing Cold War system, the narrative of a clear break from the past articulated in the Park Chung-hee syndrome and New Right scholarship has also been encouraged, shaped, and sustained, if not underwritten, by conservative mass media. Mass media's close ties with the dominant global trend is nothing new, with its spread of celebratory discourse of globalization with corporate advertisements and songs from the 1960s. This trend was intensified by the breakdown of the socialist bloc and subsequent predominance of neoliberalism.[71]

Conservative mass media in particular remained one of four entities that political scientist Jang-jip Choi [Ch'oe Chang-jip] identifies as the core power bloc—along with the military elite, chaebŏl, and technocrats of state organizations—that sustained authoritarianism in South Korea even after the 1987 democratic transition.[72] The seeming coherence and remarkable cultural and social capital that the New Right display are due in major part to mass media. It has promoted and coordinated disparate individuals and groups, including academics, literary figures, artists, social commentators, and politicians, into a unified group that has gradually cohered as the New Right. An intimate relationship between the conservative mass media and well-known conservative figures whose fictional and nonfictional writings became a foundational revisionist text of Korean history also was part and parcel of the continuing culture war.

Much as in other parts of the world, mass media sets the agenda, parameters, and terms of public discourse. It has also increasingly become what Allen Feldman calls in a different context a "historiographical apparatus," replacing or substituting professional historians' scholarship.[73] Both the Park Chung-hee syndrome and more recent debates over New Right scholarship show that the conservative mass media has become a most assiduous student of the Gramscian call for a "war of position"—a "culture war," as it were.[74]

The Postmodern Predicament and the "Failure" of Revolutions

Although perpetuation of the Cold War structure on the Korean Peninsula makes deciphering South Korea's ideological landscape a hazard, it does provide an ideological infrastructure for triumphalist discourses of the regime of discontinuity. The global end of the Cold War—the breakup of the Soviet Union and of actually existing socialism—heralded the concomitant demise of left and Marxist social theory and of political Marxism, giving rise to questioning of the premises of modernity. As philosopher Alain Badiou notes, Jean-François Lyotard's declaration of the end of "grand narratives" was a kind of "melancholic farewell to the twentieth century," which for Lyotard meant above all "the end of Marxist politics, the end of the 'proletarian narrative.'"[75]

Some of the recognized authorities on postmodern thinking such as Lyotard locate the "origin" of postmodernity in the "failure" of modernity in Europe and in the experience of mass violence and colonial counterinsurgencies, among other challenges.[76] Sociologist Jeffrey Alexander finds yet another more localized and recent "origin" of postmodern thinking in the "failure" of the 1960s; that is, many leftists who were demoralized and became uncertain about modernity's promise of grand narratives embraced postmodern theory as a way to explore the meaning of their experience of and disappointments with the 1960s.[77]

Another spin-off of the discourse of "failure" of the 1960s is the narrative of failure of revolutions found in the European academic community's discrediting of worldwide revolutionary experiences and revolutionary discourse, from François Furet's revisionist work on the French Revolution to German sociologist Wolf Lepenies's claim that "nothing happened in France in 1968,"[78] to the too-swift equation made reducing the Chinese revolution to the "excess" in China's Cultural Revolution. Given the intertwined history of modernity and revolutions, the narrative of failure has had profound consequences for the assessment of modernity.[79]

Furet's 1978 book, *Interpreting the French Revolution* (*Penser la révolution française*), one of the earliest efforts to reassess the French Revolution in the context of rising doubts about the premises of modernity, was "the history of the illusion of revolutionary politics."[80] Most significantly, it ushered in an intellectual trend of reducing major revolutionary movements of the past to "the convenient and politically paralyzing category of 'totalitarianism,'" with Auschwitz and the gulag as the presumed ultimate destinations of any project that does not align itself with the tenets of liberal democracy.[81]

As historian Geoff Eley further elaborates, for someone like Furet, the collapse of communism "confirmed the bankruptcy and final defeat of the radical democratic fantasies" of the French Revolution and any radical hopes of the leftist movements of the twentieth century, as merely "violent and irrational." In this view, Bolshevism might have been an outcome of the violent and chaotic circumstances of World War I, but the later violence of the Soviet Union came from the utopianism in Bolshevism that was inherently dictatorial and innate in the idea of revolution itself—"in the illusory belief of revolutionaries that society was available for the remaking."[82]

With *Interpreting the French Revolution*, Furet declared the revolution and its import in the French society, as well as the revolutionary ideas, was over.[83] He also offered an analysis of contemporary French society and its extremely sectarian politics by examining Jacobinism mainly in the context of, and as a genesis of, totalitarianism. The philosophical and historical linkage between Jacobinism and the post-1945 French intellectual left also contributed to the latter's demise.[84] The view of revolutionary ideas as inherently violent and dictatorial also informed the revisionist scholarship of the New Right in West Germany in the well-known instance of the historians' dispute of the 1980s. For the Holocaust denialist and historian Ernst Nolte, the French Revolution was "a dress rehearsal for Lenin's Red Terror which was a dress rehearsal for the Holocaust and the Holocaust itself as a defensive response to 'Asiatic terror.'"[85]

Postmodern and Postnational Histories

That the protagonist of the above narrative of failure is also specifically European needs no retelling.[86] Still, it should also be pointed out here that the beginning of history as a professional discipline was in part a product of revolutionary experience. The role of history was to assess the meaning of the Enlightenment and the French Revolution; both supporters and opponents of the French Revolution mobilized history as their "guide and weapon."[87] The legacy of the French Revolution was also critical in liberal historians' advocacy for radical change.[88] Historian Ch'oe Kap-su argues further that the revolutionary experiences in fact contributed to the European claim that it had experienced a true transformation of society—the claim that constituted one of the core tenets of modernity—and therefore the right to universalize its own history. The rest of the world either did not have a history (such as Africa) or had a stagnant history (such as Asia).[89] For the first half of the twentieth century and beyond, historical narratives, whether Marxist or the Annales school inspired, also projected the possibility of historical change that would take place through dynamic interactions between human and structural conditions.[90] This deeply optimistic view of history as progress, and the belief in historians' ability—as well as responsibility—to capture and explain such historical transformations, went hand in hand with a totalistic view about history: "grand narratives, rational expectation, and unitary power."[91] Such a totalistic view and belief in the emancipatory potential of historical narratives were also an expression of the self-confidence derived from Europe's experiences of historical changes through revolutions.[92]

Europe's optimism about historical progress began to wear off in the aftermath of the horror of the Holocaust and World War II. It also coincided with the emergence of formerly colonized subjects coming to the fore in the three decades of the "decolonizing era" marked by the radical and insurrectionary politics of emancipation—insurgency, revolution, nationalism, and national liberation struggle. From the beginning of the 1970s, the world system stumbled into economic recession and attendant political crisis. The consequent political reaction was to attempt "the containment and recuperation of the historic challenge from the 'Third World' that had been expressed in the struggles for decolonization in the boom years following 1945; to force a restructuring of class relations in the interests of capital in the core capitalist countries, a rolling back of the challenge represented by 'Third World' insurgency at the peripheries."[93] In the discipline of history, if previous historical writings were concerned with forces and energy that had moved history forward, then the new approaches to history began with questioning a totalistic view of history and class as a stable and unitary category through which to understand a society.[94]

Previously discussed accounts of revolutions as inherently destructive and damaging represent one of the more reactionary set of responses coming out of the post-1970 European intellectual community to these worldwide developments. These accounts, as Arif Dirlik argues, not only "call into question one of the founding moments of modernity" but also "cast doubt on all revolutions, regardless of political orientation, and the aspirations and visions that endowed revolutionary change with meaning."[95] This kind of scholarship also impedes consideration of why and how revolutions emerge—their rise as a product of sociopolitical and economic forces and their role as a voice of the aspirations of the oppressed and marginalized in society.[96]

For much of modern Korea, revolutionary transformation of society—the yearning for, the actual experience of, however partial and incomplete, and future prospects of—was indeed part and parcel of how modernity was experienced. The extreme violence, terror, and deaths that accompanied the series of "incomplete" or "passive" revolutions left most Koreans deeply traumatized, with the ensuing anti-communism as state ideology expunging society of any leftist politics by the end of the Korean War, be it in political philosophy or a social movement.[97] Starting from the late 1970s and the 1980s, however, a new generation devoted itself to the cause of reviving the previously "failed" attempt at revolution, a possibility that had seemed not only imminent but also inevitable at the time.

The insurgent demands for decolonization and self-determination among third world countries were critical for this generation's anti-authoritarian, anti-hegemonic, and anti-imperialist discourse. Minjung practitioners aligned themselves with the kind of nationalism that was taken up by the newly independent countries of Southeast Asia and Africa.[98] Some literary critics from the mid-1970s also envisioned Korean literature as a part of third world literature, which they considered the most "advanced" among world literature, holding out the promise of reinvigorating world literature.[99]

With the end of faith in the grand narrative of universal progress toward emancipation of humanity, new approaches to history both in terms of research topics and their implicit aims seemed bereft of emancipatory goals that had been previously associated with historical narratives. In the words of Ch'oe Kap-su, for historians seeking transformative politics with their history writing, "it was no longer possible to locate where to attack [for a change of society]. Each object of [the new approaches to history such as cultural history or microhistory] can be used for attack, but there is no longer a detonator that could explode the whole."[100] As the arrival of postmodernity in South Korea coincided with the demise of the minjung project, among other aspirations of societal change, it only further amplified an already pervasive sense of uncertainty about projecting any future political vision.[101] For many intellectuals, the appearance of the Korean translations of the foundational texts of postmodern thinking and postmodernism in 1992—Lyotard's *Postmodern Condition* and Jean Baudrillard's *Simulations*—were like "new machinery that had just been imported and went through customs clearance but that nobody knew how to operate yet."[102]

As elsewhere, the advent of postmodernity in Korea meant not only the end of a particular theory or ideology or certain kind of knowledge production but also, and perhaps more importantly, the end of categories of thinking with which people had long engaged the world. If the 1980s marks the end of what Alain Badiou calls the twentieth century's historical sequence, literary scholar Wang Hui identifies the end of this historical sequence "not as an end to history, nor as a willed ideological farewell, nor even as the end to the relevance of revolutionary politics altogether, but rather as the end of the possibility for twentieth-century solutions to contemporary problems."[103]

This book strives to gain a critical and comprehensive understanding of the twin trajectories of democratization and neoliberalism in post-1987 South Korea in the larger context that I have briefly discussed above, whereby the Cold War persists on the Korean Peninsula while it ended globally, while the neoliberal restructuring has been ratcheted up. Loss of faith in the grand narratives of the nineteenth and twentieth centuries led to the resulting postmodern thinking in whose political vision the twentieth century becomes the final epoch of modernity. This book integrates analyses of the nexus of neoliberal governance in political economy, culture, and society. To this end, I examine a wide range of materials such as memoirs, biographies, literary works, and academic literature, along with analyses of government policies and social movements. While paying attention to the profound and wide-ranging sociopolitical and global transformations that gave rise to the regime of discontinuity, I explore how and in what ways the regime of discontinuity functions to disavow the previous emancipatory politics of their relevance to contemporary society.

Chapter Outlines

In what follows, I discuss four separate but related developments that together constitute the regime of discontinuity. Chapter 1 tracks the conceptual paradigm shift from the people (minjung) to the citizen (simin) both in social discourse and in social movements of post-1987 South Korea. I examine how this paradigm shift ushered in primacy of the notions of "citizen" and "liberal democracy," with claims that the citizens' movement represented a new form of social movement away from the previous and more radical minjung movement.

Further scrutinizing the meaning of "citizen" in liberal democracy, I discuss how South Korea's discourse of liberal democracy widely circulated in the 1990s has been converted into a discourse of neoliberalism. Some of the neoliberal policies introduced by the newly established liberal democratic administrations were accepted as measures to correct earlier authoritarian regimes' practices. More specifically, probing the meaning of "citizen" in the case of the labor movement, I explore how the labor movement gained its social citizenship in the 1990s only to be subjected to demands of both the state and of capital.

Whereas chapter 1 is about the paradigm shift from minjung to simin at the nexus of the democratic transition and neoliberal restructuring, chapter 2 is about how these two developments brought about a shift from the political to the cultural in the 1990s. I examine *huildam* (literature of reminiscence) as symptomatic of this shift, constituting the regime of discontinuity that posits the post-1987 period as a radical departure from the previous era. Appearing in the 1990s, in the aftermath of the setback of the 1980s minjung movement, this genre deals largely with loss of revolutionary hope and vision, as well as a loss of faith in history and the future. Protagonists in these literary works are usually former undongkwŏn whose transition to sosimin (petty bourgeois) in a liberal democracy is fraught with unrelenting—in some cases fatal—self-interrogation and remorse. At the same time, I suggest that the very act of self-examination and self-exposure also functions as a Benjaminian "form of remembrance"; as it documents the unrealized hopes, dreams, betrayals, and failures of the minjung movement and the undongkwŏn, it also calls to mind the unfinished and unsuccessful struggles of the past generation as well as the ruptures in the continuity of history.

The next two chapters explore the construction of social memory and history writing of the immediate past in popular culture as well as in academia and the subsequent reorientation of history as part of a turn to the right in South Korea in the 1990s. Chapter 3 discusses the Park Chung-hee syndrome as a case of how the regime of discontinuity manifest in reconstruction of social memory of Park Chung-hee and his regime. The syndrome was not only an indictment of the Kim Young-sam government's failure to carry out its much-promised reform, nor just a case of nostalgia for the bygone days of economic boom. It was also a cocreation of powerful conservative media and a group of well-known sociopolitical and literary figures. I analyze memoirs, biographies, and literary works, showing how this vast amount of narrative labor facilitated and constituted the syndrome. The Park Chung-hee syndrome is therefore another critical site where contestation over memory and history has taken place.

With the rise of the New Right and its attempt to rewrite Korean history, the culture war in South Korea has turned into a "civil war," the focus of chapter 4. I explore how the rise of the New Right and its triumphalist discourse constitute a main pillar of the regime of discontinuity—a neoliberal disavowal of the minjung project. New Right historians' embrace of postcolonial scholarship and their critique of leftist nationalist historiography of the 1980s have pushed out the nation, only to bring back the state in its place. Intellectually and politically, the New Right's appropriation of postcolonial scholarship is a triumphal discourse that is unapologetic about neoliberal capitalist development in South Korea as well as the willful ordering of the disappearance of North Korea.

The epilogue explores the politics of time that the regime of discontinuity engages in and its historiographical and ethical implications. That is, the regime of discontinuity and the New Right scholarship discursively assign as past or anachronistic all those phenomena that do not accommodate contemporary society's hegemonic ideal. This view of temporality vindicates contemporaries in relation to injustices that happened in the past as well as to a present that has not rendered justice for past historical injustices. Informed by Benjamin's view of historical temporality that sees history as not a continuous accumulation of homogeneous empty time but as time filled with the intermingling of past and present, I suggest as an alternative a poetics of remembrance. To make amends for the previously unacknowledged suffering of the past generation and to make efforts to continue the unconcluded struggles of the past is to open up a possibility for true emancipation of society and for thinking about the limits and possibilities of a transformative political praxis as well.

1

The Paradigm Shift from Minjung (People) to Simin (Citizen) and Neoliberal Governance

The stunning result of the parliamentary election of April 26, 1988 gave rise to a phenomenon known as *yŏsoyadae* (the ruling party as the minority in the National Assembly) for the first time since 1950.[1] On January 19, 1990, however, the then-ruling party, the Democratic Justice Party of Roh Tae-woo, pushed through a merger with two other existing political parties, the conservative liberal Reunification Democratic Party of Kim Young-sam and the ultraconservative New Democratic Republican Party of Kim Jong-pil, to form the Democratic Liberal Party (DLP). With this merger, the South Korean political scene was effectively reorganized overnight.[2] Shocking the nation, Kim Young-sam, one of two emblematic figures of the democratization movement in the 1970s, had joined forces with his former oppressors, those with the "blood of the Kwangju massacre" on their hands, as it were.[3]

On the same day as the merger, thousands of labor union members and activists held the inauguration ceremony for Chŏnnohyŏp (Chŏn'uk nodongjohap hyŏbŭihoe, National Council of Trade Unions, NCTU) at Sungkyunkwan University's Suwon campus. Founded after years of preparation dating from the Great Struggle of Workers of July–September 1987, Chŏnnohyŏp was a nationwide labor organization that aimed to represent the interests of workers and to replace the government-friendly, and what many considered anti-labor, Han'guk noch'ong (Han'guk nodong johap ch'ongyŏnmaeng, Federation of Korean Trade Unions, FKTU). The ceremony ended with more than 130 labor activists and union members arrested. Chŏnnohyŏp remained "illegal" during its entire existence, with most of its leadership either on the run from police or in prison until it was dissolved in 1995.[4]

The merger of three political parties was widely decried as an "illicit union," intensifying already-simmering anti-government protests of university students and opposition forces. During one particularly large protest, Myongji University student Kang Kyŏng-dae was killed by steel pipe–wielding thugs (infamously known as white skull corps) hired by state security agencies. The death led to a nearly fifty-day-long protest that became known as the 1991 May struggle. One of the largest mobilizations of students and opposition forces since the historic June uprising of 1987, the 1991 struggle surprisingly left no visible trace or any long-lasting impact, other than an overwhelming sense of things gone awry.[5] The media's exclusive focus on "militant" responses of the movement to the state's violent suppression damaged the moral authority of the movement. Worse yet, as many noted, successful suppression of the May struggle helped to stabilize the fledgling government of Roh Tae-woo. Roh, a close associate of the widely despised former president Chun Doo-hwan, tried to distance himself from Chun and his regime, claiming to be on the side of "ordinary people."[6]

Coming on the heels of the breakdown of a cascade of Cold War structures—the Soviet Union, the "actually existing socialist" countries, the Berlin Wall—the 1991 May struggle and short-lived Chŏnnohyŏp were symptomatic of post-1987 social movements in South Korea in general and the labor movement in particular. The 1987 June uprising brought about momentous changes, the most important of which was South Korea's transition from authoritarian dictatorship to parliamentary democracy. The spectacular success of the democratic transition, however, signaled the demise of the minjung movement—the three-decade-long emancipatory movement responsible for ushering in the transition. Meanwhile, academics, journalists, political pundits, writers, and some of the former participants of the minjung movement began to circulate a discourse of the shifting paradigm from minjung (people) to simin (citizen), effectively marking the end of the minjung both in social discourse and social movement and the inauguration of a new era heralded by simin.

This chapter examines the discourse of this paradigm shift from minjung to simin in the context of the global transformation and South Korea's democratic transition and the ways in which the discourse engages with, intervenes in, or limits our understanding of the deeply transformed sociopolitical reality and subsequent transformation of social movements in South Korea. I argue that the discourse of this paradigm shift narrativizes the transition in a particular way that undermines or marginalizes the previous minjung project as no longer meaningful and relevant, hence its characterization as the regime of discontinuity. The paradigm shift ushered in the primacy of notions of "citizen" and "liberal democracy" in both public discourse and social movements, and the widely circulated discourse of liberal democracy in the 1990s was converted into a discourse of neoliberalism in the era of neoliberal restructuring. As such, this chapter is as much about implications—intellectual, political, or otherwise—of the discourse of the paradigm shift as about the paradigm shift itself. In what follows, I first provide an overview of sociopolitical developments that followed the transition that has become known as the 1987 regime or system, before going on to consider how post-1987 liberal democratic governments have adopted neoliberal policy as both South Korea's own brand of globalization and as a response to the financial crisis of 1997. I then discuss the ways in which the paradigm shift from minjung to simin in the case of the labor movement show how under the liberal-democratic state with its institutionalization of market and labor flexibility, the expansion of rights of citizens promised in the paradigm shift has also been constrained; in the labor movement, the gaining of social citizenship by labor has also been a process of self-subjectification, a process of accommodating demands of both the state and business.

The 1987 Regime (1987ch'eje) as Democratization from Above

South Korea's democratic transition in the late 1980s brought about the institutionalization of liberal democracy, which began with the election of Roh Tae-woo as president in 1987. Roh, a member of the inner circle of the authoritarian Chun Doo-hwan regime, came into power through not another military coup d'état but through a relatively free and direct election. Succeeding administrations made further significant, even historic, reforms that consolidated the liberal democratic system, such as dismantling of an unofficial private club of military officers (*Hanahoe*), one of the major mechanisms through which the military had previously intervened in politics, and restoration of the previously abandoned local government system. The growth of general political liberty was especially visible in the liberalization of the press. After 1987, the number of journals, dailies, weeklies, and monthlies mushroomed; liberalization of the press and press power grew to the point that undue exercise of media power over government and society especially since the Kim Dae-jung and Roh Moo-hyun administrations was labeled "tyranny of press."[7] All of these changes constituted what scholars later termed the "1987ch'eje" (1987 regime or 1987 system), denoting a new set of rules, norms, and ethos that has governed South Korea since 1987.

As sociologist Kim Chong-yŏp and others note, however, post-1987 developments were not without alternative formulations. As often is the case in history, social movement forces that brought down the old system were not in the position to make a new system of their own design, with their own participation. Minjung movement forces that had carried out the three-decade-long struggle against the previous authoritarian regimes of Park Chung-hee and Chun Doo-hwan had long envisioned themselves shaping the future of Korea once they removed the authoritarian regime. As sociologist and culture critic Sŏ Tong-jin remarks, the June uprising created a condition in which everything, including what might be called the "momentous," seemed possible; in this moment of a great euphoria and possibilities, what was envisioned for the future was a kind of "whole" or "complete" democracy, "the kind that cannot be reduced to what liberals talk about—democracy mainly as institutional, legal structures."[8] In the 1987 presidential election, the election platform of Paek Ki-wan, the candidate from the minjung movement, included a call for nationalization of basic industries, self-management of workers, and reunification of the two Koreas in a confederate system. These slogans, especially those calling for a socialistic mixed economy, would soon be considered "unthinkable," if not "crazy," in the post-1987 era.[9]

For some, the sense of disappointment in the aftermath of the June uprising recalled the famed poet Kim Su-yŏng's calling the April 19, 1960 uprising as "our revolution that was so humble as to be foolish."[10] As Ch'oe Chang-jip [Jang-jip Choi] and others have pointed out, one of the most notable characteristics of the 1987 system was the disintegration of the united front between the minjung movement forces (*chinbo seryŏk*), a coalition of workers, university students, and the marginalized in society, and the former opposition political parties—a separation of "substantial democracy" from "procedural democracy," as it were.[11] The split began from the very start of the 1987 system as the minjung forces were completely excluded from it. One of the first steps toward establishing a new era mandated by the June uprising was to revise the existing constitution. The revision took place without any input from minjung movement forces. None of the leaders from the Headquarters of the Citizens' Movement to Obtain a Democratic Constitution (Minjuhŏnbŏp chaengch'wi kungmin undong bonbu), the umbrella organization of more than one hundred groups that had carried out the nationwide June uprising, for example, were invited to participate in the Eight-Person Political Conference that became responsible for drafting the new constitution. Only those from the former ruling bloc, represented by the political party of Chun Doo-hwan, and the new political elite, represented by the political parties of Kim Young-sam and Kim Dae-jung, took part in the conference. Such complete exclusion of grassroots organizations in the transitional period was unusual for a case of constitutional enactment in the late twentieth century, according to political scientist Pak Myŏng-nim.[12]

In the post-1987 political sphere, the transformed political dynamics also made it difficult for minjung groups to cohere as a political force. Long accustomed to dealing with the state as the main target of their "struggles" (t'ujaeng), through which much of their demands and aspirations were to be realized, minjung groups found the transition to electoral politics difficult to adjust to.[13] The united front that had shared the "lowest common denominator" of removing the authoritarian Chun regime began to rapidly disintegrate once that goal was accomplished in 1987.

Minjung movement forces had dreamed of a world beyond liberal democracy—a world "over there," in the words of literary critic Ch'oe Wŏn-sik.[14] The vision of new political elite, hailed mostly from the ranks of former opposition politicians, had been hemmed in by the "division system"[15] and anti-communist state ideology and had remained conservative politically and socially throughout their tenure in the democratization movement. At the same time, they had gained the support of the public through their long-standing resistance against authoritarian regimes and their suffering in the process.[16] They were thus positioned to "usurp" the fruits of the 1987 June uprising as their own and entrusted to chart a new direction for South Korea's future political development.[17] University students in the minjung movement in particular had been wary of such an outcome, warning opposition politicians that they were fighting not for the opposition political parties but for "history."[18] As post-1987 South Korea became increasingly critical of the minjung forces as too radical for the changed political landscape, the new political elite feared that the continued alliance with their erstwhile allies might jeopardize their own political future. Minjung forces were excluded from the new political power structure and, as Yi Kwang-il notes, pushed to "political exile" in the new era.[19]

The political space in which former minjung forces could maneuver became even more limited with Kim Young-sam's presidency from 1993 onward. Each of the two successive liberal democratic governments since 1993 was the outcome of a compromise between the former authoritarian ruling bloc and the new political elite; the emergence of Kim Young-sam's "Civilian Government" (1993–1998)—much celebrated as the first civilian government in thirty-two years—was in fact a result of the merger of the ruling party with two other conservative parties in 1990, as noted earlier; the "Government of the People" (1998–2003) of Kim Dae-jung also came into power through a merger of Kim Dae-jung's own conservative liberal party with the ultraconservative party of Kim Jong-pil, who had been a close associate of Park Chung-hee.[20]

The second major divergence in post-1987 South Korea was between the middle class and the working class. Although the June uprising was truly a momentous event participated in by people from all walks of life, media accounts at the time and later scholarly work as well as cultural representations by and large presented it first and foremost as a phenomenon of the middle class.[21] The ubiquitous moniker *"nektie pudae"* (necktie corps)—"an explosion of the previously silent white-collar workers"—is a prime example of the association of the uprising with the middle class.[22] Although the working class was not a leading force of the June uprising, white-collar workers were not prominent participants outside of Seoul either. Blue-collar workers were the main protestors in places where industrial plants are concentrated, such as Masan, Ch'angwŏn, and Ulsan. Half of those arrested during the June uprising were workers.[23] In fact, the popular nomenclature 386 generation—referring to those who were born in the 1960s, entered university in the 1980s, and were in their thirties at the time the term was coined in the 1990s—elides the fact that many who participated in the movement were factory workers who did not and could not attend university.[24]

The country's largest protest of workers, known as the Great Struggle of Workers, erupted only a few weeks after the June uprising. For two months in July and August, workers throughout South Korea spoke up in more than 3,700 factories, including massive strikes in chaebŏl-owned industries such as Hyundai (figure 1.1) and Daewoo, as well as in small and medium-size factories and nonmanufacturing sectors. The largest mobilization and the most explosive display of working-class frustration and unity to date, with more than one million workers participating, the Great Struggle showed the working class coming together as agents of social change;[25] yet, its relative marginality in scholarship and in public discussion highlights the marginality of labor and the working class in contemporary South Korea. With the rise of the citizens' movement

FIGURE 1.1. Hyundai workers demanding to recognize their union and wage increase in Ulsan, August 18, 1987. Source: *Kyunghyang Shinmun*.

from the 1990s, the citizenship of more recent social movements has been claimed exclusively by the middle class.

A Brief History of Neoliberalism

South Korea's transition to democracy in the late 1980s and the emergence of the subsequent "1987 system" cannot be understood without an adequate understanding of neoliberalism. By the 1990s, full-fledged neoliberalism reigned in South Korea. As elsewhere in the world, neoliberalism in South Korea is not only about economic policy but also pertains to governing rationale in all aspects of sociopolitical and cultural spheres. The neoliberal rationale in economic and financial policy, however, appeared much earlier in South Korea, from the late 1970s.[26]

As is well known, Park Chung-hee's developmental-state model of economic development is characterized by the state bureaucracy's active role in economic growth and industrial transformation.[27] South Korea's geopolitical location in the Cold War international structure and its need for political stability as a bulwark against Soviet expansion made this development approach a part of US policy in East Asia.[28] Park Chung-hee initiated a series of Five-Year Economic Development Plans—considered a key component of the developmental state—beginning in 1962, with subsequent plans continuing until the 1990s. In April 1979, a few months before his assassination, Park announced the Comprehensive Policy to Stabilize the Economy (*kyŏngje anjŏnghwa chonghap sich'aek*), proposing to open the domestic market, including the financial market—South Korea's first "neoliberal" policy. At the time, South Korea faced a second oil crisis, intensification of global stagflation, and neo-protectionism of economically wealthier countries, resulting in sluggish exports, lower employment rates, and a drastic increase in prices, among other results.[29]

To stabilize the economy, Park sought to restructure existing export and investment policies and to suppress wages and prices of agricultural products. In August 1979, he announced a series of Revised Plans for Financial Institutions that sought to give financial institutions the autonomy to, among other things, adjust interest rates, develop comprehensive monetary markets, and supersize financial institutions. These goals became realized as a part of financial liberalization and open marketization in the 1980s.[30] Suppression of wages and prices of agricultural products were detrimental to the lives of the marginalized, especially factory workers and farmers. A series of massive protests erupted, such as the Pusan-Masan uprising in October 1979, which eventually led to the assassination of Park in the same month and the demise of the Park Chung-hee regime.[31]

Park Chung-hee was killed before he could implement all of his policies, but Chun Doo-hwan, his protégé who came into power with another military coup d'état shortly after Park's assassination in 1979, continued with Park's neoliberal measures. Lacking political legitimacy and faced with a severe economic crisis resulting from the second oil crisis, Chun needed first and foremost to stabilize the economy.[32] With the help of Stanford University–trained economist Kim Jae Ik [Kim Chae-ik], Chun began to draft policies that comprised in essence neoliberal restructuring.[33] These policies consisted of "a reduction in government deficit, a tight monetary policy, a restraint on the growth of wages, trade-account liberalization, relaxing control over foreign investment, privatization of major commercial banks, and phasing out of the subsidies to heavy and chemical industries."[34] These policies were also promoted by outside institutions such as the International Monetary Fund (IMF), the World Bank, and the US Department of the Treasury as the "standard" reform package for crisis-ridden developing countries, and subsequently became known as the Washington Consensus.[35] However, Chun's continuing dictatorial control of the state, as well as inertia of the state bureaucracy, also delayed full implementation of these policies.³⁶ Chun continued some of Park's interventionist and authoritarian ways even as he was introducing new policies, including the forceful dismantling of the Kukje Group.³⁷

Legitimacy of the earlier state developmentalism rapidly lost its luster as military rule fell into disrepute. Bureaucratic elites also converted to neoliberalism starting from the late 1980s. Many of South Korean economists who were trained in the United States received their PhDs at the time of "neoliberal revolution" in US academia. Convinced of the virtues of the free market, they saw developmentalism as "backward" and "mistaken."³⁸ By the 1980s, neoliberalism became hegemonic thinking among Korean elite circles including high-ranking bureaucrats.³⁹ If Park Chung-hee's economic development was modeled after the Japanese-German-led late industrialization, then Chun Doo-hwan's economic development became "Anglo-Saxonized," championed by economists trained in the United States.⁴⁰

US bilateral pressure also became a key impetus for the acceleration of economic liberalization.⁴¹ The United States was undergoing its own drastic neoliberal measures known as Reaganomics and was no longer willing to allow the protectionist trade policy of South Korea. South Korea was considered no longer a developing country and, as such, needed to be "more responsible" and give up all those "unfair" protections of its industrial and especially financial enterprises and make its market more easily accessible to the United States.⁴²

Neoliberalization and the Politics of Confusion

During the process of transitioning to democracy in the late 1980s, the state introduced more extensive neoliberal measures and managed them more efficiently than in the previous period. To be sure, there were real and meaningful overall changes since 1987, and the significance of the institutionalization of democracy in sociopolitical spheres during the first two liberal governments (Kim Young-sam and Kim Dae-jung) should not be discounted. However, the process of democratization was also the process of neoliberalization, marked by a "politics of confusion"—conflation of neoliberal measures with the democratization process.⁴³ For many Koreans who desired more than anything to get rid of the authoritarian legacy, these neoliberal measures were often seen as the dismantling of, or at least the transformation of, the previous authoritarian rule.

The economic project of liberal governments that spoke of deregulation, competition, and growth, which was also a response to the economic crisis and demands of international organizations such as the IMF, appealed to a large number of Koreans.⁴⁴ Under the authoritarian regime in the past, they would have considered these measures largely as benefiting the ruling bloc; however, launched by the reform-oriented liberal politicians who were also erstwhile democracy movement leaders, the neoliberal projects were able to gain moral and political legitimacy. That these neoliberal economic measures also required a degree of self-reform by the ruling bloc, such as the purging of corruption or the demand for corporate transparency, also helped to enhance their validity and appeal to the public.[45] In addition, the transition to democracy, as exhilarating and transformative as it was, had not been accompanied by the kind of economic growth that South Koreans had become used to under authoritarian rule. The erstwhile minjung-oriented forces did not proffer any viable alternative plan for economic growth.[46] That neoliberalism is more a conservative redistribution project than a project of growth and development, as pointed out by David Harvey, was a warning heard by few at the time.[47]

Kim Young-sam's neoliberal measures were initially announced as part of building a *sin Han'guk* (New Korea) and *segyehwa* (internationalization), South Korea's version of globalization. Kim had hoped that segyehwa would enhance South Korea's status and role in the international community in the new century. For Kim and his cabinet members, globalization was also "an inevitable process" for every nation for sustained stability and prosperity. Furthermore, South Korea's membership in the Organisation for Economic Co-operation and Development (OECD) in 1996 made it necessary to open up domestic markets.[48] Kim launched a series of reforms in six major areas: education, legal and economic, politics and mass media, national and local administration, environment, and culture.[49]

These measures, part and parcel of the Kim government's drive for its own brand of globalization and carried out in haste without necessary safeguards for the economy, set in motion a financial meltdown in the regional crisis of 1997 that has since been called the IMF crisis. The consequent financial bailout arranged by the IMF was intended not only to stabilize but also to radically restructure the domestic economy. It included "the shutdown of insolvent financial institutions, the termination of bank loans to financially distressed firms, the furthering of trade and capital-account liberalization, the establishment of a flexible labor market, and improvement in transparency and debt-to-equity ratio in the corporate sector."[50]

When Kim Dae-jung assumed the presidency in February 1998, he did not slow down the neoliberal reforms demanded by the IMF, retreating from his earlier critical stance about the conditions it imposed.[51] An iconic figure of the democratization movement and a charismatic politician with a long history of persecution, Kim had endured several years of imprisonment and house arrests, two assassination attempts, and three years of exile in the United States under the previous authoritarian regimes.[52] He was also one of the few politicians who was well versed in economic issues and consistently pointed out, since the late 1960s, the close link between political repression and financial repression—that is, the authoritarian regime's coercive capacity went hand in hand with its capacity to control the business class, which was done through financial repression. For Kim, financial liberalization was thus the most effective way to sever collusion between the state and the chaebŏl.[53] Kim Dae-jung was eager to make the most of the opportunity provided by the IMF crisis to reform chaebŏl—it would otherwise have taken another thirty years or so, he noted.[54] During the presidential election when the conservatives attacked him for being a "pro-communist," Kim deflected such criticism by saying that he was "the most prepared" candidate for solving the financial crisis.[55]

In a cruel irony of history, Kim's determination to resolve the crisis at hand, to enhance South Korea's global competitiveness, and to break from the authoritarian past resulted in further increases in unemployment, inequality, and the general suffering of ordinary people. Kim's wholesale neoliberal market-oriented reforms consisted of "orthodox structural-adjustment programs towards further financial and trade liberalization, labor-market flexibility and public sector privatization with financial recapitalization and corporate reorganization."[56] To "reform" the labor market was to increase its "flexibility," even as South Korea's labor market was already one of the most "flexible"; it had the highest ratio of temporary workers in the workforce among the OECD countries.[57] Comprehensive restructuring led to massive layoffs, increased the number of "irregular" (*pijŏnggyujik*) workers, and further eroded workers' hard-won rights and protections, causing severe economic hardship and popular resentment.[58]

Kim Dae-jung believed that participatory democracy and the market economy were mutually complementary, hence his free market restructuring under the slogan of "Parallel development of democracy and market economy."[59] Some scholars find in Kim's reforms a semblance of social democratic ideas, and there are continuing debates as to whether his reforms were truly neoliberal. However, it is undeniable that the outcome of "DJnomics," as Kim's economic policies became known, was severe and long lasting.[60] Even the Kim government's much-touted new approach to welfare, known as productive welfare, which emphasized social investment in education and human resources development, did not reduce unemployment and inequality.[61]

Chaebŏl as "a Government above the Government"

Here, we also need to heed economist Chang Ha-sŏng's caution that not all the contradictions and problems of the South Korean economy should be attributed to neoliberalism, thereby overlooking the inflection that neoliberalism takes in different contexts, both in its historical and contemporary particularities.[62] Although neoliberalism as governing rationale is globally ubiquitous, neoliberal policies have manifested differently in different spaces and over time. In the Global South, in places like Chile and Argentina, it was violently imposed through military coups and juntas; in the Euro-Atlantic world, it was carried out more subtly through transformations of discourse, law, and governmentality; in the United Kingdom and the United States, neoliberalism began with the audacious free market reforms of Margaret Thatcher and Ronald Reagan, continued with the third way of Gordon Brown and Bill Clinton, then with the ownership society of George W. Bush, and most recently with austerity politics.[63]

South Korea's capitalism has a relatively brief history, and the causes of problems associated with economy also differ from other places. More specifically, South Korea's economy has not veered toward market fundamentalism the way the United States' has.[64] This is true even as the post-IMF-crisis economy saw the role of the market greatly expanded compared to the past, and even as the flexibility of the labor market has largely followed the "American model."[65] In the course of South Korea's developmentalism, the chaebŏl have become gigantic growth machines, wielding an inordinate power over the state and society; politicians' financial dependence on chaebŏl, among other factors, has limited the autonomy of the state and its capacity to constrain the chaebŏl's relentless and reckless pursuit of expansion.[66] As economist Yu In-hak puts it, South Korea's chaebŏl is sui generis: "There is no other country in the world as in South Korea where thirty or so chaebŏl's total gross product comprises 25% of the country's GNP and their value added 12%.... The chaebŏl is one gigantic dinosaur that reigns over not only the economy but also politics, culture, and society—all aspects of South Korea."[67]

By the mid-1990s, the chaebŏl became exceedingly vocal in their call for the state to pull back from economic management, making demands "at every conceivable opportunity." In an astonishingly brazen act, the Federation of Korean Industries (FKI), the fraternity of the chaebŏl, prepared a report that encapsulated its ultra-neoliberal outlook. It called for a sweeping downsizing of the state, including the abolition of all government ministries except Defense and Foreign Affairs—a reduction of government bureaucracy by 90 percent.[68] Although a prepublication leak that set off a public uproar led to the scrapping of the report, the existence of such a report speaks to the chaebŏl's sense of staggering confidence in their power to wield influence on the state and society and to how South Korean society has been and continues to be subject to chaebŏl domination. Much like the Cato Institute in the United States, the Center for Free Enterprise, the chaebŏl's well-financed research institute, spreads the gospel of neoliberalism by publishing classical works such as Friedrich Hayek, James Buchanan, and others and sponsoring talks of influential neoliberal thinkers.[69]

During the previous era, vehement criticism against the outsized and undue influence and power of chaebŏl was integral to minjung discourse. However, the 1997 financial crisis and subsequent neoliberal dominance of the idea of market competitiveness prompted even some erstwhile minjung practitioners to believe that the way to revive the crisis-ridden economy was to revitalize and protect chaebŏl.[70] Some also argued that chaebŏl should be considered as national capital (*minjok chabon*), recalling the colonial period when ethnic Korean entrepreneurship was considered as national capital and promoted as a part of a nationalist project.[71] As Chang Ha-sŏng quips, former president Roh Moo-hyun's remark that "power has gone over to the market" should have been revised to "power has gone over to the chaebŏl." Both Roh Moo-hyun and Lee Myung-bak, each occupying the opposite end of the political spectrum, obliviously equated the market with chaebŏl. Or perhaps, as Chang retorts, "they both merely acknowledged the contemporary reality of South Korea, that the market is the chaebŏl and the chaebŏl are the market."[72] South Korea since the 1997 IMF crisis has been called Samsung Republic, and many controversial government policies and slogans during the Roh Moo-hyun administration were the product of the Samsung Economic Research Institute.[73] Some scholars consider chaebŏl's inordinate influence in society—"a government above the government"—as a source of crisis of democracy in South Korea.[74]

The Demise of the Discourse of Minjung

Given the profound transformation both globally and in post-1987 South Korea, it is inevitable that the discourse of minjung would over time become further marginalized, if not face complete demise. Although the end of the Cold War system worldwide did not end the Cold War on the Korean Peninsula, it did take away a worldview that had provided a political, ideological, and intellectual framework to the minjung movement—namely, socialism or socialist visions. For the minjung movement, perhaps more critical than the demise of the socialism as an ideology or political theory was the disappearance of a worldview that provided an egalitarian alternative to South Korea's unrelenting capitalistic development and consequent alienation and competition.

The South Korean state's anti-communism left the minjung movement in the 1980s without the benefit of knowing how socialist ideas had been practiced in the "actually existing socialist" countries, however. As former "enemies" were fast becoming not only capitalist but also political and economic partners of South Korea, any legitimacy and valence of the socialist vision in minjung discourse could not help but be taken away.[75] Some in the minjung movement initially tried to minimize the impact of the collapse by suggesting that failed socialist countries were either corrupt or practiced a state capitalism and not real socialism.[76]

During the harsh military dictatorships of Park Chung-hee and Chun Doo-hwan, a social movement needed more than just a call for political reform for its moral authority and legitimacy—it needed vision for an alternative future with a promise to overhaul the current system. Under the democratic system, however, working with the existing system became de rigueur. As the political sphere and civil society expanded and diversified, social movements also expanded and diversified. Sociologist Cho Hŭi-yŏn categorized the social movements of the 1990s broadly into minjung-oriented revolutionary movements or simin-oriented nonrevolutionary movements, or radical movements and moderate movements.[77]

South Korea's rapid capitalistic development and subsequent diversification in class structure also spurred the disintegration of minjung discourse in the late 1980s. Prior to the 1980s, capitalism in South Korea was indeed relatively undifferentiated, giving rise to the material and intellectual basis for the rise of minjung discourse.[78] Minjung practitioners considered South Korea underdeveloped and heavily foreign dependent, with its economy liable to go into crisis, if not imminent collapse, once exposed to economic fluctuations of the global capitalist system such as the 1979 second oil shock.[79]

By the late 1980s, South Korea's capitalism had become safely secured as several economic crises were put under control, which in turn provided the material basis for the differentiated class structure observed in present-day South Korea. From the time of the 1986 Asian Games to the 1988 Olympics, South Korea experienced an unprecedented level of prosperity, brought on in part by the so-called three lows—the low dollar, low price of oil, and low interest rates.[80] The middle class was also growing, helped by increases in land and property values in the aftermath of the 1988 Olympics, among other factors.[81]

The working class also became differentiated and diversified. For example, the state's promotion of capital-intensive heavy chemical industries from the late 1970s gave birth to an "aristocratic working class." These are mostly male workers in conglomerate-owned industries such as Hyundai and Daewoo. Their income level and aspirations set them apart from workers employed in labor-intensive industries that had till then formed the backbone of South Korea's export-oriented economy of the 1960s and 1970s.[82] Industrial restructuring and the resulting working-class diversification gave rise to a wide array of political perspectives and aspirations, as well as demands for a new form of social movement that differed from that of the previous era.

As elsewhere in the world, advanced capitalism in South Korea is a consumption-driven capitalism in which consumers are manufactured.[83] In contrast to the previous "era of deficiency," the radically altered, consumption-oriented 1990s was an "era of pleasure," philosopher Pak Yŏng-gyun noted. Cultural products, sports—also heavily promoted during the Fifth Republic as a way to divert public attention from politics[84]—and public discourse on sex and well-being, were initiated and mediated by mass media, coming to dominate public discussion. The discourse of minjung, constructed on and sustained in the era of deficiency, was clearly no longer tenable in the new era.[85] In sum, the discourse of minjung was a product of relatively undifferentiated capitalism and undifferentiated class structure of 1970s and 1980s Korean society.

The Rise of the Citizens' Movement (Simin Undong)

With democratization from above and profusion of emerging and multiple subjectivities and aspirations from below, it is no surprise that social movements in South Korea also went through profound changes. The 1980s minjung movement considered itself to be guided by "scientific theories" that were formulated on the analyses of the structural condition of South Korea and that was to guide the movement to its revolutionary goals. Marxism and Leninism were the most prominent among these theories, for reasons that I elaborate elsewhere, and various and strenuous efforts were made to infuse theories with praxis.[86] By the late 1990s, as I have stated before, the privileged place of such theories in social movements also came to an end. With the political liberalization that accompanied the democratization of society, social movements of the 1990s no longer had one overarching goal or even a center, ideologically or organizationally. The state was no longer the locus of power; no single issue could galvanize society as it did in the 1980s, with the ubiquitous and unifying slogan of "Down with the Chun Doo-hwan regime." In post-1987 South Korea, the previous era's "unitary confrontation of the state versus civil society" shifted to "multilevel confrontation" between the state and various actors in civil society, as sociologist Kim Ho-gi succinctly summarized.[87]

A dizzying array of new social issues began to emerge, ranging from consumer and environmental protection to educational and urban transportation issues, to women's and gay and lesbian rights, leading to the mushrooming of what became known as the citizens' movement (simin undong). The citizens' movement is composed of movements of autonomous associations, including diverse activist groups and interest groups, who pursue "universality and the public good based on democratic values and norms."[88] As procedural democratic systems were taking root in society, both the state and emerging citizens' movement proponents began to vociferously denounce the minjung movement; its goals, strategies, and tactics were out of touch with the changed sociopolitical reality—a relic of a bygone era that was no longer relevant. In the deradicalized and depoliticized 1990s, the citizens' movement was better suited to accommodate the nonrevolutionary desires of newly emerging subjectivities.[89] One of the first such organizations, Kyŏngsillyŏn (Kyŏngje chŏngŭi silch'ŏn simin yŏnhap, Citizens' Coalition for Economic Justice, CCEJ), founded in 1989 to promote economic justice and protection of the environment, along with other goals, quickly became a representative case of the new type of social movement, and other groups soon followed.

Dominant voices in this new emerging order of the 1990s demanded that the minjung movement "move over" and relinquish its erstwhile role as a catalyst and agent of social change to the middle class. In 1993, the then–general secretary of Kyŏngsillyŏn and a participant in the 1970s democratization movement, Rev. Sŏ Kyŏng-sŏk, effectively declared that the era of minjung had passed. During the authoritarian period, change in political power was deemed possible only through revolution, and the minjung had been entrusted with this historical task to bring about this revolution. In the new era, however, elections, rather than revolution, became the modus operandi to bring about social change: "If we assume that elections determine the future from this point on, our middle class, representing 70 percent of the national population, will determine the future of Korea."[90]

Here it should be noted, however, that the 1990s witnessed not only an explosion of the citizens' movement, but also at the same time what could be characterized as popularization (taejunghwa) of social movements that had continued from the 1980s, as noted by literary critic Ch'ŏn Chŏng-hwan. The labor movement made great effort to reincarnate itself to be relevant in this changed era, for example. Its persistent effort to organize unions to represent the interest of workers and to obtain basic labor rights eventually led to nationwide organizations such as Chŏnnohyŏp in 1990 and later Minju Noch'ong in 1995, which I discuss in more detail shortly. Even the university student movement, no longer with the high national profile it once had in the 1980s, made strenuous efforts to become more in tune with the general student body throughout the 1990s.[91]

The burgeoning citizens' movements in the 1990s in Korea were clearly a product of global and domestic sociopolitical and cultural transformations. At the same time, however, the citizens' movement groups in their early phase sprouted from the same soil that had nurtured the minjung movement of the previous era; as such, they were not a completely different species from the minjung movement. As sociologist Kim Tong-ch'un [Dong-Choon Kim] notes, many of the issues, strategies, and tactics of the new social movement were an outcome of the critical evaluation of real and perceived limits of the previous minjung movement: its "excess" of ideology, its exclusive focus on political issues and state power, and an overall emphasis on minjung that subordinated the rights of women and other subaltern groups, among others. If the previous minjung movement articulated a case of an American soldier's assault of a sex worker in South Korea as a manifestation of an unequal relationship between the United States and South Korea, the citizens' movement would rearticulate it as a "human rights" violation, for example. Similarly, rather than demanding the dismantling of chaebŏl in toto, which had been a persistent demand of the minjung movement in the 1980s, the citizens' movement found it more expedient, and more appealing to the public in this new era, to charge a chaebŏl with a legal infraction via a class action lawsuit.[92]

Citizen as Neoliberal Subject and the 1990s Labor Movement

As briefly mentioned in the introductory chapter and as sociologist Göran Therborn argues, the 1990s witnessed the rise of discourse of a new middle class in Africa, Asia, Latin America, and Eastern Europe.[93] This phenomenon coincided with a triumphalist discourse celebrating the "arrival of mass markets of solvent consumers." Even before the onslaught of neoliberalism, an intimate link between liberal democracy and the market had been observed, as in the work of German jurist and political theorist Carl Schmitt who noted that liberal democracy was "already a form of economizing the state and the political."[94] Citizenship and the middle class are intimately conjoined in a liberal system where, in the words of feminist theorist Mary Dietze, citizenship denotes a "right to pursue one's interests, without hindrance, in the marketplace."[95]

Even as "middle-classness" has proved to be fragile and unstable with an ever-present risk of falling into poverty, political commentators have upheld the middle class as a "promising foundation for sound economics and liberal democracy."⁹⁶ The 1990s South Korean citizens' movement constructed its emancipatory narrative based on the principal values of liberal democracy: an individual's "equality," "autonomy," and "freedom." As South Korea has become increasingly neoliberal, with the business sector perceiving politics as merely about appearance and the economy as fundamental,⁹⁷ the notion of citizen has likewise become increasingly reconfigured by market-oriented metrics such as "self-development" and "self-improvement." Sŏ Tong-jin observed that the discourse of "self-investing human capital," referring to an individual's self-motivation to increase life skill development and life competence and the state's human capital development, was especially pronounced in the 1990s.⁹⁸ Furthermore, anthropologist Jesook Song argues that in neoliberal state policies, the category of citizen has been limited in practice to those who can partake in and maintain the current liberal capitalist order and its class structure.⁹⁹

One of the most trenchant observations about the modern liberal-democratic state was made by Michel Foucault, who noted that it has emerged historically with the parallel development of "a whole network of disciplinary mechanisms whose ultimate effect was to induce self-discipline as an integral dimension of subject-formation."¹⁰⁰ In Foucault's analysis of the panopticon, a model prison designed in the late eighteenth century, each inmate "becomes to himself his own jailer." Foucault saw in the perpetual self-surveillance of the inmate "the genesis of the celebrated 'individualism' and heightened self-consciousness that are hallmarks of modern times."¹⁰¹ Foucault summed up this central problematic concerning the relationship between the modern subject (i.e., citizen) and the modern state as "the intimate relation and reciprocal tension between subjectivity and subjection."¹⁰² Another corollary observation about citizenship as the foundational principle in a liberal democracy is its tendency to limit politics to activities oriented to the state. Political theorist Kirstie McClure argues that the construction of the citizen as the "subject of rights" assumes the institutions of the modern constitutional state to be "a privileged expression of political community and hence as the principle [sic] and necessarily privileged site of political action."¹⁰³

South Korea's labor movement, especially in the context of global neoliberalism and the state's institutionalization of market and labor flexibility, illustrates this tension between subject formation and state subjection. In the trajectory of the post-1987 labor movement, one can follow how the process of the labor movement's gaining of social citizenship, as it became accepted as a formal political subject, was simultaneously a process of subjection to the state and to the corporate sector. The case of the Minju noch'ong (Chŏn'guk minju nodongjohap ch'ongyŏnmaeng, Korean Confederation of Trade Unions, KCTU), one of South Korea's two national umbrella union organizations, illustrates this point most clearly.

The Great Struggle of Workers in 1987 was the largest-ever mass strike of the working class in Korea. For the first time since 1945, laborers who had existed until then mostly as "wage slaves" burst onto the national scene as a working class—the struggle was indeed the "workers' self-declaration as human beings."[104] Through unity and persistence, the labor movement achieved remarkable gains, pushing pay increases to double digits in 1987 and organizing more than two thousand new democratic unions in 1988.[105] Equally important as tangible and organizational gains was the new sense of confidence workers had in their own collective power. After decades of defeat and betrayal, the struggle showed the possibility of the working class gaining its own rights and influencing the future direction of Korean society.

Having experienced exhilarating solidarity since the struggle but increasingly faced with unrelenting repression from the state and business, especially under a revised labor law that would enable management to lay off workers easily, workers came together to form Chŏnnohyŏp, mentioned at the beginning of this chapter. Chŏnnohyŏp aimed to be a central organization of the labor movement that would forge nationwide solidarity among workers to repeal the revised labor law, to obtain wage increases, and to support newly established democratic unions in each plant. Built on workers' independent activities, Chŏnnohyŏp's organizational and operating principles set it apart from the regime-friendly Han'guk noch'ong (FKTU) with its management-accommodating tendencies.[106]

From the moment Chŏnnohyŏp was founded, it faced attack from both the state and business and had to fight to defend its very existence. State repression of Chŏnnohyŏp took a variety of forms such as inspections of the activities of unions affiliated with Chŏnnohyŏp, putting leaders on wanted lists or imprisoning them, and penalizing workers' exercise of legal rights by means of the policy of "no work, no pay." South Korea's labor unionism was enterprise based—the organization of a single trade union within one plant rather than by trade or industry. This type of unionism makes it difficult for unions to represent the interest of all workers, especially those in nonstandard arrangements, and to resist state and capital's labor flexibilization strategies. Faced with the difficulty of carrying out any joint action on a national scale, Chŏnnohyŏp decided to transform existing enterprise-based unions into industry-based unions. Toward this goal, Chŏnnohyŏp members formed Minju noch'ong (KCTU) on November 11, 1995, with the participation of 866 unions nationally and 410,000 union members.[107]

It was not until 1999 that the Minju noch'ong gained full citizenship, only after demonstrating its strength by carrying out a nationwide general strike during a bitter winter from December 1996 until January 1997. The largest strike since 1987, it aimed to do away with the revised labor law that made dismissal of workers easier for employers and severely limited labor-organizing rights. Both blue-collar and white-collar workers, including those in the financial sector and clerical jobs, joined in the strike. Even the management-friendly Han'guk noch'ong participated in the strike for the first time in its history.[108] As a result, the government was forced to amend the laws. In 1999, the state also relented and legalized Minju noch'ong, four years after its founding.

As I have briefly discussed before, and as Pak Yŏng-gyun and many others have pointed out, democracy, rationality, and liberalization constituted the cornerstones of the passive revolution from above in post-1987 South Korea. These ideas became institutionalized and legalized in social, political, and economic spheres, with the contractual relationship between management and labor systematically built in. The legalization of Minju noch'ong, though due in part to labor's growing strength, as the state could no longer control it through overt coercion, was also the first full-scale attempt by the state and the corporate sector to institutionalize neoliberal management-labor relations.[109]

Once the democratic labor movement now represented by Minju noch'ong gained social citizenship, however, it immediately found itself in a "crisis" and to respond to demands of the state and corporate sector to redeem itself. The crisis stemmed from Minju noch'ong's "too radical" and "selfish" position—it needed to modify its egocentric position and become more responsible for the common good of society.[110] In the previous era, the "democratic" labor movement, along with the student movement, had been a central component of the anti-authoritarian and pro-democracy movement.[111] Its moral authority in the minjung movement derived in large part from its position as militant and uncompromising as well as a valiant history of organizing and maintaining "democratic unions" in the face of state suppression and "yellow unions" (company friendly, or *ŏyong*). Since the early 1990s, in part due to the strength of the labor movement, management has abandoned its previous tactic of not recognizing democratic unions or threatening existing democratic unions and has instead adopted a strategy of accommodation and co-optation. Under the slogans of "Reconciliation between management and labor" and "Industrial peace," the management began to co-opt "democratic union" leaders and members. As a result, the previously clear-cut distinction between "democratic unions" and "yellow unions" was no longer so distinct on the shop floor.[112] At the same time, the state, business, and citizens' movement all demanded that the labor movement reform and be more responsive to the welfare of the society as a whole.[113]

The demand for reform, that labor "participate and self-reflect" (*ch'amyŏ wa sŏngch'al ŭi nodong undong*)—one of the more ubiquitous slogans at the time—was also a practical and discursive struggle for the control of labor. In the face of unrelenting pressure from the state and business sector, Minju noch'ong relented, putting forth various strategies to accommodate such demands, as expressed in slogans such as "The labor movement that is with the citizens" (*kungmin kwa hamkke hanŭn nodong undong*) and "Society-oriented labor unionism" (*sahoejŏk nodong chohap chuŭi*).[114] Such efforts by labor did not stop the sheer magnitude of the neoliberal tide, however.

The ease with which demands for labor to reform gained currency at the time indicated that both the state and the corporate sector were able to control labor and carry out the policy of labor flexibility. At its core, this demand for reform was a call for Minju noch'ong to recognize and accept the fundamental principles of liberal market competition.[115] In fact, all three liberal democratic governments (Kim Young-sam, Kim Dae-jung, and Roh Moo-hyun) demanded that both business and labor compete on an equal footing, as if they were on the same playing field.[116] The 1997 IMF crisis further intensified the call to accede to demands of liberal market competition. The prime example of an institutional framework promoting such market competition based on the principle of equal partnership of labor and corporate sectors was the Korea Tripartite Commission in 1998.[117]

By inviting labor to participate in the tripartite commission, the Kim Dae-jung government hoped, among other goals, to recognize labor as an essential partner in production and to give it a voice at the bargaining table with business.[118] The key issue that eventually forced the Minju noch'ong to withdraw from the commission was a set of revised laws that would make layoffs and employment of dispatched workers to replace temporary vacancies easier for corporations. In return for agreement on these laws, the government promised to expand public expenditures for the social safety net and to improve basic labor rights.[119] The rank and file of Minju noch'ong saw these laws as a way for the state and business to advance the goal of labor market flexibility.[120] Even as the commission was deliberating, the Kim government announced and eventually carried out a series of neoliberal policies, such as privatization of public industries and closure of underperforming banks and corporations. Minju noch'ong was powerless to compel the state to execute the promised reform.[121] Minju noch'ong was absent when its government and business-friendly counterpart

Han'guk noch'ong signed an agreement ultimately giving consent for the state and corporate sector to control labor.[122]

As we have seen, the paradigm shift from minjung to simin starting in the late 1980s was part and parcel of both socioeconomic transformations of global scale, as well as epistemological shifts that such profound and wide-ranging changes accompany. The discourse of minjung, conceived at a time when Korean capitalism was still developing, could not sustain its vitality and function with the advance of capitalism and resulting differentiation in class structure, followed by the subsequent proliferation of multiple subjectivities and desires. Whether as an emancipatory narrative or as critique, minjung discourse seemingly became no longer viable or compatible with the increasing emphasis on individual identities and needs, with the public defined exclusively as citizens in a liberal democracy, even as opportunities for self-identification multiplied and diversified.

Since 1997, South Korea has faced an explosion of economic crises, massive unemployment, and an increasing gap between the rich and the poor, among other challenges. At the same time, structural conditions and quality-of-life issues raised by neoliberalism and mounting socioeconomic problems have confirmed what historian Arif Dirlik observed—the very structures of contemporary capitalism are the "new authoritarianism" that exercises "unprecedentedly powerful means of supervision and control."[123] Even as the issues faced by post-1997 South Korea are essentially the same problems that previous social theories set out to solve, the push to do away with minjung discourse has made those problems illegible.[124] The widely circulated discourse of liberal democracy of the 1990s has been recast as a discourse of neoliberalism. Standing notions of "citizen" and "liberal democracy," though capturing the new dynamics found in transformed post-1987 South Korea, have been inadequate to respond to the challenges of neoliberal capitalism. The discourse of the paradigm shift, while proffering much-needed and justified criticism of minjung discourse, has also functioned, however inadvertently, to legitimize contemporary structures of power. The following chapter continues the discussion of the paradigm shift from minjung to simin in the sphere of culture.

2

The Paradigm Shift from the Political to the Cultural and Huildam Literature

In 1997, Pang Hyŏn-sŏk, known for his memorable "labor literature" (*nodong sosŏl*) of the 1980s, blasted the contemporary literary field.¹ Noting that that year's recipient of the Nobel Prize in literature was Italian playwright Dario Fo, whose work is regarded as a powerful critique of social injustice and inequality, Pang lamented that South Korean literature was running in the opposite direction.² The targets of his high-voltage criticism were not only commercially successful novels but also those characterized as "literature of reminiscence" (huildam).

Pang Hyŏn-sŏk's vehement indignation was more specifically directed to the ways in which huildam portray the 1980s in general and 1980s undongkwŏn in particular. As he saw it, the 1990s huildam invoke undongkwŏn to mark its wholesale indictment as misguided and no longer irrelevant. What began as a compelling need to assess the 1980s became a melodramatic distortion of truth for Pang; huildam of the 1990s treated both the ruling bloc and undongkwŏn as one and the same—as victims of the oppressive regime. The ruthless authoritarian military dictatorship, which trampled human and civil rights and the dignity of the people, and the undongkwŏn, who had fought against them with dedication and sacrifice, were treated equally as victims in huildam. An amorphous group usually portrayed as tender hearted (*yŏrin simjŏng*) and good natured (*sŏllyanghan*), the victims in huildam were "all of us"; there was no effort to distinguish those who sacrificed themselves for democracy from those who were simply waiting out the time and getting by or those who were content to seek their own personal comfort and material gain, ignoring the exigency of the era. As all of them were simply victims, there was no one left to take stock of the era or to take responsibility for mistakes of the 1980s. Furthermore, Pang lamented, undongkwŏn were portrayed usually as fatally and inherently flawed individuals who caused "all of us"—the "good people"—the pain and anguish from which they still suffer and thus deserved to be condemned.[3]

Literary critic Chŏng Hong-su summed up Pang's predicament: "What does it mean to look back on the life of a generation whose erstwhile political commitment has been reduced to an index of ideological excess and utter failure, subjected to ongoing insults, their past wounds still fresh, and their own deeply felt remorse and self-reflection still ongoing?"[4] Huildam emerged in the 1990s as a widespread sense of setback among the generation of the 1980s minjung movement that their revolutionary hope and vision, faith in history and the future were disappearing fast. The outcome of the June uprising of 1987, itself also a culmination of nearly three decades of the persistent democratization movement, was far from what they had envisioned and hoped for, especially as the post-1987 political leadership was still in the hands of those who were closely affiliated with the Chun Doo-hwan regime. The 1990s was for many a time of a different kind of crisis from the earlier authoritarian era, a kind faced when "the old is dying and the new cannot be born,"[5] when the energies unleashed by the minjung movement were swiftly contained and the revolutionary wave was turned back—a time Alain Badiou in a different context referred to as "the switching between the epic and the tragic."[6]

Huildam by and large deal with memories of the 1980s by the generation who lived through it. That huildam writers, many of whom had been involved in or sympathetic to the 1980s movement, were writing in the deeply and radically transformed 1990s by itself was taken to be an indication that their work was mostly about reevaluating their own past convictions and the worldview that they had inhabited. Some of them, to some degree, were also thought to have capitulated to the changed reality, the reality of wholesale globalization and neoliberalism.[7] Huildam literature was clearly a phenomenon of the 1990s, although it is not unusual to find literary works published well into the 2000s and even later that could and would be characterized as huildam.

Although Pang's criticisms were directed at huildam in general for their sweeping condemnation of undongkwŏn from the vantage point of former undongkwŏn, critics who were themselves sympathetic to the minjung movement tended to criticize huildam for a different reason—as a case of self-renunciation or self-pity of the undongkwŏn, or as a gesture of "exaggerated despair" with the seeming suggestion that any resistance was no longer possible.[8] Although none of the critics mentioned it by name, their overall criticisms amounted to what Walter Benjamin called left-wing melancholy: a melancholia of the former revolutionary who self-indulgently wallows in memories of the revolution's failure and refuses to come to terms with the transformed present. This refusal or failure is rooted on the notion of history as "empty-time" or "progress." For Benjamin, the most critical point was that the narcissistic attachment to one's past allegiances and identity leads to inaction and complacency.[9]

Authors and protagonists of huildam were more often than not former undongkwŏn who were undergoing the paradigm shifts in their own lives—from minjung to simin, from the revolutionary to petite bourgeoisie. Their huildam is replete with loss, regret, passion, and meaninglessness—the stuff of melancholy. In this context, huildam constitutes, however unwittingly, the regime of discontinuity that posits post-1987 as a radical departure from the previous era, suggesting the finality of the paradigm shift. At the same time, however, a more keenly contextual and attentive reading of some of the huildam suggests the possibility of reconceptualizing huildam as a "form of remembrance"—that is, it explores the archive of unrealized hopes, dreams, betrayals, and failures of the minjung movement and the undongkwŏn when society was in haste to disavow the movement in toto. Even as Benjamin excoriated the self-absorbed melancholy that is not interested in the world of human actors but the world of dead objects, he also suggested a possibility of embracing dead objects as a way to "redeem" them.[10] Although his notion of redemption is open to multiple interpretations and my own understanding is highly schematic,[11] what is central for this chapter is his suggestion that history be viewed as a sort of counterhistory of the defeated, forgotten, and oppressed.[12] It is a redemption of the "destructive energies" of the former struggle, both the unknown stories and the as-yet-unfulfilled hopes and desires, "a mode of articulating the past that is co-extensive with the defeatism and quietism" inaugurated by the transformed world.[13] Huildam writers whom I discuss here, and especially women writers, were dismissed by critics by and large as hypersentimental, as they return to the past and self-interrogate persistently and uncompromisingly. Rather than offering comforting platitudes about the inevitable historical advance of progressive forces in the face of defeat, I submit, they perform an act of record keeping, the task of a chronicler for a redemptive interruption of the paralyzing course of history.

Neither a survey of huildam literature nor a comprehensive summation of critical work on it, this chapter examines huildam literature as symptomatic of both the shift from the political to the cultural in Korean society in general and among the minjung movement in particular while simultaneously practicing a politics of active remembrance of unfulfilled promises of the minjung movement. Aside from the authors' shared background as former undongkwŏn, which each text handles differently, the works I discuss are linked by their preoccupation with the failures of the 1980s revolution. In what follows, I first discuss debates surrounding the "crisis of literature" of the 1990s, moving the previous chapter's discussion of the paradigm shift of minjung to simin to the literary domain. I then examine the rise of huildam in the context of the changing role of literature and writers in the 1990s. The third part of the chapter focuses on discussing huildam as suggesting a mode of remembrance that cannot be reduced to melancholy devoid of any relation to the present.

Crisis of Literature

The radical transformation of Korean society from the late 1980s and the widespread sense of loss, confusion, and despair that greeted the democratization movement convulsed the literary field as well. Writers who had believed that it was their responsibility to represent the lives of minjung in all of their entirety and complexity and who had taken pride in partaking in the democratization movement through their literary production felt an overwhelming sense of powerlessness—"as if disarmed soldiers."[14] For an eminent scholar of Korean literature, Ch'oe Wŏn-sik, the previous era's national (minjok) or people's (minjung) literature had been "an arsenal open to all, where the poor and the weak daily resorted for arms."[15] Kong Chi-yŏng, a novelist of numerous best sellers, ruefully echoed this sentiment: "I have borne a heavy responsibility on behalf of Korean literature . . . in the last twenty years. This is not because I was someone with a particularly strong sense of responsibility nor because I was an unduly serious person [*mugŏun in'gan*], and I was not the only one carrying this burden. [The sense of responsibility] was like a uniform given to me as someone who happened to be a writer in that era."[16]

In the 1990s, however, as literary critic Kim Myŏng-in noted, literature was "taken over" by writers whose worldview did not contain, or was devoid of, such heavily loaded terms as "minjung," "history," "subjectivity," and "emancipation," that had preoccupied writers of the previous era. In the 1990s, everyday life replaced historical, individuality replaced communality, post-enlightenment and the post-political that of enlightenment and the political. In this circumstance, "a writer speaking of minjung again . . . needs to brace herself for the silent stigma of being anachronic."[17]

Kim Pyŏng-ik, another well-known critic writing in 1995, captured the paradigm shifts taking place in the field of literature:

> We are in the middle of the 1990s, and our topics have changed so very much from ten years ago, so much so that not only have the mountains and rivers changed, but also it feels as if I myself have become the mountain and the river. The [topics of] stories have moved on: from revolution to a [social] movement, from praxis to desire, from political economy to cultural studies, from progressive to pluralistic, from the theory of dominant versus dominated to post-centrism and deconstruction, from analysis of class systems to exploration of signs [kiho], from minjung to mass, from nation [minjok] to globalization, from Marx to Foucault and Baudrillard, among others.[18]

The regime of discontinuity that I discuss in the introduction, the narrative of break—epistemological, aesthetic, and political—from the 1980s was also one of the most pronounced tropes of literature of the 1990s. In a roundtable discussion that aimed to take stock of the literary field of the decade, participating critics Hwang Chong-yŏn, Chin Chŏng-sŏk, Kim Tong-sik, and Yi Kwang-ho all agreed that the field had changed completely and dramatically since the 1980s.[19] Most notably, the faith in the possibility of radical change, a sentiment that was common in the 1980s, had disappeared. Literature in the 1980s had been a constitutive part of the radical movement, and as such was produced and consumed in the nexus of the political goal of radical change. This particular circumstance had also allowed writers to nurture and sustain the hope—or the fantasy—that literature could capture and represent the world holistically, Hwang Chŏng-yŏn opined. In this context, larger historical-philosophical aspirations of the work took priority over literary maturity and sophistication, however such notions may have been defined. The works of representative writers of the 1980s, such as Pak No-hae and Hwang Chi-u, were also a kind of "open text," inviting readers to actively engage with them, rather than a product of aspiration for literary perfection.[20]

The notion of writer as socially engaged—the Sartrean notion of committed literature (*littérature engagée*)—goes back over a century to Émile Zola's essay "J'accuse," written at the time of the Dreyfus affair in 1898. It is by now passé to mention George Orwell's dictum that "the attitude that art should have nothing to do with politics is itself a political attitude."[21] The attempt to separate the aesthetic from the political is usually found in conservative literary circles,[22] but minjung writers by and large were also keenly aware of, and expressed their concern about, the presumed "lack of aesthetic" in minjung literature. Some were more explicitly concerned about the political, however. Kim In-suk, for example, whose earlier novels in the 1980s dealt with major themes of Korean history and society, was concerned about her novels' approximation to "historical truths" rather than about their aesthetic achievement (*mihakjŏk wansŏngdo*); she was concerned that her work might inadvertently "fabricate facts or delete important parts of facts for novelistic convenience" and, furthermore, that she might "distort historical developments" due to her "own limited perspective."[23]

By the 1990s, the above four critics in the roundtable concluded, the nexus of literature and radical change that had provided an anchor for writers of the 1980s no longer existed or had lost much of its utility. The literature of the 1990s had to stand on its own, as it were, based on its own raison d'être and identity, in the midst of rough challenges posed by the culture industry and the commodity aesthetic, among others. It was no longer feasible to claim that literature still had an enlightenment function or that it would holistically reflect or represent the life or the era in which one lived. In the 1990s, literature was undergoing a fundamental change of delicate "functional differentiation" as it was developing its own independent and autonomous realm.[24] Kim Chŏng-nan, a poet and critic, in another roundtable discussion assessing the literature of the 1990s, also echoed this sentiment: "In the 1990s, the long-standing illusion about literature [as an agent of societal change] has been demolished as literature can no longer rely on politics or society for its raison d'être; literature has to return to literature and compete solely within its own terms."[25]

For critic Hwang Chong-yŏn, Ku Hyo-sŏ's novel *A Way to Cross a Swamp* (*Nŭp'ŭl kŏnnŏnŭn pŏp*) was one of the most symptomatic of crises that literature faced in the 1990s. In Ku's novel, a man tries to find out the truth about his birth, which he knows to have been surrounded by some unclear circumstances. The more he tries to find out the "truth," however, the deeper he falls into a labyrinth, and he ultimately fails to get any firmly established facts about his birth. The moral of the story is clear, according to Hwang: it is no longer profitable to question origin, the fundamental, or history; there is no longer a narrative that anchors and guarantees one's firm identity.[26] Hwang continues:

> It became difficult for people in the 1990s to trust in history or narrative.... Whether it was nationalism, minjung-ism, or Marxism, these narratives [of the pre-1990s] had the public's trust [kongsinnyŏk].... But in the 1990s they became suspect. The demise of actually existing socialism took away the faith in the progress and progressiveness of history, and as the postmodernism fad spread, distrust in the grand narrative intensified. That the grand narrative through which a particular individual and societal experience became universalized has lost its authority—this is the most critical condition in which the literature of the 1990s existed.[27]

A pervasive sense of the uncertain role of literature also explains in part the high-profile reception of Kojin Karatani's *The End of Modern Literature* in South Korea. Literature is no longer capable of taking on sociopolitical issues as it was in the past, Karatani argues, as the specific historical conditions in which modern literature had emerged have been transformed. In particular, the emergence of global mass culture following the development of new media technology, along with other developments, has contributed to the demise of the novel.[28] Following this development is the loss of the intellectual and ethical role that literature of modern society had assumed until recently. For literary critic Kim Chong-ch'ŏl, literature was no longer able to provide answers to resolve some of the contradictions of society; it had become too narrowly focused to be able to deal with sociopolitical issues. In fact, Karatani cites the case of Kim, who quit being a critic and founded a journal focusing on environmental issues, as symptomatic of the end of modern literature.[29] Karatani claims that in South Korea, literature functioned more or less like a student movement—that is, in the absence of other forces to fight for social justice and equality, literature has had to carry more than its share of social and political responsibility. In his earlier *Origins of Modern Japanese Literature*, Karatani also suggested that political disillusionment following the failure of the 1920s people's rights movement and the subsequent disappearance of political possibilities in Japan were closely linked with the appearance of landscape and interiority—"the inner life." In other words, the turn to interiority in literature was the product of a specific historical order.[30]

While critics and scholars debated vociferously whether Karatani's prognosis about modern literature is correct or whether he was exaggerating the case of South Korea, it is undeniable that the transformation wrought by the demise of South Korea's once-vibrant social movement and the concomitant emergence of neoliberal governance gave rise to the crisis, if not yet the end, of literature. In Germany as well, following the breakdown of the Soviet Union and German reunification and as the intellectual life was no longer dominated by Cold War logic, writers of the 1968 generation were criticized for having taken the country too far down the path of political correctness at the expense of the political and moral stability of the country.[31]

Literature as Commodity and the Commercialization of Literature

It should be noted that not everyone, including those who were considered writers of minjung orientation, agreed that the 1990s represented a crisis in literature; in fact, some saw the paradigm shift and the changing scene as liberating and as an opportunity to explore new literary developments. Ku Hyo-sŏ, who was regarded in the 1980s as a minjung writer, noted how the previous era, driven by the desperation of having to confront injustice and the oppressive authoritarian regime, had made unduly excessive—and unmerited—demands on writers. Being a writer meant taking up such demands, and there was not even any serious discussion as to whether writers had such responsibility, according to Ku. In the 1990s, however, writers themselves wanted to be freed from all that fierce and burdensome social reality. Ku acknowledged that there was a great deal of confusion among writers in the 1990s. But even this kind of confusion was welcome, because in the past, "[writers] were not even allowed to be confused." In the 1990s, however, individuals and groups were confronted with various interests and demands that were self-driven and not dictated by sociopolitical concerns, which for him was a good thing. He hoped that a new kind of literature would emerge out of the transitional period, out of the process of taking stock of what had happened and of reflecting on and exploring new ways to understand the era.[32]

Literary critic Kwŏn Sŏng-u also took the stance that the 1990s represented a break from the previous era.[33] Rather than the "fossilized ideology" that dominated the literature of the 1980s, the literature of the 1990s would show more of the immediacy of life and the abundance of existential issues in the varied experiences of people. The 1980s literature that dealt with major sociopolitical issues, such as the division of the country or the oppression of labor, would move away from its sharp-edged and narrow sense of the political world and show us a world with a more complex, existential, and expansive view of humanity, the world, and history. This, according to Kwŏn, would mean overcoming the narrow parameters of subject matter that the 1980s literature was concerned with. In the 1990s, the author's own unique perspective on the subject matter and her method of representation would be important criteria by which literary merit was considered, Kwŏn opined.[34]

Hwang Chong-yŏn was another critic who greeted the crisis of literature as a natural and positive outcome of historical development. Upending the prevailing sentiment about literature of engagement, he declared that it was actually the "underdevelopment" of Korean society that had accorded literature the high esteem, authority, and influence that it had enjoyed until the 1990s. He questioned the merit of accolades that some of the works, especially those known for their political engagement, had received.[35] He suggested that the kind of undue influence of literature that marked the previous era is anachronic and should be dispensed with in the 1990s.[36] Novelist Ch'oe Yun also welcomed the changed environment in which authors have to navigate the place of literature and writers in society on new terms as distressing but also meaningful and even joyous.[37]

At the same time, concern about the commodification and commercialization of literature, both in the realm of production and consumption, was an oft-discussed topic from the 1990s onward and was considered part and parcel of the larger trend, the rise of mass consumption. Mass consumption was considered to be one of the most conspicuous changes in popular culture of the late 1980s. To be sure, every decade has witnessed a great change in popular culture and the parallel rise of mass consumption, each with its representative cultural icons: draft beer, blue jeans, and acoustic guitar in the 1970s and pro baseball, color TV, and the liberalization of school uniforms in the 1980s, for example. However, the kind of transformation in mass culture and the rise of consumption culture in the 1990s was in no way comparable to what had appeared before.[38] To critics, the blurring of the divide between reality and fantasy[39] as well as the dazzling urban sophistication shown in the literary works of the 1990s was mostly a result of the rise of mass consumption.[40]

Commercialization and commodification of literature, as well as the commercialization of publishers, also meant a changed role for literary critics, of which literary critic Kim Myŏng-in was perhaps one of the most vocal critics. Publishing literature in the 1990s had become a commercial enterprise, Kim protested, requiring the same kind of enterprising mindset and skill as producing a trendy commercial product; literary criticism had also fallen to the level of mere packaging or decoration of a product. If an "excess of ethics" characterized the literary criticism of the 1980s, then a lack of ethics characterized the literary criticism of the 1990s; this void of ethics was an index of literature's subjugation to commercialism as well as the disappearance of its political consciousness, according to Kim.[41] Kim argued that literary critics had become mainly cheerleaders or promoters for publishing houses, whose survival depended on publishing a steady stream of best sellers; critics were mobilized to carry out what amounted to literary journeywork; to issue spurious criticisms, to write anything from blurbs of book covers to newspaper advertisements to postscripts and commentaries, among others.[42] For Kim Chŏng-nan, critics were also becoming the "caretakers of celebrity authors."[43] The critics' neglect of their duties to properly examine literature left the task to the commercially driven machinery of the advertising industry.[44] Contemporary literary journals were also criticized for their market orientation and for catering to rising star writers, rather than discovering and nurturing talented but unknown writers.[45] The fact that many recently successful writers were graduates of creative writing programs at universities, unlike the writers of the previous era who did not follow a requisite course to become writers, was also seen as yet another indication of the changing, commercialized scene in the field, according to critic Sŏ Tong-jin.[46]

Furthermore, Kim Chŏng-nan argued, the literary community tends to regard highly those critics who use Western theories—postmodernism being the most-often-cited theory—as a barometer by which to evaluate literary work. Many of these critics know theories but do not know how to read the texts, Kim charged.[47] Kim went even further, suggesting that these critics, with their indiscriminate adoption and application of theories without considering the specific context of South Korean society, contributed to the 1990s "great cultural bubble."[48]

The sense that commercial enterprises, such as newspapers, were playing an unduly powerful and negative role in the literary field had been simmering for a while; it exploded in public on July 20, 2000, with the publication of the "Hwang Sŏk-yŏng Manifesto" in the newspaper *Hangryore*. Hwang Sŏk-yŏng, the doyen of minjung literature, characterized the conservative *Chosun Ilbo*'s administration of its Tong'in Literary Prize and other practices as not only an expansion of the commercialism that was already rampant in the literary field but also, and more problematically, as a strategy of cultural domination: the newspaper's extreme conservative positions on political and social issues; its strategy of "appeasement," which promoted cultural diversity in theory but in practice stifled genuine diversity; sensationalist reporting of its sister magazine, *Sports Chosun*—all of these were conscious strategies to lure, in the manner of starfish (*pulgasari*), the young and the old alike to its conservative fold.[49] The power wielded by *Chosun Ilbo* over intellectuals and the cozy relationship some of them had with the newspaper became yet another fault line for the literary community, further intensifying the division in an already-fractured literary field.[50]

The term *literary power* (*munhak kwŏllyŏk*), which had previously circulated only within the literary field (*mundan*), surfaced into public view as well. In

August 2000, an influential newspaper, *Kyunghyang Shinmun*, carried out a survey of forty-one literary figures and concluded that "literary power" was indeed real and that its impact on the literary field was far reaching and pernicious.[51] Literary power here was characterized as practices including long-standing nepotism and favoritism in the field; editors' requests for stories, articles, columns, and reviews only from certain authors; editors' and publishers' protection of authors from criticism; monopoly and favoritism in the management of literary prizes; and the forming of inner circles among literary figures.[52] Literary prizes were monopolized and given to those who were commercially successful rather than those who were trying new ideas and topics—writers who "ferociously" depicted reality were completely ignored by the literary field.[53] Again, this criticism of the media's collusion with writers or writers cooperating with one another to boost sales of literary work is not unique to South Korea or to the 1990s; in West Germany as well, for example, writers, critics, and publishers were often alleged to have created literary controversies in order to increase sales long before the 1990s.[54] In South Korea, all of the developments that were regarded as tied to the commercialization of literature erupted in the 1990s all at once and were seen as an unassailable indication that the role of literature as a whole had radically changed.

Huildam and Undongkwŏn

The 1990s huildam emerged as the literary field was in the throes of intense debates about the changing role of literature and of writers in society. That the trajectory of huildam followed that of political development is not a surprise. The term *huildam* was reputedly first coined in the 1990s by Kim Yun-sik, the well-known literary scholar, to refer to a literary development following the dissolution of the leftist cultural organization KAPF (Chosŏn p'ŭrollet'aria yesulga tongmaeng, Korea Artista Proleta Federacio) in the 1930s due to intensified Japanese suppression.[55] Although Kim does not explain why, he considered the early 1990s to be similar to the case of the 1930s when a large number of intellectuals and artists renounced their political commitment to the leftist cause.[56]

The disillusionment, frustration, as well as utter sense of failure of the generation that had fought for the long-anticipated revolution were the main themes of huildam, leading one scholar to characterize it as a literature of trauma.[57] Indeed, the dominant ethos of huildam was "shock, pain, and despair" as well as a sense of loss and nihilism.[58] The protagonist in Kong Chi-yŏng's short story "Decency toward Human Beings" ("*In'gane taehan yeu*") laments that the 1990s were a time "when no one sings the movement songs anymore even during a drinking gathering . . . when no one cares who's being wanted by police, who's left in prison and having to endure the chill of cold early spring weather; when everyone laughs when someone says, 'What, you still talk of the movement?'; when people talk about not what is right and what is wrong but what they like and [what they] don't like."[59]

In "Aftereffect" ("*Hyuyujŭng*"), a poem by Kim Yŏng-hyŏn, "I," a man who's "worn-out and behind the times," get up in the middle of the night, puzzled that "other people seem to go on as if nothing unusual has happened. . . . [I] answer to no one in particular. . . . Letting out a low roar as if I'm an old wolf . . . suffering anxiety, fretfulness, nausea, and loneliness by myself."[60] In Pang Hyŏn-sŏk's novel *A Form of Existence* (*Chonjaeŭi hyŏngsik*), the protagonist Chae-u, who had served a prison term for his labor activism, lashes out when he is told that he needs to file a petition to the court to clear his name from the criminal record: "Who the hell has the right to judge us as to whether our actions were honorable? We are dishonorable not because of the [labor activism we were involved in in the] past but because of what we [have become] in the present."[61]

Another ubiquitous theme in huildam is the characters' sense of loneliness and emptiness; their lives had once been filled with active and passionate engagement and the sacrifice of their own individual goals and plans for a larger purpose. In the changed era, they had become just the kind of ordinary petite bourgeoisie, any trace of which they had vigorously tried to shake off before. Moreover, the change in the political system—the democratization from above—did not bring about the anticipated change in society as a whole. Huildam is therefore a "self-confessional report," as it were, of the 1980s generation on the "humiliating existence" they were forced to carry on after the 1980s revolutionary fervor has been dissipated. Appearing in large numbers in the 1990s, huildam shares a certain set of characteristics that sets it apart from other works, so that critics consider it a genre of its own.[62]

Although the dominant public image of the 386 generation is male and some of the well-known huildam authors were also male, female writers burst onto the literary scene en masse in the 1990s and some of them, such as Kong Chi-yŏng and Kim In-suk, became not only popular writers but also well-known huildam authors. More often than not, these authors entered university in the early 1980s and were baptized by the passion of the era's revolutionary ideals and ethos, which remained formative, even foundational—regardless of the depth or the duration of their involvement—in their own personal trajectories as individuals and as writers. These authors have also borne the brunt of criticism for their reputed narratives of the depressed narcissist, their "regressive nostalgia" for the past, or their formulaic representation of the 1980s.[63]

For authors who were labeled as huildam writers, it is not only a gross injustice to be called as such, but the whole notion of huildam is anathema. For Pang Hyŏn-sŏk, the label belongs to other writers whose works treat undongkwŏn unfairly:

> Is it fair to treat the undongkwŏn, who paid dearly for their resistance to the ruling regime, as an object of ridicule and eradication, in the same way as the former authoritarian rulers whose crime stained the 1980s with blood? Why should those who remain at the front of the movement and nurture hope, even in the late 1990s . . . who had not run away from the demands of the era, be subjected to disdain? I have not yet met anyone [among the former undongkwŏn], except a few that I can count on my fingers, who has given in to the powers that be, who has received unfair benefit by leveraging their undongkwŏn past, or who is elevated unduly in their professional field because of their background as an undongkwŏn.⁶⁴

Pang was not alone in this sentiment. Kim Yŏng-hyŏn, also a former undongkwŏn and regarded by critics as one of the representative huildam writers of the 1990s, was bitter about the characterization of his literary output as huildam. He felt that the label reflected society's attitude toward the 1980s as an object to be eradicated (*ch'ŏngsan*), remembering the era only terms of their own weariness and the "torrent of Molotov cocktails and tear gas."⁶⁵ Germany in the 1990s also experienced a similar treatment of former activists. So intensely has the literature condemned the "68ers," participants in the German student movement, not only by the right but also by those within their own ranks, that they were "principally identified with shrill, moralizing accusations."⁶⁶

Kim Yŏng-hyŏn's personal trajectory as both an undongkwŏn and a published author encapsulates the literary itinerary of a huildam author for whom the paradigm shift from minjung to simin in the 1990s posed fundamental, something akin to existential, challenges. His literary work in the 1990s betrayed all the confusion and anxiety that such challenges brought about, even as he believed his writerly self to have remained the same as before. Born in 1955, Kim had been an undongkwŏn since his university days, spending the late 1970s in prison, then in "forced military conscription" (*kangje chingchip*), and the 1980s on the streets amid Molotov cocktails and tear gas.⁶⁷ He published his first short story, "Deep River Flows Far Away" ("*Kipŭn kangŭn mŏlli hŭrŭnda*"), in 1984, and in 1990 published a collection of short stories with the same title. These stories, usually woven into a family saga, dealt with the major events of Korean history as well as the experience of young people who immersed themselves in the student or labor movement. Many of the stories were based on Kim's personal experience.⁶⁸

Kim's *Deep River Flows Far Away* has received acclaim for both its realistic representation of historical events and periods and for its "lyrical romanticism," as well as for the sensitive portrayal of undongkwŏn characters as complex and multidimensional. Critic Kwŏn Sŏng-u, writing in 1990, was probably most effusive, praising Kim's work as having created a rich and complex world of the undongkwŏn embedded in their everyday lives and for its characters' intricate and delicate interiority. Unlike other huildam, Kim's stories were not encumbered by an excess of ideology; Kim's characters were full of individuality and life, and their stories—even as they dealt with the era's most urgent sociopolitical and ideological issues—dynamic and dramatic, according to Kwŏn.[69]

In Kim's works produced in the 1990s, however, some critics saw a distance from his previous "healthy historical consciousness and faith," along with the romanticism and poetic prose he had shown in his earlier works. As the previously clear division between friend and enemy was being dismantled, a great deal of confusion and perplexity ensued, and protagonists in Kim's later works lost their fighting spirit and tended to become uncertain and disjoined from their commitments, according to a critic.[70] In a short story titled "A Government in Exile in My Heart" ("*Naemaŭmŭi mangmyŏngjŏngbu*"), published in 1992, the protagonist dreams of emigration; his current world is devoid of any meaning, as he no longer thinks that he can change the world—an "imagination" that had previously provided him with much joy. The world to which he can devote his life had collapsed. Words such as "progressive," "revolutionary" have lost meaning, and any mention of changing the world would be considered a joke.[71]

One critic suggested that the characters in Kim's *And Never Said a Word* (*Kŭrigo amumaldo haji anhatta*), a collection of short stories published in 1995, have difficulty carrying on, let alone coming to grips with their lives, after their surroundings had changed so much. The critic implied that perhaps it was not that the author did not have the wherewithal to think about how to adapt to the changed reality but rather that he did not even acknowledge that the reality had changed. In one of the stories in the collection, "Wisteria" ("*Tungkkot*"), a character's friend, lovingly portrayed as the embodiment of purity of an undongkwŏn, is having a crisis in his marriage; his "longing" for "the past condition of solidarity that was full of passion and hope" makes it difficult for him to adapt to his current life.[72] There seems to be no trace of such passion or hope left in the present, and as the characters are becoming middle class and middle aged, they feel that their lives are meaningless and frivolous.[73]

As far as Kim Yŏng-hyŏn was concerned, however, even as he professed his desire to remain a fighter (*t'usa*) rather than "domesticated as a [professional] writer" (*chakkarosŏ kildŭryŏjinŭn'gŏtpoda*), and even as he talked of the need for writers to think of literature "as a weapon" to engage with contemporary social issues, he has always believed that literature should engage with issues that are universal and existential for humanity. As long as literature is a form of art, it has to reflect reality, but at the same time it has to create a world of its own, however unfamiliar to the reader. For him, the prison, forced military conscription, and tear-gas filled streets were sites where he confronted his existential issues in the 1970s and 1980s, issues many of his characters also faced as they confronted the authoritarian regime. But even in these stories, such as "Insect" ("*Pŏllae*") and "A Faraway Encounter" ("*Mŏlgo mŏn haehu*"), Kim thought that he was more concerned with the existential needs of his individual characters than the needs of the movement at the time and that he "rejected [literature's] instrumental role—its role as a weapon [of social change]." He further thought that true literature should be about the "existential needs of individuals," which he also understood as "the true manifestation of realism."[74]

Kim acknowledged that during the authoritarian period his literature was about the fighting (*ssaum*) and about the dark and lonely journey of intellectuals in the midst of that turbulent era. The older generation of writers before Kim had wrestled with existential issues dealing with their experience of the Korean War, and the younger generation of writers are currently experimenting with various forms to deal with their own issues. His generation, however, Kim protested, has not had a chance to learn a way to narrate their own experiences—they had fast become an object to be eradicated (*ch'ŏngsanŭi taesang*). His generation's traumatic memories do not disappear just because society wishes to forget them. Kim consigned himself to the role of healing the trauma of those who still have to live with the memories of their fellow classmates or comrades who burned to death in their protest against the authoritarian regime, who fell off buildings to their deaths, and who died in prison. To get rid of all the memories, however painful or ugly—as the society seemed wont to do—he claimed, is a historical loss.[75]

From Undongkwŏn to Sosimin (Petite Bourgeoisie)

Even as Kim Yŏng-hyŏn protested society's disavowal of the 1980s, and as critics carped about huildam as narcissistic and hypersentimental, huildam, and representations of the 1980s in huildam, abounded. In particular, undongkwŏn women protagonists populated huildam. Many of them are disillusioned not only by the fact that the revolution for which they had devoted their entire youth had not arrived but also that they themselves were fast becoming petite bourgeoisie (sosimin) once the revolution seemed no longer on the horizon. Both Kim In-suk and Kong Chi-yŏng, two of the most representative of the 386-generation female huildam authors, had themselves been involved in the student movement and became authors while still in their twenties. Their female protagonists are by no means stock figures of self-pity and hysteria, however; in fact, even as they share disappointments and disillusionment about what the 1990s brought about, some of their responses to the changes are unpredictable and even ferocious, demanding further critical analysis rather than dismissal. It is in their persistent return to the 1980s that the huildam female protagonists enunciate the break, thus partaking in the discourse of the paradigm shift; at the same time, in their tenacious, indeed what one critic calls dogged, return to the 1980s, huildam simultaneously perform a record-keeping function for the era.

Born in 1963 and an undongkwŏn during her university years, Kim In-suk's identity as a writer is deeply rooted in her experience of the 1980s. As one of her characters describes the 1980s, there was a "specialness" to the era, to the extent that she thought even "corruption was [an expression of] passion."[76] Most of Kim's literary work published in the 1980s embodied and reflected the worldview and ethos of the day, as her characters mostly dealt with issues that were closely rooted in the decade, such as the student movement, the labor movement, the 1987 presidential election, and the alternative teachers' union (Chŏnkyojo, Korean Teachers and Educational Workers Union), among others.[77] Her realist approach, considered to be the most suitable form for expressing the demands of the time, was also aligned with the era.[78]

In the midst of confusion and the search for meaning in the changed circumstances of the 1990s, however, most of her protagonists cannot completely erase or subjugate the memory of the 1980s at their own will. They involuntarily confront memories of the 1980s, causing panic whenever it occurs—while having sex, watching a movie, or just walking down the street.[79] Having devoted their youth to the 1980s movement and now living mostly as housewives in high-rise apartment buildings in metropolitan cities, they are overwhelmed with meaninglessness, boredom, and a vague sense of longing.[80] In a short story in the collection published in 2001, "To a Fellow Hide-and-Seek Player" ("*Sullaeege*"), the main character calls 911 out of sheer boredom, nonchalantly lying to the responder that her husband has had a heart attack. As the ambulance—and the excitement that would accompany its arrival—fails to materialize, she muses that gazing at the glow of the sky as the sun is about to set is perhaps enough of a pastime for an evening.[81] She has a brief, unmemorable affair with a neighbor, an event she cannot even be sure has actually occurred or not. Most symptomatic of her unhinged mind is when she cannot stop acting hysterically—laughing, clapping, and jumping up and down for no purpose—after winning the jackpot in a casino on her trip away from home.⁸² Her boredom has so deeply penetrated her life that she likens it to a tapeworm in her body that she is unable to get rid of.⁸³ Kim's characters all suffer from a sense of not belonging, "as if they are a plane that has made an emergency landing in an unknown place."⁸⁴ They do not actively protest their current status but are either resigned or make desperate gestures to fill the void they feel.⁸⁵

In "Glass Shoes" ("*Yuri kudu*"), a short story first published in 1993, former undongkwŏn Yu-sŏn refuses to engage in any kind of "normal" relationship with a fellow former undongkwŏn, "I," with whom she reconnects years later and wants only to have sex. When "I" jokingly says "I love you," mimicking the character of a porn movie they were watching together, Yu-sŏn replies, "No, you sex me."⁸⁶ Both Yu-sŏn and "I" had devoted their youth to the movement in the 1980s—"the era of anger and despair"—during which they felt that "it was necessary to justify even their existence at every moment. Perhaps even corruption [*t'arak*] was also a form of justification. But there was a specialness to that time. There was passion that one could devote to that specialness."⁸⁷ Yu-sŏn realizes one day that there is nothing that she can devote her passion to. At the age of thirty, sex seems to be the last possibility left for her: "Not because sex is great but because it is done in a closed room. . . . The passion of the public square . . . the possibility of dedicating that passion no longer exists."⁸⁸

To replace love with sex, to replace the passion of the public square with the passion of the bed, as it were, is perhaps to indict the excess of politics of the past era and the undongkwŏn's monitoring of her personal desires, as critic Kim Ŭn-ha noted.⁸⁹ To be sure, Yu-sŏn's "wickedness," whether feigned or not, can be dismissed as a case of self-pity and desperate gestures to fill the void, but this extreme gesture cannot be adequately understood outside of the historical and cultural context of the puritanical extreme to which the undongkwŏn pushed themselves in the 1980s. As I write elsewhere, the central aspiration and ethos around which undongkwŏn intellectuals and university students cohered was the intellectual as "a watchman in the darkness" and the consequent sense of self-abnegation and sacrifice.⁹⁰ The sense of self-negation, along with what was considered to be the historical demand of the era, drove mostly petit bourgeois college students to believe—or at least they had appeared to believe—that they had to shed themselves of every trace of their class background and to forgo personal happiness and pleasure, however small, to devote themselves to the cause of the minjung revolution.

Kong Chi-yŏng, a former undongkwŏn christened the bard of her (386) generation by the press and critics, also dealt in the 1990s mostly with themes and topics that reflected the ethos of the revolutionary 1980s, much as Kim In-suk had.⁹¹ Kong's novels are populated by women who have been deeply scarred by their involvement with the movement and who still carry the wounds. After her first short story in 1988, "Dawn Is Coming" ("*Tongt'ŭnŭn saebyŏk*"), which dealt with university students in the labor movement,⁹² she published in rapid succession a series of novels that dealt mostly with the 1980s. Her earlier novels focused on female characters from well-to-do families with fathers or families with compromising pasts, who plunge themselves into the student or labor movements. In her first novel published in 1989, *There Is No More Beautiful Wandering* (*Tŏ isang arŭmdanun panghwang'ŭn ŏpta*), Minsu, from a privileged family with a father with a politically checkered past, chooses to become a factory worker. She feels that she is faced with only three paths before her: "prison [for her involvement in the student movement], a factory, or [her own] betrayal [of the movement]."⁹³ *And Then There Is Their Splendid Beginning* (*Kŭrigo kŭdŭrŭi arŭmdaun sijak*, 1991) also focuses on a female protagonist who is from a well-to-do family, beautiful, and smart—thus born with "original sin."⁹⁴ In her later novels of the 1990s, these female protagonists, confronted with the "end of ideology," face their own petit bourgeois tendencies, which had been deeply suppressed during their undongkwŏn years.

Critics by and large dismissed Kong Chi-yŏng's earlier work in the 1990s as stoking "cheap nostalgia" and as a case of infantile narcissism and questioned whether she was the right choice to be a literary spokesperson of the 1980s.⁹⁵ There is even a suggestion among critics, as literary scholar Kim Myŏng-in observes, that the sentimentality of Kong's work—the 1980s was the "era of fierceness" but also the "era of the beautiful"—was responsible for the speed with which the 1980s was quickly consigned to memory without proper historical reckoning. It was as if her novels, Kim notes, functioned as "an indulgence" for the public to forgo dealing with the memories of the 1980s. Even so, "without her infamous sentimentality, the 1980s would have disappeared without a trace in our literature," Kim protests. Whereas those who had considered themselves to be at the center of the movement proved reluctant to confront, or even disavowed, the memory of the 1980s, Kong has had the courage to confront it "honestly and persistently."⁹⁶

Kong's 1994 novel *Mackerel* (*Kodŭngŏ*), which sold more than 700,000 copies, has a memorable, oft-cited passage in which the author marks the 386 generation as those who "felt guilty even admiring the beauty of the river" when they walked down the banks of the Han River.⁹⁷ For many critics, this passage functioned as an index of the author's excess of sentimentality that brought the work to the level of melodrama; Kong's literary works, filled with "exaggerated and embellished language," they argue, seemed to testify less to the brutality and pain of the era than to serve her desire for self-aggrandizement.⁹⁸

On the other hand, it was her protagonists' steadfast dedication to the goals of the movement well into the 1990s that led to some critics' weary reactions. The female protagonist Ŭn-lim in *Mackerel* shows up at Myŏng-u's place seven years after they last saw each other. Both had been in the same movement organization, but Myŏng-u had left the organization and Ŭn-lim after having a brief affair with her, unable to face reproach from his comrades. Ŭn-lim, however, stayed and dedicated herself to the movement even after her husband was imprisoned for his labor activism, her brother was institutionalized due to torture during his imprisonment for his activism, and her mother had emigrated to the United States.

When Ŭn-lim reappears with her health greatly deteriorated, Myŏng-u gives up his comfortable middle-class life and new girlfriend to care for her. Whereas Ŭn-lim's presence reminds Myŏng-u of his own guilt and cowardice in having fled the movement and her, Ŭn-lim is able to face her impending death with an aura of transcendence, having punished herself for her previous transgression thoroughly.⁹⁹ However, the tenacity of Ŭn-lim, who does not compromise with reality even as she is faced with death, also deeply moves Myŏng-u. He no longer writes "dead letters"—ghostwriting other people's autobiographies for money; he has rediscovered strength and energy to write "living letters," about people such as Ŭn-lim who have devoted their lives to change the world.¹⁰⁰

Literary scholar Kim Ŭn-ha takes her fellow critics to task for their glib indictment of Kong; before chastising Kong for her reputed hypersentimentality, Kim urges, one should first ask why she resorted to such exaggerated postures.¹⁰¹ The ethos of the "overpoliticized" 386 generation was such that they could not just take in the beauty of the Han River—for the "tears, sweats, and the long-accumulated suffering" of minjung must have percolated into the waters in different parts of the country that eventually merged into the Han River.¹⁰² For Kim Ŭn-ha, the embellishment in Kong's prose figures not as an embarrassing exaggeration or an inflated ego, as many critics charged, but as a genuine case of self-reflection and as an ethical stance.¹⁰³ In Kong's 1993 short story "What Is to Be Done" ("*Muŏsŭl halgŏsin'ga*"), the female protagonist "I" had deeply fallen for her undongkwŏn senior (*sŏnbae*) and he for her, although he refused to acknowledge it because he was already engaged to marry a fellow undongkwŏn. His fiancée is half-paralyzed from a fall from the university library building while being chased by police during a protest. "I" hears that he is currently working at a relative's golf store and is about to marry his paralytic fiancée. The classmate who relays the news said, "That sŏnbae . . . he was truly the most promising of us all. . . . It seems that only those of us who had shrewdly dropped out [of the movement] early are doing fine."[104] "I" is seized with guilt about having left the movement; she would have given up her life for love, but she would not have given her life up for the movement—to endure the day-to-day grinding undongkwŏn life had seemed at the time so much more arduous than giving up one's life for love.[105] As Kim Ŭn-ha suggests, this guilt and self-reproach was an honest sentiment of those who had either left the movement before its demise or faced the sense of utter failure and loss from its demise in the 1990s. In case of Kong's character, the self-reproach is also a way to prove Kong's "authenticity," that she has not lived in comfort and security after leaving the movement.[106]

The authenticity of the characters is also indicated by their refusal to submit to the changed era. Even if they no longer hold the aspirations and passion of the previous era, they do not necessarily search for a way out of the radical changes that the 1990s thrust into their midst.[107] In fact, they feel they still owe something to the movement. The previously mentioned protagonist in "Decency toward Human Beings" is besieged by a sense of debt to her fellow undongkwŏn for having left the movement early: "I have run away from the long tunnel, having left those who had fallen to the ground. . . . I have run away by myself."[108]

The guilt of the middle-class undongkwŏn was a common trope in Kong's work, but this guilt is not simply or only due to the protagonists' middle-class background. Kong's protagonists' guilt is often expressed as fear, akin to that of a mouse being chased by a cat, or a cry of the possessed, Kim Ŭn-ha observes. It was violence that drove Kong's female protagonist away from the movement initially in the story above, for example, especially sexual violence that affected women disproportionately, in addition to the physical and emotional violence that all undongkwŏn were exposed to. The protagonist "I" in "What Is to Be Done" had earlier decided to leave the student movement the day after hearing the rumor that plainclothes policemen had gang-raped activist women students on her campus. She had also witnessed a fellow female activist (who becomes her sŏnbae's fiancée, it turns out) falling from a balcony of the university library.[109]

The 1980s was drenched in violence, whether it was the kind of violence involved in street protests, police interrogation, imprisonment, and torture or the kind of emotional violence inflicted by fellow undongkwŏn. The pervasiveness of violence was such that the violence experienced by women was not readily recognized or acknowledged in the movement let alone in the general society. In her relentless pursuit of the past in all of its variegated dimensions, Kong Chi-yŏng reveals gender-inflected experiences of women that male authors have overlooked or ignored.

Huildam as the Recovery of the Social

As contextual and attentive readings of works of Kim In-suk and Kong Chi-yŏng reveal more complex and multilayered challenges in the 1990s and the characters' responses to these challenges, I suggest that we consider what might be called a recovery of the social as another perspective from which to approach some of the huildam, rather than dismissing them all simply as a case of regressive nostalgia or of hopeless self-pity. Here, as a representative illustration of this way of reading, I focus on the previously mentioned Kim Yŏng-hyŏn short story "And Never Said a Word" ("*Kŭrigo amumaldo haji anhatta*"), published in 1994.

This story centers on an artist, To Chae-sŏp, who is deeply pessimistic about the future of his own life and of his art. His young daughter has recently been killed in a car accident; his wife, who has shown symptoms of epilepsy, has left home; and a close friend and former undongkwŏn, Chŏng-min, has recently committed suicide. Chae-sŏp's affair with his hubae (one's junior in school or in a workplace) Yŏng-ae does not relieve him from the sense of despair and spiritual desolation that surrounds him. Chae-sŏp is asked to draw a mural at a Catholic retreat center, an assignment he takes up reluctantly.

His friend Chŏng-min had left a note before his suicide, lamenting how he was confused and dejected about the political turnaround of a respected and well-liked sŏnbae (in this case, one's senior in the movement), how he was overwhelmed with agony about how to live a meaningful life, and how the longer he lived, the less confident he became that he could go on. Chŏng-min had said, when Chae-sŏp saw him not long before his suicide, "I can live with the fact that revolution is no longer. But I cannot live with the fact that there is no longer an absolute [value] worthy [*chŏldaejŏk kach'i*] of devoting all my existence to."[110]

The title of Kim's story is the same as that of the German novelist Heinrich Böll's *And Never Said a Word*, which depicts the bleak and hopeless milieu of postwar West Germany. In fact, Kim frequently quotes passages from Böll's novel in his story.[111] The main protagonists in Böll's novel are a couple who are isolated from other human beings and from each other. The husband—timid, unstable, eking out a living as a telephone operator in a Catholic church, and living separately from his wife and children as the story unfolds—feels pity and guilt toward his wife because he is unable to provide for her and the family.[112]

Critic Han Chŏm-tol suggests that Böll, faced with both existential and social crises from both his own personal predicament and the historical experiences of Nazism and World War II, does not resort to the "existential transcendence" that was prevalent in Europe during the time. Rather, it is the recuperation of the love of family—the recovery of sociality—through which he anticipates the possibility of reconstructing German society. In Kim's novel, the painter Chae-sŏp similarly faces both existential and social crises that result from the collapse of ideology and the social world that had constituted his world, leading to the collapse of human relationships around him in the present. It is through recovery of the social, however, Han suggests, that Chae-sŏp anticipates overcoming his own existential crisis, by recapturing the existence of a great chain (*taeyŏnswae*) of human beings, a humane order of things different from what is dictated by the current existing order.

Chae-sŏp has not completely lost faith in the cause of his devotion. Rather, the cause has shifted in accordance with historical circumstances. One's task in changed times is to explore new attitudes and find ways to align oneself harmoniously (*wŏnyungjŏgŭro*) with the new direction of one's object of devotion.[113] As Chae-sŏp is about to finish with the mural, he experiences "a sense of absoluteness," the kind of absoluteness that was akin to the devotion that his generation had to the revolutionary ideals of the previous era. He returns home, anticipating a reunion with his wife.[114] In another reading of this story, critic Kang Sang-hui suggests that even as Chae-sŏp's previous object of allegiance had disappeared, he has continuously engaged with society through his art, that his continuous process of thinking and rethinking to finish his piece—even as he was enveloped in despair and hopelessness in doing so—signals a reconciliation and an honest reckoning with the changed reality.[115]

Huildam as Rupture of History

In Kwŏn Yŏ-sŏn we find yet another writer whose work cannot be discussed outside the context of the 1980s, even as they are considered too unwieldy to conform to the usual parameters of huildam. Unsparing in her critique of undongkwŏn for their "mendaciousness" and "hypocrisy," Kwŏn nonetheless provides a privileged opportunity for their self-reflection and "penance" (*kohae sŏngsa*), as it were, in her novel *Legato* (*Regat'o*). Although this novel was published in 2012, later than most of the literary work I discuss in this chapter, I include it here to point out in part that huildam's literary itinerary did not end with the 1990s. More importantly, the text speaks to the need to reconstruct the present through a continuous engagement with the past. Even though individual characters in *Regat'o* seem to be partaking in the regime of discontinuity with their changed lives, the novel as a whole calls for remembrance,

I contend. Although the author was not an undongkwŏn herself, she was surrounded by undongkwŏn.[116] The paradigmatic Kwangju uprising took place in the author's first year in university, and in her fourth year a close friend and undongkwŏn plunged to her death in the Han River.[117] Several of Kwŏn's published novels and short stories, including her 1996 debut novel, feature undongkwŏn university students and intellectuals as protagonists.

Kwŏn's characters are noted for their intricate, multilayered, and sensitive self-understanding as well as their uninhibited display of wounds and baseness (*piruham*)—what Kim Ŭn-ha calls their "masochistic performance."[118] In her stories, the past does not remain obediently waiting to be discovered, scanned for a particular meaning and then securely deposited away; rather, it is freshly rediscovered and torn asunder each time. Trauma and guilt ooze out as if from an untreated sore, never giving one a chance to completely wipe them out. It is as if Kwŏn's characters gain emotional consolation only by insulting and punishing themselves.[119] Memory in her novels is also decidedly unstable and unreliable. Fragments of uncomfortable pasts are revealed only as a crack in the process of reconstructing "twisted" (*twit'tulligo*) and subjective memories of protagonists.[120]

O Chŏng-yŏn, the protagonist in *Regat'o*, joins an underground student movement circle[121] at a university located in Seoul in 1979. She is raped by the circle leader, In-ha, gets pregnant, drops out of university, returns home to a farming village in Chŏlla Province, gives birth, and disappears during the Kwangju uprising in May of the following year. The trajectory of Chŏng-yŏn's life is unrelentingly violent and tragic even by standards of the early 1980s—a time of "sheer insanity."[122] Chŏng-yŏn's withdrawal from the movement is prompted mostly by her fellow comrades' indifference to her torment and anguish, however; unaware that her voracious appetite was induced by her pregnancy, they are appalled by her gluttonous grab for the last remaining chicken wing at the chicken rotisserie where they last met before her disappearance; for them, this was yet another sign of her having become greedy and also lax in her commitment to the struggle.[123]

Thirty years later, Chin-t'ae, Chŏng-yŏn's erstwhile classmate and a fellow circle member, learns from Chŏng-yŏn's mother why she'd left the university and disappeared. He buries himself in deep remorse after learning the reasons.

> Why were they [the circle members] so accusatory toward her [Chŏng-yŏn] that she had to leave the chicken rotisserie without finishing the last chicken piece? . . . Why did they, so emotionally dried up and ignorant [*maemarŭgo mujihan chŏngsinŭro*], insist on putting up a gesture of

the extreme kind, a gesture of severance? ... As youth of every age do, Chin-t'ae's soul at that time was seized with the manic, excessive determination to live up to the dictates of the era [ŏdisŏgŏn che unmyŏng ŭl ilgŏnaegoya malgetdanŭn]. How much of Chin-t'ae's memory was fabricated to give himself peace of mind? Was the forgery of his memory the Pandora's box that he had been so fearful of all this time?[124]

The excuse for their immature behavior was, on the one hand, the fight that they were waging against the violent authoritarian regime as well as the passion for minjung liberation that they could not give up under any circumstances; on the other hand, it was their youth itself—after all, they were a "bundle of abstract thoughts, immaturity, and inflexibility." Looking back now, was not In-ha, the leader of the circle who was at the time looked up to by fellow students as "really somebody" (*taedanhan*), only a youth in his early twenties? Without their youthful ardor, abstract thoughts, and purity, how could they have fought so ferociously in the 1980s? However, their struggle also inevitably led to hurting not only themselves but also those around them. Who gave them the right to scorn and hold in contempt those who were not in the movement or those who, as in the case of Chŏng-yŏn, were afraid of getting caught and sent to prison, or torture, for something as mundane as distributing pamphlets in the street?[125]

They (circle members and by extension undongkwŏn as a whole) had discussed and agonized endlessly over the suffering of the abstract notion of minjung. Yet, they were unaware of the embarrassment, fear, and hunger of their friend who was among them: "Why were they in such a hurry, and what were they so busy about that they had not noticed the change [in Chŏng-yŏn]? Why did they all ignore the sorrow in her eyes when she hurriedly left the chicken rotisserie?"[126]

Perhaps, as critic Chŏng Hong-su suggests, it would have been impossible at the time to demand the kind of self-reflection that they eventually came to ask of themselves many years later. Their justification for the shortcomings and failings would have been their youth, the dictates of the era (*tangwisŏng*), and their devotion to the movement. In *Regat'o*, Chŏng Hong-su further suggests, the self-reproach and self-questioning of former members of the underground circle are an inescapable prelude to the ultimate repentance—and redemption— that the author allows them. Reappearance of the long-lost Chŏng-yŏn reminds members of the era, and only through reencountering with Chŏng-yŏn, while facing their own erstwhile cowardice and heartlessness, could members see the past and present meet or have the gap smoothed out—as legato functions in a musical piece—before they move on with their lives.[127]

In an interview, the author questioned why and how, given that the literary form of the novel in general travels between past and present, only huildam that deal with the 1980s are considered by critics to be backward and anachronistic.[128] She also noted how the male character Chin-t'ae immediately realizes his own complicity when he learns of what has happened to Chŏng-yŏn. However, this realization is not the kind that proclaims loudly, "Let's all reflect, forgive, and regroup"—the kind that is oriented toward another ideology or "ism," another critic Sim Chin-kyŏng notes. Rather, it is the sort that "pours out from within himself, tearing his own self apart, the kind that empathizes most sincerely [chŏljŏrhan konggam] with the other, that makes him genuinely face his own complicity."[129]

Through the character of Chin-t'ae, the reader learns that the decision to become an undongkwŏn could have been a sheer-chance decision and not necessarily an outcome of sustained ideological conviction and that this chance decision has been mythologized as undongkwŏn's dedication.[130] Many mistakes were committed in the name of the collective, including the mythologizing of the role of undongkwŏn in the 1980s.[131] Critic Chŏng Hong-su also suggests that it is the guilt of the author and her generation that interpolates O Chŏng-yŏn as an emblem of the era.[132]

Thirty years after her disappearance, Chŏng-yŏn reappears, her soul and body ravaged—she has lost her memory and her legs. Her former comrades have all but forgotten her, as have the rest of "us" in society, as critic Cho Yŏn-chŏng points out. Cho suggests Chŏng-yŏn's reappearance is a powerful jolt to the true meaning of a community. With the reappearance of Chŏng-yŏn, whom they had long assumed dead, and her daughter, whose existence they did not even know about, the members of the circle have gained an opportunity to reflect on how they "so powerlessly abdicated to reality," leaving behind their mistakes and their guilt until now. They now have a chance to respond to her earlier entreaty, in the days of their underground circle—"Would you take care of me if something were to happen to me—if I die or if I become an invalid?"[133] Chŏng-yŏn returns not to punish her former comrades for the violence inflicted on her but to confront the violence of memory that has fossilized her existence—and the Kwangju uprising—as a past event.[134]

The huildam writers' insistence on digging into the past entails "rupturing" the continuity of history, as suggested by Walter Benjamin. Although Benjamin's Angel of History cannot wake the dead and redeem what is lost because of the sheer force of the wreckage and debris of history,[135] he suggests that one view history "against the grain," from the point of view of history's "losers," in an attempt to rescue from the collective past images that have the power to startle one onto a course of action. Even as huildam partake in the discourse of the paradigm shift from the political to the cultural and from minjung to simin, the texts' dogged dwelling on loss, the past, and political failures, what one might call a kind of "splenetic melancholy,"[136] also compel a return to the past that has the potential to redeem what was lost, a potential to give rise to interest and action in the present world. I elaborate this issue further in the epilogue.

3

The Park Chung-hee Syndrome, Mass Media,
and "Culture War"

The specter of Park Chung-hee has been haunting South Korea ever since the rise of the "Park Chung-hee syndrome" in the late 1990s. As I discuss in the introduction, the syndrome began rather humorously with a number of university students selecting Park Chung-hee as a historical figure they wished to clone in March 1997.[1] A month later, a daily paper's survey showed that 75.9 percent of the respondents chose Park as a "president who performed his duties well," far above the percentages selecting Chun Doo-hwan (6.6 percent) and Kim Young-sam (3.7 percent).[2] Promptly described as the Park Chung-hee syndrome, a series of public debates ensued about the meaning and implications of the syndrome in academic symposia, newspaper commentaries, readers' opinions, and, most intensively, on the internet. Enterprising individuals were quick to jump on the bandwagon of the syndrome, from presidential contenders trying to woo voters by promising to construct a Park Chung-hee memorial, to another candidate highlighting his physical resemblance to Park, to fashion designers capitalizing on the rediscovered appeal of the 1970s' sartorial style.[3] Cultural and literary products extolling the virtues of Park also began to appear from the late 1990s.[4]

My purpose in discussing the syndrome in this chapter is neither to reconstruct the course of this widely discussed phenomenon, nor to substantiate or disprove the relative truth of the claims and counterclaims of historical representations of the Park Chung-hee period.[5] I explore the syndrome mostly as a case that manifests the regime of discontinuity that the 1990s represents a break from the past and as a critical site where various contending forces vied to reconstruct the memory of Park Chung-hee and his regime. I argue that both literary and nonliterary texts produced during this period by well-known figures functioned as a foundational revisionist text of the Park Chung-hee period and, by extension, of post-1945 Korean history. To this end, I examine biographies, memoirs, and literary works on or related to Park Chung-hee, showing how the vast amount of narrative labor has in fact facilitated and constituted the syndrome. Contrary to the mass media's representation of the syndrome as "spontaneous" and a "grass roots," it was—and continues to be—coproduced by the combined forces of conservative mass media and well-known political and literary figures, the gatekeepers of South Korea. Indeed, the syndrome was one of the first instances that clearly showed an interlocking relationship between the two groups. In what follows, I first provide an overview of the sociopolitical developments that gave rise to the syndrome. I then discuss the emergence of mass media in South Korea as a critical agent of memory construction of Park Chung-hee and his regime and the role of the three major conservative media and literary works of well-known novelists in the making of the syndrome.

Park Chung-hee

Park Chung-hee remains one of the most controversial and most enigmatic political leaders of South Korea. He ruled South Korea for over eighteen years, first two years as a supreme leader of the military junta after carrying out a military coup on May 16, 1961, against a democratically elected government and then as an elected president of the country from 1963 onward. In October 1972, he decreed the Yusin Constitution which wiped away what little democratic procedure was left in the country.[6] As a series of protests against his authoritarian rule mounted, he was assassinated by his right-hand man and then-director of the Korea Central Intelligence Agency (KCIA) on October 26, 1979.

Park Chung-hee, with his meteoric rise from a humble background and his seemingly unlimited ambitions, led an extraordinarily checkered life; he graduated from the Japanese Manchurian Military School at the age of twenty-eight, was accused by the South Korean government of being a secret military agent for the South Korean Communist Party and sentenced to death (later commuted) at the age of thirty-two, reinstated into the military two years later at the outbreak of the Korean War, led the military coup d'état at the age of forty-five, and ruled South Korea until his assassination at the age of sixty-three. His social revival began with the democratization of South Korea in the 1980s and reached its climax with the Park Chung-hee syndrome in the late 1990s. In 2012, his daughter became the president of South Korea—she was impeached in 2017 for corruption and abuse of public office—giving rise to South Korea's short-lived presidential dynasty.[7] For many Koreans, Park's personal story was to a certain degree their own as well as their country's; his successes and his failings, his humble background, his ambitions, and his kaleidoscopic life in some way reflected their own and that of the country itself.[8]

Assessments of Park Chung-hee since his death have tended to fall into one of two extremely opposite views, as divergent as "heaven and hell": on the one hand, he accomplished spectacular economic development and, with his staunch anti-communism, saved the country from the threat of North Korea; on the other hand, he undermined not only the country's democratic development with his Yusin declaration and emergency decrees but also a "normal" development of the economy by deviating from the market economy and pursuing state-directed economy.[9] Obviously, the complexities of the Park era cannot be captured by binaries of authoritarianism versus democracy or domination versus resistance that characterized much of the scholarship until the late 1990s. The Park Chung-hee era was decidedly an era of violence, represented by its draconian Yusin Constitution, emergency measures, and its policy of accelerated economic development at the expense of all else. His will was imposed and realized through the suppression of civil and human rights; during his era, an able-bodied person "living an idle life" was considered a criminal.[10] Under Park Chung-hee, South Korea endured almost nine years—half of Park's rule—of either martial law, emergency measures, or garrison decrees. In fact, the Park Chung-hee regime began with a declaration of martial law following the May 16 military coup d'état in 1961 and ended with a declaration of a garrison decree following the Pusan-Masan uprising in 1979.[11]

At the same time, however, the Park regime was the first and most effective modern state in Korea in terms of both its governing structure and mode of operation, and active organization of its support base. The state's mobilization of its citizenry to participate in its modernizing and economic projects were not only through coercion and suppression but also, and perhaps more effectively, through the production and circulation of discursive practices. The narrative of egalitarianism was one such discursive practice that proceeded along with the discourse of modernization, conjoining the widespread desire and collective will of Koreans to eliminate poverty and live a better life, with its ubiquitous slogans such as "Let us live better lives."[12] As such, and as historian Hwang Pyŏng-ju argues eloquently, Park's playbook featured not only the politics of repression but also the politics of desire.[13] If the previous leaders of Korean politics flaunted their elite background and tried to distance themselves from the ordinary people, Park's repertoire was that he was a son of poor peasants and therefore one of "the people."[14]

Park's conflicting and seemingly irreconcilable legacies have become all the more salient and controversial for South Korea since the 1990s, especially since the economic crisis of 1997 and later his daughter's presidency of the country (2013–2017). Park's brutal authoritarianism carried out concurrently with spectacular economic development has been a source of both the persistent political strife and an immense pride for a large number of Koreans. These clashing memories of the Park regime have also shaped the ways in which the public responded to rebuilding democracy in post-1987.[15]

By now it would be redundant to say that Park Chung-hee's place in South Korean history and the Korean public's memory of him since his death have undergone significant evolutions, along with social and political changes in South Korea. It is not surprising that until the late 1980s, assessments of Park had been nearly absent and what little there was had been predominantly negative. When Chun Doo-hwan came into power after Park's assassination through another military coup d'état (known as the December 12 coup), he quickly consigned the memory of Park to history: he erased mention of the "May 16 revolution," as Park's military coup of 1961 was called, in the constitution; he barred many members of Park's erstwhile political party (Democratic Republican Party) and his former cabinet members from political activities; he sought to distance himself and his regime by characterizing Park's period as a time of "corruption, depravity, and absurdity" and claimed that his government would aim to establish a "society of justice" (*chŏngŭi kuhyŏn*).[16] The Chun government also discouraged any public events related to Park, including anniversary ceremonies for the 1961 coup and public commemoration of Park.[17] For the South Korean public at large, Chun Doo-hwan's military coup in the immediate aftermath of Park's death in 1979 and the subsequent decade of his harsh rule had robbed them of an opportunity for historical assessment and, especially for those who had suffered under Park's rule, to pursue any retroactive justice.[18]

"Rectification of History"

By the late 1980s, the political situation had turned yet another dramatic corner, creating conditions that made a more positive reevaluation of Park in public discourse possible. Ironically, it was the democratization of Korean society from the late 1980s onward that expanded the political sphere that made it possible for Park's followers to reenter politics. Kim Jong-pil, the former close associate of Park Chung-hee and a distant relative by marriage, formed the New Democratic Republican Party (NDRP) in 1987 with the clearly articulated goal of inheriting the legacy of Park Chung-hee. The creation of NDRP, with most of its members from the rank and file of Park Chung-hee's cabinet and former political party, was the beginning of the political revival of Park Chung-hee.[19] In October 1988, Park Geun-hye, daughter of Park Chung-hee, launched a commemorative organization and published a book that highlighted Park Chung-hee's achievements. On the tenth anniversary of Park's death in 1989, one thousand adults over twenty years old were surveyed on Park's accomplishments as president of the country. Over 61 percent responded that Park's accomplishments outweighed his mistakes.[20] It was not until 1997, however, that the hagiography of Park Chung-hee in various genres began to appear in earnest, beginning with major newspapers publishing memoirs and personal recollections of various individuals who knew Park personally or who had served in his regime.

The immediate political context of the emergence of this revisionism clearly has to do with the public's disappointment with the Kim Young-sam government's failure to follow through on its promises of reform. Kim Young-sam, much like Kim Dae-jung, was a well-known dissident politician in the 1970s and 1980s with a long-standing opposition to the Park and Chun regimes. His was the first civilian government in more than thirty years, and his reform drives were met with great euphoria and enthusiasm by the public, who gave him an unprecedented approval rating of 90 percent, a few months into his presidency. However, the united front of conservative forces—mass media, the conservative members of his own ruling party, and high-ranking government officials—vehemently opposed his reforms. A series of corruption cases involving his own son further undermined his efforts at reform, and his own authoritarian manner, along with other issues, left the people deeply disillusioned with his government.[21]

The Kim government's reform drive included "rectification of history" (*yŏksa paro seugi*), a campaign to deal with various colonial and authoritarian

FIGURE 3.1. Demolition of the former Japanese governor-general building, Seoul, 1996.

legacies of the previous era, including the punishment of those responsible for the 1980 Kwangju massacre. The campaign initially took off with a clear signal to dismantle the authoritarian remnants. A secret military club called Hanahoe (Group of One), whose members were responsible for the December 12 coup of 1979 and the Kwangju massacre of 1980, was disbanded in 1993, and the building that had housed the former Japanese general government was demolished in 1996 (figure 3.1).[22] Most remarkably, two former presidents, Roh Tae-woo and Chun Doo-hwan, were indicted for their roles in the December 1979 coup d'état and the brutal massacre of the people of Kwangju in 1980, respectively.[23]

What had appeared to be swift action toward acceding to the public's demand for justice, what historian Bruce Cumings commended as "a fine moment for Korean democracy . . . vindicating the masses of Koreans who had fought for democratic rule over the past fifty years,"[24] however, needs further scrutiny of its motives and its reputed historical significance. The Kim Young-sam government's call for "rectification of history" was clearly a part of its much-anticipated reform movement. At the same time, Kim's Faustian bargain with heirs of the Chun Doo-hwan regime earlier[25] made it crucial that he distance his government from previous authoritarian regimes. He began to emphasize that his government's legitimacy rested in past democratic events in the history of Korea, including the May 18 Kwangju people's uprising of 1980.[26]

Kim Young-sam took up the task of investigating the Kwangju massacre reluctantly and belatedly, however. As in Spain after the death of Francisco Franco—where both sides of the political spectrum tacitly agreed to put the past behind them and forget the traumatic history of the division of the Spanish people since the civil war of 1936[27]—Kim Young-sam initially did not demand an investigation, nor did he press for the punishment of those responsible for the massacre. He called for reconciliation instead, declaring that his administration would not pursue insurrection charges against Roh and Chun. The truth of the Kwangju massacre, along with the military junta's guilt, he said, should be reserved for "future historical judgment" and that punishment might lead to renewed conflict by publicly retelling the "shameful story of the dark age."[28]

Only after numerous groups, including those of the family members of victims of the massacre, vociferously and persistently demanded to identify and punish those responsible for the massacre did Kim finally change his mind.[29] Kim's volte-face came about mainly due to the dictates of realpolitik: his party suffered a major defeat in local elections in June 1995, and in November, Roh Tae-woo was found to have a secret slush fund of "astronomical sums," generating widespread speculation that Kim Young-sam had benefited from this money as the successor of Roh's political party.[30] The subsequent Special Law on the Kwangju Massacre provided the basis to convict the two former presidents of treason, homicide for the purposes of treason, mutiny (for their illegal seizure of power with the 1979 December military coup and in May 1980), and corruption. In the final decision of the Supreme Court on April 17, 1997, Chun was sentenced to life imprisonment and Roh to seventeen years. Both Chun and Roh were pardoned by Kim Young-sam immediately prior to his leaving office, with the approval of the then-president-elect Kim Dae-jung.

The Return of Park Chung-hee

By the late 1990s, as the Park Chung-hee syndrome was in full swing, debates continued among various individuals as to the possible meaning and implications of the syndrome. Journalists, scholars, and social commentators each put forth their own analyses of the syndrome, which are summarized by political scientist Chŏng Hae-gu as follows: Some argued that the syndrome was an arrival of what was long overdue, that Koreans were finally acknowledging the extraordinary leadership of Park Chung-hee whose push for economic development had made it possible for South Korea to enter the ranks of "advanced countries" (sŏnjin'guk). An opposing view held that the syndrome was manufactured by the conspiracy of conservatives who wish to maintain the status quo.

Another view saw the syndrome as a reaction to the disappointment over the failure of the Kim Young-sam government for its sluggish reform drive. The fourth view looked for reasons in the subconscious of Koreans, that despite the emergence of a civilian government and a high level of institutional and political democratization, the psychic makeup of South Koreans still tended to depend on a charismatic strongman; that the downfall of the prestige of the presidency with a series of scandals involving Kim Young-sam's own family members reawakened a subconsciously held dependence on the authoritarian Park Chung-hee.[31]

Those who deplored the appearance of the syndrome also suggested that it was the absence of "objective" scholarly representation of the Park Chung-hee regime that gave rise to public "mass amnesia" that easily forgets the line between the good and the evil, and to Koreans' lingering wish for a "strong man" in politics.[32] If Friedrich Nietzsche called nineteenth-century Germany a case of "hypertrophy of history,"[33] then these commentators were suggesting that the Korean public of the 1990s was suffering from a hypertrophy of memory and that a more "objective history" should be its antidote.

What South Korea has witnessed during the syndrome and what continues until now—whether one calls it a hypertrophy of history or memory—is an all too familiar story globally. For historian Ann-Louise Shapiro, contemporary society in general is in a slightly "schizophrenic moment"; that is, there is both considerable worry about "historical illiteracy, cultural amnesia, and intractable presentism—the loss of meaningful history—and an equally powerful sense of history as everywhere present" in films, museum exhibits, and theme parks, among others. She states that these worries—too little and too much of history—are in fact not two different sets of problems but aspects of the same larger concern: that the wrong kind of history (wrongheaded or simply wrong) is producing an unfortunate kind of historical consciousness. As Shapiro puts it, "the issue is not that people have forgotten the past, but that they misremember it all too well; not that they don't care about history, but that they don't or can't discriminate among the available versions."[34] In a different context, literary scholar Andreas Huyssen also notes how in contemporary society there is simultaneous popularity of museums and the resurgence of the monument and the memorial and at the same time there is an "undisputed waning of history and historical consciousness."[35]

As in other cases of public debates, professional or academic historians did not define the terms of this debate. The syndrome clearly indicated that historians' claim to a privileged role in shaping national identity that was popularly accepted in the 1970s and the 1980s was no longer the case; this claim sprang largely from the historically specific experience of the period in which intellectuals, especially those who had aligned themselves with the minjung movement, played a critical role in shaping the historical consciousness of university students and their fellow intellectuals. During the height of the democratization movement in the 1970s and 1980s, critical reevaluation of modern Korean history was an integral component of the social movement. Korean history had become a site of intense contestation between the state and the oppositional minjung movement and between established academic scholars and the newly rising independent minjung-oriented scholars. The democratization movement was therefore very much a process of discursive contestations such as between socially sanctioned memory and countermemory, between the state discourse of dominant nationalism and the minjung movement's oppositional nationalism. During this period, the historical experience of Koreans was interpreted in absolute binary categories: state memory and countermemory—what historian John Bodnar calls official memory and vernacular memory, with all the attendant problems that such a neat dichotomy entails.[36] As I discuss further below, the syndrome showed that such binary categories were no longer tenable, and the lines of judgment between authoritarian rule versus democracy began to blur.

Mass Media as Historiographical Apparatus

Although the syndrome may have been mass-based and widespread, it was clearly not a case of a spontaneous or grassroots movement, as the media would have led one to believe. Nor should the causes of the syndrome be found only in the political failures of the Kim Young-sam government or the forgetfulness of the Korean people. As in the case of the rise of the New Right, it was the conservative mass media that became the most critical agent of reconstruction of memory in the case of the Park Chung-hee syndrome. The status and role of mass media have undergone dramatic changes with the democratic transition and neoliberal restructuring, as I briefly discussed in the introduction. The media's collusion with the authoritarian regime began in the Yusin period, when media was reduced to "a public relations agency" in exchange for special benefits that eventually would lead to its mammoth size and elevated status, wielding unduly powerful influences in society.[37]

The conservative mass media was increasingly becoming uncomfortable with Kim Young-sam's reform drive and vehemently opposed the reform measures. Numerous public opinion polls and surveys conducted by mass media, begun prior to the full-fledged appearance of the syndrome in the spring of

1997, in fact came to constitute the syndrome. As philosopher Hong Yun-gi suggested, by juxtaposing Kim Young-sam's weakness and incompetency against Park Chung-hee's aura of the strongman, the conservative mass media seemed to sow doubt in the public not only about the process of democratization but also the value of democracy itself.[38]

Philosophers of history such as Hayden White and Paul Ricoeur argue that events in history become historical when they are narrated. They also remind us of the critical importance of social and political contingencies in acquiring historical knowledge and in narrating history, regardless of the medium one employs. Representations of the past are deeply entangled with the vicissitudes of life and enacted through the narrator's "social and personal perspectives, standpoints, and positions that both constrain and create meaning—the trinity of place, time, and person gives birth to shifting and multiple historical perspectives."[39]

In the same vein, scholars have also analyzed how social memory is culturally reconstructed, with the decisive roles played by the above-mentioned trinity.[40] Paul Connerton in particular stresses the social aspect of memory formation by highlighting social actors' intention and mediation that intervene in the meaning making of the present.[41] Social and political conditions are thus critical for cultural memory, as they provide either possibility for, or constraints on, the social capacity to narrate the past.[42]

Many of the media that have in recent decades become active in producing and narrating the past have increasingly become, as previously mentioned, "historiographical apparatus," which can and do function as "a prosthetic" for professional historians' scholarship.[43] During the height of the Park Chung-hee syndrome, the conservative newspapers became central in the production of social memory of Park Chung-hee himself and his era.[44] As such, they became the main site where the regime of discontinuity played out.

JoongAng Ilbo (*Chung'ang Ilbo*), along with *Chosun Ilbo* (*Chosŏn Ilbo*) and *Dong-A Ilbo* (*Tong'a Ilbo*), three papers forming the troika of media conservatism known as Cho-Joong-Dong, became instrumental and most active in articulating and promoting this revisionist assessment of Park. Personal reminiscences, memoirs of those who were a part of Park's government or were personal associates, and biographies of Park led an effective campaign for revisionist history from 1997. Starting in 1997, the *JoongAng Ilbo* serialized "Veritable Record, Park Chung-hee," containing recollections of various individuals who were associated with Park; this collection is most notable in justifying most of Park's egregious policies and behaviors as historically and politically legitimate.[45] In addition, the *JoongAng Kyongje Shinmun* (a sister paper of *JoongAng Ilbo*) began to serialize *Thirty Years of Korean Economic Policy*, a memoir of Kim Chŏng-nyŏm who had served in the Park Chung-hee government for ten years as minister of finance and secretary-general of the Blue House.[46] This serialization, which detailed various aspects of the economic policies implemented in the 1960s and 1970s, was yet another hagiographic treatment of Park, extolling Park for his "perspicacious foresight and greatness."[47] From April 27 until May 19, 1997, Kim Chŏng-nyŏm also serialized his political memoir, *Ah Park Chung-hee* in the *JoongAng Ilbo*. In sharp contrast to the diminished reputation of then-president Kim Young-sam, whose political failures and personal shortcomings gave rise to a widely shared sense of disillusionment about his government, Park was presented as "a revolutionary, a solider, an educator, and administrator"; a masterful and strong political leader in all areas of economic development, diplomacy, defense, as well as a model of self-discipline, thrift, and diligence.[48]

Along with the *JoonAng Ilbo*, the ultraconservative *Chosun Ilbo* also began to serialize Cho Kap-che's long-awaited Park Chung-hee biography, *Spit on My Grave* (*Nae mudŏm e ch'im ŭl paet'ŏra*).[49] Cho Kap-che's personal itinerary from an investigative reporter known for his uncompromising and highly respected reportage of the 1970s and the 1980s, including the exposé of the corruptions of the Park Chung-hee regime, to his metamorphosis since the late 1980s into a far-right polemicist, is well known.[50] His conversion seemed to have been triggered by what he considers to have been the negative effects of the democratic transition.[51]

Cho's previous publications had appraised Park Chung-hee as a statesman and a president focusing on his accomplishments and shortcomings as such. In his 1987 *The Posthumous Work*, for example, Cho is even-handed in his treatment of Park, pointing out Park's shortcomings as well as his achievements: Cho considers Park to be an important historical figure as a "Confucian pragmatist," whose achievements "will remain in our history in thick Gothic font," but also cautiously notes the lack of worldview and perspective that would have granted him with strength at times of his loneliness and nihilistic disquiet.[52]

In *Spit on My Grave*, however, Park Chung-hee was elevated to almost a superhuman and a mythic figure.[53] Park Chung-hee accomplished what no other leader in Korea has been able to achieve—the two of the most urgent tasks faced by the nation, industrialization and modernization. This was possible not only because Park was an able stateman but also because he was a revolutionary figure who possessed the highest degree of integrity—Park was "an incarnation of justice." Most importantly, Park is presented as an ardent nationalist who, embodying the Korean people's *han* (long-accumulated suffering), was able to "sublimate his plebian but uncompromising spirit for the nationalist cause." That Park was assassinated by his trusted right-hand man only augments his aura of a

FIGURE 3.2. Participants of the commemorative ceremony of Park Chung-hee bowing before his statue, Kumi, North Kyŏngsang Province, November 14, 2016. Source: OhMyNews/Cho Chŏng-hun.

tragic revolutionary martyrdom.[54] Cho's accolades of Park seem to have no limit and often verge on comical: Park is described as a "superhuman who held his spirit high," a "first-rate thinker," "a bashful hero," a "superhuman with much tears," a "plebian everyman," and finally, a true "indigenous Korean."[55]

In fact, this image of himself as larger than life was what Park Chung-hee often turned to during his lifetime to justify his political actions or policy. As he flagrantly defied democratic rules, Park repeatedly claimed that he was indifferent to public opinion or pressure—he was above any popularity contest, as it were. Indeed, as Hong Yun-gi quips, Park imputed that his political acts were directed from the will of "another super-reality called national history" (*minjoksa*). He defended his 1961 military coup d'état by stating that it was necessary to quell the "social chaos" created in the aftermath of the April 19 uprising, that it was his sense of responsibility to congeal (*ŭnggyŏl*) the will for national salvation that led to the coup: "If this chaos continues it is inevitable that our country will be communized, our five thousand years of history and tradition will suddenly disappear, and I would be ashamed to face the lofty spirit of our forerunners, who wished to make their descendants prosper through bringing national revival."[56] As Hong Yun-gi points out, Park Chung-hee here likens himself to a shaman who has received a divination from Korea's five thousand years of history.[57] In Cho's *Spit on My Grave*, South Korea's history has manifested a Hegelian trajectory, with the will of the individual Park infused with predetermined national destiny.[58]

Monumental History and Literary Gatekeepers

In its unrestrained embellishment of Park Chung-hee, Cho's *Spit on My Grave* also performs what Nietzsche characterized as "monumental" history. In his "On the Uses and Disadvantages of History," Nietzsche chastises historians for their tendency to present historiography as a scientifically ordered analysis of history, thereby obscuring its actual value-driven and selective nature.[59] Monumental history arises in a situation when one is dissatisfied with one's own time, when one wishes to flee the present and seeks comfort in the past, serving to uncritically beautify and distort one's view of the past.[60] It identifies with the famous and powerful, "overpower[ing] the marginal, dark, and vanishing aspects of past."[61] It becomes "free poetic invention" that produces a stimulating "mythical fiction."[62] In doing so, it also brings about unwarranted disappointment about the present, which is likely to cause more complacency and cynicism than critical engagement.[63] Huyssen also notes a similar phenomenon in his study of memory in contemporary society, noting that novelty is associated with new versions of the past rather than with visions of the future.[64] During the Reagan and Thatcher eras as well, literary scholar Colin Hutchinson suggests that the widespread concern about insecure future and inconsistency between the reality and what was promised was addressed by the "promise of a return to the values and certainties of a comforting, mythical past that is consistent with the age and social conservatism of both leaders."[65]

As South Koreans in the 1990s were increasingly becoming dispossessed of a sense of their place in history and feeling uncertain about what the future would bring, as briefly discussed before, writers also searched in the past for more ideal and appealing alternatives to the present. Best sellers of the 1990s were mostly past oriented, literary critic Han Man-su notes, and this phenomenon contrasts with the 1980s when the novels of note were mostly future oriented.[66] Cho's *Spit on My Grave* aside, a number of literary works in the 1990s also performed monumental history.

Yi In-hwa's *A Man's Road* (*In'ganŭi kil*), appearing in 1997, is a historical novel loosely based on Park Chung-hee. As in the case of Cho's *Spit on My Grave*,

Park's individual life is infused with a Hegelian manifestation of a supreme spirit, as Park is depicted as transcending his individuality for the higher call of historical responsibility. As Hong Yun-gi perceptively suggests, Yi's literary representation of Park Chung-hee verges on a kind of mythic, religious transcendence (*ch'owŏlsŏng*) as well as a metaphysical foray into death.[67]

Yi In-hwa belongs to that much-celebrated—and much-maligned—generation that led the democratization movement of the 1980s. Yi's glorified portrayal of Park as someone who "possessed the wisdom and foresight to intuit what the era demanded and led [the nation] to fulfill the [people's] aspirations"[68] is thus one of the first cases of a "countermemory" to that generation. It may also be the first literary expression of the New Right.[69]

Yi In-hwa had aspired to write a novel with a broad appeal to the Korean public, and he found his model in Shiba Ryōtarō's *Ryōma Goes His Way* (*Ryōma ka kanda*), a well-known work that juxtaposes the life of Sakamoto Ryōma, a key figure in the movement to overthrow the Tokugawa shogunate, with the nation-building process of Meiji Japan.[70] During numerous interviews with news media, Yi told how he was interested in pursuing only stories related to Park Chung-hee and not the issues of "freedom or democracy or such things of civil society," and how he had given all of himself to the task of writing this novel.[71] His singular focus on Park stemmed from his faith and confidence that Park was a true great man and, as such, worthy object of his devotion: "We learn from the individual whom we think is truly great and emulate his thinking and action. That way might be the only factor for progress for humankind. When an individual endowed with genius shows the way and becomes a role model, many choose and follow his path."[72]

In *A Man's Road*, Korea's historical developments that intersect with the personal life of Park are rendered to highlight his greatness. Those who fought against the Japanese, those who stood on the opposite side of Park during the colonial period, are portrayed simply as losers who had never managed to put up any meaningful and effective resistance against the Japanese—they were "hangers-on of the Kuomintang [Chinese Nationalist Party], smugglers, gamblers, and opium addicts." Their nationalist pride had prevented them from engaging in a more effective strategy to win against the Japanese; they would rather be killed by the Japanese and "disappear as yellow dust in the vast land of Manchuria" than to modify their strategies and tactics to adapt to a changing situation. Being killed, like those who perished while resisting Japan's colonial regime in Korea, "is something that anyone with pride can do."[73] On the other hand, Park Chung-hee's decision to enter the Japanese military academy and become a military officer—whose primary task was to hunt and eliminate Korean and Chinese resistance fighters—was motivated by a spirit of rebellion, an act of true insurgence against the Japanese.[74]

Should Park's stint as a Japanese imperial officer blemish his otherwise pure "nationalist" credential, he more than found redemption in his subsequent devotion to the Korean state and with his ultimate sacrifice for the nation—assassination by his right-hand man. Park's moral blemishes are sublimated to the power of death that drove him to run toward the "narrow and treacherous road of state interest [*kug'ik*] without looking back; only the urgent [*chŏlbakhan*] task of the era—that is, the nation's prosperity—showed a way for individual salvation for Park."[75] In the face of this superhuman transcendence based on the metaphysics of death, Yi suggests, any rational and mundane interest in political legitimacy—the lack of which had plagued Park's regime especially since the declaration of Yusin in 1972—would only be an object of ridicule as far as Park was concerned.[76]

One literary critic dubbed *A Man's Road* a "courageous" move,[77] given the near absence of any literary treatment of Park and the less-than-positive appraisal of Park especially in the intellectual community at large at the time of the novel's publication. Yi also unabashedly relies on folklore elements to portray Park as a larger-than-life figure. Park's conception is foretold by his father's dream, for example, in which a red dragon baby jumps out of his body. The chapter in which this dream is told is titled "Reappearance of Yu the Great" ("*Taeuhyŏnsin*"), Yu the Great being a legendary ruler in ancient China. The implication that Park Chung-hee is a reincarnation of Yu the Great cannot be more obvious.[78] Much as in the family saga of Kim Il Sung, Park's mother is also endowed in the novel with an unusual gift—she communicates with spirits. Not only do the spirits stay away as soon as she becomes pregnant with Park; everywhere she goes, spirits residing in the area run away in fear of the unborn baby![79]

Although Yi In-hwa's *A Man's Road* was perhaps the most obvious hagiographic treatment of Park among literary works published in the 1990s, there were a number of other works that captured the public's imagination and spawned public debate over Park's legacy. These texts signaled a move to the right that was taking place among South Korea's cultural gatekeepers. In these literary works, the 1970s and the 1980s are reconstructed as a period of egalitarianism where everybody was poor but lived and worked harmoniously together to bring about their own individual prosperity as well as that of the nation, under the leadership of Park Chung-hee and the ubiquitous slogan of "Let us live better."

Kim Chin-myŏng's *The Rose of Sharon Has Blossomed* (*Mugunghwa kkoti p'iŏtsŭmnida*) was published in 1993 and became immensely popular, with three million copies sold within the first year of its publication, the highest number of any title in the history of South Korea up to that point.[80] One of the protagonists is a US-based ethnic Korean nuclear physicist, Dr. Yi Yong-hu (based on a real-life theoretical physicist, Dr. Benjamin Whisoh Lee), who returns to South Korea—thereby giving up the prospect of receiving a Nobel Prize—to help Park Chung-hee realize his quest for nuclear weapons development. An erstwhile opponent of Park's authoritarian rule, Dr. Yi is deeply touched by Park's earnest devotion to the nation and is convinced by Park's appeal that to possess nuclear weapons is the only way for Korea to survive a volatile world dominated by two superpowers. He is killed in a mysterious auto accident (the real Dr. Lee was also killed in an auto accident in the United States), and Park himself is also killed less than a year before the scheduled day of underground nuclear testing (the real Park Chung-hee was assassinated by his KCIA director in 1979 and there was no nuclear testing scheduled).[81] The author attributes both deaths to the work of the American CIA to prevent South Korea from developing nuclear weapons.[82]

Published before the full-fledged appearance of the Park Chung-hee syndrome, Kim's novel anticipates it, giving a glowing portrayal of Park as a deeply astute politician, fervent nationalist, and a man of compassion who is "readily moved by tears." Park's obsession with nuclear weapons development is attributed to his deeply nationalist longing to see Korea survive the uncertain world of the post-détente geopolitical configuration; his steadfast determination and stealthy maneuvering to make atomic weapons is met with frequent meddling by the United States in the novel. Park's authoritarian measures are explained away as stemming from his desire to bring prosperity and national security to Korea.[83] In the novel, Park pledges to Dr. Yi that he will declare an end to his presidency and the Yusin Constitution on the day of successful underground nuclear testing.[84] As literary critic Mun Hŭng-sul notes, the author's portrayal of the Park Chung-hee period is statist and militarist, justifying possible nuclear proliferation in the name of national defense and the future of Korea.[85] The unstated wish for the emergence of a strong leader matching the reputed leadership and charisma of Park also permeates the novel.[86]

Yet another popular novel in the 1990s was Kim Chŏng-hyŏn's *Father* (*Abŏji*), published in 1996. A "portrait of fathers who are tired and abandoned"[87]—having fallen from the previously exalted position of "industrial soldier"[88]—it sold a million copies within six months of its publication. The novel opens with the father, the protagonist, diagnosed with a terminal illness, his pain so severe that he seeks to have an assisted suicide. His life had been dictated by the mandate to bring about economic development at all costs; he is one of the ubiquitous absentee fathers in South Korea whose wife and children treat him as if he's just a boarder. He has been using a separate bedroom from his wife for several years and does not even realize that the audio set in the living no longer has a turntable but instead a CD player.[89] Only with the gradual revelation of his illness does his family come to realize the sacrifice he has made for the family and reconciles with him—his wife even lets him continue his extramarital affair with a much younger woman.[90] With his imminent death, all of his past wrongdoings are forgiven and the erstwhile family conflict is resolved. As critic Cho Myŏng-gi remarks, the father's impending death here stands in as a silent threat to the family to obey and put their faith in the dominant culture and value system—the ruling ideology.[91]

As in other parts of the world, the father figure has occupied a vexing and often conflicted position in the literature of Korea, from the figure that demands absolute obedience to the object of compassion and pity, or as an object of intense scorn and hatred, even leading to a plot of patricide.[92] In the 1990s, however, many literary sons were mostly comforting and paying homage to fathers for their sacrifices for family and nation, waxing nostalgic for the good old days, when reputedly everyone sacrificed for South Korea's economic development and modernization.[93] *Father* was a particularly problematic case of fanning patriarchal nostalgia and whitewashing the often-violent past of Korea. Critics also rebuked the novel as a reaction against the rise of feminism in South Korea.[94]

All three novels discussed here participated in constituting the Park Chung-hee syndrome and performed, however inadvertently, a number of historical displacements. Yi In-hwa's portrayal of Park Chung-hee as singlehandedly responsible for South Korea's modernization and industrialization accompanied the backgrounding of the history of the "dark side of the miracle"—the multifold negative side effects of quick-paced industrialization. By doing so, Yi glosses over the Korean people's participation and their many sacrifices in the process of industrialization. It also pushes into the background crucial aspects of the historical context, such as the Cold War arrangement for South Korea to exchange military dependency on the United States for economic aid and political support, for example.[95] It is as if the country's economic development overrides any of the concerns with Park Chung-hee's abuse of civil and human rights committed during authoritarian rule, as the three-decade-long democratization movement recedes into the background.

The Cho-Joong-Dong Literary Complex and the Ascendance of Neoconservatism

The immense popularity of these novels had to do with the authors' storytelling gifts and thematic resonance, among other literary factors. At the same time, the previously mentioned troika of conservative newspapers, what one may call the Cho-Joong-Dong literary complex, also played a significant role with their energetic promotion of the authors, sponsoring and organizing book reviews, author interviews, and talk shows with the writers. Yi In-hwa in particular received inordinate attention from the mass media, which also helped to catapult him to visibility as a poster child of the revisionist assessment of Park Chung-hee.[96] Yi In-hwa's earlier *Everlasting Empire* (*Yŏngwŏnhan cheguk*, 1993), a historical novel set in late eighteenth-century Korea that superimposed the reform-oriented king Chŏngjo onto Park Chung-hee,[97] was glowingly reviewed by none other than Yi Mun-yŏl, the famed novelist and an outspoken champion of conservatism.[98]

In fact, the conservative mass media provided cultural gatekeepers such as Yi Mun-yŏl with various platforms to comment on the major issues of Korean society. Yi is known for an arresting writing style and dazzling display of erudition, especially with his frequent references to classical literature in his novels which have enjoyed both critical and commercial success.[99] As philosopher Kim Yŏng-min notes, Yi is truly one of the few literary figures in South Korea who could be said to have a personal "literary power" (*munhak kwŏllyŏk*), discussed in chapter 2.[100] Yi has wielded his powerful position as a famous novelist and a celebrity figure to voice his opposition to the progressive governments of Kim Dae-jung and Roh Moo-hyun and to comment on various social topics through not only his own literary works but also in numerous interviews with the mass media. Yi was especially outspoken about the Roh government's attempt to introduce legislative laws to deal with legacies of the colonial and the authoritarian past, a project that became known as "cleanse the past" (*kwagŏ ch'ŏngsan*).[101]

Roh's predecessor Kim Dae-jung initiated efforts to examine "unresolved issues" related to Japanese colonialism, the division of the peninsula, and the decades-long anti-communist dictatorships. After much resistance from conservative parties, the Truth and Reconciliation Commission (TRC) was founded in 2005 to investigate incidents of "the sufferings of the colonial rule of Japan, the indescribable loss of civilian lives from massacres during the Korean War, human rights abuses under the authoritarian regimes, a search for truth, and finally to achieve justice."[102] During the Roh Moo-hyun government, the effort to deal with Japanese legacies resulted in the 2005 passage of the Basic Act for Coping with Past History for Truth and Reconciliation.[103]

In a 2006 interview with *JoongAng Ilbo*, Yi Mun-yŏl likened the Roh government's legislative acts to the Cultural Revolution: a crude, spasmodic, and superficial political slogan driven by mindless nationalism.[104] Countries that had put forth nationalism as political ideology, such as Nazi Germany and interwar Japan, had had a disastrous backlash. It would be acceptable to investigate and assess the collaboration historically and culturally, but to make a political issue by enacting a law was not only disagreeable but also had no practical benefit. Its only aim would be to punish the descendants of the collaborators by applying *yŏnjwaje* (guilt by association) or to "provide yet more of a boost to the political legitimacy of the Kim Il Sung regime," Yi opined.

According to Yi Mun-yŏl, the Roh government's attempt to rectify the past was also at its core an expression of anti-Americanism held by leftists who occupied critical positions in the government. From Yi's perspective, the leftists' critique of the United States' role in post-1945 South Korea is unfounded, as the United States bore no responsibility for the trajectory of South Korean history: at the time of the US Military Government in Korea (1945–1948), it had no choice but to rely on the existing Japanese colonial structure, as it had no basic information about the country before arriving in Korea in September 1945. But the more the anti-American perspective spread in South Korea, the more it would benefit North Korea, as the political legitimacy of the north's regime derives from Kim Il Sung's anti-colonial resistance and anti-US stance, Yi argued. For Yi, the logical conclusion of the rectification of past wrongs pushed by the Roh government was to legitimize the Korean War as a righteous war to reunify the two Koreas.

In the same interview, Yi declared that the most important educational goal of elementary and middle school is to raise future citizens whose duty is to protect the "state system" (*kukka ch'eje*). He then lamented that current education had been taken hostage by the teachers' union Chŏnkyojo (Korean Teachers and Educational Workers Union), whose goal he claimed was to raise future citizens fit not for the Republic of Korea based on the 1948 constitution but rather for another republic—North Korea.[105] As far as he was concerned, all of the ways in which the Roh government and "leftist forces" were dealing with issues of historical justice were ultimately an attempt to benefit North Korea. His indiscriminate label of "pro–North Korea" for anything that he finds distasteful or irksome included the campaign to boycott *Chosun Ilbo* in the 1990s.[106]

Yi Mun-yŏl's self-designated role as arbiter of social issues was also prominently displayed in his literary works. When the Kim Dae-jung administration launched an investigation of the conservative media giant *Chosun Ilbo* and a number of other mass media outlets for tax evasion, there was an uproar among conservatives that Kim was trying to muzzle critical media.[107] In his 2001 novel that was a blatant and loud protest against this investigation, Yi called the government officials "dogs" and those who called for press reform "Red Guards," while the owners of the media outlets were praised as *"ŏn'gwan,"* high-ranking government censors during the Koryŏ (918–1392) and Chosŏn (1392–1910) periods who were responsible for keeping the court record free of fabrication or bias.[108] His 2006 novel *Homo Executans* is yet another political jab at the governments of Kim Dae-jung and Roh Moo-hyun as pro–North Korea and nationalist.[109]

Earlier in 1997, Yi also published a novel, *Choice* (*Sŏnt'aek*), that was widely considered to be a rebuke to contemporary feminist women—those "who follow feminism with vulgar and superficial understanding" and who "shout vulgar slogans of revenge and propagate naked selfishness."[110] *Sŏnt'aek* proposes a counterimage for contemporary women in an aristocratic woman from Korea's past—Lady Chang, from a prominent elite (*yangban*) family in the mid-Chosŏn period (1392-1910) and revered as a model of "wise mother, good wife" (*hyŏnmo yangch'ŏ*) in the region of Yŏngnam, where Yi was born. Despite her initial resistance to social mores dictated by the Confucian patriarchy, Lady Chang acquiesces and steadfastly defends them. Yi presents Lady Chang's life as a series of "choices" she made on her own: giving up the pursuit of scholarship, marriage, devotion to her husband and parents-in-law, giving birth, rearing children, and devotion to the needy in her old age. There is no sense in the novel of any historical, socioeconomic, or cultural constraints that might have been, or were certainly at play, for her choices. In one of the most problematic passages in the novel, Lady Chang urges implicitly that the women of today follow her life trajectory.[111]

Even as Yi Mun-yŏl continued to enjoy the privileges that come as an arbiter of sociopolitical issues with support from the troika of conservative mass media, he maintained his posture as the anguished intellectual and dissident—politically persecuted by leftist governments and misunderstood by the public, with the uproar caused by the novel *Choice* as evidence, for example.[112] Performed as gestures of self-resignation and self-flagellation, his posture veils the degree to which he relies on his stature as a cultural icon, while recycling hackneyed Cold War anti-communist and statist rhetoric as well as patriarchal values.

Pok Kŏ-il is another well-known novelist and conservative commentator who, much as Yi Mun-yŏl, is frequently called on by the media to comment on various contemporary issues.[113] Much like Yi Mun-yŏl, he also plays the self-styled nonconformist and the outsider.[114] Pok's numerous publications extol the virtues of his own brand of liberalism, a unique brand that at times contradicts itself, and a kind that writer and journalist Ko Chong-sŏk—who, along with Pok, is one of the few public figures who identifies himself as a liberalist (*chayujuŭija*)—characterizes as a liberalism that serves only "the strong and the exceptional."[115] Pok considers himself to be one of the few, even among liberalists, who are truly committed to the principles of "economic liberalism" (*kyŏngjejŏk chayujuŭi*), which for him constitutes the foundational principles of capitalism and which has developed the most rigorous and refined theories from among many variations of liberalism.[116] His firm belief in economic liberalism, the distillation of which for him is that competition is the most efficient way a society produces value, has led him to suggest that South Korea adopt English as an official language. His other suggestion was that the country expand eligibility for the presidency to foreigners with proven leadership, with Margaret Thatcher and Ronald Reagan given as examples of such proven leadership.[117]

Pok Kŏ-il is one of the first public figures to reduce the historical meanings of the democratization movement in general, and the 1987 June uprising in particular, to fit the trajectory of conservative ideology of the post-1987 period. In his 1990 publication *Reality and Future Aim* (*Hyŏnsil kwa Chihyang*), Pok interprets the 1987 democratic transition as the "victory of conservatism" while at the same time designating Marxist and leftist ideology as the source of all problems that Korean society faces.[118] Not surprisingly, Pok has also emerged as a public defender of chaebŏl. In his 2007 publication *Power of Ideology* (*Inyŏmŭi him*), Pok argues that current criticisms directed at Samsung, the largest Korean chaebŏl, are part of a larger scheme of leftists to "demolish the system" (*ch'eje hŏmulgi*), unproblematically equating chaebŏl with the South Korean regime. As far as he is concerned, anyone criticizing Samsung is a leftist who is automatically defined as a follower of totalitarianism.[119] From the 1990s and well into the early 2000s, much as with the case of Yi Mun-yŏl's indiscriminate labeling of "pro-North Korea," Pok's specialty was to indiscriminately throw around the label of "totalitarianism" to refer to politically progressive forces as threatening the liberal order of South Korea.[120] That many of his writings were in fact published by the Center for Free Enterprise, a chaebŏl-funded research institute that churns out numerous neoliberal publications, shows the deep intertwinement, if not symbiosis, among chaebŏl, the conservative mass media, and intellectuals who align with these two forces.[121]

Much like Yi Mun-yŏl, Pok is not above deploying his much-admired literary skill to attack those he considers to be his political nemesis. In 2001, Pok published "A Collection of Maxims from Jupiter" ("*Moksŏng chamŏnjip*"), a science fiction tale set on an imaginary planet in the future. The planet's leader and the main protagonist is clearly modeled on the former president Kim Dae-jung: "Having served too long as an opposition party leader to be president of the country . . . he has pursued the Sunshine Policy unreasonably; but the policy was so unrealistic and ended in a complete failure, leaving only a deep scar of the division of public opinion."[122] As one blogger–cum–literary critic notes, Pok Kŏ-il's well-deserved reputation as a preeminent science fiction novelist is put into question with this novel, as it reads more like a political pamphlet peddled by the likes of the previously mentioned Center for Free Enterprise than bona fide science fiction.[123]

Yi Mun-yŏl has protested that he has no social influence in society, asking that the public indulge in his free-floating novelistic imagination without impugning any political motives in his literary works.[124] Pok has also inveighed against literature's engagement with political issues, claiming that to do so is "the worst kind of contempt to literature and writers."[125] At the same time, they not only use literature as "a personal weapon against their adversaries"[126] but also suggest that their prestige should exempt them from any charge of partisan politics—the talented writer would not have stooped to put out a mere potboiler or political vendetta. In the 1980s, writers whose literary works dealt with contemporary sociopolitical issues were regarded with suspicion as "minjung-oriented"—that is to say, political. However, few of those labeled as such would have retreated from public scrutiny with a claim that they were "only" novelists. Yi and Pok, on the other hand, masquerade their sloganeering under the facade of "pure literature."[127]

In fact, both Yi and Pok were elevated as public intellectuals from the 1990s onward by the troika of Cho-Joong-Dong. Until the 1990s, the notion of public intellectual referred to a small number of intellectuals who were willing to forgo their own personal interests and welfare in the pursuit and defense of what they perceived to be the truth and universal values. During the authoritarian era, their pursuit of the truth meant to speak against political repression, economic inequality, the collusion between the state and corporate conglomerates (chaebŏl), low wages and harsh working conditions for workers, degradation of environment, and other injustices. In most cases, these intellectuals commonly paid a high price for being dissidents, as they were considered to be subversive by the state and dismissed from their jobs, placed under house arrest, detained, tortured, imprisoned, and even murdered.[128]

Since the late 1980s, the status and role of intellectuals in Korean society have undergone a radical shift, following the previously discussed global transformation in general and, more specifically, the profusion of consumer culture, rise of the internet and consequent advent of the information age, and the high number of university graduates, among other factors. An intellectual was no longer seen as—and the society seemed no longer to need—a prophetic voice and a seeker of truth. Some of the well-known intellectuals who were active in social movement went into politics, becoming high-ranking officials of the administration or National Assembly members, a phenomenon encapsulated in the widely circulated term *polifessor*, a portmanteau of "politics" and "professor."[129] The disdain with which the term was frequently invoked by conservative mass media—who coined the term in 2012—seemed to have been directed mostly at former undongkwŏn who entered politics after their stint as academics. Some of the iconic public intellectuals of the previous era also took a turn to the right, such as Kim Chi-ha. A celebrated dissident of the 1970s known for his biting satire of the Park Chung-hee regime, under whose watch he was imprisoned several times and received a death sentence (which was later commuted), Kim's public support for the presidential aspiration of Park Geun-hye, the daughter of Pak Chung-hee, was considered by many to be tantamount to disavowing his own past.[130]

Given the transformed place and role of intellectuals and the rise of the New Right among the rank and file of former undongkwŏn that I discuss in the following chapter, it seems as if a wholesale discrediting of the previous generation of public intellectuals became de rigueur. The status and role of mass media have also undergone drastic changes, as I briefly discuss earlier.[131] The combined processes of the declining status of the previous dissident public intellectuals and the unparalleled new power of the conservative mass media also gave rise to the emergence of neoconservatives such as Yi and Pok as new public intellectuals.

The cases of Yi Mun-yŏl and Pok Kŏ-il illustrate the ways in which the conservative mass media and well-known literary figures work in tandem to yield their power as cultural gatekeepers and powerbrokers, by relying on their reputed brilliant intellect and "culturedness" (*kyoyang*). That their outsized role as such has not been scrutinized has been also in part due to their status among the privileged ranks of cultural producers in South Korea.[132] Their literary output as well as their public pronouncements on various sociopolitical issues have functioned as revisionist texts of the Park Chung-hee period and by extension post-1945 South Korean history.

As I have shown in this chapter, the Park Chung-hee syndrome was much more than a spontaneous and grassroots expression by ordinary Korean people. It was the combined efforts of conservative mass media providing platforms for various figures of note that produced the syndrome. The narrative exertion that facilitated and constituted the syndrome included not only biographies of Park and memoirs authored by those who were close to Park Chung-hee but also literary outputs such as Yi In-hwa's *A Man's Road*, Kim Chin-myŏng's *The Rose of Sharon Has Blossomed*, and Kim Chŏng-hyŏn's *Father*, all published within a few years of each other in the 1990s.

Throughout the rise and sustainment of the Park Chung-hee syndrome, it became clear that mass media, with their vast and influential platforms, have become the most critical agent for reconstructing the memory of Park Chung-hee, one of the core elements of the Park Chung-hee syndrome. From conducting numerous public opinion polls to providing various platforms to novelists and other visible figures of culture to comment on current affairs, to serializing and publishing memoirs of the individuals associated with Park Chung-hee, the mass media has produced and narrated the past, becoming more powerful and effective than any professional historians' scholarly works. By functioning as agents of memory and providing spaces where such memory is articulated and conveyed, the conservative newspapers became the main medium through which revisionist views of Park Chung-hee were articulated and spread.

One of the more significant outcomes of the Park Chung-hee syndrome has been the blurring of the lines of distinction between authoritarianism and democracy. The controversy sparked by the syndrome indicates the extent to which the previously existing social paradigm of authoritarianism versus democracy was in danger of losing its essential functions as the interpretive framework of the society, as well as the broker between what was considered to be the two main political cultures until the 1990s. Although this binary framework of authoritarianism versus democracy risks perpetuating a certain set of received ideas and myths about the 1980s and possibly foreclosing a more critical examination of the period,[133] its blurring has also given rise to a new set of intellectual, historical, and political challenges, which the following chapter on the rise of New Right historiography examines.

4

The Rise of New Right Historiography
and Its Triumphalist Discourse

In 2006, the occasion of the publication of *Reunderstanding Pre- and Post-liberation History* (*Haebang chŏnhusa ŭi chaeinsik*, hereafter *Reunderstanding*) (figure 4.1) was a much-anticipated media event, akin to the release of a long-awaited sequel of a popular novel. Mass media's extensive coverage even before publication stirred a great deal of curiosity among those in the know, with rumors of how reviews were being kept secret. Editors of the volume, although denying that they had any intention to engage in current politics, made it clear that their work was a refutation of, and a counternarrative to, the six-volume *Understanding Pre- and Post-liberation History* (*Haebang chŏnhusa ŭi insik*, hereafter *Understanding*) (figure 4.2).[1] Published between 1979 and 1989—the first volume in 1979 at the height of the "Frozen Republic" of the Park Chung-hee regime—*Understanding* was considered a must-read among progressive intellectuals in the 1980s. Its

FIGURE 4.1. *Haebang chŏnhusa ŭi chaeinsik* (*Reunderstanding Pre- and Post-liberation History*), 2006.

editors were also unequivocal that their aim was to critique not only the authoritarian regimes of Syngman Rhee and Park Chung-hee but also the state anti-communism, skewed state-led economic development at the expense of equitable distribution of wealth, South Korea's subservience to the United States, and perpetuation of the Cold War on the Korean Peninsula, among others.[2]

The editors of the 2006 *Reunderstanding* saw *Understanding* as a distillation of the minjung perspective and its problems, which they characterized as the tendency to see nationalism as the deus ex machina of all of Korea's problems, belief in the inevitability of a minjung revolution, and a radical interpretation of post-1945 Korean history.[3] They also believed that *Understanding*'s perspective unjustifiably dominated the field of Korean history and contemporary society and saw it as their responsibility to transform the way fellow historians and society think about Korean history.

Although Yi Yŏng-hun, one of the four editors, soon became a star in the neoconservative firmament and more recently the impresario of the New Right, it would be unfair and too simplistic to characterize the whole volume

FIGURE 4.2. *Haebang chŏnhusa ŭi insik (Understanding Pre- and Post-liberation History)*, 1979–1989.

as New Right. A major scholarly publication with twenty-eight contributors from both in and outside of South Korea, with wide-ranging topics written by scholars in various disciplines including historians of Europe and Japan, the publication deserves much more than the kind of sensational, media-driven reception it has had so far.[4] Not every contributor would have agreed with the editors' framework or could have anticipated the controversy the volume has given rise to.[5] However, the editors' arguments in the introduction to the first volume and their roundtable discussion in the second volume certainly read like a manifesto to revise "leftist" scholarship of the previous era, as well as a clarion call for a New Right history that would soon emerge. Two years later, a New Right group of scholars called Textbook Forum (Kyogwasŏ p'orŏm) published *The Alternative Textbook: Modern and Contemporary Korean History* (*Han'guk kŭn-hyŏndaesa: Taean kyogwasŏ*) with a similar goal as the editors of *Reunderstanding*: to remove "distorted" representations of the past in contemporary history textbooks and to proffer a more positive view of Korean history.[6] The debates following these publications assumed the character of a national dispute.

Historiography and historical revisionism constitute an important site for the organization of collective memory; they reconfigure the relationship between collective memory and national identity, among other relationships.[7] The debates following the publication of *Reunderstanding* and *The Alternative*

Textbook, as with previous debates on "colonial modernization"[8] and the Park Chung-hee syndrome, became contested terrain where individuals or groups contend, guided or compelled by their present political orientations, to reshape their national pasts.[9] As before, both sides of the debate also antagonistically accused the other side of grinding an ideological axe rather than being genuinely scholarly, but the stakes this time seemed much higher than before and more consequential. The self-understanding of participants in these debates stems from the different ways in which they have dealt with or understood the tumultuous experience of Korea's twentieth century: colonialization, division, the Korean War, and South Korea's economic development and democratization processes in the context of the still-divided Korean Peninsula, and other major episodes in the country. The debates were thus as much about the past itself as about how a nation reconciles with or overcomes the still-lingering legacies of Japanese colonial rule and more recent legacies of Park Chung-hee's authoritarian regime.

My main purpose in this chapter is not to provide a detailed analysis of the New Right's arguments or its organizations, which numerous scholars have already done with more thoroughness than I can deliver.[10] Rather, I explore how New Right historiography partakes in the reconstruction of collective memory and rewriting history, situating it in the context of global transformation and neoliberal restructuring. I argue that the New Right, through circuitous critique of nationalist and leftist orientation of previous scholarship, recasts the centrality of the state by way of bringing the primacy of the market to the fore, not only in economics but also in the evaluation of public life. It also recycles anti-communist developmentalist arguments and tropes while taking up the language of liberalism; it obscures the mutual constitution of South Korea and North Korea and turns the north's economic problems into cultural difference, much as in colonial discourse, which then justifies its eventual demise. I further argue that New Right revisionist scholarship and the historiographical debates that have ensued, despite having generated much public attention to issues of critical importance, have not suggested alternative ways to formulate one's self- or national identification in relation to collective memory.

The Rise of the New Right

As with the Park Chung-hee syndrome, the mass media has been integral to the rise of the New Right. Mass media coined the term *New Right*, which was later adopted by its proponents themselves. Even the debates generated by publication of *Reunderstanding* were in large part due to the media's extensive—

inordinate, some would argue—coverage.[11] The inauguration of the Liberty Union (Chayujuŭi yŏndae) on November 23, 2004 seems to have marked the beginning of the many organizations that openly characterized themselves as New Right. *Dong-A Ilbo*, one of the troika of conservative newspapers, began to cover extensively the emergence of the New Right, including serialization of a special report from February 2005.

The inaugural statement of the Liberty Union was quite clear about what was at stake for the New Right:

> Our beloved motherland is faced with a crisis that has reached a dead end. As the very principle of liberal democracy and market economy, the ideological justification and historical legitimacy of South Korea, has been questioned by the [current] ruling power, the country's identity has been damaged.... At this time when mobilizing the wisdom of the entire nation and marching toward construction of an advanced country [*sŏnjin'guk*] is called for, Roh Moo-hyun government hangs its fate on the "war with the past" by spreading the history of self-torment [*chahaksagwan*], to [forcefully] change the existing order and to reconfigure the ruling bloc.[12]

The statement also called for the primacy of democratic liberalism in Korean society for its future, as South Korea has achieved the twin goal of industrialization and democratization: "The *Geist* of the twenty-first century is not the authoritarianism of industrialization forces, nor the minjungism of some democratization forces; it is a twenty-first-century-style liberalism that fits with the reality of South Korea and that will fully realize globalization [*segyehwa*], informatization [*chŏngbohwa*], and liberalization [*chayuhwa*]."[13]

The immediate context of this statement was clear. The previous government of Kim Dae-jung (1998–2003) initiated efforts to examine "unresolved issues" related to Japanese colonialism, the division of the peninsula, and the decades of anti-communist dictatorships, as discussed in chapter 3. Roh Moo-hyun, a former human rights lawyer, succeeded Kim Dae-jung as president in 2003; in June 2004, Roh's political party took the majority in the National Assembly—the first time a progressive party had won a majority of seats in the history of South Korea's general elections. Tensions between conservatives and progressives intensified and the sense of crisis among conservative elements reached its height. To them, the Roh government's extensive reform agenda and continued move toward rapprochement with North Korea—including high-level military talks and offers of economic assistance and independence from the Bush administration on a range of issues including relations with North Korea—were "nothing less than class warfare."[14] In particular, the Roh government's proposal of four legislative reforms (*sadae ipbŏp*) and a series of enactments of new laws addressing state violence committed during the old regime made the Liberty Union claim that the Roh regime was at "war with the past."[15]

At the same time, the economic crisis that eventually brought about International Monetary Fund (IMF) intervention and South Korea's drastic neoliberal transformation also strengthened the already-prevalent discourse of sŏnjin'guk, "advanced country." The desire to escape from the category of *hujin'guk* (backward country) and to become a sŏnjin'guk has informed national identities and worldviews of South Koreans during the developmental stage.[16] In what appears to be the twenty-first century version of the Darwinian notion of survival of the fittest, the discourse of sŏnjin'guk became revitalized as South Korea was undergoing neoliberal transformation. Embedded in hierarchical and binary logic—such as the advanced and the backward, the normal and the abnormal—sŏnjin'guk discourse was appropriated by conservatives to promote neoliberal policies. The conservatives' principle of "liberal democracy" was transposed to neoliberal ideas and practices: downsizing of government, privatization of public enterprise, deregulation, pro-business policy, and the open market. For conservatives, the contemporary Kim Dae-jung and Roh Moo-hyun governments were not small enough and were not doing enough to promote the market economy.[17]

The South Korean New Right is not like the skinheads in jackboots and leather jackets in North America or Europe, where the right-wing populist movements are decidedly anti-elitist; they are mostly elites in society—politicians, journalists, novelists, professors, lawyers, and historians.[18] Many of the sixty or so founding members of the Liberty Union were also former undongkwŏn: Sin Chi-ho was a labor activist, Hong Chin-p'yo a reunification movement activist, and Ch'oe Hong-jae a president of Korea University's Student Association, a position that was usually occupied by an undongkwŏn until about the mid-1990s. In fact, the "New Christian Right" is a prominent group composed of former minjung or liberation theology practitioners who adopted neoliberal thinking within the New Right.[19] A flurry of memoirs by former undongkwŏn intellectuals confessing their erstwhile allegiance as a mistake and as a relic of the past began with Sin Chi-ho's "Are You Still Dreaming of Revolution?" and "Confession," both published in 1992.[20]

Since the 1990s and early 2000s, a sea change in the relationship between politics and intellectual legitimacy occurred, as evidenced by an increase in the number of polemical and literary works that urgently sought to comprehend former political allegiances and identities. In many cases, these efforts amounted to nothing more than explaining away one's now-discredited ideological pasts. Consequently, claiming delegitimation of the previous paradigm

FIGURE 4.3. Former president Park Geun-hye (*second from left*) attending the first anniversary of the founding of the Nationwide Coalition of the New Right, Changch'ung Stadium, Seoul, November 9, 2006. Source: *Hankyoreh*.

of the minjung movement and all of its attendant historiography, that one had been vaccinated from Marxism or more generally leftist ideas, became a source of political legitimacy in the intellectual community. In particular, having overcome their erstwhile capitulation to the lure of *chuch'e sasang* has been the political cache of the representative figures of the New Right.[21]

Such a Damascene conversion of intellectuals is not unique or specific to South Korea. Nor is it due to only personal proclivities or failings, or to be condemned outright; it is also the radically transformed sociopolitical and economic circumstances that push one to undergo such a transformation in outlook.[22] Perhaps society remembers only the most extreme cases, such as those who participated in 1968 in France who have become "managers of capitalism" with a "deep ethical and political gap" in their lives,[23] or former leaders of the 1970s radical Zenkyoto movement who became Japan's leading neoconservative ideologues.[24] In South Korea, the democratic transition, the persistence of the Cold War on the Korean Peninsula, North Korea's failing economic system, South Korea's embrace of neoliberalism, and other factors made the disavowal of North Korea a rite of passage for these former *undongkwŏn*.

Kim Yŏng-hwan's personal itinerary from "the founder" of the *chusap'a* (followers of North Korea's chuch'e sasang) in the 1980s to a human rights activist advocating for regime change in North Korea in the 1990s testifies to the persistence of the Cold War structure in Korea as well as the place of North Korea as a legitimating and enabling factor in the rise of the New Right.[25] In 1986, during the height of the minjung movement, Kim rose to prominence for his underground pamphlets known as the *Kangch'ŏl* series, which helped to spread chuch'e sasang—which he called "a true revolutionary path, for it combined the best of Marxism-Leninism with the best of Korea's nationalism"—as a model for the South Korean minjung movement.[26] Arrested in 1986 for the violation of the National Security Law, he was released in 1988. He then went on to found an underground organization, Anti-imperial Youth Alliance (Panje ch'ŏngnyŏn tongmaeng), which was reorganized later as the Revolutionary Party of National Democracy (Minjok minju hyŏngmyŏngdang).

In 1991, he sneaked into North Korea on a semi-submarine and met with the then-leader of North Korea, Kim Il Sung, and scholars of chuch'e sasang. This meeting, which should have been the most exciting event of his activist life, and which many of his fellow undongkwŏn in the 1980s could have only dreamed of, proved to be an utter disappointment for Kim—neither Kim Il Sung nor the scholars around him, as far as Kim was concerned, knew much about chuch'e sasang. Starting from around 1995, with revelations of mass starvation in North Korea and the defection of Hwang Chang-yŏp, the reputed architect of chuch'e sasang, among others, Kim saw the scales fall from his eyes, exposing him to the true enormity of the sin of "actually existing socialism" of North Korea. Contra Kim Il Sung, Park Chung-hee had been right all along. Accordingly, it was time to embrace capitalism. His conversion was so extreme that for him, Margaret Thatcher—of the infamous declaration, "There is no such thing as society; only individual men and women and family"[27]—became his ideal political leader. Kim also considered the current form of capitalism to be the highest form of civilization, carrying with it its own Korean brand of "civilizing mission."[28]

Although Kim's case is perhaps one of the most dramatic turnarounds among the undongkwŏn, the adoption of neoliberalism among former undongkwŏn of the New Right has been swift. It is in part due to their commitment to liberal democracy and market economy that they engage in various efforts to "save" North Korea from communism and its leadership. North Korea, having pursued a socialist planned economy, was hit by both human-made and natural disasters that plunged the country into tragic upheaval. The government's human rights violations and nuclear weapons development, and consequent worsening of relations with the United States, provided the conservatives with a powerful reason for demanding a tough policy against North Korea. Against South Korea's unprecedented economic development and current status as an economic global powerhouse, North Korea's failure is all the more glaring, as well as inevitable, to New Right intellectuals.

New Right Scholarship and the History War

It is safe to say that the New Right as the kind of social movement envisioned by the Liberty Union has not yet materialized as of this writing, perhaps due to the elitist makeup of the New Right leadership and for reasons other scholars have discussed.[29] However, the New Right as both a source of social discourse and as a historiographical movement to revise Korean history has persisted, despite some views to the contrary.[30] The underlying sense of crisis and urgency, ushered in by the Kim Dae-jung and Roh Moo-hyun governments' various reform measures that prompted organization of the Liberty Union, is also shared by editors of the 2006 volume *Reunderstanding*, notwithstanding their claim to be free of any political motive.[31] To the editors of *Reunderstanding*, Roh Moo-hyun and his supporters are of the generation influenced by the scholarship in *Understanding*, which they vehemently decry as nationalistic and anachronistic. They believe that it was time to reconsider their perspectives in light of the progress that South Korea has made. Furthermore, it was necessary to expose the harm caused to society by the views expounded in *Understanding*.[32] The reception of the 2006 publication was also clearly bifurcated along the lines of what South Koreans call the logic of encampment (*chinyŏng nolli*); the conservatives, including conservative mass media, exulted the publication of *Reunderstanding* and helped to boost its commercial success.[33] Those on the left, but also some of those who may not associate themselves with either the left or the right, were equally united in their dismissal of the publication, given to understanding that its editors, though not all contributors, aimed to target the current "progressive" policies of the Roh government and of progressive forces at large.[34] Some historians have suggested that elitist backgrounds of New Right historians also explain the degree to which they vehemently denounce the anti-colonial critique of the nationalist and minjung scholarship.[35]

With the publication of *Reunderstanding* as the opening salvo, a veritable history war started over reinterpretations of the modern and contemporary history of Korea. Although *Reunderstanding* editors did not claim themselves to be of the New Right, a series of organizations and publications that shared the outlook of the editors of *Reunderstanding* and identified as New Right soon emerged. In 2008, the previously mentioned Textbook Forum published *The Alternative Textbook*, with the goal of revising existing textbooks. These textbooks reputedly focused on negative and painful history and neglected achievements of South Korea since its foundation, among its other problems.[36] In keeping with their effort to emphasize the legitimacy of the Republic of Korea and to rebrand its state-directed economy as market-oriented, the authors of *The Alternative Textbook* suggest that colonial rule helped to develop the "social capacity that Koreans needed to establish a modern nation state."[37] In their scenario, Park Chung Hee's "modernization revolution" (*kŭndaehwa hyŏngmyŏng*) was also responsible for the market economy, which was modeled on earlier colonial development. Downplaying the dictatorship and all other violations of human and civil rights under his regime, the oppressions were presented as an unavoidable—and possibly even small—price to pay for South Korea's inexorable march toward a modern market economy.[38] Historian Owen Miller calls *The Alternative Textbook* a form of "neoliberal historiography" that revises historical assessment of imperialism and authoritarianism "in order to reinvigorate the fortunes of the South Korean Right."[39]

More publications of the New Right followed. In 2007, Yi Yŏng-hun published *The Story of the Republic of Korea: Lectures on* Reunderstanding (*Taehanmin'guk iyagi: Haebang chŏnhusa ŭi chaeinsik ui kangŭi*), a summary of the themes and arguments of *Reunderstanding*. In 2011, the contributors to the New Right journal *Geist* (*Sidae chŏngsin*) put together an edited volume, *Origin and Future of South Korea's Democracy: The Conservatives Have Been Leading Democracy* (*Han'guk minjujuŭi ŭi kiwŏn kwa mirae: Posuga ikkŭlda*), a hagiographic treatment of Syngman Rhee and Park Chung-hee.[40]

As historian Yun Hae-dong reminds us, the six-volume *Understanding*, the main target of the editors of the 2006 *Reunderstanding*, was the product of a long process of historians' challenges to the ways in which the discipline of history had accommodated dictates of the state. Since liberation of Korea from Japanese rule simultaneously brought about the division of Korea, any real experience and meaning of liberation was stripped for most Koreans. Suppression of civil and human rights, along with an unrelenting drive for economic development aided by anti-communist state ideology and draconian authoritarian rule inspired an oppositional movement. This was accompanied by a process of reinterpreting post-1945 history "in terms of powerful binaries" by the 1980s: "genuine nationalism versus mindless anti-communism, and minjung (people)-oriented democracy versus mere formal democracy."[41] In this context, *Understanding* was not only a critique of authoritarian regimes but also of Cold War mentality and politics, encapsulated most clearly in anti-communism as the state ideology. *Understanding* was also a criticism against the authoritarian state for its appropriation of history for its own goal of state-building, which included teaching history only with state-approved textbooks.

Ultimately, *Understanding* challenged all that was considered taboo in South Korean society at the time, such as any positive appraisal of socialism and communism. *Understanding* was therefore a process of the scholarly community finally coming to express its own voice, a process of gaining intellectual citizenship, as it were, at a time when scholarship remained dominated by a Cold War mentality and anti-communism.[42] The state's violent killings of the people of Kwangju in 1980 brought closer to home what these historians have known, that the division of the country and subsequent tension between the two Koreas have been used repeatedly to justify authoritarian rule in South Korea. They felt that their responsibility was to contribute to overcoming the structure of division and to bring about reunification by highlighting such efforts in their own scholarship.[43]

Historiographical binaries of previous decades came crashing down in the 1990s with the democratic transition and consequent demise of the minjung movement; the breakdown of the Soviet Union and actually existing socialism, which, among other factors, in turn contributed to North Korea's rapid economic downfall;[44] and a series of reform projects carried out by the liberal governments of Kim Dae-jung and Roh Moo-hyun. Whereas North Korea has become an international pariah, South Korea has become one of the economic powerhouses of the world, with accompanying political prestige in the global community. The contrasting developmental trajectories of the two Koreas have become a core element of self-understanding as well as a measure of historical consciousness and moral standards among New Right scholars. The divergence of two Koreas has also become the most critical element in reframing the narrative of Korean history by the New Right.

Yi Yŏng-hun, one of four editors of *Reunderstanding*, characterizes this contrasting outcome to be a case of "justice":

> Democracy and the market economy of South Korea started extremely precariously ... but the promotion without limit of freedom and egoism—human beings' most innate qualities—have brought the highest degree of material and spiritual achievement since the beginning of civilization on the Korean Peninsula.... There were a few prophetic leaders among those who, even as they were stubborn and foolish [in other matters], understood that history moves along only when [people are given] freedom and when [people are free to exercise] egoism. These [leaders] are the ones who established the Republic of Korea on the principles of democracy and market economy. Their establishing the republic was an act of "justice" itself from the beginning, because their choice

of the principle of democracy and market economy has been shared by humanity of the modern era [and understood] as "justice" through the experience of the long history of civilization.[45]

It is a remarkable statement, its grandiosity of scale matched perhaps by Francis Fukuyama's triumphalist discourse of the end of history in which liberal democracy—seen in its institutions of representative government, free markets, and consumerist culture—had become universal, and history had reached its goal.[46] Aside from Yi's problematic notion of justice, to which I will return in the next chapter, the complete absence of crucial global and historical context in this statement is equally remarkable. For history was not so obliging; crucial to South Korea's economic development takeoff was the normalization of relations with Japan and participation in the Vietnam War in the Cold War structure, where the United States was a hegemon. Normalization with Japan was intimately related to the United States' overall strategy of integrating East Asia as an anti-communist alliance, militarily and economically. The Vietnam War also provided an opportunity for economic development for Japan, South Korea, Taiwan, and other East Asian capitalist states at the time. The United States let South Korea pursue export-oriented economic development while simultaneously implementing protective trade policy and import substitution industrialization, as South Korea was viewed as an exhibition case of the free world bloc and in competition with North Korea.[47]

Neither does the flagrant disregard of democratic values and rule of law by the authoritarian leaders figure as a concern in Yi Yŏng-hun's idea of "justice." Yi's history is as unbalanced as the other right-wing scholars whose hagiographic treatment of Syngman Rhee and Park Chung-hee completely neglects the violation of civil and human rights of these leaders. Without considering the sociopolitical as well as cultural, not to mention psychic, price that South Korea has paid for its relentless push for economic development above all else, Yi Yŏng-hun's notion of justice offers South Korean economic development a kind of valediction: the mission of a liberal market economy, though in reality achieved by means other than a market economy approach, had been accomplished.

No less celebratory of the market economy and the state's role in it, the New Right intellectuals who founded the Textbook Forum in 2005 made clear that their aim was to revise current history books on modern and contemporary Korea. Existing history books, they argued, influenced by minjung historiography, are leftist, nationalist, and in collusion with the then-ruling "leftist" regime. Their leftist perspective not only discourages more "objective" historical views but also promotes self-doubt and self-torment in the younger generation. The task of the New Right is therefore to bring a "balanced" historical understanding of history that had privileged anti-Japanese resistance of the colonial period and the anti-authoritarian struggles in the post-liberation period at the expense of promoting the legitimacy of the Republic of Korea and celebrating its achievement.[48] The statement from the inauguration of the Textbook Forum reads,

> Our future generation is learning from their middle and high school history textbooks ... that the Republic of Korea should not have been born.... But the Republic of Korea can be proud of accomplishing "the mission impossible."... These textbooks ... do not contain what [a textbook] should naturally contain: the image of ourselves who have done our best to establish, defend, and nurture our country, a portrait of ourselves who have shed blood and tears to improve the quality of our lives. [In these textbooks] there are only accounts of dictatorship and oppression, and pitiful [ch'amdamhan] contradictions of capitalism. For how long should the future generation of the Republic of Korea wear a scarlet letter?[49]

As in the case of Yi Yŏng-hun's remarks about "justice," North Korea looms large here despite its absence in name; the reference that youth in South Korea are learning to question the legitimacy of their own country is inescapably related to the place North Korea has occupied in the historiography of South Korea since the 1980s which the New Right has castigated as "leftist" and "nationalist." It is undeniable that *some* of the erstwhile minjung historians and the undongkwŏn in the 1980s—here it is important to note that not all undongkwŏn of the 1980s followed chuch'e sasang—regarded North Korea as truly nationalist, in large part due to Kim Il Sung's anti-colonial resistance against Japan. They also regarded North Korea as having followed a path of true decolonization and as more autonomous and independent than South Korea in its relationships with superpowers. All of this led North Korea to become considered as a positive counterpart to South Korea among some of the 1980s undongkwŏn.[50]

Even for a discipline that has resisted new theoretical interventions, postcolonial theories were a welcome respite to many newly minted and more openminded historians; the particular appeal was its offer of a trenchant critique of nation and class, the central categories of modern historiography, as totalizing and undemocratic. Some of the New Right scholars, such as historian Yi Yŏng-hun, have also embraced postcolonial scholarship for its focus away from nation; for Yi, the postcolonial approach has enabled him to "recenter" the "individual" as a category of historical analysis.[51] However, New Right historians have pushed out the nation only to bring back the state in its place, a case of what cultural studies scholar Lisa Yoneyama terms the "'warping' of politics," an appropriation of critique in a different context and for a different purpose.[52]

The centrality of the state and the market economy are some of the most conspicuous aspects of New Right scholarship, as noted by other scholars, which also leads to the consequent barbarization and "otherization"—and eventual disappearance—of North Korea.[53] North Korea's political position as a pariah of the world and the country's economic woes have become equated with cultural difference, as in the Japanese colonial discourse about Korea, justifying its subordination vis-à-vis South Korea. Another notable aspect of New Right scholarship is hagiographical treatments of Park Chung-hee and Syngman Rhee. Park Chung-hee has been elevated to a mythical figure, singularly responsible for the "modernization revolution" of South Korea, without giving due acknowledgment of the political and physical violence committed in the process of state building and modernization.[54] Syngman Rhee has also been reborn not only as the "founding father" of the Republic of Korea but also as the staunch defender of liberal democracy, completely overlooking his rampant disregard of liberal democratic principles that the New Right claims to cherish as foundational principles for South Korea. The "liberalism" that the New Right champions is yet another iteration of anti-communism, bereft of any vision or advocacy of sociopolitical and economic justice that liberalism in principle stood for.

Revival of Syngman Rhee and Park Chung-hee and the Return of the State

Syngman Rhee, the first president of South Korea, is one of the most controversial political figures in Korea's modern history. Born in 1875, he spent thirty-nine years of his adult life outside Korea to engage in various activities to regain Korea's independence. As a young man he participated in the Independence Club in Korea and was later elected to be the president of the Korean Provisional Government (KPG) in Shanghai that was created after the March 1 movement of 1919. By the time he entered his forties, Rhee had become a key leader of the rightist nationalist forces. He became the first president of the Republic of Korea in 1948 at the age of seventy-four and ruled the country for twelve years until he was forced to resign in 1960 by the April 19 student movement.

Rhee stood "at a crossroad between tradition and the contemporary world, between Korea and the world," and left a distinctive trace at each of the critical moments of Korea's modern and contemporary history.[55] South Korea had been in the shadow of Syngman Rhee for so long that the political order that he helped to create in the immediate post-1945 period did not change until the late 1980s. No other political leader in Korea since 1876 has had the impact on Korea's political development as Rhee.⁵⁶ Given this, any effort to reassess his life and his legacy would involve "a head-on clash" with the entirety of South Korea's political history.⁵⁷ In fact, as sociologist Chŏn Sang-in notes, the question of how to evaluate the legacy of Syngman Rhee has remained the most difficult and still the most divisive issue among scholars, even more so than the Korean War. Opposing views on Rhee have remained a sharply drawn battle line, in part because these views are directly related to historical lineages and political legitimacy in contemporary politics.⁵⁸ During his lifetime, Rhee's followers proclaimed him a great revolutionary and patriot who devoted all his life to Korea's freedom and independence; he was also a politician of strong will who had prevented communism from taking over all of the Korean Peninsula. On the other hand, his political opponents and critics lambasted him as a divisive figure of outsized egotism and self-righteousness, an expert schemer in "palace politics," a fanatical anti-communist and Cold War warrior whose extreme views were responsible for continuing the division of the country, as well as an autocrat who behaved as an absolute monarch and trampled over his people. Even after his death, the divided appraisal of Yi continued among scholars.⁵⁹

The first wave of scholarly assessment of Rhee started with reassessment of post-1945 Korean history that began in earnest from the late 1970s and early 1980s, which became part and parcel of the revisionist scholarship on the Korean War. Of this, Bruce Cumings's two-volume *The Origins of the Korean War* is the most representative as well as the most well-known work.⁶⁰ Chŏn Sang-in summarizes his interpretation of Cumings's characterization of Rhee as the following: "Rhee was a prototypical Machiavellian, who was too dependent on the United States to be even called a nationalist, and the scourge of the Korean people, for whose sake he should not have returned to South Korea. Furthermore, his return to South Korea was arranged as a political scheme between the US general Douglas MacArthur and Rhee, mainly to provide political legitimacy to the Korea Democratic Party whose members were mostly former collaborators."⁶¹

The scholarly assessment of Rhee by and large was scathing: Rhee was an authoritarian ruler whose oversized ego seemed to have no bound, however acute his political instincts for survival. Song Kŏn-ho, a former journalist and one of the editors of the first volume of *Understanding*, charged Rhee with the following: his refusal to punish collaborators after Korea's liberation from Japan, his sabotage of the work of the US-Soviet Joint Commission immediately after liberation to prevent the formation of a unified coalition government, and his taking the lead in manipulating anti-communist discourse to establish a separate state in the south, thus making the division of Korea as long lasting as it has been.[62]

Song also characterized Rhee as a troublesome politician who continued to loom large in Korean society long after his death, someone who caused so much harm to the Korean nation, listing his "harmful" activities in three separate categories: first, his overseas activities for the independence of Korea; second, his advocacy of establishing a separate government alone in South Korea in the post-liberation period; and third, his protection of collaborators with Japan (*ch'inilp'a*).[63] Song's indictment of Rhee is as follows: Rhee's participation in the Independence Club was not due to his nationalist self-esteem but rather to his emotional anti-Japanese sentiment and in part a reaction to his repeated failure to pass the civil service examination. His independence movement activity in the United States was also mostly conducted as a petition drive to the US government—a diplomacy of petitions, as it were. Given the geopolitical condition of the time and the United States' own imperialist ambition, there was no reason to believe that the United States would consider seriously Rhee's petition of self-rule, however urgent and earnest his appeal; he was seen merely as colonized subject. Rhee is commonly known as anti-Japanese, but he is in fact South Korea's foremost pro-Japanese figure, as he protected the collaborators and let the pernicious colonial influence continue to hurt Korean society, leaving its nationalist conscience paralyzed. His staunch anti-communism also led him to push for the establishment of a separate government in the south, rather than trying to overcome the division by negotiating with the Soviet Union and establishing a unified government. He opposed formation of a unified coalition government at the US-Soviet Joint Commission in 1946, believing that it would be dominated by communists and leftists excluding the collaborators. Rhee also sought exclusively for the United States to be an ally and supporter of the Republic of Korea. His anti-communism, which he rationalized as a defense of South Korea from communism, was used not only for the extension of his power but also to make the division permanent.[64]

It is fair to say that scholarly research on Rhee had been meager despite his critical role in Korean history, as noted by scholars of conservative bend.[65] Starting from the late 1990s, Syngman Rhee's political fortune was reversed, however, just as the Park Chung-hee syndrome was reaching its height. From the early 2000s onward, there has also been a steady outpouring of scholarly monographs, numerous biographies in various genres, including graphic novels, as well as educational institutes devoted to Rhee.[66] The collapse of actually existing socialism, the emergence of the civilian government in South Korea, the death of Kim Il Sung and subsequent deterioration of North Korea, the emerging scholarly challenge to revisionist scholarship on the Korean War, the all-powerful machinery of conservative mass media, as well as the availability of new historical sources on and about Rhee have all contributed to the second round of revisionist scholarship on Syngman Rhee.[67]

The worldwide transformation and South Korea's turn to the right should have anticipated the reversal of Rhee's historical place, as Chŏn Sang-in intimates; Rhee, who had advocated for—and anticipated—the collapse of communism and the crisis of North Korea, had been right all along, according to New Right scholars.[68] Yi Yŏng-hun says, "After the liberation from Japan many people in Korea demanded the establishment of a unified government through collaboration with the left and right. President Syngman Rhee opposed it. The history of many countries in the world testifies to the fact that a country that collaborated with communists would become a communist country."[69] Journalist Yi Han-u also credits the rise of the New Right for the spread of the positive assessment of Syngman Rhee, along with positive historical appraisals of post-1945 South Korea, against the leftists' "unilateral denouncement of contemporary history."[70] In fact, one of the New Right internet newspapers, *New Daily* (*Nyudeilli*) also founded the Syngman Rhee Studies Center (Yi Sŭngman yŏn'guso) in 2011. In addition to research activities, the center also operates the Syngman Rhee Forum and Syngman Rhee Academy, both of which carry out educational programs about Syngman Rhee for students from elementary school to university.[71]

Efforts to rehabilitate Rhee were also facilitated by various academic research institutes that began in the 1990s. In 1997, Yu Yŏng-ik [Young Ick Lew], a well-known historian who has devoted himself to research on Rhee since the early 1990s, founded the Institute for Modern Korean Studies (IMKS, Hyŏndae Han'gukhak Yŏn'guso) at Yonsei University with a multibillion-won fund provided by the Samsung Group.[72] In 2011, Yu Yŏng-ik set up the Syngman Rhee Institute (Yi Sŭngman Yŏnguwŏn), a separate and autonomous entity from IMKS, to focus its research exclusively on Rhee. Yu Sŏk-ch'un, another New Right scholar, has headed the institute since 2011. Under the helms of both Yus, a veritable revival, as well as hagiography, of Rhee has been undertaken through research, publishing activities, and educational programs for the public.[73]

Yu Yŏng-ik alone has authored several monographs and numerous journal articles on Syngman Rhee between 1997 and 2019.[74] His appraisal of the "real Syngman Rhee" can be summarized as a person of sui generis talent and ability, an extraordinary thinker and writer, a genius, a devoted Christian who continued to keep his faith throughout his life, a person with a strong sense of responsibility and work ethic, a person of great diplomatic skills with an extensive network of individuals from diverse national, class, and gender backgrounds, and a true independence fighter and patriot who believed that South Korea could and would become a model Christian democratic country such as or even surpassing the United States.[75] Yu's scholarly dedication to Rhee can be shown in his massive biography of Rhee, *Making of the First Korean President*, in which a vast amount of sources are mobilized to portray Rhee as a great statesman and patriot.[76]

It would be safe to say most New Right scholars share the same assessment of Syngman Rhee as Yu Yŏng-ik. Yi Yŏng-hun, introduced earlier as one of four editors of *Reunderstanding* and founder of yet another educational outlet for the general public, the Syngman Rhee School (Yi Sŭngman Haktang), sums up the arguments put forth by many of these scholars:

> Without Syngman Rhee, there would have been no Republic of Korea, or it would have become a different country [a communist country that would have met its demise by the 1990s]. President Rhee laid the foundation for the state that continues until today. His achievements as the founder of the Republic of Korea—such as establishment of a presidential system of government, implementation of land reform, defense of South Korea against the communist North Korea, the signing of the U.S.–South Korea military alliance, development of base industries for the state economy—will shine in history for a long time. Despite all this achievement, our citizens' assessment of Rhee is rather stingy, due to little understanding of our history's true character. Therefore, South Korea's future as a free republic is not bright at all.[77]

Historian Kwŏn Hŭi-yŏng repeats the familiar refrain "only Syngman Rhee could have pulled it off" by emphasizing Rhee's reputed political acumen, ingenuity, persistence, and diplomatic successes. As Kwŏn would have it, it is Rhee's political acuity—"he was able to see clearly the true color of the communists much more so than the Americans at the US Military Government in Korea or the US government"—and not his virulent anti-communism as he had been accused of, that led him to refuse to work with communists to create a unified government immediately after Korea was liberated. Rhee's unwavering confidence in himself, as well as his ability to align himself with the right kind of ally, the United States, made it possible for him to establish the Republic of Korea.[78] Kwŏn also reiterates another oft-repeated argument that the negative historical assessment of Syngman Rhee had been largely influenced by the leftists' negative view of post-1945 history.[79]

However, as even their fellow New Right scholar Chŏn Sang-in acknowledges, much of the views expressed above are cases of presentism, a conclusion reached only in the 1990s and from the perspective of a victor in the Cold War that had been waged globally since 1945. As Chŏn himself asks, would it be still possible to hold Syngman Rhee in such positive regard had there been no collapse of socialism and no dysfunctional state of North Korea?[80] Yu Yŏng-ik also acknowledges that it is through witnessing the end of the Cold War and the collapse of communist states in 1989 that he gained a new perspective on Syngman Rhee and his role in post-1945 South Korea.[81] Historical revisionism is often occasioned by such change in circumstances, or newly discovered archival material, or the scholar's new perspective gained from the passage of time, and none of these by itself should be cause for alarm or disdain.

But as New Right scholars elevate Syngman Rhee as a paragon of democratic rule, they resort to playing fast and loose with historical evidence, to a high-wire dance of tautological and teleological arguments, in which Rhee's authoritarianism is justified by both the contemporary political condition and by the present status of South Korea as a democracy and as an economic powerhouse. An Pyŏng-jik, editor of *Origin and Future of South Korea's Democracy* and the doyen of New Right scholars, claims that the particularity of the immediate post-1945 South Korea, such as the absence of a middle class and the presence of communist North Korea with its goal of overtaking South Korea, was responsible for Syngman Rhee's authoritarianism: "In an underdeveloped country such as South Korea, modernization was launched at a time when all the conditions for it were not developed. South Korea imported a political system of an advanced country first, and then tried to create conditions for such a system to be realized.... It was inevitable to apply methods that were in contradiction to the spirit of that system."[82] An then asks, "Could South Korea have been protected [from North Korea] had it not been for the anticommunism of Syngman Rhee?"[83] An even attributes the April 19 student uprising that brought down the Rhee regime to be a by-product of Rhee's establishment of liberal democracy and the nurturing of talent through education.[84]

Efforts to rehabilitate Syngman Rhee were not limited to glossing over his flagrant and violent disregard of liberal democratic values but also upgraded Rhee's policy, crediting it with laying the foundation for South Korea's market economy. An cites the land reform and disposal of government-vested properties (properties that had been owned by the Japanese until the end of World War II) as responsible for laying the groundwork for establishing a market economy in South Korea. This is yet another case where An conveniently overlooks the sociopolitical context of such a policy, let alone the fact that what South Korea had was clearly not a market economy. Among the factors contributing to the push for land reform was the need for the

US government and Rhee to win the "hearts and minds" of the people in the aftermath of so much bloodshed in the process of the founding of the republic.[85]

Even some of the more blatant cases of Rhee's repressive measures were not true cases of repression, according to Yi Chu-yŏng, another contributor to *Origin and Future of South Korea's Democracy*. In 1954, Rhee rammed through a constitutional amendment giving himself a third term in office through an absurd scheme known as *sa-sa o-ip* constitutional revision,[86] and in 1958, he tried to revise the National Security Law to suppress his critics. In 1959, Rhee forcibly shut down the newspaper *Kyunghyang Shinmun* that was critical of him. None of these measures, however, stopped the existing media from criticizing Rhee or stopped the public from electing the country's vice president from the opposition party (the vice presidency had been won by Chang Myon [Chang Myŏn] of the opposition party in the 1956 presidential election), according to Yi—hence the claim that there was no true repression during Rhee's presidency.[87]

New Right scholars' wish to elevate Syngman Rhee's political and historical place in South Korean history leads them to force historical facts and developments to fit their monocausal explanation for repression as justified by Rhee's reputed espousal and upholding of liberal democracy. As such, the scholarship risks "a caricature of real history," as in the case of some of the more virulent anti-communist scholarship on communism.[88] Resting heavily on Cold War anti-communism, New Right scholarship is more about Rhee's anti-communism and his recourse to ideology and political maneuverings and less about historical context, complexities, and deeper understanding of the choices that Rhee had to make.

Park Chung-hee and New Right Scholarship

Much like the New Right scholars who focus on Syngman Rhee, New Right scholars working on Park Chung-hee continue to undermine their own scholarship by a one-sided concern with making the case for Park Chung-hee's economic development, hence explaining away all of the problems associated with his regime as an inevitable outcome of any societal transformation of the magnitude that South Korea underwent. An Pyŏng-jik and contributors to the volume *Origin and Future of South Korea's Democracy* also apply the same circuitous argument that they use for Syngman Rhee to justify Park's dictatorship; the logical conclusion of their argument is that Park Chung-hee was dictatorial in order to protect the liberal democratic system and to pursue economic development.[89] An characterizes Park Chung-hee's authoritarianism as a case of "purposive rationality" (*mokchŏk hamnisŏng* or *Zweckrationalität*)—that is, it was driven by the demands of economic development that the country needed in order to achieve liberal democracy.[90] An then goes on to argue, while acknowledging that the democratization movement played a role in the democratic transition of 1987, that Park Chung-hee's economic development and adoption of liberal democratic ideals laid the groundwork for the democratic transition. Accordingly, it is the conservatives who have led South Korea's democracy; even now in the 2000s, the conservatives are the ones who are safeguarding democracy.[91]

In the same vein as An Pyŏng-jik, political scientist Kim Se-jung argues that Park Chung-hee's military coup in 1961 ultimately protected liberal democracy—that is, it was the transition from the military government to civilian government in 1963 that contributed to the restoration of the constitution and rule of law in South Korea. Park, who since 1961 had ruled the country as head of the military junta, the Supreme Council for National Reconstruction, donned civilian clothes to run for the 1963 presidential election and won. Even the Yusin system, a case of outright violation of the constitution and democratic rule, was ultimately to protect liberal democracy, according to Kim.[92]

Kim further argues that Park Chung-hee's prioritization of industrialization was to ultimately pave the road for liberal democracy in South Korea. As the country in the 1960s was in a perpetual competition with North Korea and relied on the United States for more than half of the state budget and most of the defense budget, industrialization was crucial to bring not only prosperity but also security to South Korea.[93] For Park Chung-hee, economic development was the most efficient way to provide the conditions for establishing liberal democracy; it helped to overcome traditional values and still-existing authoritarian practices that were in the way of modernizing the country. Kim also credits Park for developing a "Korean" version of liberal democracy, referring to the problematic "Korean-style democracy" (*Han'gukchŏk minjujuŭi*) that Park proclaimed during his presidency and by which he justified his authoritarian rule. Park repeatedly expressed his doubt about whether liberal democracy, originated and cultivated in the West, and with its "inherent quality of allowing or causing instability and chaos," would be suitable for an efficient process of carrying out modernization and industrialization.[94]

Much as the case with Syngman Rhee, Kim treats Park Chung-hee's blatant attempt in 1969 to revise the constitution to permit a third run for presidency, known as *samsŏn kaehŏn* (literally, "revision of the constitution for a third term"), as a case necessitated by the exigencies of the era: "Park Chung-hee at the time was the most decisive figure, as well as a symbol and embodiment, of state-led economic development, for whose smooth continuation Park was necessary. Accordingly, Park's extension of his rule—even through unlawful constitutional revision—was not simply a case of a power grab but was to ensure long-term continuation of the developmentalist system."[95]

Kim also mobilizes well-known American scholars in development studies such as Alice H. Amsden, Robert Wade, and Stephan Haggard to legitimize his argument that a repressive authoritarian regime was unavoidable for, or at least instrumental in, the fast-paced economic development of South Korea. However, Kim either misrepresents their main points and arguments or cites nonexistent passages.[96] Even if one sets aside Kim's work as an extreme case of scholarly sloppiness, New Right scholars' cavalier dismissal of the historical context of their subject matter and their logical inconsistencies, among other things, undermine their own credibility, haphazardly and in some cases even blithely crisscrossing the line separating scholarship from sloganeering.

August 15, 1948—Day of Liberation or Foundation?

All of these efforts to reassess and rehabilitate Syngman Rhee and Park Chung-hee went hand in hand with the New Right's push to designate August 15, 1948 as the founding (*kŏn'guk*) day of the Republic of Korea. The establishment of the government of the Republic of Korea (*chŏngbu surip*) in 1948 has been celebrated along with the liberation of Korea from Japan in 1945 in official annual commemoration of the Day of Liberation (*kwangbokchŏl*).[97] During the sixty-third anniversary of Independence Day, in 2008, then-president Lee Myung-bak also added celebration of the "sixtieth anniversary of the founding of the Republic of Korea" (*kŏn'gukchŏl*), to the confusion of many in the public.[98]

It was none other than Yi Yŏng-hun who first suggested in 2006 that August 15 be renamed as the day of foundation of the republic. Yi lamented that the history textbooks of South Korea did not teach children when their republic was founded; if it was mentioned at all, it was only as an unfortunate event that should not have taken place, for the republic was not the unified government that many Koreans had hoped for. Despite Koreans' exaltation of the independence movement of the colonial period, Koreans did not achieve independence by themselves; it came about as a by-product of the new world order emerging at the end of World War II, Yi argued. To celebrate the date of foundation is therefore to get rid of the absurd notion that the "founding of the Republic of Korea was a mistake" and to celebrate the achievements of South Korea, as well as to be future-oriented.[99]

The Founding Day campaign was yet another case of willful misrepresentation of both existing scholarship and the general public's view on the topic. To emphasize the importance of the independent movement is not to suggest that it led to independence of Korea; in fact, the emphasis all along had been precisely the opposite—that is, despite the persistence of anti-colonial movements during the colonial period, Korea was in the end liberated by Allied powers and became subject to the emerging world order headed by the United States. This widespread view gave rise to a pervasive sense of what I call the "crisis of historical subjectivity" among intellectuals and university students in post-1945 South Korea, which also galvanized them to push for democratization of the country.[100]

As expected for such a controversial topic as the proposal to establish a kŏn'gukchŏl, there appeared an array of divergent views, arguments, and approaches, including the view that the time of Tan'gun should be considered the founding moment of the Republic of Korea.[101] Here, I condense the various arguments and views into the two main opposing perspectives following the schema developed by political scientist Pak Myŏng-nim: the "foundation discourse" (kŏn'guk tamnon) that emphasizes August 15, 1948 as the day of founding of the Republic of Korea and its subsequent development in South Korea as an example of success and victory, and the "division discourse" (pundan tamnon) that is critical of the division of the country and its failure to bring about a "unified nation-state." The "division discourse" recognizes the year 1919, when the KPG in Shanghai was founded in the aftermath of the March 1 movement, as the founding year of the Republic of Korea.[102]

New Right scholars, who are the most vocal proponents of the foundation discourse, have been arguing that South Korea must overcome the previous era's tendency to view post-1945 Korea as a history of the division and the unification of two Koreas as a national goal.[103] To them, South Korea's claim to have received the mantle (pŏpt'ong) of the KPG, as stated in the constitution, faces a major problem—that is, Korea was colonized by Japan for thirty-five years, and therefore the KPG did not fulfill the three requisite criteria by which a modern nation-state is constituted: the territory, the people, and sovereignty.[104] Historian Yang Tong-an agrees that the South Korean government inherited (kyesŭng) the KPG in terms of its ruling ideology (t'ongch'i inyŏm) and in that many of the members of the KPG participated later in the establishment of, or declared their loyalty to, the Republic of Korea. He argues, however, that since the KPG was merely "a preparatory" one and not an actual government, to insist that the establishment of the KPG was the moment the Republic of Korea was founded is rather akin to insisting that one's engagement date is one's wedding date.[105]

For the New Right, to claim the lineage of the KPG poses another major problem: the historical legitimacy of South Korea. It currently occupies only half of the peninsula, despite what article three of the constitution says: "The territory of the Republic of Korea shall consist of the Korean Peninsula and its adjacent islands."[106] Furthermore, it also makes the current status of North Korea—"an anti-state organization of the Republic" according to the constitution—ambiguous, given that it, too, could claim its origin from the same 1919 KPG.[107]

To proponents of division discourse, to designate 1948 as the year of the foundation of the republic is to reduce the long history of Korea to a mere sixty-some years and to downplay or ignore the spirited history of Koreans' anti-colonial resistance. It also violates the spirit of the constitution of the republic, which states that it inherits the spirit and the legacy of the KPG, even deriving its current name of Taehanmin'guk from it; therefore, the beginning of the Republic of Korea should be the date when the KPG of 1919 was founded.[108] Deeply suspicious of the motive of the foundation discourse proponents, some even went so far as to suggest that the whole idea behind the proposed name change was a conspiracy by the descendants of collaborators with the Japanese colonial regime (ch'inilp'a) to sidetrack attention away from the contemporary debate about ch'inilp'a.[109] One commentator opined that the foundation discourse proponents' sense of urgency stems from their misguided notion that South Korea has denigrated its own state by not properly designating the day of its foundation, unlike North Korea, which has its own foundation day.[110]

Historian Pak Sŏng-su, who is no friend of "leftist" historians, also reiterates the previously mentioned argument that to insist 1948 as the year of the foundation of the republic is to play down the existence of the provisional government and the legacy of the independence movement: "We have set up a government with the flag . . . that was stained with the blood [of the independence movement activists]; our history should not be recorded as if we had just set up a government flying a flag that has not even been exposed to dust."[111] The sum of Park's argument is captured in the following by political scientist Yi Wan-bŏm: "The Republic of Korea did not just fall from the sky. Nor was it simply a gift from a powerful foreign power [United States], or a product of the willpower of one or two great political leaders [Syngman Rhee]. Korean society should not denigrate the history of the independence movement that became the basis for the establishment of the Republic of Korea; it was founded by the sacrifice of numerous patriots who devoted their lives to restore the country in the harshest of conditions."[112]

The debate moved over to the National Assembly in July 2008, when the members of the then-ruling party, the Grand National Party (Hannaradang), proposed to change August 15 to the Founding Day of the Republic of Korea, with the same arguments put forth by New Right scholars. Hyŏn Kyŏngbyŏng, one of the co-introducers of the bill, stated that the reason for proposing the bill was "to celebrate the history of Korea as a history of victory and glory instead of the history of defeat and despair."[113] To opponents of this bill, this legislative move, which they argued was prompted by the New Right, is only further proof of the New Right's effort to thwart ongoing historical evaluation of the ch'inilp'a and to whitewash authoritarian and violent history of the Syngman Rhee government and elevate him as the founding father of the Republic of Korea.[114] Faced with widespread and vehement opposition, drafters of the 2008 bill withdrew it within a year.[115]

The debates following the publication of *Reunderstanding* and *The Alternative Textbook*, as well as the more recent controversy concerning designation of the day of founding of South Korea, have become sites where historians, individuals, and groups have articulated historical issues as public issues, with high stakes for contemporary South Korea. Despite the heated reactions that the debates generated among participants and to a certain degree the general public, however, the debates have not offered any new insight into how one might think of one's self-identity or national identity, as they have stayed within the existing binary framework. In debates concerning the foundation controversy, for example, most of the vocal participants, whether they are aligned with the foundation discourse or the division discourse, were beholden to their overriding concern about present implications of their viewpoints for political legitimacy, as noted by historian Chi Su-gŏl.[116]

Revisionist history should and can have the potential to perform the kind of history that Walter Benjamin contemplated in his much-quoted passage: "to articulate the past historically does not mean to recognize it 'the way it really was' [*Ranke*]. It means to seize hold of a memory as it flashes up at a moment of danger."[117] Benjamin believed that there is a possibility for the historian to paradigmatically alter the way we read the present, by bringing the present into contact with an unexpected—and often jarring—past, to interrupt the present, to serve as a wake-up call. Despite the New Right scholars' claim to be postnational and their criticism of nationalist historians for focusing on the nation and not on individuals, the New Right revisionist histories, especially those of Syngman Rhee and Park Chung-hee, participate in constructing what Prasenjit Duara calls "national history"[118]—that is, their scholarship is shaped in large part by the desire to affirm the sovereignty of the nation-state, although in their case, it is more about the legitimacy of the state than of the nation. In trying to narrate the recent history to fit contemporary political goals of affirming the state, New Right scholars have shown, quite contrary to their aims, how precisely the kinds of debates that they are engaged in, debates over contemporary goals and historical realities, shape the past.[119]

The New Right's modern Korean history is a narrative that sees history as linear, teleological, progressive—history with a capital *H*, with the South Korean state as the subject of this history. In this narrative, the South Korean state has successfully withstood various challenges, à la Hegelian development of the individual and the state from enslavement to freedom, to arrive at the present moment of democracy and economic success.[120] This narrative is by its nature exclusionary. The suffering, pain, and injustice that the past generation had to endure is missing in this narrative, and many of the potentialities and possibilities that had existed alongside the ones that have become dominant in contemporary society disappear as no longer meaningful. The following chapter further engages with these issues.

Epilogue

The Politics of Time and the Poetics of Remembrance

For the greater part of history there has been a belief that the past sets the pattern for the present, that it provides a pathway for a myriad of issues facing contemporary society. As historian Eric Hobsbawm notes, the inclusion of history in every modern education system shows the sense of the past as a collective continuity of experience. Even revolutionary movements of Marxist orientation with their supposed avowal of irrelevance also harken back to past movements for inspiration and examples.[1] In fact, Hobsbawm attributes the rise of linear historical consciousness to the existential problem of the need to anchor meaning in continuous transformation of society: "Paradoxically, the past remains the most useful analytical tool for coping with constant change."[2]

Since around the 1960s, however, the sense of the past providing a guide for the future has been shaken, particularly in advanced industrial societies.[3]

Although this sense of loss of direction might be most prevalent in academia, where the notion of modernity "as a key concept for cultural self-interpretation" has been widely challenged, society at large has also experienced much of skepticism about the notion of history as a teacher and guide for living, offering perspective on the future.[4] Historian Jörn Rüsen suggests that historiography has responded to the challenge in various ways that can be summed up as consisting of two different modes: one mode is to continue to rely on the existing belief that historical interpretation of the past would elucidate the current predicament; it searches for "a point to cast anchor in the cataracts of progress."[5] This mode still believes that in the process of modernization, historical reference points delineated over the years provide guidance to negotiate its current crisis. One such reference point is the historical category of the nation. It is a familiar mode of thinking that historical understanding and knowledge provide a stable form of national identity, which in turn provide direction for contemporary life.[6]

The Contentious Present and Historical Counterimages

The second mode of response is to critically reassess the narrative of progress that has been embedded in historiography until recently, by both looking for historical cases of rupture in the rapid process of modernization and at the same time critically reexamining each case "against the grain of its own ideology of progress." Rüsen contends that this kind of critical investigation has ambiguous results, however: "The critique of progress can lead to a flight of historical memory from the orientational problems of the current age into more or less elaborated historical counterimages."[7] That is, the challenges experienced in the present day are negotiated in the examples of life from long ago. The more contemporary society wrestles with conflicts and dilemmas, and the more our present lives seem to offer little in the way of meaning, the more the past seems appealing as an alternative way to engage in historical identification. Thus, for example, in historian Carlo Ginzburg's *The Cheese and the Worms*, intellectual disappointment in the outcome of the 1960s uprising in Europe crystallizes in a sixteenth-century miller, Menocchio, an uneducated peasant and independent thinker. Ginzburg finds the origin of the radical, materialist worldview of Menocchio in an ancient oral tradition, which he represents as popular culture of the sixteenth century. The anticipated future that failed to materialize in the aftermath of the 1960s uprising has now become a radical worldview of a peasant in the past.[8]

Examples of the search in the past for the present abound, whether in historiography or in national politics. In West Germany, the arrival of the new approach of history of everyday life (*Alltagsgeschichte*) also saw some of its practitioners who study Nazism "[taking] refuge in the consoling rediscovery of the *Heimat* [homeland]."[9] In France, the real and perceived crisis of national identity that began in the Mitterrand era gave rise to the study of collective memory famously known as *Les lieux de mémoire*. This was a conservative case of "reinvent[ion] of France through memory, in which it could still be one and indivisible, thereby thwarting the political and cultural projects of both neo-nationalists and multiculturalists."[10] During the Reagan and Thatcher era, widespread insecurity about the present and future, and deep contradictions between what was promised and what was delivered, were appeased by the political leadership's "promise of a return to the values and certainties of a comforting, mythical past."[11] More recently, the slogan of "Make America Great Again" and the rising white nationalist movement in the United States also involve an extreme admiration of the past, a search in the past for a more ideal and more appealing alternative to the present, as individuals are increasingly becoming dispossessed of a sense of one's place in history.[12] As historian Charles Maier has cautioned, this kind of politics of time has also the potential to lead to a certain "aestheticizing of politics—a revived distaste of mass democracy, a covert celebration of elites disguised by an appeal to folk culture and artisanship."[13]

In one of the cruel ironies of history, South Korea's historic transition to parliamentary democracy was soon followed by the country's violent thrust into the world of neoliberalism, as I have discussed before. In the words of one scholar, the history of neoliberalism "was written in shocks."[14] Large-scale collective trauma followed the economic downturn known as the International Monetary Fund (IMF) crisis of the late 1990s. As elsewhere in the world, violence and coercion, certainly of different kinds from the ones administered by past authoritarian regimes, but equally, if not more, painful and pernicious for ordinary Koreans, marked the process of neoliberal "reform." In what I have discussed as a politics of confusion in chapter 1, and in another example of the irony of history, the policies of the politically progressive government of Kim Dae-jung, whose promotion of labor and corporate restructuring was in large part to break from the past authoritarian state's collusion with the chaebŏl, led to massive layoffs, causing severe economic hardship and popular resentment. In the "reformed" labor market that was designed for increased "flexibility," for example, workers' strikes are calculated mainly on the basis of economic gain or loss and mainly as an issue of legalistic strategy. Corporations no longer pursue negotiations via labor law with striking workers but bring lawsuits against union leaders and rank-and-file members to claim compensation for the damage caused by strikes.[15]

The "return" of Park Chung-hee in the late 1990s as seen in the Park Chung-hee syndrome also reflects in part the people's need to alleviate the uncertainty and anxiety of the present. Many of the best-selling works of the 1990s also returned to the mythic past to find inspiration for counterimages to the present, whether in the steadfast devotion to Confucian womanhood of an eighteenth-century yangban woman in Yi Mun-yŏl's *Choice* (*Sŏnt'aek*) or in the reincarnation of Park Chung-hee as a fervent nationalist whose clandestine plan to build nuclear weapons was to safeguard Korea's future against capricious superpowers in Kim Chin-myŏng's *The Rose of Sharon Has Blossomed* (*Mugunghwa kkoti p'iŏtsŭmnida*). In these retellings of Korean history in novelistic form, alternative pasts are presented as "one's own 'true' time," as the present is perceived to be increasingly antagonistic and alienating.

Post-1945 South Korean history encompasses both extreme destruction and violence of the war and overall destitution on the one hand and wealth, progress, and the phenomenal success of achieving parliamentary democracy and economic development on the other. The seeming incommensurability of both trajectories in one generation, while still surrounded by the continuous Cold War structure, poses a challenge for scholarship. Compression of the modernization process, debates over the role of the "colonial" period in that process including whether it was the "origin" of South Korea's capitalist development, the global end of the Cold War that has been seen by many as a victory of one political trajectory over the others, among other factors, raise high the political, emotional, and intellectual stakes of interpreting post-1945 Korean history. From the vantage point of six decades after the liberation of Korea, a contemporary history whose interpretive framework was conceived when the country was undergoing rapid economic development under authoritarian regimes and beset with contradictory developments might be seen as distinctly dispiriting and, furthermore, unsuitable as guidance for the radically transformed present.

New Right historiography has thus the appearance of responding to the predicament faced by contemporary South Korea, especially the uncertainty about the role of history in charting the future. Its triumphalist narrative also masks a sense of urgency, a worldview besieged by a sense of crisis. In the radically transformed post-1997 IMF South Korea, the Darwinian notion of survival of the fittest became once more the mantra of the day, especially among conservatives. The discourse of *sŏnjin'guk* (advanced country) that was pervasive especially in the late 1990s and early 2000s and closely associated with neoliberalism gives a sense of what is at stake for conservatives: the contemporary world is a place in which relentless and unceasing competition forces South

Korea to face only two options: "to aggressively participate in the limitless competition system or to join the group of grumblers falling behind the competition."[16] The already-pervasive anxiety of conservatives was further heightened by political and cultural ascendance of the previously marginalized and persecuted left: two former presidents, Kim Dae-jung and Roh Moo-hyon, had deep ties with democratization movements; their cabinet members and inner circle of advisers had roots in the progressive politics of an earlier period, alarming the conservatives as if these administrations would put their previous utopian dream back on the national agenda. The cultural scene also increasingly turned to the left, not in the least because many former university student activists began to occupy positions of influence in the cultural sphere.[17] All of these developments were profoundly destabilizing for the right. New Right scholars began to locate the cause of a deeply polarized South Korea in the "lack of an established history of the state," a history that can be agreed on by all citizens, a history "that the older generation can proudly pass on to the next generation."[18]

As Rüsen suggests, however, historical counterimages do not always open up perspectives on the future that can serve to envision a different future from the present and to guide action to establish that future. Proffering counterimages or alternative images from a bygone era mostly provide, much like Friedrich Nietzsche's monumental history discussed in chapter 3, solace in the embellished and idealized past and a negative orientation to one's own present.[19] They may alleviate temporarily the widespread sense of loss of meaning in contemporary society, but they do not help eliminate or overcome it. Rather, these historiographical images provide the appearance of an alternative, masking over the serious sense of loss of direction experienced in contemporary society while obscuring the depth and shape of the present predicament.[20]

The New Right scholarship's attempt to promote a positive view of history that encourages a strong identification with the Korean state and its argument that only a positive image of history would provide historical lessons—hence its lament about young generations wearing a scarlet letter—is closely bound up with the idea that historical knowledge and traditions nurture and sustain one's self- and national identity. This idea also explains the charge of "self-flagellation" directed by the right against scholarship and public efforts at seeking retrospective and transitional justice, whether in Germany, Japan, or South Korea.[21]

Historiographical debates generated in the aftermath of key publications of New Right scholarship in South Korea share a number of commonalities with the West Germany's historians' dispute of the late 1980s. I do not imply at all that the historical events that each debate was concerned with and their respective import in each society are in any way comparable. I suggest only that these debates were less about what happened in the past than about how to evaluate or contextualize what had taken place. Furthermore, both debates were as much about interpretation of the past as about the shaping of the present and future of these countries.[22]

The West German historians' dispute can trace its beginning to 1959 when Theodor Adorno started a series of debates with an essay "What Does Coming to Terms with the Past Mean?" in which he called for public discussion of the Nazi period.[23] Given the prevailing belief that the past nourishes self-understanding in a nation, the issue of whether a repeated reminder of a dark past, however carefully and reflectively conducted, does any good, has been a question for West German society ever since. This question was also at the center of the 1986 dispute, which began with the charge made by philosopher and sociologist Jürgen Habermas against "apologetic" tendencies in the writing of German contemporary history. The West German right, like conservative movements elsewhere, has been keen to foster positive identification with the national past in order to create a stronger sense of national identity. They worried that constant reminder of Germany's Nazi past would have a destabilizing effect; rather than focusing on a disturbing past, Germany should seek to mobilize pasts that can accommodate present needs and aspirations and allow for easier identification with the German nation.[24] In the words of one conservative historian, "How long the petrified guest from the past should be permitted to veto civic virtue and love of the fatherland, both in the future and in the past?"[25]

As Maier has pointed out, both sides of the dispute took on enlightenment arguments; they assumed that more empirical historical work would help reach a definitive conclusion, that more knowledge would raise the critical consciousness of the public.[26] Habermas was considered by many to be squarely on the side of enlightenment thinking during this discussion, especially due to his conviction that knowledge can change politics and society.[27] However, he also suggested that we rethink the ancient topos of history as teacher and guide for living—that is, we usually think of learning from history if it tells us "something positive, something worth imitating."[28] Individuals and societies learn not only from positive experience but also negative ones and even from disappointments, Habermas contends: "We learn historically chiefly from the way historical events challenge us, showing us that traditions fail, and that we and the convictions that heretofore guided our actions have gone aground on the problems that must be solved."[29] To learn from history is not to brush aside any unresolved or uncomfortable issues from history but to remain open to their ability to provide us with critical insight, by providing history's "counterevidence . . . [and] shattered expectations."[30]

Additionally, finding historical examples to constitute one's identity, whether personal, cultural, or national, is itself not the problem, but the "limitations placed on identity" are.[31] As suggested above, one's identity should be a process of actively engaging with history, rather than passively accepting some ideal history, and accepting responsibility when presented with "historical choices, not just *faits accomplis*."[32] This call to engage with repressed elements of the past to make possible their critical appropriation for the present recalls Walter Benjamin's idea of history as "remembrance"—his injunction to "brush history against the grain."[33] These insights have much relevance for assessing the recent historiographical debates of South Korea.

The Poetics of Remembrance

For Benjamin, having lived through World War I and writing in 1940, a time Victor Serge called "midnight in the century," the very notion of history as progress was a "cruel illusion."[34] From his perspective, the past is not a gradual accumulation of conquests or victories but an interminable series of catastrophic defeats. He sought to capture the sense of endangerment in his famous image of the Angel of History: "The angel would like to stay, awaken the dead, and make whole what has been smashed. But a storm is blowing from Paradise; it has got caught in his wings with such violence that the angel can no longer close them. This storm irresistibly propels him into the future to which his back is turned, while the pile of debris before him grows skyward. This storm is what we call progress."[35] Even as pessimism and resignation reign all around him, however, Benjamin tried to uphold a vision of possibility that resides beyond the fallen and desolate landscape of the present.[36] For him, it is in the present, what he calls "now-time" (*Jetztzeit*), that the possibility of redemption, however faint, resides.[37] With this notion of redemption or the idea of remembrance, Benjamin challenges the regime of historicity by suggesting "a different relationship with history, a different historical temporality."[38] For Benjamin, the kind of utilitarian view of the past, the kind that "increases the accuracy of our inferences, and thus our knowledge of the future," the kind that is usually invoked as the reason for remembering the past, which also involves the belief that history is continuous, stems from the mistaken idea of historiography as progressive and objective, what he calls "historicism." The historicist attempt to narrate the past "as they really were" is in fact a form of forgetting,[39] or, much worse, a way of defending a certain kind of history, through the process of "binding or suppression of aspects of the past that are not conducive to the notion of progress."[40] There is no "neutral" historian who can access the "real" facts without taking sides.

Simply put, Benjamin's notion of historicism is identified with the historian who sides with the "victor," with the "triumphal procession of the powerful."[41]

Benjamin instead proposes that historians "brush history against the grain." Historians are urged to be "in solidarity with those who have fallen beneath the wheels"[42] of the development that is usually viewed as achievement, and out of which triumphalist and national epic is crafted. That is, the past has to be reclaimed from those who distort it and claim for their own purposes. For Benjamin, the past "does not lie in inert states passively waiting to be uncovered."[43] The past is not to be understood as "an object to be known, but as a subject, an active partner in the construction of meaning."[44] The past also encompasses not only what happened but also what was only dreamed about and envisioned but failed to materialize—"both the unknown stories and the as yet unfulfilled hopes and desires; the underside of history is marked by loss, regret, passion, envy and hope of redemption."[45] In other words, past and present are intermingled.[46] History therefore is not a continuous accumulation of homogeneous, empty time—"the sequence of events like the beads of a rosary"—which keeps accumulating more information "void of redemptive potential"[47] but time filled full by now-time. Now-time is a real historical time that happens only when there is "a dazzling conjunction between the past and the present."[48] Benjamin wrote, "It's not that what is past casts its light on what is present, or what is present its light on what is past; rather, image is that wherein what has been comes together in a flash with the now to form a constellation."[49]

To catch this moment, the moment when an image of the past suddenly breaks out of the continuum and flashes into the present, is what Benjamin calls a "historical materialist" approach. This approach "cuts through historicism" to reveal the labor that made possible the progress, and to bring out consciousness of the past injustice to fuel further actions challenging the status quo; "the energy of the past comes from the negation of events as they are currently known."[50] Even failed history, as it were, endows its future—that is, the present—with redemptive possibilities when it is "recognized, grasped in the present, making a new connection."[51] That is, redemption is a task assigned to the present, by past generations, a "moral claim" that the past makes on the present, a point to which I will return shortly.[52]

Rescuing the past entails rupturing the continuity of history. Unlike Karl Marx, who suggested that humanity must learn to part with its past by "let[ting] the dead bury their dead," Benjamin proposes that contemporary society actively and constructively engages with the past; remembrance of past events, knowledge of the past, including the "not obvious, unwritten, as well as the unaccomplished," is crucial to accurately understand the present and to envision future.⁵³ Although Marx excoriated the French revolutionaries for "performing revolution in Roman costume and with Roman phrases," for example, Benjamin was willing to explore what they were doing and why with their seemingly outlandish actions. The revolutionaries were dealing with an unprecedented situation in which "time suddenly seemed to speed up," no past event was available to illuminate their current situation, and the future was unpredictable.⁵⁴ They were "working with an image of the past which captured their own concerns in the now and at least recognized that historical tradition might be part of the terrain of class struggle."⁵⁵

How the past is told, presented, and depicted makes a difference for how the future might be shaped: "Only that historian will have the gift of fanning the spark of hope in the past who is firmly convinced that *even the dead* will not be safe from the enemy if he wins."⁵⁶ This is so because only then, in the words of Benjamin's explicator Michael Löwy, "the comfortable, lazy vision of history as uninterrupted 'progress' dissolves. The danger of a current defeat sharpens the sensitivity to preceding ones, arouses interest in the battle fought by the defeated, and encourages a critical view of history."⁵⁷

The Politics of Time

The New Right's view of history as that which contributes to constructing one's cultural and national identity, which in itself may not be cause for concern, also engages in the politics of time. The previously discussed notion of "justice" of Yi Yŏng-hun in chapter 4 serves as a case in point. According to Yi, South Korea was established by "a few prophetic leaders" on the principles of liberal democracy and market economy, which global history of the modern era has shown to be a successful case of historical development⁵⁸—a conclusion reached, presumably, in the aftermath of the collapse of the Soviet Union and the Eastern European socialist bloc. If Georg Wilhelm Friedrich Hegel's idea of history was to "reveal the truth of the human spirit,"⁵⁹ Yi sees "freedom" and "egoism"—two qualities that he characterizes as the "innate nature" of human beings and that which reputedly have been promoted by the Korean state, in return making possible South Korea's eventual democratization and economic development—as the truth of the human spirit, with the South Korean state as its "carrier."⁶⁰ Aside from Yi's essentialist notion of the subject whose inner essence is unchanging—it gradually reveals itself as "freedom"—a teleological logic where history moves toward a predetermined goal, and the absence of global and national contexts in his analysis, which I discuss in the previous chapter, this narrative is also exclusionary, erasing the suffering and pain of the past generation.

Erasure of the past generation's suffering is most evident in the recent publication by Yi Yŏng-hun and his fellow New Right scholars. In their edited volume, *Anti-Japanese Tribalism: The Origin of South Korea's Crisis* (*Panil chongjokchuŭi: Taehanmin'guk wigiŭi kŭnwŏn*), contributors present the colonial period without colonialism.[61] Few topics bring into relief the New Right's display of "the arrogance of those who come later [that] preens itself with the notion that the past is dead and gone"[62] as clearly as the volume's discussion of the Japanese colonial period. Dismissing "military sexual slavery" and "forced labor" as a product of Koreans' distorted historical consciousness and Koreans' "innate propensity to lie,"[63] New Right scholars reconfigure the "comfort women," young women who were drafted for military sexual slavery by the Imperial Japanese Army during the Fifteen Years War (1931–1945), and those who were conscripted forcibly for other forms of industrial labor as exclusively as Homo economicus; Yi argues that the "comfort women" (*wiwanbu*) "followed their own choice and their own will" and that being "comfort women" was a merely a job that they performed in the comfort station (*wiwanso*); as they had the right and freedom to stop working whenever they wished, they cannot be called "sexual slaves."[64] Another contributor to the volume, Yi U-yŏn, denies that during the colonial period there was any forced conscription of Koreans for labor in factories and mines, nor was there any discrimination against Koreans as has been claimed by nationalist historians; Koreans by and large received equal wages to that of Japanese workers, and there could not have been "forced mobilization" or "forced labor" as such terms did not exist in the lexicon during the colonial period.[65]

The aspiration for empirically robust and balanced scholarship—Yi Yŏnghun repeatedly states history needs to be "scientific," that "history is science and can only be science"[66]—and to correct what the New Right scholars consider to be too narrow a nationalistic interpretation of the colonial period, is not at all my point of contention. Providing more facts, more empirical research on the colonial era or on the post-1945 era, however, does not resolve the issue of how individuals, historians, and society as a whole *should* regard past injustices such as the cases of "comfort women," or the other forcibly conscripted laborers during the colonial period, or those whose human and civil rights were violated or whose lives were taken unjustly by the state in post-1945 South Korea. New and more facts, although promoting further historical discourses and historical awareness, do not by themselves lead to "truth"—not least because there is a lack of "a rule of judgement," as philosopher Jean-François Lyotard discusses in a different context, that can equitably resolve conflicting interpretations of different sides.[67] In his *Differend*, Lyotard develops a powerful argument of how the empirical demonstration of facts in the case of the denial of the Holocaust/

Auschwitz further drowns out the pain and anguish of the victims, that, in contrast to litigation, the wrongs experienced by the victims cannot be presented adequately; a victim is not just someone who has been wronged but someone who has also lost the power to present this wrong.[68]

When issues such as the "comfort women" and forced industrial laborers are pursued strictly as a historiographical issue in terms of historical facts alone, and in the case of the New Right as Homo economicus without consideration for the pain and injustice suffered by said individuals, history becomes "homogeneous, empty time," a sequence of events like the "beads of a rosary"—growing longer as it amasses more and more empirical facts without redemptive potential. How do we engage with a past that, for the victims of the injustice, is not and cannot remain a part of the past without getting mired in hopelessness and negativity, but in a way that brings the society together to work toward a horizon of possibility and hope, to be able to envision a shared emancipatory present and future? The importance of engaging with the past is underscored by the fact that the suffering and pain of the past generation is not limited to the victims of injustice but also extends to immediate families, friends, neighbors, and to the anguish of the entire society.[69] In *Haunting the Korean Diaspora*, sociologist Grace M. Cho traces how the profound trauma of the Korean War is unconsciously passed on to the next generation through silence and secrets; how Koreans living in the United States have continued to suffer from traumatic effects of the accumulation of oft-unacknowledged grief of the Korean War—what she calls "transgenerational haunting."[70]

Remembrance as Emancipatory

Here, the previously discussed Benjaminian notion of remembrance proffers some insight. Benjamin suggests that there is an indissoluble connection between the injustice of the past and the emancipatory chances of the present. For Benjamin, remembrance of the past injustice is not only a necessary condition but the only possible way for true emancipation of the present. Benjamin thus writes of a moral debt to the historical process: "Like every generation that preceded us, we have been endowed with a weak Messianic power, a power to which the past has a claim."[71] As philosopher Axel Honnet further explains, the "claim" here is a kind of moral right that past generations have put on the present generation to acknowledge and to recompense for the injustice endured by a past generation:

> Every present is enriched by the material and symbolic goods which the preceding generations created in "anonymous toil" without ever having

been compensated for their sacrifices and privations. Thus, every historical process is pervaded by a chain of moral entanglements, one in which every unatoned suffering of the past further increases the objective debt of the present generation. To be freed from this growing debt is, however, for Benjamin a condition to which the success of human emancipation as a whole is attached; for without an appropriate atonement for all the wrongs that precede every present, no generation can know itself to be "free," in a sense which includes the freedom of an unforced agreement with oneself.[72]

Benjamin's insistence that fulfilling the moral obligation of the present for the past is crucial for society to attain true emancipation has been critical for recent scholarly attempts to think through the issue of restitution of historical injustices.[73] Historian Berber Bevernage, in particular, has put forth a compelling argument that to seek retrospective justice for the victims of past injustices does not have to lead to negative effects; that is, retrospective measures such as reparations for the victims of past wrongdoings or a nation's admission of its own guilt does not have to come at the cost of future-oriented politics or utopian and emancipatory visions for the future. He calls the tendency not only to posit the past as negative but also to treat negatives as anachronistic or as only belonging to the past a "temporal Manichaeism."[74]

The concern that to acknowledge past wrongs and injustices would lead to negative consequences for the present and future stems from a particular type of historical thought or philosophy of history, Bevernage argues, as the discussion above shows. This view of history treats the relations between past, present, and future in "antinomic terms" and treats them as "discrete and mutually exclusive entities," which also prevents us from understanding injustices and responsibilities across different time periods.[75] In this view, all of the political and historical alternatives that were not part of the successful present moment are consigned to the past or at least considered an anachronism. Francis Fukuyama's thesis of the end of history is a case of this negative logic par excellence; he argues that the present moment of liberal democracy represents the end of history primarily by claiming that all other alternatives to political forms of liberal democracy have failed.[76] In this line of thinking, the structural continuities between past and present are missing, which also explains why reflection on the past injustice seldom leads to moral responsibility for those in the present.[77] On the contrary, it is considered undesirable to keep harping on past injustices as is often done by victim and survivor groups.[78]

Bevernage calls attention to the practice that "'performatively' treats as past or anachronistic all those phenomena that do not conform to the contemporary society's dominant liberal-democratic ideal."[79] This vision of temporality that sets the past against the present and the future has a specific function: that of vindicating contemporaries in relation to injustices that happened in the past, as well as in relation to a present that has not rendered justice to past historical injustice. Philosopher Jacques Rancière has also called attention to a politics of time that functions to make certain experiences of the past illegible or obscure in the present.[80]

Bevernage calls for a different vision of temporality, a different philosophy of history that rethinks historical temporality in such a way that it no longer lends itself to these "antinomic" or "dualist" approaches.[81] The groups who seek retrospective justice that Bevernage examines resist such dualist visions of temporality and even notions of temporal distance. The South African Khulumani Support Group bases its ongoing struggle for justice on the argument that for the victims and survivors "the past is still in the present."[82] For the Mothers of the Plaza de Mayo in Argentina, even after more than thirty years, the disappearance of their children cannot be consigned to the past.[83] For these individuals, their own lived experience as victims or relatives of the victims of the past injustice do not render the past, present, and future as separate. Their embrace of "radical noncontemporaneity" is also what Benjamin calls "redemption" or "remembrance," as I have discussed above.

Returning to South Korea's New Right scholarship, Yi Yŏng-hun has repeatedly asserted in publications and public pronouncements that his insistence on calling the "comfort women"—itself a disturbing and misguided euphemism and a direct translation used by the Japanese state—"professional prostitutes" is to expose the problematic nationalist framework and the continuing systematic violence against women, to urge Korean society to awaken to "its own comfort women in its midst."[84] What might have been a compelling critique has become in Yi Yŏng-hun a straw man argument. He not only ignores the use of force with which many of the women were recruited at the time but also the development of public discourse and scholarly work that are critical of, and go beyond, the nationalist and binary frameworks that overlook the deeply entrenched patriarchal system and everyday gender violence in Korean society, as well as the interlocking relationship of global human trafficking, sex crimes, and violation of women.[85] This kind of understanding has been articulated in cultural productions as well. As Chŏng Kyŏng-a, author of a well-received graphic novel *"Comfort Women" Report ("Wiwanbu" rip'ot'ŭ)* states, the redress movement for "comfort women" is neither simply a case of the formerly colonized seeking justice from the colonizer, nor just a case of historical rectification (*yŏksa ch'ŏngsan*); the issue of "comfort women" is an "issue for us," precisely because of the ongoing and various forms of gendered structural violence in South Korea and globally.[86]

New Right scholars also object to the timing of this redress movement. Chu Ik-chong questions why the "comfort women" issue became public only in the late 1980s when people had been aware of its existence from early on, arguing that no newspaper or textbook mentioned the issue earlier. He then goes on to intimate that it was the Chŏngdaehyŏp (Korean Council for the Women Drafted for Military Sexual Slavery by Japan) that had mobilized the issue as a way to push its own nationalist agenda.[87] Here again, he ignores the historical context of how during the authoritarian regimes the issue of "comfort women," along with many other past historical injustices, could not be brought up in public. Globally, too, demands for transitional justice in general could be brought up only after each country transitioned to democracy.[88]

To dismiss the demand for redress for "comfort women" by arguing that the "comfort women" system was a part of the "age old" history of humankind and that its practice continued into post-1945 South Korea[89] is not only to dismiss the physical violence the women endured but also to engage in the epistemic violence that consigns the lived experience of individual "comfort women" as no longer relevant for the present. It engages in a politics of time that treats the past injustices in terms of historical discourse alone, thereby creating distance between one's own present day and the allegedly past event.[90] This distance serves to evade historical responsibility and "qualify, relativize, and unburden" not only the Japanese state but also Korean society of the debt owed to the victims of the past injustice.

This kind of politics of time, which performatively designates what they perceive as undesirable phenomena and persons in the chronological present to the past, is not limited to the New Right scholarship. It also operates most egregiously in the form of public denunciation and humiliation of victims and their family members by elements of the right. The "comfort women" and their supporters, and victims and family members of the Kwangju massacre and more recently those of the Sewol Ferry, among others, are told that they need to accept that the past is past and to move on. Furthermore, they are scorned for being "obsessive" and "unseemly" for their unwillingness to be silent.[91]

I have tried to show in this book how neoliberal rationality and the politics of time combined has given rise to various attempts to deny or obscure past emancipatory projects as illegible and to various performative announcements against the possibility of historical change, which I characterize as the regime of discontinuity. I have examined how the regime of discontinuity has operated at various levels and fields, both at the level of state policy and as a part of public discourse, as well as in cultural production and in the field of history. The regime of discontinuity, as practiced under the now-dominant neoliberal restructuring, has extended the notion of economization to previously non-economic spheres and practices as a process of remaking knowledge, as shown in the case of New Right historiography. In New Right historiography, modern Korean history is reconstructed exclusively as a history of Homo economicus, reconfiguring individuals as marching progressively from extreme destitution toward economic development and liberal democracy, with "freedom" and "egoism" contributing to the common prosperity of all Korean people. At the center of this narrative of progress is also the primary subjectivity of the South Korean state, as shown in the recent controversy regarding the New Right's attempt to designate August 15 as the date of the foundation of South Korea.

The politics of time operates in such a way that it announces or marks not simply that the "times have changed" but also that what was before "an idea of time as a set of possibilities" is now no longer possible.[92] This politics of time is also not unique or specific to the New Right in South Korea. In the global annals of democracy, for example, the discourse of de-democratization has dominated, which asserts that "despite the hegemony of democratic rhetoric, democracy today has been entirely emptied of meaning to the point of being reduced to a floating signifier by unregulated capital, the separation of the economy from the political, and substitution of the political rationality of neoliberalism for democratic rationality."[93] As I discuss in the introduction, a widespread sense of disillusion and disenchantment stemming from less-than-satisfactory reforms and drastic neoliberal measures has been such that "progressive politics" have been brushed aside as out of sync with the demands of the time in post-1987 South Korea.

A different understanding of time, a Benjaminian view of history where history does not progress according to a prescribed linear trajectory, history as a dialectic process that unfolds "in a temporal tension between continuities and discontinuities, ruptures and closures, advances and retreats" is required to map out often-contradictory contours of critical interventions and outcries against the status quo.[94] As I discussed in chapter 2, the efforts of women huildam writers to chronicle the unfulfilled dreams and aspirations, failures and limitations of the minjung movement and the undongkwŏn, were excoriated for being self-absorbed and melancholic. Yet by documenting the wounds and scars so nakedly of the failed revolution, they also refused the banality of progress of history and the inevitable victory of progressive forces. In their refusal, in the process of contemplating their defeat, and the severe pain that accompanied it, might lie what we may call a Benjaminian poetics of remembrance, the memory of the lived experience as a resource for thinking about the limits and possibilities of a transformative political praxis.

What had been suppressed, forgotten, or pushed away in the process of attaining the current dominant system persist and endure, and these submerged possibilities continue to function as political and social pressures and often express themselves as a social movement. The three-decade-long redress movement by, and on behalf of, the "comfort women" in South Korea and elsewhere, including the Wednesday noon protest held in front of the Japanese embassy in Seoul since 1992 is one such example. More recently, the movement to install the "Statue of a Girl for Peace" (Sonyŏsang) around the world has also generated active participation of silenced victims of sexual violence and the general public.[95] As Lisa Yoneyama has powerfully shown in *Cold War Ruins*, at the forefront of the emergence of a "transborder redress culture" in the 1990s were those who had been formally consigned to the realm of the "inauthentic" and the "ineligible"—former colonial subjects, racialized minorities, sexual and gender minorities, migrants and diasporic people, and others, challenging established narratives with their "insurgent memories, counterknowledges, and inauthentic identities."[96] The redress movement is also built on the "ruins" of the Cold War—the failures of transitional justice that had put the Cold War security agenda ahead of individual victims.

Despite a pervasive sense of defeat and the marginalization of organized labor that had been the backbone of social movements of the previous era, for example, there exists an equally persistent current of resistance against the dominant system put forth by various individuals and groups, from the "irregular" (*pijŏnggyujik*) workers to youth and to the most recent candlelight protest participants.[97] As these cases show, the progress of history has been built out of the web of constant and vigorous tensions of various possibilities and potentialities, some of which submerge only to reappear at a different time, which also in large part explains the dynamic history of the country.

Notes

INTRODUCTION

1   Chŏng Hae-gu, "Pak Chŏng-hŭi sindŭrŏm."
2   This is of course not unique or specific to South Korea. The New Left of the 1960s was criticized by Hannah Arendt on similar grounds that they sought to comprehend the reality of the twentieth century through political categories of the nineteenth century, such as the concept of progress. Arendt, *On Violence*, 88.
3   Rancière, "In What Time Do We Live?"
4   Löwy, *Fire Alarm*, 44–45.
5   See, among others, Kim Ch'ang-nam, "Taejung munhwa 10nyŏn"; Kim Ch'ang-nam, "90nyŏndae sinsedae munhwaŭi aik'on."
6   Foucault, *Birth of Biopolitics*; Brown, *Undoing the Demos*, 30.
7   Brown, *Undoing the Demos*, 30–31.
8   See, among others, Duggan, *Twilight of Equality?*; Hong, *Death beyond Disavowal*; Povinelli, *Economies of Abandonment*.
9   Hong, *Death beyond Disavowal*, 19–20.
10 Dirlik, *Postmodernity's Histories*, 51.
11 Kim Chong-yŏp, "Chagi kyebarŭl nŏmŏsŏn chayuŭi ŭijirŭl wihayŏ," 292–93.
12 Kim Chong-yŏp, "Chagi kyebarŭl nŏmŏsŏn chayuŭi ŭijirŭl wihayŏ," 293. Historians have recently begun to examine the 1960s and 1970s from the perspective of Michel Foucault's idea of neoliberalism as governing rationality. See, for example, Yi Sang-nok, "Sanŏphwa sigi 'ch'ulsse.'"
13 Miller, "Idea of Stagnation," 10.
14 Halbwachs, *On Collective Memory*; Connerton, *How Societies Remember*.
15 Choi, *Democracy after Democratization*, 131.
16 Feldman, "Political Terror."
17 Nora, "Between Memory and History," 17; see also Schwarz, "Memory, Temporality, Modernity."
18 Mercer, "Moral Rearmament," 108.
19 Mercer, "Moral Rearmament," 107–8.

20 Fukuyama, "End of History?" 4.
21 Such events include the Korean War in 1950, April 19 student uprising of 1960, self-immolation of Chŏn T'ae-il in 1970, Kwangju uprising in 1980, and the historic summit between North and South Korea in 2000. The IMF crisis in 1997 was the most critical event of the 1990s.
22 Varon, Foley, and McMillian, "Time Is an Ocean," 1.
23 "What Was Revolutionary about the French Revolution?" *New York Review of Books*, January 19, 1989, 10; quoted in Varon, Foley, and McMillian, "Time Is an Ocean," 1.
24 See Lee, *Making of Minjung*, 294–95.
25 More specifically, the 1987ch'eje denotes the regime governed by the revised constitution of 1987, as well as all the changes that were brought about since, both worldwide and in South Korea. Kang Wŏn-taek et al., "6wŏl hangjaeng 30chunyŏn," 72.
26 Kim Ho-gi, "1987nyŏn ch'eje," 13.
27 See, among others, Kyŏnghyang sinmun t'ŭkpyŏl chwijaet'im, *Minjuhwa 20nyŏn ŭi yŏlmang kwa chŏlmang*.
28 *Han'guk minjok munhwa taebaekkwasajŏn*. See also Song, *South Koreans in the Debt Crisis*.
29 From 1986 to 1988, the rates of GDP growth was at 12 percent annually, the highest in the world. Eichengreen, Perkins, and Shin, *From Miracle to Maturity*, 44–45. The average growth rate during the Chun Doo-hwan regime (1981–1987) was 8.7 percent and the national GDP reached $100 billion. Heo et al., "Political Economy," 10.
30 Pak Yŏng-gyun, "Minjung undong," 16.
31 For more detailed discussion of this term, see Lee, *Making of Minjung*, 8–9, 147–86.
32 Im Tae-sik, "*Haebang chŏnhusa ŭi chaeinsik* ŭl p'yŏlch'yŏbon kandanhan sohoe," 12.
33 Kim Kyu-hang, *B-kŭp chwap'a*, 272.
34 Coined in the 1990s, it refers to those who were born in the 1960s, went to college in the 1980s, and were in their thirties at the time.
35 See Lee, *Making of Minjung*, 14.
36 Lim and Jang, "Between Neoliberalism and Democracy," 8.
37 Lim and Jang, "Between Neoliberalism and Democracy," 9.
38 Povinelli, *Economies of Abandonment*, 25–26.
39 Duggan, *Twilight of Equality?*
40 Duggan, *Twilight of Equality?*; quoted in Ferguson and Hong, "Sexual and Racial Contradictions of Neoliberalism," 1058.
41 Hong, *Death beyond Disavowal*, 19–20.
42 Brown, *Undoing the Demos*, 30–31.
43 Park, *Capitalist Unconscious*.
44 Therborn, "New Masses?" Historian Yi Sang-nok argues that the discourse of the middle class (*chungsanch'ŭng*) in South Korea was in full swing by the 1980s, in which the growth of the middle class was seen as a preemptive measure against any radical movements. Yi Sang-nok, "1980nyŏndae chungsanch'ŭng tamnon," 292–94.
45 Yi Sang-nok, "1980nyŏndae chungsanch'ŭng tamnon," 282.
46 Cohen, "Finding Uncommon Ground," 124.
47 Thatcher, "AIDS, Education, and the Year 2000!"
48 These films include *Shiri* (1999), *Joint Security Area* (2002), *Tae Guk Gi: The Brotherhood of War* (2004), and *Welcome to Dongmakgol* (2005). *Tae Guk Gi: The Brotherhood*

of War, narrating the Korean War from the point of view of two brothers who each end up joining the opposite side, reportedly drew over ten million moviegoers—approximately one out of four South Koreans. See, among others, Lee, "South Korean Blockbuster."

49 As will be discussed in chapter 1, Kim Young-sam's presidency was made possible in part due to the merger of his political party with the ruling party in 1990.

50 See, among others, Ha Sang-bok, "Ŭijehyŏngsŏngŭi chŏngch'ihak." On the evaluation of the Kim government's effort, see, among others, Sŏ Chung-sŏk, Sajin kwa kŭrim ŭro ponŭn Han'guk hyŏndaesa; Cho Yong-hwan, "5.18 t'ŭkpyŏlbŏpkwa Chŏn-No chaep'anŭi munjejŏm."

51 See, among others, Chŏn Myŏng-hyŏk, "Han'gugesŏ kwagŏch'ŏngsanundongŭi yŏksa"; Kim Chu-wan, "Cho Tu-nam ch'inil nonjaeng kyŏnggwabogo"; De Ceuster, "Nation Exorcised," 219–22.

52 The drama was so popular that it was said that streets were empty during the time it aired in the late evenings. The 1980 Kwangju uprising is a pivotal event in the lives of the protagonists, and the mass media would refer to this generation as "the generation of the *Sandglass*." See Kim Chong-wŏn, "Urinŭn moraesidae sedaeigirŭl kŏbuhanda." Hye-rin, one of the three main protagonists and a university student activist from a wealthy family, pretends to come from a poor family and lives in a one-room rental out of guilt about her privileged background. She delivers one of the most memorable television dialogues capturing the ethos of the 1980s *minjung* movement, the self-denial of the intellectual at the sight of the suffering minjung: "I bought this sack of rice with money . . . while female workers [at Tong'il Textile] are waging a hunger strike, risking their lives" (episode 5, broadcast on January 15, 1995). More recent television dramas such as *Respond 1988* (broadcast in 2016) and films such as *A Taxi Driver* and *1987: When the Day Comes* (both released in 2017), dealing with the Kwangju uprising and the 1987 June uprising, respectively, were also immensely popular, the two films drawing more than ten million and seven million moviegoers, respectively. Park, "'A Taxi Driver' Attracts 10 Million Viewers."

53 Crane, "Memory, Distortion, and History."

54 For similar cases of other countries, see, among others, Friedman and Kenney, *Partisan Histories*.

55 See, among others, Huyssen, *Twilight Memories*.

56 The official name of the body formed to investigate is the Presidential Committee for the Inspection of Collaborations for Japanese Imperialism. On collaboration and South Korean historiography, see, among others, De Ceuster, "Nation Exorcised"; Tikhonov, "Rise and Fall," 9–14.

57 President Kim Young-sam initially refused to bring the two former presidents to trial, saying that history would make a final judgment about their role in the massacre of civilians in the Kwangju uprising. I discuss this issue in more detail in chapter 1.

58 Coronil, "Towards a Critique," 351.

59 Coronil, "Towards a Critique," 354.

60 See, among others, Kyogwasŏ p'orŏm, *Han'guk kŭn-hyŏndaesa*; Kim Tong-gil, Pok Kŏ-il, and Yi Ch'un-gŭn, *Pukhan chayu sŏnŏn*.

61 Yi Ch'ŏl-hŭi, "Posunŭn wae Kim Dae-jungboda," 26.
62 See, among others, Kwon, *The Other Cold War*.
63 Yi Ch'ŏl-hŭi, "Posunŭn wae Kim Dae-jungboda," 27. Many accounts of the 2016–2017 candlelight protests that led to the impeachment of President Park Geun-hye, Park Chung-hee's daughter, suggest that this base may have been shattered for the first time by the protests.
64 First enacted in 1948 and revised several times since, South Korea's NSL mandates harsh felony punishments for "any person who has organized an association or group for the purpose of . . . disturbing the state or who prepared or conspired to do so." Quoted in Shaw, *Human Rights in Korea*, 184. Even the joint membership in the United Nations since 1991 did not change the enemy status of North Korea until the June 2000 summit meeting.
65 See Lee, *Making of Minjung*, 70–108.
66 Ko Chong-sŏk, *Ko Chong-sŏk*, 42.
67 During the first year of Kim Dae-jung's presidency, the number of those who were arrested for violation of the NSL and the number of political prisoners increased fourfold compared to the first year of the previous Kim Young-sam government. Son Ho-ch'ŏl, *Sinjayujuŭi sidae*, 157.
68 See, for example, Doucette and Koo, "Distorting Democracy." The trajectory of the discourse of *chongbuk chwap'a* is more complicated than rendered here, as the term first originated within a leftist political party to denounce its members who were seen as intransigent followers of North Korea's *chuch'e sasang*. Chŏng Yŏng-t'ae, *P'abŏl: Minjunodongdang chŏngp'a kaldŭngŭi kiwŏn'gwa chongmal* [Factions: Origin and end of the factional strife within the Democratic Labor Party] (Imaejin, 2012), 217; cited in Kim Chŏng-in, "Chongbukp'ŭreim," 212.
69 This does not mean the two administrations were immune from criticisms by the left. The left became highly critical of the government's neoliberal economic policies as well as other acts such as Roh Moo-hyun's decision to send troops to Iraq in 2003. See, among others, Yu Pyŏng-mun, "Kim Se-gyun Min'gyohyŏp sangimgongdongdaep'yo"; French, "Despite Protests."
70 See, among others, Pak T'ae-gyun, "Haetpyŏt'chŏngch'aek."
71 Coronil, "Towards a Critique," 352n1.
72 Choi, *Democracy after Democratization*, 131.
73 Feldman, "Political Terror," 63. Feldman's use of the term is in the context of how, in the case of Northern Ireland, retributive violence, such as revenge, retaliation, or punishment, acted as a way to construct a certain memory of the country's immediate past and to settle some contentious historical disputes.
74 Gramsci, *Prison Notebooks*, 168.
75 Badiou, *Century*, 208n19. Historian Ammar Ali Jan elaborates this point further: "For a significant part of the 20th century the word 'Marxism' denoted a global movement for a radically different world from the prevalent order, one that brought together diverse struggles of workers, peasants, women, anti-colonial fighters and civil rights activists, to engage in the collective project of emancipation. Since the late 1980s, however, the dominant memory of these struggles is one of a pedagogical project that ended in a 'totalitarian' disaster signified by the 'gulags.'

Against the authoritarianism of Communist politics, the contemporary liberal ethic emphasizes the futility (and danger) of any project that aims to radically alter the 'essence' of man, and instead privileges the 'protection' of citizens from the excesses of totalitarian projects through a discourse of human rights enforced by powerful states ('western' states in the global arena). Revolutionary thought, a crucial pillar of politics in the 20th century, became unthinkable at the end of the century, since it was deemed to be neither possible nor desirable by the dominant consensus." Jan, "'Beyond Good and Evil.'"

76 I thank Lisa Yoneyama for this point.
77 Therborn, "After Dialectics," 71; Alexander, "Modern, Anti, Post, Neo," 82.
78 Quoted in Ross, *May '68*, 19.
79 Dirlik, *Postmodernity's Histories*, 46.
80 Christofferson, "Antitotalitarian History," 572.
81 Jan, "'Beyond Good and Evil.'"
82 Christofferson, "Antitotalitarian History," 557. For example, Richard Pipes, historian of Russia and the Soviet Union, compares the Russian Revolution to a "virus." Pipes, *Russian Revolution*, 132–33. Furet's 1995 book *Le passé d'une illusion* (*The Passing of an Illusion: The Idea of Communism in the Twentieth Century* [Chicago: University of Chicago Press, 1999]), as well as other publications in the late 1990s, such as Stéphane Courtois et al., *The Black Book of Communism* (Cambridge, MA: Harvard University Press, 1999), also share the same view of a substantial identity between Nazism and Bolshevism, the former resulting in "racial genocide" and the latter in "class genocide," as "epiphenomena of equivalent ideological essences." Traverso, "Totalitarianism," 111.
83 Mercer, "Moral Rearmament," 108.
84 Christofferson, "Antitotalitarian History," 557.
85 Heilbrunn, "Germany's New Right," 85.
86 I thank Lisa Yoneyama for reminding me of this important point.
87 Appleby, Hunt, and Jacob, *Telling the Truth*, 42.
88 Appleby, Hunt, and Jacob, *Telling the Truth*, 42–43.
89 Ch'oe Kap-su, "Yŏksaesŏ pyŏnhyŏgiran muŏsin'ga," 41. Historians Mike Haynes and Jim Wolfreys write that the French Revolution was also "a self-conscious appeal to the world. The Declaration of the Rights of Man embodied part of this wider claim. It was, said Mirabeau, 'applicable to all times, all places and all climes.'" Haynes and Wolfreys, "Introduction," 2–3.
90 Ch'oe Kap-su, "Yŏksaesŏ pyŏnhyŏgiran muŏsin'ga," 42.
91 Maxwell, "Political Economy," 491.
92 Ch'oe Kap-su, "Yŏksaesŏ pyŏnhyŏgiran muŏsin'ga," 41–42. Susan Buck-Morss points out that the Black slaves of San Domingo "surpassed the metropole in actively realizing the Enlightenment goal of human liberty, seeming to give proof that the French Revolution was not simply a European phenomenon but world-historical in its implications." Buck-Morss, *Hegel*, 39; quoted in Tassone, "It Is Not Over Yet," 343. As Tassone adds, this did not mean that history of San Domingo was incorporated into history of Europe. Tassone, "It Is Not Over Yet," 343.
93 Lazarus, "'Third Worldism,'" 3–4.

94 For the history of emergence of cultural history, see, among others, Appleby, Hunt, and Jacob, *Telling the Truth*, 217–23; Eley, "History in a Moment of Danger?" 11–13.
95 Dirlik, *Postmodernity's Histories*, 46.
96 Dirlik, *Postmodernity's Histories*, 46.
97 See, among others, Dong-Choon Kim [Kim Tong-ch'un], *Unending Korean War*. On the notion of passive revolution, see, among others, Thomas, "Gramsci's Revolutions."
98 See Paek Wŏn-dam, "Asiaesŏ 1960-70nyŏndae pidongmaeng."
99 Yi Chin-hyŏng, "Minjok munhak," 125, 136–38.
100 Ch'oe Kap-su, "Yŏksaesŏ pyŏnhyŏgiran muŏsin'ga," 43–44. The military metaphor here, as problematic as it is, is also symptomatic of both the sense of importance historians used to attach to their own profession in the 1980s as well as the sense that historical writing, much as literary work, was considered a "weapon" to be used for social change.
101 Kim Chong-yŏp, "P'osŭt'ŭmodŏn sahoe iron?" 265.
102 Kim Chong-yŏp, "P'osŭt'ŭmodŏn sahoe iron?" 265. For a powerful critique of postmodernist history, see, among others, Eley, "History in a Moment of Danger?"
103 Karl, "Foreword," viii.

1. THE PARADIGM SHIFT FROM MINJUNG (PEOPLE) TO SIMIN (CITIZEN) AND NEOLIBERAL GOVERNANCE

1 Kim, "1988 Parliamentary Election," 480.
2 The thirteenth general election of April 1988 took place soon after the presidential election of December 1987, which was won by Roh Tae-woo and resulted in the ruling Democratic Justice Party winning only 87 seats out of 224. As a result of the 1990 merger of three parties, though, the DLP became a supersized ruling party, taking 216 seats and leaving the Peace Democratic Party headed by Kim Dae-jung as the only minority party.
3 Details of the merger have yet to be disclosed, but it was widely speculated that Kim Young-sam made a political bargain to grant impunity to Chun Doo-hwan and Roh Tae-woo in return for their financial and political backing needed to defeat Kim Dae-jung in the 1992 presidential election. West, "Martial Lawlessness," 103–4.
4 From 1988 to 1995, over 1,877 workers were arrested for their union activities. Kim, "Rethinking the New Beginning," 496.
5 Twelve university students committed suicide as a protest, prompting Kim Chi-ha, an erstwhile dissident and well-known poet, to publish the now-infamous "Clear away the shamanic ritual of death!" Kim Chi-ha, "Chugŭmŭi kutp'an."
6 Chŏn Chae-ho, Kim Wŏn, and Kim Chŏng-han, *91yŏn 5wŏl t'ujaengkwa*, 16.
7 Kang Nae-hŭi, "Munhwa wa sijang," 243.
8 Sŏ Tong-jin, *Pyŏnjŭngpŏp ŭi natcham*, 200.
9 Sŏ Tong-jin, *Pyŏnjŭngpŏp ŭi natcham*, 200.
10 Kim Myŏng-hwan, "1987nyŏn 6wŏl hangjaeng," 225.

11　Choi, *Democracy after Democratization*, 157–71; Kang Wŏn-t'aek et al., "6wŏl hangjaeng 30chunyŏn," 80–81.
12　Kang Wŏn-t'aek et al., "6wŏl hangjaeng 30chunyŏn," 78–79.
13　Kim Chong-yŏp, "87nyŏn ch'ejeŭi kwejŏkgwa nonjaeng," 362.
14　Ch'oe Wŏn-sik, "Munhak kwa chinbo," 150.
15　Historian Kang Man-gil is the first to designate post-1945 as an "era of division" (*pundan sidae*) to denote the centrality of peninsular division affecting South Korea's society. Since then, literary scholar and public intellectual Paek Nak-ch'ŏng [Paik Nak-chung] has further elaborated on this idea as the "division system" (*pundan ch'eje*). See Kang Man-gil, *Pundan sidae ŭi yŏksa insik*; Nak-chung Paik, *Division System in Crisis*.
16　I think it is accurate to characterize the oppositional political parties during the authoritarian regime as "conservative liberal," following Yi Kwang-il's formulation in his book *Pak Chŏng-hŭi ch'eje*.
17　Kim Chong-yŏp, "87nyŏn ch'ejeŭi kwejŏkgwa nonjaeng," 365.
18　Ch'oe Chin-sŏp, "6wŏlhangjaeng chuyŏktŭrŭi hyŏnjuso," 81.
19　Yi Kwang-il, "Minjujuŭi ihaeng kwa simin undong," 330; Kang Wŏn-taek et al., "6wŏl hangjaeng 30chunyŏn," 78.
20　See, among others, Kim Tong-ch'un, "Han'guk sahoe undong hyŏnjuso"; Yi Kwang-il, "Minjujuŭi ihaeng kwa simin undong."
21　*Hankook Ilbo*'s calling the June uprising a "middle-class revolution" is a representative case; cited in Kim Se-jung, "Pak Chŏng-hŭi sidae," 66. The 2017 film *A Taxi Driver* is an exception to the majority of the cultural production dealing with the 1980s democratization movement in that the main protagonist is a taxi driver and not a middle class or an intellectual. See also Kim Wŏn, *87nyŏn 6wŏl hangjaeng*, 161–75.
22　Kim Wŏn, *87nyŏn 6wŏl hangjaeng*, 168; Ch'oe Chin-sŏp, "6wŏlhangjaeng chuyŏktŭrŭi hyŏnjuso," 85.
23　Kim Wŏn, *87nyŏn 6wŏl hangjaeng*, 168; Nam Chong-sŏk, "87nyŏnch'ejewa nodong undong."
24　Han Hong-gu, *Taehanmin'guksa*, 4:236.
25　On the Great Struggle, see, among others, Koo, *Korean Workers*; Ch'oe Yŏng-gi et al., *1987nyŏn ihu Han'guk ŭi nodong undong*.
26　The term *neoliberalism* was first mentioned in South Korea in 1994 in a conference where presenters defined the Kim Young-sam government's New Economy Policy as such. In 1996, when the Kim government revised the labor laws to make dismissal of workers easier, there was a nationwide protest calling the government policies "neoliberal." Kang Nae-hŭi, "Munhwa wa sijang," 239n2.
27　See, among others, Woo-Cumings, *Developmental State*; Lim and Jang, "Between Neoliberalism and Democracy," 1.
28　See, among others, Pak T'ae-gyun, *Wŏnhyŏnggwa pyŏnyong*.
29　Kang Nae-hui, "Sinjayujuŭi sidae," 281.
30　Kang Nae-hui, "Sinjayujuŭi sidae," 282.
31　See, among others, Kim Wŏn, "Pumahangjaenggwa tosihach'ŭngmin."
32　Lee, "Institutional Reform," 9–10.

Notes to Chapter One　143

33 Kim, "Kim Jae-Ik."
34 Lee, "Institutional Reform," 10.
35 The key words of the consensus include "fiscal discipline, appropriate public expenditure priorities, tax reform, financial liberalization, appropriate exchange rate policy, trade liberalization, abolishment of barriers to foreign direct investment, privatization, deregulation, and property rights." Lee, "Institutional Reform," 10.
36 Economist Chung H. Lee argues that the only group to oppose the reform was the government bureaucrats who had much to lose from establishment of a market economy. Lee, "Institutional Reform," 3.
37 Kukje Group, the seventeenth largest chaebŏl in 1985, went bankrupt when the state-owned bank stopped honoring checks written by the company. It was widely believed that the owner of Kukje did not contribute enough funds to various projects that Chun Doo-hwan's family members were involved with. See, among others, Sin Chun-yŏng, "Simch'ŭngch'ujŏk: Chŏn Tu-hwan," 47–48; Yi Sŭng-gu et al., "Chŏnggyŏngsanmaek."
38 Shin and Chang, *Restructuring Korea Inc.*, 68.
39 Shin and Chang, *Restructuring Korea Inc.*, 68. The majority of South Korean holders of nondomestic PhDs in economics have received their degrees in the United States. Economists Jang-Sup Shin and Ha-Joon Chang found that between 1987 and 1995, about 9.7 percent of those who had received PhDs in economics in the United States had Korean-sounding names. In no less than three out of the nine years (1991, 1992, 1994), over 10 percent of the names could be identified as Korean, with Korean-sounding names accounting for 12.1 percent of the list in 1991 (114 out of 946). The majority of those PhDs returned to South Korea to assume positions in universities and government bureaucracy. Shin and Chang, *Restructuring Korea Inc.*, 68n20.
40 Lee, "Institutional Reform," 3.
41 Gills and Gills, "South Korea and Globalization," 220.
42 Kang Nae-hŭi, "Munhwa wa sijang," 241; Shin and Chang, *Restructuring Korea Inc.*, 70.
43 Lim and Jang, "Between Neoliberalism and Democracy," 22. For further discussion of different kinds of politics of confusion, see, among others, Bourdieu, *Acts of Resistance*, 94–105.
44 Kim Chong-yŏp, "87nyŏn ch'ejeŭi kwejŏkgwa nonjaeng," 363.
45 On Kim Young-sam government's initial policy to deconcentrate chaebŏl, see Gills and Gills, "South Korea and Globalization," 207.
46 Kim Chong-yŏp, "87nyŏn ch'ejeŭi kwejŏkgwa nonjaeng," 364.
47 Harvey, *Brief History of Neoliberalism*, 16.
48 Lim and Jang, "Between Neoliberalism and Democracy," 10.
49 Gills and Gills, "South Korea and Globalization," 202.
50 Lim and Jang, "Between Neoliberalism and Democracy," 11.
51 Lim and Jang, "Between Neoliberalism and Democracy," 12.
52 Kim Dae-jung [Kim Tae-jung], *Kim Tae-jung chasŏjŏn*.
53 As Bruce Cumings notes, many of Kim's economic advisers had long criticized the concentration of economic activity in the chaebŏl. Cumings, "Asian Crisis, Democracy," 39.

54 Son Ho-ch'ŏl, *Sinjayujuŭi sidae*, 211. On history of the chaebŏl, see, among others, Yu In-hak, *Han'guk chaebŏrŭi haebu*.
55 Han Yun-hyŏng, *Ant'i Chosun undongsa*, 73.
56 Lim and Jang, "Between Neoliberalism and Democracy," 12.
57 Shin and Chang, *Restructuring Korea Inc.*, 56.
58 South Korea's unemployment rate had been around 2.5 percent from 1988 through 1997. In 1998, it shot up to 6.9 percent. In the same year, 590,000 jobs were shed in the manufacturing sector alone; in the construction sector, 346,000 jobs were lost. These two sectors, which had played a major role in sustaining South Korea's rapid economic growth, accounted for almost one million job losses in 1998 alone. Lee and Lee, "Will the Model of Uncoordinated Decentralization Persist?" 149.
59 Kim Dae-jung, *Kim Tae-jung chasŏjŏn*, 341; Ryu Tong-min, "Kim Tae-jung ŭi kyŏngjesasang," 160–66. On Kim Dae-jung's thoughts on the economy, see, among others, Ryu Tongmin, "Kim Tae-jung ŭi kyŏngjesasang"; on his notion of "economic democracy," see pp. 144–47.
60 Some would argue that DJnomics, due to its introduction of welfare policies, was closer to German social market–styled "order liberalism" or a third way version than neoliberalism. See Ryu Tongmin, "Kim Tae-jung ŭi kyŏngjesasang," 168–69; Kim, "DJnomics," 472. For Kim Dae-jung's own views of DJnomics, see Han'guk kaebal yŏn'guwŏn, *Kungmin kwa hamkke*.
61 Kim Dae-jung, *Kim Tae-jung chasŏjŏn*, 341; cited in Ryu Tongmin, "Kim Tae-jung ŭi kyŏngjesasang," 168–69. There was no welfare policy to speak of in South Korea until Kim Dae-jung's administration. Political scientist Meredith Woo-Cumings suggests that the five largest chaebŏl, employing more than 600,000 workers, performed an indispensable welfare function in a society largely bereft of a social safety net. Woo-Cumings, "State, Democracy," 124. For a further discussion of welfare during the Kim Dae-jung government, see Song, *South Koreans in the Debt Crisis*.
62 Chang Ha-sŏng, *Han'guk chabonjuŭi*, 97.
63 Brown, *Undoing the Demos*, 20–21, 47–49.
64 Chang Ha-sŏng, *Han'guk chabonjuŭi*, 97.
65 Kim, "DJnomics," 476.
66 Gills and Gills, "South Korea and Globalization," 205.
67 Yu In-hak, *Han'guk chaebŏrŭi haebu*, 5. These figures are from prior to 1991.
68 Shin and Chang, *Restructuring Korea Inc.*, 69.
69 Shin and Chang, *Restructuring Korea Inc.*, 69. Hayek was invited to South Korea by the Federation of Korean Industries as early as September 9, 1978. During his stay, he actively promoted neoliberal policies, such as ending the central bank's monopoly to issue bank notes and calling for competition with privately owned banks. The chaebŏl's demand for the state to retreat from managing economy also started from around this time. See Hwang Pyŏng-ju, "Yusin, chabon'gwaŭi kongmo hogŭn taegyŏl," 37–39. James Buchanan is the subject of the historian Nancy MacLean's *Democracy in Chains*, which exposes how Buchanan with corporate and right-wing foundations carried out persistent campaigns to eliminate unions, suppress voting,

privatize public education, and restrain democratic majority rule. For a sample of scathing attacks on the book by neoconservatives in the United States, see, among others, Bernstein, "Some Dubious Claims."

70 Kim Kyu-hang, "Samsŏngŭn uriege muŏsin'ga," 23–24. Kim argues that Koreans' attitude toward chaebŏl has changed dramatically from disdain to respect and envy since the 1990s; that since 1987, intensified competition in society has made money the one and only barometer by which to measure one's happiness. He suggests that the changed attitude toward chaebŏl resulted in the election of Lee Myung-bak, a former CEO of Hyundai Engineering and Construction, as president in 2007. Kim Kyu-hang, "Samsŏngŭn uriege muŏsin'ga," 23–24.
71 Chang Ha-sŏng, Han'guk chabonjuŭi, 101–3.
72 Chang Ha-sŏng, Han'guk chabonjuŭi, 137–38.
73 Kim Sang-jo, "Samsung konghwaguk," 39; Kim Kyu-hang, B-kŭp chwap'a, 270.
74 See, among others, Kim Sang-jo, "Samsung konghwaguk," 33–40.
75 Kang Wŏn-t'aek et al., "6wŏl hangjaeng 30chunyŏn," 92.
76 Cho Hŭi-yŏn, "Minjung undong," 301.
77 Cho Hŭi-yŏn, "Minjung undong," 301.
78 Pak Yŏng-gyun, "Minjung undong."
79 Lee and Kim, South Korean Democratization Movement, 85.
80 Eichengreen, Perkins, and Shin, From Miracle to Maturity, 44–45.
81 See, among others, Cho Hŭi-yŏn, "Minjung undong," 240; Choi and Heo, "Economic Changes," 1855–58.
82 See, among others, Ch'oe Yŏng-gi et al., 1987nyŏn ihu Han'guk ŭi nodong undong.
83 Lefebvre, Critique of Everyday Life, 2:10.
84 See, among others, MBC (Munhwa Broadcasting Corporation), "Sŭp'och'ŭro chibaehara!"
85 Pak Yŏng-gyun, "Minjung undong," 14.
86 Lee, Making of Minjung, 162–65. For a different view on Marxism's hold on the 1980s intellectual community and social movement, see Kim Wŏn, "80nyŏndae taehan 'kiŏk.'"
87 Kim Ho-gi, "Siminsahoe ŭi kujo wa pyŏndong," 72. For a differing view on the notion of the demise of the minjung movement, see, among others, Kim, "Left Out."
88 Choi, "Democratization, Civil Society," 35.
89 Choi, "Democratization, Civil Society," 34–36.
90 Sŏ Kyŏng-sŏk, "Minjung sinhak," 197–98.
91 Kang Wŏn-t'aek et al., "6wŏl hangjaeng 30chunyŏn," 93. In the late 1980s, the student movement was considered to be one of the most important political actors in South Korean society, second only to the military, leading a government official to remark that the country was "at the brink of choosing either a military republic or a student republic." Quoted in Lee, "South Korean Student Movement," 132. On changing strategies and tactics of the student movement to respond to the changing situation, see Kim Chong-wŏn, "Pyŏnsin mosaekhanŭn haksaengundong hyŏnjuso"; Yi In-yŏng, "Haksaengundong."
92 Kim Tong-ch'un, "Han'guk sahoe undong," 22.

93 Therborn, "New Masses?" For a further discussion of "citizen" in the context of the 1987 June uprising and the Workers' Great Struggle, see Kim Wŏn, *87nyŏn 6wŏl hangjaeng*, 150–75.
94 Schmitt, *Crisis*, 24–26; quoted in Brown, *Undoing the Demos*, 32.
95 Dietz, "Context Is All," 67.
96 Therborn, "New Masses?" 10. For an ethnographical study of the rising middle class and social stratification in South Korea, see Lett, *In Pursuit of Status*.
97 Sŏ Tong-jin, *Pyŏnjŭngpŏp ŭi natcham*, 146.
98 Sŏ Tong-jin, *Chayuŭi ŭiji*. Sŏ's examination of the literature of self-improvement is one of the most insightful analyses of how neoliberalism provides both discourse and techniques to manage oneself; he analyzes how the emphasis on self-management and self as entrepreneur—the individual thinks of oneself as a corporation and as always self-employed—has the effect of removing the category of working class or employment from social discourse. Yi Sang-nok suggests that the discourse of "self-improvement" has been spreading in a limited way among white-collar workers since the 1970s. Yi Sang-nok, "Sanŏphwa sigi."
99 Song, *South Koreans in the Debt Crisis*, 14.
100 Foucault, *Discipline and Punish*, 195–228; quoted in Koschmann, *Revolution and Subjectivity*, 179.
101 Koschmann, *Revolution and Subjectivity*, 179.
102 Foucault, *Discipline and Punish*, 195–228; quoted in McClure, "On the Subject of Rights," 110.
103 McClure, "On the Subject of Rights," 110.
104 Nam Chong-sŏk, "87nyŏnch'ejewa nodong undong." Historian Han Hong-gu relays an episode at an early large gathering of workers during the Great Struggle at Ulsan. The biggest grievance among gathered workers was not about low wages or the lack of a union; it was that they did not have the freedom to select and wear their own hairstyle and work clothes. Han Hong-gu, "Toesaranan ch'inil seryŏk," 19–20.
105 Ch'oe Yŏng-gi et al., *1987nyŏn ihu Han'guk ŭi nodong undong*. More than two-thirds of workers in large enterprises of the heavy and chemical industry sector were organized by 1989. Lee and Lee, "Will the Model of Uncoordinated Decentralization Persist?" 146.
106 Kim Se-gyun, "1987nyŏn ihu," 208.
107 Kim Se-gyun, "1987nyŏn ihu," 208.
108 See, among others, Koo, "Dilemmas of Empowered Labor."
109 Pak Yŏng-gyun, "Minjung undong," 23.
110 No Chung-gi, "Wigi ŭi nodong undong," 53.
111 From the 1970s to the 1990s, a labor union organized as an alternative to the existing company union was called a "democratic union" (*minju nojo*). Most unions or labor organizations organized by labor activists were also called "democratic" unions or "democratic" labor organizations. After the Great Struggle of Workers in 1987, many workers went back to factories and began to demand "democratization" of factory life, raising issues from managers' rude language to workers, to what workers perceived to be the remnants of militarism. Nam Chong-sŏk, "87nyŏnch'ejewa nodong undong."

112 No Chung-gi, "Wigi ŭi nodong undong," 53.
113 The labor movement's crisis was not only manufactured by the state and management. The increasing number of temporary workers also divided the working class, among other reasons for the crisis. No Chung-gi, "Wigi ŭi nodong undong," 52.
114 Nam Chong-sŏk, "87nyŏnch'ejewa nodong undong."
115 No Chung-gi, "Wigi ŭi nodong undong," 47.
116 Pak Yŏng-gyun, "Minjung undong," 23.
117 Pak Yŏng-gyun, "Minjung undong," 23; Kim Yŏng-su, "Nosajŏngwiwŏnhoe," 83.
118 Gills and Gills, "South Korea and Globalization," 214. The other aims of the commission were to strengthen national competitiveness and to equalize the severe impact of the IMF crisis. Lee and Lee, "Will the Model of Uncoordinated Decentralization Persist?" 158.
119 Lee and Lee, "Will the Model of Uncoordinated Decentralization Persist?" 158.
120 It should be noted that Minju noch'ong was by no means unified within on its positions, strategies, and tactics, especially regarding whether to participate in the commission. In the commission's first round of agreements in 1998, Minju noch'ong in effect consented to the revised laws. For details, see, among others, Kim Yŏng-su, "Nosajŏngwiwŏnhoe," 83; No Chung-gi, "Minju nojo undong."
121 No Chung-gi, "Minju nojo undong," 237; Kim Yŏng-su, "Nosajŏngwiwŏnhoe," 89.
122 For details, see No Chung-gi, "Minju nojo undong."
123 Dirlik, *Postmodernity's Histories*, 22.
124 Sin Hyŏn-jun, "Sahoe kwahak ŭi wigi?" 161.

2. THE PARADIGM SHIFT FROM THE POLITICAL TO THE CULTURAL AND HUILDAM LITERATURE

1 Pang Hyŏn-sŏk, "Huildam munhak," 144.
2 The Swedish Academy described Dario Fo as someone "who emulates the jesters of the Middle Ages in scourging authority and upholding the dignity of the downtrodden." Swedish Academy, "Dario Fo"; Pang Hyŏn-sŏk, "Huildam munhak," 144.
3 Pang Hyŏn-sŏk, "Huildam munhak," 146.
4 Chŏng Hong-su, "Kohae ŭi chari," 346.
5 The full quote is from Antonio Gramsci, *Selections from the Prison Notebooks*, 276: "The crisis consists precisely in the fact that the old is dying and the new cannot be born; in this interregnum a great variety of morbid symptoms appear."
6 Badiou, *Century*, 22.
7 Yi Myŏng-wŏn, *Maŭm i sogŭm pat*, 225.
8 Sim Chin-kyŏng, "Kwŏn Yŏ-sŏn," 355.
9 Benjamin, "Left-Wing Melancholy." As Wendy Brown further elaborates, the irony of melancholia "is that attachment to the object of one's sorrowful loss supersedes any desire to recover from this loss, to live free of it in the present, to be unburdened by it." Brown, "Resisting Left Melancholy," 19.
10 Benjamin, *Origin of German Tragic Drama*, 157; Plass, "From Left-Wing," 151.

11 Benjamin, "Theses on the Philosophy of History," 257–58. Although I discuss Benjamin's concept of redemption more in the epilogue, I readily acknowledge that it demands much more fine-grained analysis than what I can provide here, and I also do not deal with its complexities and various interpretations, of which I am aware.
12 Plass, "From Left-Wing," 151–52.
13 Hayes, "Historico-poetic Materialism," 127.
14 Kim Myŏng-in, *Hwanmyŏl ŭi munhak*, 201.
15 Tocqueville, *Democracy in America*, 4; quoted in Ch'oe Wŏn-sik, "Munhak kwa chinbo," 157. On the socially engaged writers of the 1970s, see Ryu, *Writers of the Winter Republic*.
16 Kong Chi-yŏng, "Salmŭi pop'yŏnjŏk t'ongch'arŭl," 188–89.
17 Kim Myŏng-in, *Hwanmyŏl ŭi munhak*, 201.
18 Kim Pyŏng-ik, "Sinsedae wa saeroun salmŭi yangsik," 665; quoted in Yang Chin-o, "90yŏndae munhak pipyŏng," 172.
19 Hwang Chong-yŏn et al., "90yŏndae munhak ŏttŏke polgŏsin'ga."
20 Hwang Chong-yŏn et al., "90yŏndae munhak ŏttŏke polgŏsin'ga," 19–20.
21 Orwell, "Why I Write," 11; quoted in Parkes, *Writers*, 1.
22 Parkes, *Writers*, 19.
23 Kim In-suk, *'79-'80: Kyŏuresŏ pom sai*, 1:3–5; quoted in Kim Nam-ok, "'386' sedae," 288.
24 Hwang Chong-yŏn et al., "90yŏndae munhak ŏttŏke polgŏsin'ga," 20–21.
25 Hwang Chong-yŏn et al., "90yŏndae munhak ŏttŏke polgŏsin'ga," 38.
26 Hwang Chong-yŏn et al., "90yŏndae munhak ŏttŏke polgŏsin'ga," 22. First published in a literary journal *Munye Chung'ang* (Spring 1991), *Nŭp'ŭl kŏnnŏnŭn pŏp* was published in book form a few months later and republished in 2014 by *Munhak tongne*.
27 Hwang Chong-yŏn et al., "90yŏndae munhak ŏttŏke polgŏsin'ga," 22.
28 Kim Chŏng-nam, "Kŭndae munhak," 117.
29 Kim Chŏng-nam, "Kŭndae munhak," 117–18.
30 Karatani, *Origins*, 39; see also Chŏng Chi-hwan, "Kim Yun-sik," 53.
31 Parkes, *Writers*, 181–89.
32 Ku Hyo-sŏ et al., "Uri sidae ŭi chakkadŭrŭn," 294–96.
33 Kwŏn Sŏng-u, "Perŭllin, Chŏnnohyŏp," 256.
34 Kwŏn Sŏng-u, "Perŭllin, Chŏnnohyŏp," 262.
35 Hwang Jongyon [Hwang Chong-yŏn], "After the Apocalypse," 120. His examples of the underdevelopments are "the overall low quality of college learning and education in general; cultural crudeness and the technical backwardness of mass media; the severe control over public communication by a succession of authoritarian regimes; the age-old legacy of Confucian culture, which affords men of letters elite privilege; and a social system characterized by a monopoly of worldly success held by a well-educated class." Hwang, "After the Apocalypse," 120.
36 Hwang, "After the Apocalypse," 120–21.
37 Ku Hyo-sŏ et al., "Uri sidae ŭi chakkadŭrŭn," 303.
38 Yi Chae-hyŏn, "'Huildam hyŏnsang,'" 186. Yi notes the resurgence of Korean film industry in the 1990s was also a significant part of mass culture.

39 Hwang Chong-yŏn et al., "90yŏndae munhak ŏttŏke polgŏsin'ga," 75–76.
40 Kim Myŏng-in, *Hwanmyŏl ŭi munhak*, 201.
41 Kim Myŏng-in, *Hwanmyŏl ŭi munhak*, 322.
42 Kim Myŏng-in, *Hwanmyŏl ŭi munhak*, 184.
43 Kim Chŏng-nan et al., "90yŏndae munhak," 31.
44 Kim Chŏng-nan et al., "90yŏndae munhak," 31.
45 Kim Myŏng-in, *Hwanmyŏl ŭi munhak*, 322; Kim Yŏng-hyŏn, "'Riŏllijŭm munhak,'" 147.
46 Sŏ Tong-jin, "Munhwa ŭi t'aja," 273. Someone like Kim Yŏng-hyŏn, one of the representative huildam writers who debuted in the mid-1980s, for example, did not have the time or the wherewithal to nurture his aspiration to be a writer, which began in his early twenties: "All I did was participate in the movement, go to prison, and continue in my movement after I was released from prison." Ku Hyo-sŏ et al., "Uri sidae ŭi chakkadŭrŭn," 296.
47 Kim Chŏng-nan et al., "90yŏndae munhak," 32.
48 Kim Chŏng-nan et al., "90yŏndae munhak," 44.
49 Kim Myŏng-in, *Hwanmyŏl ŭi munhak*, 291. This newspaper's anti-communism and anti–North Korea stance is such that when the film *Welcome to Dongmakgol* was released in 2005 and was popularly received, the paper's internet news columnist derided it by calling it "Welcome to Kim Il Sung Kingdom" for its reputedly positive portrayal of North Korean soldiers, among others. Chin Sŏng-ho, "Welk'ŏm t'u Kim Ilssŏng wangguk." Earlier in 1998, the *Chosun Ilbo*, along with the *JoongAng Ilbo*, was responsible for forcing Professor Ch'oe Chang-jip [Jang Jip Choi] from his post as head of the Presidential Policy Planning Committee for his characterization of Kim Il Sung as "more of a nationalist than a communist." See, among others, Lee, *Making of Minjung*, 61, 74; Kotch, "Chosun Ilbo," 443–44.
50 Kim Myŏng-in, *Hwanmyŏl ŭi munhak*, 292. For further discussion of this case, see Han Yun-hyŏng, *Ant'i Chosun undongsa*, 196–97.
51 "Mundane agyŏnghyang 'munhakkwŏllyŏk' itta" [There is "literary power" that is pernicious for the literary field], *Kyunghyang shinmun*, August 24, 2000; quoted in Kim Myŏng-in, *Hwanmyŏl ŭi munhak*, 304.
52 Kim Myŏng-in, *Hwanmyŏl ŭi munhak*, 304.
53 Kim Yŏng-hyŏn, "'Riŏllijŭm munhak,'" 147.
54 Donahue, "Revising '68," 295.
55 On KAPF, see, among others, Hughes, *Literature and Film*, 19–60; Park, *Proletarian Wave*.
56 Yi Chae-hyŏn, "'Huildam hyŏnsang,'" 182; Yi does not provide citation, and I have not been able to find any of Kim Yun-sik's work that defines what huildam is, other than his remark that the significance of huildam literature of the 1990s in Korean literary history is comparable to that of 1930s "conversion literature" among KAPF writers. Kim Yun-sik, "Huildam munhakkwa sosŏlga," 323–24.
57 Kim Po-kyŏng, "Kiŏgŭn hegemoni ŭi yongmang," 132. There are other similar genres, such as "scar literature" or "literature of the wounded," which emerged after the Cultural Revolution in China and dealt with the suffering of cadres and intellectuals during the Cultural Revolution. A former Red Guard's literary exposé of the excess of ideology during the Cultural Revolution, Dai Houying's

Stones of the Wall, was translated into Korean in 2005 (*Sarama a sarama*) and was hugely popular.
58 Kim Ŭn-ha, "386 sedae yŏsŏng huildam," 113–14.
59 "In'gane taehan yeu," 92–93; quoted in Sŏ Ŭn-kyŏng, "Kong Chi-yŏng non," 171–72. This and other short stories are collected in *In'gane taehan yeŭi*, published in 1994.
60 Kim Yŏng-hyŏn, *Namhae yŏpsŏ*, 26.
61 Pang Hyŏn-sŏk, *Chonjaeŭi hyŏngsik*, 56.
62 Kim Ŭn-ha, "386 sedae yŏsŏng huildam," 101.
63 See, among others, Hwang Chong-yŏn, "Chinchŏngsŏng ŭi inyŏm kwa sosŏl," 313.
64 Pang Hyŏn-sŏk, "Huildam munhak," 146–47. Writing in 1997, Pang seems to have anticipated a number of novels published in the early 2000s whose denouncement of undongkwŏn was much more strident than the typical huildam of the early 1990s; for example, Pae Su-a's *Tokhakja* (An autodidact), published in 2004 (Yŏllimwŏn), portrays undongkwŏn as unethical, hypocritical, incompetent, and irrational and calls the student activists as a whole "a shock troop of drunkards." Pae Su-a, *Tokhakja*, 118; see also Kim Po-kyŏng, "Kiŏgŭn hegemoni ŭi yongmang."
65 Kim Yŏng-hyŏn, "'Riŏllijŭm munhak,'" 146.
66 Donahue, "Revising '68," 293.
67 Male students who were involved in the student movement were often conscripted into compulsory military service without even letting their family know; see Lee and Kim, *South Korean Democratization Movement*, 228–32. Kim spent a year and a half in solitary confinement before he was drafted forcibly into military service and tortured during the Kwangju uprising. Kim Yŏng-hyŏn, "'Riŏllijŭm munhak,'" 144.
68 Hwang Kwang-su, "90yŏndaeŭi chinghwa tu sosŏljip," 414.
69 Kwŏn Sŏng-u, "Perŭllin, Chŏnnohyŏp," 263.
70 Kang Chin-ho, "T'ŭmsaewa konggan saie," 77–78.
71 "Naemaŭmŭi mangmyŏngjŏngbu" in Kim Yŏng-hyŏn, *Naemaŭmŭi mangmyŏngjŏngbu*; Yang Chin-o, "Mangmyŏngŭi yongmang," 367.
72 "Tungkkot" in *Kŭrigo amumaldo haji anhatta*, 67–69; quoted in Kang Sang-hui, "Sosŏljŏk chinjŏngsŏng," 425–26.
73 "Tungkkot," 67–69.
74 Kim Yŏng-hyŏn, "Tasi 'Kim Yŏng-hyŏn,'" 57.
75 Kim Yŏng-hyŏn, "'Riŏllijŭm munhak,'" 146.
76 Kim In-suk, "Yuri kudu," 26.
77 Kim In-suk, *'79–'80: Kyŏuresŏ pom sai*; Kim In-suk, *Hamkke kŏnnŭn'gil*.
78 Kim Nam-ok, "'386' sedae," 286–87.
79 Kim Nam-ok, "'386' sedae," 291.
80 Kim Ŭn-ha, "386 sedae yŏsŏng huildam," 107.
81 Kim In-suk, "Sullaeege," 253–54.
82 Kim In-suk, "Sullaeege," 257–59, 254–55.
83 Kim In-suk, "Sullaeege," 255.
84 Kim Ŭn-ha, "386 sedae yŏsŏng huildam," 107.
85 Kim Ŭn-ha, "386 sedae yŏsŏng huildam," 107.
86 Kim In-suk, "Yuri kudu," 17.

87 Kim In-suk, "Yuri kudu," 26.
88 Kim In-suk, "Yuri kudu," 30; quoted in Kim Ŭn-ha, "386 sedae yŏsŏng huildam," 108. Christopher Lasch also discusses a similar trend of how North Americans, after the turmoil of the sixties, retreated to the private and the individual, such as in psychic self-improvement, as they felt that they had no hope of improving their lives in meaningful ways. Lasch, *Culture of Narcissism*.
89 Kim Ŭn-ha, "386 sedae yŏsŏng huildam," 108.
90 Lee, *Making of Minjung*, 16.
91 Kim Nam-ok, "'386' sedae," 291. Kong's *Go Alone like a Rhinoceros* (*Musoŭi ppulch'ŏrŏm honjasŏ kara*, 1993) is one of the few novels she published in the 1990s that do not have former undongkwŏn as the protagonists. It became one of her most successful novels, remaining popular well into the 2000s, and was also made into a film, a play, and a musical.
92 "Tongt'ŭnŭn saebyŏk" in Kong Chi-yŏng, *In'gane taehan yeŭi*, 279–314.
93 Kong Chi-yŏng, *Tŏ isang arŭmdanun panghwang'ŭn ŏpta*, 279.
94 Kong is from a well-to-do family and is also known for her attractiveness, which she said had made her feel "unfit" for the puritanical undongkwŏn culture of the 1980s.
95 Kim Myŏng-in, "Kamsangesŏ sŏngch'allo," 538.
96 Kim Myŏng-in, "Kamsangesŏ sŏngch'allo," 538–39.
97 Kong Chi-yŏng, *Kodŭngŏ*, 186.
98 Chŏng Mun-sun, "T'ongsok kwa chagi yŏnmin"; quoted in Kim Ŭn-ha, "386 sedae yŏsŏng huildam," 103.
99 Kim Ŭn-ha, "386 sedae yŏsŏng huildam," 106.
100 Yi Chŏng-hui, "Kŭnyŏŭi arŭmdaun sijak," 137.
101 Kim Ŭn-ha, "386 sedae yŏsŏng huildam," 104.
102 Kong Chi-yŏng, *Kodŭngŏ*, 186.
103 Kong Chi-yŏng, *Kodŭngŏ*, 186; Kim Ŭn-ha, "386 sedae yŏsŏng huildam," 104.
104 "Muŏsŭl hal kŏsin'ga" in Kong Chi-yŏng, *In'gane taehan yeŭi*, 116.
105 "Muŏsŭl hal kŏsin'ga" in Kong Chi-yŏng, *In'gane taehan yeŭi*, 113.
106 Kim Ŭn-ha, "386 sedae yŏsŏng huildam," 104.
107 Sŏ Ŭn-kyŏng, "Kong Chi-yŏng non," 172.
108 "In'gan e taehan yeui" in Kong Chi-yŏng, *In'gane taehan yeŭi*, 70; quoted in Sŏ Ŭn-kyŏng, "Kong Chi-yŏng non," 172.
109 "Muŏsŭl hal kŏsin'ga" in Kong Chi-yŏng, *In'gane taehan yeŭi*, 101; Kim Ŭn-ha, "386 sedae yŏsŏng huildam," 104. During the 1980s, plainclothes policemen were stationed at major universities to monitor students and faculty. Although there is no officially reported case of rape by them on campus, there were cases where women students who were taken to police stations for questioning were sexually abused. There were also several cases in the 1980s where student activists fell from school buildings as they were being chased by plainclothes policemen or riot soldiers; a few of them died as a result. See, among others, Lee and Kim, *South Korean Democratization Movement*, 261–62, 270–75.
110 Kim Yŏng-hyŏn, *Kŭrigo amumaldo haji anhatta*, 10–11; quoted in Yi Sŏng-uk, "Sosŏl munhak," 347.

111 *Und sagte kein einziges Wort*. Its Korean translation is rendered as *Kŭrigo amumaldo haji anhatta*. Han Chŏm-tol, "Han'guk e mich'in Togil chŏnhu sosŏl," 276.
112 Han Chŏm-tol, "Han'guk e mich'in Togil chŏnhu sosŏl," 275.
113 Yi Sŏng-uk, "Sosŏl munhak," 347.
114 *Kŭrigo amumaldo haji anhatta*, 10–11; Han Chŏm-tol, "Han'guk e mich'in Togil chŏnhu sosŏl," 270.
115 Kang Sang-hui, "Sosŏljŏk chinjŏngsŏng," 427.
116 Sin Chun-bong, "Chingjingjingjing ulmyŏnsŏ."
117 Sin Chun-bong, "Chingjingjingjing ulmyŏnsŏ." Even though the author does not reveal her friend's name in this interview, a fourth-year Seoul National University student by the name of Pak Hye-jŏng committed suicide in 1986 chastising herself for being "cowardly and insincere" about her commitment to the movement. Kim Myŏng-u, "Hollo sidaerŭl kominhaettŏn."
118 Kim Ŭn-ha, "386 sedae yŏsŏng huildam," 111.
119 Kim Ŭn-ha, "386 sedae yŏsŏng huildam," 112.
120 Chŏng Hong-su, "Kohae ŭi chari," 346.
121 Referring to extracurricular clubs at universities, many "circles" were movement oriented, places where politically conscious students would come together to conduct teach-in seminars for one another and to discuss current affairs. State surveillance forced circles to operate underground from the 1970s until the mid-1980s. In the 1980s, circles also existed in factories, farming villages, and slum areas as the basic organizing units of grassroots activism.
122 Chŏng Hong-su, "Kohae ŭi chari," 347.
123 Cho Yŏn-chŏng, "'Kwangju'rŭl hyŏnjaehwa," 120.
124 *Regat'o*, 391; quoted in Cho Yŏn-chŏng, "'Kwangju'rŭl hyŏnjaehwa," 121–22; also quoted in Chŏng Hong-su, "Kohae ŭi chari," 347.
125 *Regat'o*, 64; cited in Chŏng Hong-su, "Kohae ŭi chari," 347.
126 *Regat'o*, 391; quoted in Chŏng Hong-su, "Kohae ŭi chari," 347.
127 Chŏng Hong-su, "Kohae ŭi chari," 348. Legato is a musical performance technique that produces "fluid, continuous motion between notes."
128 Sim Chin-kyŏng, "Kwŏn Yŏ-sŏn," 354.
129 Sim Chin-kyŏng, "Kwŏn Yŏ-sŏn," 357.
130 *Regat'o*, 391; Cho Yŏn-chŏng, "'Kwangju'rŭl hyŏnjaehwa," 122.
131 Cho Yŏn-chŏng, "'Kwangju'rŭl hyŏnjaehwa," 122.
132 Chŏng Hong-su, "Kohae ŭi chari," 348.
133 *Regat'o*, 234; Cho Yŏn-chŏng, "'Kwangju'rŭl hyŏnjaehwa," 117, 121.
134 Cho Yŏn-chŏng, "'Kwangju'rŭl hyŏnjaehwa," 101–2.
135 Benjamin, "Theses on the Philosophy of History," 257–58.
136 Flatley, "Modernism," 65.

3. THE PARK CHUNG-HEE SYNDROME, MASS MEDIA, AND "CULTURE WAR"

1 Sin Tong-ho, "Pak Chŏng-hŭi," 21.
2 Sin Tong-ho, "Pak Chŏng-hŭi," 21.

3   Kim Dae-jung, one of the 1997 presidential candidates who had been persecuted by Park Chung-hee in the 1970s, pledged to fund the construction of the Park Chung-hee memorial building if he were elected. Another candidate, Yi In-je, tried to woo voters by emphasizing his facial resemblance to Park. Some designers also came up with modified "Saemaŭl jackets" that used to be worn by government bureaucrats and village leaders during the 1970s new village movement (*Saemaŭl undong*), one of Park's signature policies; art collectors' demand for Park's calligraphy rose, and the number of visitors to the house where Park was born and spent his youth increased dramatically. Cho Ŭn-hŭi, "Pak Chŏng-hŭi hyungnaenaemyŏn," 35; Han Ki-hong, "'Kakha,' tangsini kŭripsŭmnida," 33–34; Kim Ho-sŏp, "Nuga Pak Chŏnghŭirŭl," 31.

4   The "revival" of Park Chung-hee also included a production of an opera titled *A Superman with Much Tears* (*Nunmulmanhŭn ch'oin*), written by Yi In-hwa, the author I discuss later in the chapter. O Mi-hwan, "Pak Chŏng-hŭi tarun op'era."

5   There are numerous scholarly and popular works on the Park Chung-hee syndrome. See, among others, Han'guk chŏngch'i yŏn'guhoe, *Pak Chŏng-hŭi rŭl nŏmŏsŏ*; Hyŏndaesa charyoban, *Pak Chŏng-hui p'yŏngga*; Chŏn Chae-ho, "Pak Chŏng-hŭi robut'ŏ yŏksa rŭl"; Kang Chun-man, "'Pak Chŏng-hŭi sindŭrŏm'"; Seungsook Moon, "Cultural Politics of Remembering Park Chung Hee," *Harvard Asia Quarterly* 11 (Spring/Summer 2008): 26–44.

6   See, among others, Lee, *Making of Minjung*, 34–37.

7   For a similar case with Mussolini's granddaughter in Italy, see Robert A. Ventresca, "Mussolini's Ghost: Italy's Duce in History and Memory," *History and Memory* 18:1 (2006).

8   Cho Kap-che, *Yugo!* 1:5.

9   Kim Pyŏng-ju, "Ch'ŏndanggwa chiongmank'ŭm," 33. On various assessments of Park and the period, see, among others, Hyŏndaesa charyoban, *Pak Chŏng-hui p'yŏngga*; Chŏn Chae-ho, *Pak Chŏng-hŭi tae Pak Chŏng-hŭi*; Kwŏn Podŭrae et al., *Pak Chŏng-hŭi modŏnijŭm*; Lee, *Developmental Dictatorship*; Kim and Sorensen, *Reassessing the Park Chung Hee Era*; Kim and Vogel, *Park Chung Hee Era*.

10 Son Ho-ch'ŏl, "Pak Chŏng-hŭi chŏnggwŏn," 41.

11 During his eighteen years of rule, Park Chung-hee declared martial law three times, lasting a total of thirty-one months; a garrison decree (*wisuryŏng*) three times, lasting for five months; and nine emergency measures, which were in place for sixty-nine months. O Pyŏng-hŏn, "Kunbu tokchae ŭi k'al," 500; quoted in Chŏng Sang-ho, "Pak Chŏng-hŭi sindŭrŏm," 90. A garrison decree is usually issued as "a military contingency and has almost the same effect as martial law, except that it allows the continued functioning of civil administration and 'freedom of the press' in the affected area." Lee and Kim, *South Korean Democratization Movement*, 88n12.

12 Hwang, "Ruling Discourse," 12–20. In 1961 when Park took state power with his military coup, annual per capita income of South Korea was $92, putting the country 78th in the world. In the next eighteen years, its yearly average rate of growth was 8.3% and in 1979 annual per capita income was $1,747, 48th in the world. Chang Ha-sŏng, *Han'guk chabonjuŭi*, 89.

13 Hwang, "Ruling Discourse," 12.

14 Hwang, "Ruling Discourse," 12. For a scholarly effort to reassess the Park Chung-hee period centered on the concept of mass dictatorship that argues that there was widespread support for Park, see Im Chi-hyŏn [Lim Jie-Hyun] and Kim Yŏng-u, *Taejung tokchae*.
15 See, among others, Ham Chae-bong et al., "Pak Chŏng-hŭi." For a cultural and social history of the 1970s, see, among others, Kwŏn Podŭrae et al., *Pak Chŏng-hŭi modŏnijŭm*.
16 Chŏn Chae-ho, "Pak Chŏng-hŭi robut'ŏ yŏksa rŭl," 37; Chŏng Sang-ho, "Pak Chŏng-hŭi sindŭrŏm," 75–76.
17 Chŏng Sang-ho, "Pak Chŏng-hŭi sindŭrŏm," 77–78. Chun Doo-hwan ordered cancellation of a large-scale commemoration event of Park Chung-hee that the Association of Friends for National Restoration (Minjok chunghŭng tongjihoe) was organizing in 1985. Minjok chunghŭng tongjihoe was founded in December 1984 to memorialize Park's legacy and included former members of the ruling Democratic Republic Party, former cabinet members of the Park government, and high-ranking military officers who had served during his regime, as well as members of Yusin chŏng'uhoe (usually abridged as Yuchŏnghoe). Park Chung-hee appointed one-third of the National Assembly members according to the 1972 Yusin Constitution, many of whom became members of Yuchŏnghoe. It functioned primarily as Park's private political party to influence the legislature and also its members performed as "Royal Guards" in the National Assembly, often engaging in physical confrontations with opposition party members. It was disbanded in 1980 at the start of the Chun Doo-hwan administration. Hwang Tong-il, "'Ŭngdang chon'gyŏngbadŭlmank'ŭm padŭlppun'"; Chŏng Un-hyŏn, "Pak Chŏng-hŭi sidae," 172–74.
18 Chŏn Chae-ho, "Pak Chŏng-hŭi robut'ŏ yŏksa rŭl," 37.
19 Chŏng Sang-ho, "Pak Chŏng-hŭi sindŭrŏm," 78–80.
20 Chŏn Chae-ho, "Pak Chŏng-hŭi robut'ŏ yŏksa rŭl," 38. Only 13.7 percent responded that he made more mistakes than accomplishments.
21 Yi Ch'ung-hun, "'Yŏngung' ŭi chŏngch'ihak," 252. Chŏng Sang-ho, "Pak Chŏng-hŭi sindŭrŏm," 83–86.
22 Hanahoe was composed of the eleventh and twelfth classes of the Korea Military Academy (Yukkun sakwan hakkyo). Doo-hwan and Roh Tae-woo were the leaders of this club since the 1979 coup, and their positions in key positions in the military since then put them in command during the Kwangju massacre. Chun had become the head of the Defense Security Command as well as the director of the Korean Central Intelligence Agency (KCIA) by May 1980, while Roh Tae-woo had become the commander of the Capital Security Command, one of the key military security positions. Kim Chae-gyun, *5.18 kwa Han'guk*, 137. On the demolition of the former Japanese general-government building, see, among others, Kim Sŏng-nye, "P'ungsuwa singminji sigi"; Ha Sang-bok, "Ŭijehyŏngsŏngŭi chŏngch'ihak."
23 For further details on the process of and the reasons for the Kim Young-sam government enacting the Special Acts Concerning the May 18 Democratization Movement, see, among others, Lee, "From the Streets," 60–69.
24 Cumings, *Korea's Place*, 391.
25 I discuss this in length in chapter 1.

26　Pak Wŏn-sun, "Paesangŭi ch'ŭngmyŏnesŏ," 145.
27　See, among others, Aguilar, *Memory and Amnesia*.
28　"Kimdaet'ongnyŏng t'ŭkpyŏldamhwa ŭimi"; Pak Wŏn-sun, "Paesangŭi ch'ŭngmyŏnesŏ," 147. Kim Young-sam further declared, "We cannot allow our unfortunate past to forever shackle [us], preventing us from progressing forward.... There should not be any retaliatory vent to satisfy one's grudge [*popokjŏkin hanp'uri*]. Let us not forget [history] but let us courageously forgive and reconcile." Quoted in Pak Wŏn-sun, "Paesangŭi ch'ŭngmyŏnesŏ," 147. See also Kang Chŏng-gu, "Kim Yŏngsam chŏnggwŏn."
29　For further details, see Lee, "From the Street," 62–63.
30　The sum was speculated to have been over 500 billion won (US$650 million), of which 170 billion won (US$215 million) was reputedly remaining in the coffer of the ruling party when Roh left office in February 1993. Kim Chae-gyun, *5.18 kwa Han'guk*, 179; Han, "Kwangju and Beyond," 1006.
31　Chŏng Hae-gu, "Pak Chŏng-hŭi sindŭrŏm," 60–64. Yi Chae-hyŏn, a literary critic, opined that "at the core of the Park syndrome is a sense of betrayal." See Kim Ho-sŏp, "Nuga Pak Chŏnghŭirŭl purŭnŭn'ga," 31.
32　Hong Se-hwa, "Pak Chŏng-hŭi sindŭrom," 47.
33　Nietzche chided that Germans had an excessive attachment to the past, believing that there was a reason for everything that happened. Cited in Huyssen, *Present Pasts*, 3.
34　Shapiro, "Whose (Which) History," 1–3.
35　Huyssen, *Twilight Memories*, 9; quoted in Olick, *Politics of Regret*, 183.
36　Lee, *Making of Minjung*, 23–69; Bodnar, *Remaking America*, 13–20.
37　Choi, *Democracy after Democratization*, 128–31. It was only a small group of journalists who went on to organize a movement to democratize the press. They, along with a small number of lawyers, gave rise to the discourse of human rights that became the moral backbone of the human rights and democratization movement of the 1970s. See, among others, Chang, *Protest Dialectics*.
38　Hong Yun-gi, "Tagŭkjŏk hyŏndaesŏng," 62n4.
39　White, *Tropics of Discourse*; Ricoeur, *Time and Narrative*; Feldman, "Political Terror," 61.
40　Literature covering this topic is far too numerous to mention all, but see, among others, Halbwachs, *On Collective Memory*. On some of the problems of collective memory studies, see, among others, Kansteiner, "Finding Meaning in Memory."
41　Connerton, *How Societies Remember*; Feldman, "Political Terror," 61.
42　Feldman, "Political Terror," 61.
43　Feldman, "Political Terror," 63.
44　*Chosun Ilbo* has continuously invoked Park Chung-hee and his policies as a role model for other countries. During the 2010 earthquake in Haiti, describing the catastrophe as a typical case of a third world country, a former South Korean ambassador to Colombia wrote in *Chosun Ilbo*, "The core of the problem is how to awaken the people's consciousness buried for a long time in the habitual routine of poverty and to help them regain hope." He offered the new village movement of the Park Chung-hee regime as a solution: "If the *saemaul* movement was about reforming people's minds and giving them back their dreams, it might be exactly

what these people need." Cho Kap-tong, "Aitie saemaŭrundong"; cited in Ha, "Mass Dictatorship," 50.
45 Chŏn Chae-ho, "Pak Chŏng-hŭi robut'ŏ yŏksa rŭl," 44.
46 Kim Chŏng-nyŏm, Ch'oebin'guk esŏ sŏnjin'guk.
47 Chŏn Chae-ho, "Pak Chŏng-hŭi robut'ŏ yŏksa rŭl," 42–43.
48 The serialization was later published as a monograph. Kim Chŏng-nyŏm, *Kim Chŏng-nyŏm chŏngch'i hoegorok*; Chŏng Hae-gu, "Pak Chŏng-hŭi sindŭrŏm," 55.
49 Cho Kap-che first serialized *Nae mudŏm e ch'im ŭl paet'ŏra* in *Chosun Ilbo* and *Wolgan Chosun* (Monthly Chosun) and later published as a monograph in eight volumes. In 2006, Cho published a revised version in thirteen volumes as *Biography of Park Chung-hee* (*Park Chung-hee chŏn'gi*, Cho Kap-che tatk'om).
50 See, among others, Yu In-gyŏng, "Pan'golgijaesŏ kŭgunon'gaegŭro." Incidentally, it is believed that Park Chung-hee used to dodge journalists' questions by saying, "Spit on my grave," the title of Cho Kap-che's biography. No Chae-hyŏn, "'*Nae mudŏme ch'imŭl paet'ŏra*.'" Cho's refusal to acknowledge any misrule of Park Chung-hee after his death seems to have provided him with a sense of moral high ground, a badge of honor, as it were, which also elicited a certain degree of fascination about Cho among the public as well. Jürgen Habermas notes that for Carl Schmitt and Martin Heidegger, their public refusal to admit their guilt or their political mistake committed during the Nazi period lent them a certain cachet among the young intellectuals whom they continued to influence in post-1945 West Germany. Schmitt infamously asked, "Which was actually more indecent, supporting Hitler in 1933 or spitting on him in 1945?" Habermas, *Berlin Republic*, 108.
51 Cho writes, "The process of democratization in the last ten years was a process of pursuing regional interest, individual interest, partisan interest in the name of democracy, freedom, equality, and human rights, thereby destroying national and public interest." *Nae mudŏm e ch'im ŭl paet'ŏra*, 1:13; quoted in Chŏn Chae-ho, "Pak Chŏng-hŭi robut'ŏ yŏksa rŭl," 45.
52 Cho Kap-che, *Yugo!* 1:5–6; quoted in Chŏn Chae-ho, "Pak Chŏng-hŭi robut'ŏ yŏksa rŭl," 44. *Yugo!* is considered by many commentators as a work that still bears the mark of Cho Kap-che as an investigative journalist, before he turned to a hagiographer of Park Chung-hee.
53 Cho's first attempt at writing Park's biography began with the publication of *Park Chung-hee: Time of Discontent and Misfortune* (*Pak Chŏng-hŭi 1: Pulman'gwa purunŭi sewŏl*) in 1992 (Kkach'i). He had planned to publish a multivolume work but stopped after only the first volume was published. Then he began the serialization of *Nae mudŏm e ch'im ŭl paet'ŏra* in *Chosun Ilbo* from 1997.
54 Cho Kap-che, *Nae mudŏm e ch'im ŭl paet'ŏra*, 1:140; Hong Yun-gi, "Tagŭkjŏk hyŏndaesŏng," 75. On Park Chung-hee's nationalism, see, among others, Chŏn Chae-ho, *Pak Chŏng-hŭi tae Pak Chŏng-hŭi*, 225–54.
55 Cho Kap-che, *Nae mudŏm e ch'im ŭl paet'ŏra*; quoted in Chŏn Chae-ho, "Pak Chŏng-hŭi robut'ŏ yŏksa rŭl," 44.
56 Pak Chŏng-hŭi, *Minjokŭi chŏryŏk*, 119; quoted in Hong Yun-gi, "Tagŭkjŏk hyŏndaesŏng," 76n26.
57 Hong Yun-gi, "Tagŭkjŏk hyŏndaesŏng," 76n26.

58 Hong Yun-gi, "Tagŭkjŏk hyŏndaesŏng," 76.
59 Nietzsche, "On the Uses and Disadvantages of History," 72.
60 Jenkins, "Nietzsche's Use of Monumental History."
61 Lindroos, *Now-Time Image-Space*, 70; This myth of monumentality is also aided by, for instance, national holidays and ceremonies, and the celebration of victims of war on memorial days.
62 Nietzsche, "On the Uses and Disadvantages of History," 70–71; quoted in Jenkins, "Nietzsche's Use of Monumental History," 173.
63 Jenkins, "Nietzsche's Use of Monumental History," 173; Han Man-su, "90yŏndae pesŭt'ŭsellŏ sosŏl," 202. Here, Han does not mention monumental history at all, but his analysis of the novels of the 1990s encapsulates Nietzsche's notion of monumental history.
64 Huyssen, *Twilight Memories*, 9.
65 Hutchinson, *Reaganism, Thatcherism*, 19–20. Hutchinson writes that there was also an effort to reconstruct the 1940s and 1950s in a way to minimize "centrist consensus and state intervention" and to emphasize individual effort to bring their own prosperity without state regulation or welfare. Hutchinson, *Reaganism, Thatcherism*, 20.
66 Han Man-su, "90yŏndae pesŭt'ŭsellŏ sosŏl," 200. Four out of five best sellers of the 1990s that Han discusses were also authored by men.
67 Hong Yun-gi, "Tagŭkjŏk hyŏndaesŏng," 76. Critic Chin Chung-gwŏn goes so far as to suggest that Yi In-hwa's *A Man's Road* as well as Cho Kap-che's biography "contain all of the aspects of fascist aesthetics." Chin Chung-gwŏn, "Pak Chŏng-hŭiwa angmajuŭi," 587n8. Kim Chŏng-nan, a literary critic, also finds fascist aesthetics both in Yi's novel and Cho's biography. Kim Chŏng-nan, "Nuga yŏng'ungŭl ch'annŭn'ga," 384–89.
68 Yi In-hwa, *"In'gan ŭi kil* e nat'anan," 276; quoted in Yi Ch'ung-hun, "'Yŏngung' ŭi chŏngch'ihak,'" 254.
69 See Chin Chung-gwŏn, "Chugŭn tokchaejaŭi sahoe," 359.
70 Kang Yŏng-hŭi, *"In'gan ui kil* ro," 81. In this interview, Yi mentions the title as *The Grand Dream (Taemang)* rather than *Ryōma Goes His Way*. In its Korean translation, *The Grand Dream* comprises three volumes that detail political, economic, cultural, and military dimensions of Japan's nation-building process from the time of Tokugawa to the Russo-Japanese War. Only the third volume of *The Grand Dream* is attributed to Shiba Ryōtarō. *Ryōma Goes His Way* was first serialized in the newspaper *Sankei* from 1962 to 1966 before being published as a book.
71 Ha Chŏng-il, "P'asijŭm ŭi sinhwa," 67; Kang Yŏng-hŭi, *"In'gan ui kil* ro," 80. Yi said that he had aspired to write a *kungmin sosŏl* such as *The Grand Dream*, but it is not clear what he means by kungmin sosŏl, which is different from *kungmin munhak*. There are two types of kungmin munhak (national literature), both of which arose during the colonial period. One type arose mainly as a reaction against the leftist literature of the KAPF (Korea Artista Proleta Federacio) and is considered "nationalist" as opposed to the KAPF'S class-oriented bent, and includes well-known writers such as Yi Kwang-su and Ch'oe Nam-sŏn. Another category refers to literary works considered "imperial subjects literature," such as that of Chang

Hyŏk-chu and Hyŏn Yŏng-sŏp. See, among others, Hughes, *Literature and Film*, 25; Ha Chŏng-il, "Minjok munhak"; Kim Yun-sik, "Han'guk kŭndaemunhaksa." Yi In-hwa's notion of kungmin sosŏl most likely refers to a novel that has popular appeal.

72 Yi In-hwa, "Chakkaŭi mal," in *In'gan ŭi kil*, 1:6; quoted Ha Chŏng-il, "P'asijŭm ŭi sinhwa," 70–71.

73 *In'gan ŭi kil*, 1:193; quoted in Ha Chong-il, "P'asijŭm ŭi sinhwa," 69.

74 *In'gan ŭi kil*, 1:194–95; Ha Chong-il, "P'asijŭm ŭi sinhwa," 69. The bulk of the novel's second volume is devoted to Park's alleged plan to organize a guerrilla unit among the rank and file of Korean soldiers serving in the Japanese military in Manchuria. A popular TV drama titled *The Eyes of Dawn* (*Yŏmyŏngŭi nundongja*), which aired from late 1991 until early 1992, also features Park as leading a contingent of ethnic Korean soldiers in the Japanese Manchurian military to Korea during the colonial period. Historians, as well as former armed resistant fighters of the colonial period, have denied that Park was ever involved in any such plan, but the claim has persisted. See No Tong-hyŏn, "Pak Chŏng-hŭiŭi Kwangbokkun naet'ongsŏrŭl kŏjit"; Yi Chun-sik, "Pak Chŏng-hŭiga Kwangbokkun?"

75 Yi In-hwa, "Sŏnak ttwiŏnŏmŭn chinjŏnghan chidoja."

76 Hong Yun-gi, "Tagŭkjŏk hyŏndaesŏng," 78.

77 Ha Chŏng-il, "P'asijŭm ŭi sinhwa," 65.

78 Yi In-hwa, *In'gan ŭi kil*, 1:96; cited in Ha Chŏng-il, "P'asijŭm ŭi sinhwa," 67–68.

79 Yi In-hwa, *In'gan ŭi kil*, 1:116–17; cited in Ha Chŏng-il, "P'asijŭm ŭi sinhwa," 68. Usually, humans run away from spirits, not the other way around.

80 It was also voted "Best Book Chosen by Readers" for two years in a row in 1993 and 1994, and a 2000 Gallup survey found Kim as the second-most-liked author by Koreans. Yi Hae-nyŏn, "T'alssingminjuŭi," 225n7.

81 Concerned about the Nixon doctrine's policy to reduce US military presence in Asia and to utilize the nuclear option as a bargaining chip with the United States, among other reasons, Park Chung-hee authorized a program to develop nuclear weapons technology in late 1974, which was suspended by December 1976 under immense pressure from the United States. For further details on Park's nuclear quest, see, among others, Hong, "Search for Deterrence." According to Peter Hayes and Chung-in Moon, who examined the declassified documents released by the CIA in 2005, Park's proliferation activity continued for at least another two years. Hayes and Moon, "Park Chung Hee."

82 Kim Chin-myŏng, *Mugunghwa kkoti p'iŏtsŭmnida*, 1:474, 2:117. There was a widespread rumor in South Korea that the CIA was involved in Park's assassination to halt his nuclear weapons development. See, among others, Hayes and Moon, "Park Chung Hee," n14; Cho Kap-che, *Yugo!* 1:4. Nam Chae-hŭi, a former journalist and minister of labor during the Kim Young-sam administration, also said in an interview that he believed the United States might have been behind Park's assassination. Nam Chae-hŭi, "Wŏllo ŏllonin chŏngch'iin Nam Chae-hŭiga pon taet'ongnyŏngdŭl," pt. 3.

83 In the novel, Madame Sin, the owner of a high-end bar/restaurant that Park frequents, relates the story that Park once told her, of how he was moved to tears twice during his visit to [West] Germany. The first when he saw the long and straight highways of Germany which reminded him of the dirt-covered and barren

land of Korea. The second time was when Korean residents in Munich gave him a warm welcome; many of these Koreans were leading difficult lives as migrants working as miners and nurses. Both events made him further resolve to dedicate his life to improve the situation of Korea and to bring prosperity to the Korean people. Kim Chin-myŏng, *Mugunghwa kkoti p'iŏtsŭmnida*, 2:140.

84 Kim Chin-myŏng, *Mugunghwa kkoti p'iŏtsŭmnida*, 2:141–42.
85 Mun Hŭng-sul, "Minjokchuŭi irŭm," 131. A positive review of this novel praised it as an expression of postcolonial nationalism. See Yi Hae-nyŏn, "T'alssingminjuŭi." Kim Chin-myŏng went on to publish a number of novels that deal with nationalist themes and were highly popular. See Yi Hae-nyŏn, "T'alssingminjuŭi," 224n6.
86 Mun Hŭng-sul, "Minjokchuŭi irŭm."
87 Yi Hye-wŏn, "Chich'igo pŏrimbadŭn."
88 Kim Chŏng-nan, "Nuga yŏng'ungŭl," 380.
89 Kim Chŏng-hyŏn, *Abŏji*, 34, 36–37.
90 Cho Myŏng-gi, "90nyŏndae taejung," 133.
91 Cho Myŏng-gi, "90nyŏndae taejung," 133.
92 There is as of yet no outright rebellion of children against fathers in Korean cultural output, and any discussion of such rebellion or patricide concerns collaborators with the Japanese during the colonial period. For example, Pak Chŏng-sŏk's "Kill the Father" (*Abŏjirŭl chugyŏra*) is a play loosely based on the organization called Patricide Society (*Salbukye*) that reputedly was founded with an aim to kill fathers who collaborated with Japanese. "Abŏjirŭl chugyŏra," written and directed by Pak Chŏng-sŏk, performed by Kŭktan paramp'ul, Yŏn'gŭksirhŏmsil, Seoul, March 21–April 1, 2007. It appears that the actual Patricide Society existed not during the colonial period but in the immediate post-1945 period, and its aim was to eliminate fathers who were either collaborators with the Japanese or who opposed communism. Sohaengsŏng, "Abŏjirŭl chugyŏra." In Han Sŭng-wŏn [Sung-won Han]'s 1989 novel *Father and Son* (*Abŏji wa adŭl*), the main protagonist, a university student movement activist in the 1980s, declares to his own conservative father that he feels affinity for the sons of the Patricide Society that was organized sometime between 1945 and 1950. In the novel, the murder of some "reactionary elements" are attributed to the Patricide Society. Han, *Father and Son*, 147–48, 152. In a 2015 film *Assassination* (*Amsal*), the daughter, a first-rate sniper and a leader in the resistance movement based in Manchuria during the colonial period, finds that her target is her own biological father. A ruthless collaborator, the father had killed his own wife (the sniper's mother) earlier for her assistance to the nationalists and is even willing to kill his own long-lost twin daughter—the sniper. The daughter cannot bring herself to pull the trigger aimed at her father—he is eventually killed by a former member of the Patricide Society, who had betrayed the cause and became a hired assassin but decides to help the sniper. *Amsal*, directed by Dong-hoon Choi [Ch'oe Tong-hun], Showbox (2015).
93 A filmic representation of this is *Ode to My Father* (*Kukche sijang*), released in 2014.
94 See, among others, Han Man-su, "90yŏndae pesŭt'ŭsellŏ sosŏl," 193.
95 On the issue of South Korea's geopolitical location in the Cold War structure and US support for South Korea's economic development, see, among others, Cumings, "Asian Crisis, Democracy."

96 Numerous critics point out the mass media's overzealous reaction to this novel. See, among others, Kang Chun-man, "Wae Pak Chŏng-hŭi." For the role of *Chosun Ilbo* in promoting Yi In-hwa, see, among others, Han Yun-hyŏng, *Ant'i* Chosun *undongsa*, 195-96.
97 Chin Chung-gwŏn, "Chugŭn tokchaejaŭi sahoe," 344.
98 Sŏl Chun-kyu, "Somunnan chanch'i," 425-26.
99 On Yi Mun-yŏl, see, among others, Yi Nam-ho, *Yi Mun-yŏl*; Yi Myŏng-wŏn, "Yi Mun-yŏl nonjaeng." Literary critic Cho Yŏng-il calls Yi the "most erudite novelist" (*kajang paksikhan sosŏlga*) in South Korea. Cho Yŏng-il, "Mŏnamŏn segyemunhak," 268. Yi Mun-yŏl also reportedly sold the highest numbers of novels in South Korea as of 2001. Ku Pon-gwŏn, "Yi Mun-yŏl sosŏrŭi 'pisu'rŭl majŭn kŏsŭn?"
100 Kim Yŏng-min, "Yŏ Un-hyŏng, Yi Mun-yŏl," 139.
101 For further discussion of various special laws enacted during this period, see, among others, Cho, "Transitional Justice"; Kim, "Long Road toward Truth."
102 Kim, "Long Road toward Truth," 525. Kim Dae-jung established the first truth commission in 2000. When this commission completed its work in 2004, the National Assembly felt that a further, much broader Truth and Reconciliation Commission was needed, and in 2005 it passed a law establishing the Truth and Reconciliation Commission (TRC). See, among others, Cho, "Transitional Justice," 607-10; United States Institute of Peace, "Truth Commission."
103 The Basic Act calls for inquiry into the following: "(i) the anti-Japanese liberation movement before and under the Japanese Occupation, (ii) the history of overseas Koreans who have maintained the sovereignty of Korea or enhanced national capability since the Japanese Occupation, (iii) the unlawful killings of civilians from August 15, 1945, to the Korean War, (iv) death, injury, and disappearance as a result of unlawful or conspicuously improper exercises of state authority, such as conduct destructive to constitutional order, serious human rights violations and cases of fabricated facts from August 15, 1945 through the period of authoritarian rule, (v) terror, human rights violations, violence, massacre, and suspicious deaths committed by those who denied the legitimacy of the Republic of Korea or were hostile to the Republic of Korea from August 15, 1945 to the period of authoritarian rule, and (vi) cases for which the Truth and Reconciliation Commission has recognized the necessity of investigation." Cho, "Transitional Justice," 608.
104 Pae Yŏng-dae, "Yi Mun-yŏl ege tŭnnŭnda." This and the next three paragraphs, including the quotes, are from the interview.
105 Chŏnkyojo was founded in 1989 as an independent nationwide teachers' union to serve as an alternative to the existing, officially sanctioned Association of Teachers, with the goal of creating a "nationalistic, democratic and humane" education system; it was not legalized until 1999. In 2016, it was declared illegal once again and in 2020 made legal. Yi Mun-yŏl calls the teachers of Chŏnkyojo and undongkwŏn "evil spirits" in his medium-length story, "Runaway Evil Spirit" ("*Taranan angnyŏng*"), in *Sultanji wa chanŭl kkŭrŏdanggimyŏ*, 42-133.
106 Kim Yong-gyu, "Sidaewaŭi hwahaerŭl," 443.
107 For further details, see Han Yun-hyŏng, *Ant'i* Chosun *undongsa*, 164-82.

108 "Sultanji wa chanŭl kkŭrŏdanggimyŏ" in *Sultanji wa chanŭl kkŭrŏdanggimyŏ*, 159–61. See also Kim Tong-min, "Tasi Yi Mun-yŏl." On *ŏn'gwan*, see, among others, Ch'oe Sŭng-hŭi, *Chosŏn ch'ogi ŏn'gwan, ŏllon yŏn'gu*.
109 *Homo eksek'uttansŭ*. Yi has coined the term *homo executans* to refer those who ruthlessly eliminate their political opponents once they ascend to a position of power, and the obvious target of his fury was the previously mentioned 386-generation politicians in the Kim Dae-jung and Roh Moo-hyun administrations.
110 *Sŏntaek*, 224, 75–76; quoted in Kim Chŏng-in, "Sŏntaek," 31, 34.
111 Lady Chang: "Without doubt many things in life do change, but there are certain things that do not. Some such [values] overcome the destructive power of time and survive [to present day], and some principles overcome the vicissitudes of an era and still apply [to contemporary situations]. Such [values and principles] are to be kept in mind as one follows the path of a daughter." *Sŏntaek*, 18–19; quoted in Sin Sŭng-hŭi, "*Sŏntaek* kwa 'Ingmyŏng ui sŏm,'" 57.
112 Considering himself to be an iconoclast standing against the main currents of the contemporary society, he said that readers' criticisms of *Choice* were the price he pays for his "refusal to comply with the dominant currents of the era." Yi Mun-yŏl, *Sidaewaŭi purhwa*, 66; quoted in Kim Yŏng-min, "Yŏ Un-hyŏng, Yi Mun-yŏl," 139.
113 For further discussion on Pok's science fictions, see, among others, Pok To-hun, "Han'gugŭi SF."
114 See, among others, Kim Sŏng-dong, "Siryue panyŏkhanŭn." Here, journalists also play a key role in portraying Pok as such. For example, the journalists credit Pok's previous 1992 publication *Hyŏnsil kwa chihyang* as responsible for the "coming out" of the erstwhile "lonely" liberalists at the time—due to the reputed dominance of anti-capitalistic, socialist tendencies of intellectuals at the time. Kim So-jŏng and Kim Kyu-t'ae, "Chisigindŭre taehan Pok Kŏ-il ŭi tangbu."
115 Ko Chong-sŏk, *Ko Chong-sŏk*, 13. In 2017, Pok wrote and directed a play about Park Chung-hee titled *The Path of Park Chung-hee* (*Pak Chŏng-hŭiŭi kil*) on the occasion of Park's one hundredth birthday, extolling Park's pursuit of economic development that was "led by the state but executed according to market principles." Chŏng Chang-yŏl, "Pak Chŏng-hŭiwa Yi Pyŏng-ch'ŏrŭi mannami Taehanmin'gugŭi unmyŏngŭl pakkwŏtta." The play was also published as a book in Korean and Japanese: *Pak Chŏng-hŭiŭi kil* (Pugaenp'ip'ŭl, 2017).
116 Pok Kŏ-il, "Kyŏngjejŏk chayujuŭijadŭrŭi kwaje," 3–7.
117 See *Kukcheŏ sidaeŭi minjogŏ* [National language in the era of international language] (Munhakkwa chisŏngsa, 1998); Kim Sŏng-dong, "Siryue panyŏkhanŭn."
118 Pok Kŏ-il, *Hyŏnsil kwa chihyang*, 13.
119 Pok Kŏ-il, *Inyŏm ŭi him*, 179, 191.
120 Pok Kŏ-il, *Chindan kwa Ch'ŏbang*, 141; Han Su-yŏng, *Sosŏl kwa ilsangsŏng*, 308–11.
121 Pok's books published by the Center for Free Enterprise include some sensational titles such as *Ways to Repel Minjung-ism* (*Minjungjuŭirŭl maganaenŭn kil*, 2002), but the majority deal with issues related to liberalism in South Korea such as *Liberalism in South Korea* (*Han'guk ŭi chayujuŭi*, 2007) and *Trials of Liberalism* (*Chayujuŭi ŭi siryŏn*, 2009).

122 Pok Kŏ-il, *Moksŏng chamŏnjip*, 234, 238; quoted in Kang Chun-man, "Pok Kŏ-il ŭi sosŏl," 185.
123 Chang Kang-myŏng, "Pyŏnmyŏng ŭl ch'ajasŏ." Pok Kŏ-il has also discoursed on the issue of collaborators with Japanese colonial regime, which I think is one of the more reasonable approaches presented by conservatives. See Pok Kŏ-il, "Chaengjŏm."
124 Yi Mun-yŏl, *Sidaewaŭi purhwa*, 305.
125 Pok Kŏ-il, "Hondon'gwa chilssŏ," 355.
126 Kim Yong-gyu, "Sidaewaŭi hwahaerŭl," 444.
127 Kang Chun-man, "Yi Mun-yŏl ŭl almyŏn," 138. Pok's other titles of "political" novels include *The Unseen Hand* (*Poiji annŭn son*, Munhakkwa chisŏngsa, 2006), which promotes market economy and *Ground Zero* (*Kŭraundŭ chero*, Kyŏngdŏk ch'ulp'ansa, 2007), also another political jab at the Kim Dae-jung government's policy toward North Korea.
128 For a further discussion of the evolution of the ideas, roles, and characteristics of the public intellectual in South Korea, see Lee, "Public Intellectuals." On Chang Chun-ha, one of the public intellectuals who is widely presumed to have been killed by Park Chung-hee's order, see, among others, Pak Kyŏng-su, *Chang Chun-ha: Minjokchuŭijaŭi kil* [Chang Chun-ha: The path of a nationalist] (Tolbegae, 2013).
129 Lee, "Public Intellectuals"; Kim and Chang, "Entry of Past Activists."
130 Novelist Hwang Sŏk-yŏng, the doyen of literature of the downtrodden, also briefly associated with the Lee Myung-bak government in 2008 but soon distanced himself.
131 The conservative mass media's cozy relationship with chaebŏl is not only ideologically driven but also economical, as they rely heavily on revenue from chaebŏl advertisements to make up for losses in the increasingly competitive media market. See Kim Sang-jo, "Samsung konghwaguk," 36–38.
132 Kang Chun-man characterizes this phenomenon as a "tendency to privilege culture" (*munhwa t'ŭkkwŏnjuŭi*): "it is the kind of sentiment [that is prevalent in Korean society] that takes for granted that those in cultural sphere can intervene in societal issues without any accountability, with the belief that they do not enjoy as much political power or earn as much as those who work in political and financial spheres." Kang Chun-man, "Yi Mun-yŏl ŭl almyŏn," 137.
133 I point out some of these issues in *Making of the Minjung*, 294–99. See also Kim Wŏn, "80nyŏndaee taehan 'kiŏk,'" 12–13; Yi Sang-nok, "1980nyŏndae chungsanch'ŭng tamnon," 279–82.

4. THE RISE OF NEW RIGHT HISTORIOGRAPHY AND ITS TRIUMPHALIST DISCOURSE

1 Pak Chi-hyang et al., "Mŏrimal," 12.
2 See, among others, Em, "Historians."
3 Pak Chi-hyang et al., "Mŏrimal," 12.
4 See Im Tae-sik, "*Haebang chŏnhusa ŭi chaeinsik*," 12–13.
5 On the postpublication developments concerning some of the contributors to the volume whose positions depart from that of the New Right, see Pak T'ae-gyun, "Nyurait'ŭŭi tŭngjang," 295–99.

6 Kyogwasŏ p'orŏm, *Han'guk kŭn-hyŏndaesa*.
7 Levy, "Future of the Past," 51.
8 See, among others, Chŏng Yŏn-t'ae, "'Singminji kŭndaehwaron' nonjaengŭi pip'an'gwa sin'gŭndaesaronŭi mosaek"; Chŏn Sang-in, "Singminji kŭndaehwarone taehan ihaewa ohae"; Cho, "Colonial Modernity Matters?"
9 Levy, "Future of the Past," 52. Political use of the past in political conflicts cuts across the ideological spectrum globally, as there are plenty of cases of the left's use of the past for its political purposes. Some examples include East Germany's instrumentalization of memories of communist resistance to the Third Reich and Spain's Socialist Party who broke a truce over the use of history for partisan purposes when it feared losing a national election in 1993. Friedman and Kenney, Introduction to *Partisan Histories*, 5.
10 See, among others, a collection of articles on the New Right in "Kin'gŭpchindan"; Tikhonov, "Rise and Fall."
11 Im Tae-sik, "*Haebang chŏnhusa ŭi chaeinsik*," 12–13.
12 Chayujuŭi yŏndae, "Chayujuŭi yŏndae." In the process of preparing the 2013 Korean history textbook that New Right scholars published (Kwŏn Hŭi-yŏng at al., *Han'guksa*), the scholars insisted that any mention of "democracy" should be replaced with "liberal democracy" in history books of South Korea. Hong Sŏng-nyul, "Naengjŏnjŏk yŏksasŏsul," 85–86. Historian Hong Sŏng-nyul characterizes the New Right's perspective on liberal democracy as Cold War anti-communism and "Cold War liberalism," informed by discussion of the American case of liberalism during the Cold War in Anthony Arblaster, *The Rise and Decline of Western Liberalism* (Oxford: Basil Blackwell, 1984); Hong Sŏng-nyul, "Naengjŏnjŏk yŏksasŏsul," 85–88. In fact, a more accurate description of Cold War liberalism in the American context would be "left-liberal anti-communism"—that is, its ideological orientation was based on the alliance of leftist and liberalists united in their anti-communism: democratic socialists, New Deal liberals, and anti-Stalinist leftists (former Trotskyists). Their union underwent a number of reconsolidations and fractures until it foundered in the late 1960s. Furthermore, and as historian Ari Cushner argues, despite their "anti-totalitarian" position and support of Cold War foreign policy, they remained committed to the civil rights and labor movements, advocated social and economic justice, and pursued a domestic agenda of progressive reform attached to the legacy of the New Deal. Cushner, "Cold War Comrades." It would be difficult to say that the "democratic liberalism" that the New Right speaks of has any history of pursuing even a modest form of social and economic, let alone political, justice. It is a straightforward "Cold War anti-communism" than "Cold War liberalism."
13 Chayujuŭi yŏndae, "Chayujuŭi yŏndae."
14 Pastreich, "Balancer," 9–10. Roh's policies toward North Korea and his more independent views about South Korea-US relations were also virulently attacked by the American right. Pastreich, "Balancer," 11–12.
15 The four legislative reforms were to abolish or revise the following four laws: the National Security Law, Private School Law, Press-Related Laws, and the Law to Investigate Past Wrongdoings.

16 On the history and characteristics of the discourse of sŏnjin'guk in South Korea, see Kim, "Discourse of *Sŏnjin'guk*."
17 Editorial, "Han'gugesŏn oemyŏndanghan '2006 sŏnjin'guk t'ŭrendŭ'" ["Advanced countries" trends in 2006 ignored in South Korea], *Dong-A Ilbo*, December 26, 2006; cited in Kim, "Discourse of *Sŏnjin'guk*," 178.
18 They include former politicians such as Sin Chi-ho, well-known historians such as An Pyŏng-jik and Yi Yŏng-hun, Christian leaders such as Kim Chin-hong, and journalists and editors of newspapers such as Cho Kap-che and Ch'oe Hong-jae.
19 Suh, "Generational Dynamics," 22–23.
20 Sin Chi-ho, "Tangsinŭn ajikto 'hyŏngmyŏng'ŭl kkumkkunŭn'ga." There has been a steady stream of publications of this kind. See, among others, Kim Mun-su, *Ajikto nanŭn nekt'aiga ŏsaekhada*; Ch'oe Hong-jae, *386 ŭi kkum, kŭ sŏngch'arŭi iyu*; Yi Chong-ch'ŏl and Yi Kwang-baek, *Naŭi kobaek*; Kim Yŏng-hwan, *Tasi Kangch'ŏllo sara*. Many internet sites also offer confessions from former chusap'a. See, among others, Sŏ Sŏk-ku, "Ch'inundonggwŏn pyŏnhosaŭi kobaek"; Hong Chin-p'yo, "Han kolssu 386 chusap'a ch'ulssinŭi ch'ehŏmjŏk kobaek." New Right groups also have an array of their own publication outlets, such as the quarterly *Sidae Chŏngsin* (*Geist*), a web magazine called *Polizen*, and an internet newspaper, *New Daily*, in addition to publishing companies such as Sidae chŏngsin.
21 They include historian An Pyŏng-jik; columnist Yu Kŭn-il (of *Chosun Ilbo*); politician Sin Chi-ho; the "founder" of the 1980s chusap'a (followers of North Korea's chuch'e sasang), Kim Yŏng-hwan; and a fellow former chusap'a, Hong Chin-p'yo. See, among others, An Pyŏng-jik, "Chŭngŏn: Minjuhwa undonggwa minjujuŭi" [Testimony: Democratization movement and democracy], in An Pyŏng-jik, *Han'guk minjujuŭi*, 143–83; Yu Kŭn-il and Hong Chin-p'yo, *Chisŏnggwa panjisŏng*; Sin Chi-ho, *Nyurait'ŭŭi sesangikki*; Kim Yŏng-hwan, *Sidaejŏngsinŭl marhada*.
22 See, for example, Benjamin, *Understanding Brecht*, 91; cited in Plass, "From the Left-Wing," 159–60.
23 Löwy, "On May '68," 15.
24 Koschmann, *Revolution*, 247.
25 This brief account is from Kim Yŏng-hwan, *Tasi Kangch'ŏllo sara*, 120–66.
26 Kim Yŏng-hwan, interview with the author; cited in Lee, *Making of Minjung*, 135.
27 Thatcher, "AIDS, Education, and the Year 2000!"
28 Kim Yŏng-hwan, interview with the author. It is not clear why Thatcher, more than Reagan, is frequently mentioned among New Right intellectuals as their role model; it is likely due to the fact that Reagan was closely tied to the much-hated Chun Doo-hwan regime.
29 See, among others, Chŏn Chae-ho, "2000nyŏndae Han'guk posujuŭiŭi."
30 Historian Vladimir Tikhonov contends that the New Right as a social and an academic movement has met its demise with the fall of the Park Geun-hye government in 2017. Tikhonov, "Rise and Fall."
31 Yet, the editors made clear in their introduction to the volume that the Roh government's enactment of a series of laws to investigate past wrongdoings instigated them to put together the volume. Pak Chi-hyang et al., "Mŏrimal," 11.
32 Pak Chi-hyang et al., "Mŏrimal," 12.

33 See, among others, Yi Chu-ho, "*Haebang chŏnhusa*"; Yi Yŏng-hun, *Taehanmin'guk iyagi*, 6.
34 See, among others, Im Tae-sik, "*Haebang chŏnhusa ŭi chaeinsik*"; Chŏng Hae-gu, "Nyurait'ŭ undong"; Ye Tae-yŏl, "Nyurait'ŭwa t'algŭndaeron"; Ha Chŏng-il, "*Haebang chŏnhusa*." Some of the major charges leveled by the editors of *Reunderstanding* against *Understanding* were a straw man argument. That there was a single, unified understanding or interpretation of post-1945 history among contributors to the six volumes is beyond credibility. Furthermore, very few of those contributors still maintain the position expressed in their chapters. In fact, not a few have since been rebaptized by postcolonial and postmodern theories that have swept up the academic community from the late 1980s. Nor did editors of *Reunderstanding* evidence an in-depth and comprehensive understanding about the sociopolitical context in which the reputed radical views that they vociferously denounced arose, as they lumped all of the views expressed in *Understanding* as "nationalist" and "leftist."
35 See, among others, Tikhonov, "Rise and Fall"; Han Hong-gu, "Toesaranan ch'inil seryŏk."
36 Kyogwasŏ p'orŏm, *Han'guk kŭn-hyŏndaesa*, 7.
37 Miller, "Idea of Stagnation," 10.
38 For more detailed and critical analysis of the textbook, see, among others, Han Hong-gu, "Toesaranan ch'inil seryŏk."
39 Miller, "Idea of Stagnation," 10.
40 An Pyŏng-jik, *Han'guk minjujuŭi*.
41 Em, "Historians," 670.
42 Yun Hae-dong, "Chedorosŏŭi yŏksahak," 164.
43 Em, "Historians," 670–71.
44 See, among others, Chŏng Han-gu, *Soryŏn Tongyurŏp sahoejuŭiŭi punggoewa Pukhanŭi changnae*.
45 Yi Yŏng-hun, "Wae tasi Haebang chŏnhusain'ga," 63; quotation marks in the original.
46 Fukuyama, "End of History?"
47 See, among others, Hong Sŏng-nyul, "Taehanmin'guk 60nyŏn," 61; Chŏn Chae-ho, *Pak Chŏng-hŭi tae Pak Chŏng-hŭi*, 28–31; Pak T'ae-gyun, *Wŏnhyŏnggwa pyŏnyong*; Cumings, "Asian Crisis, Democracy"; The United States was not always in sync with the specifics of the South Korean government's economic plan, however. See, among others, Pak T'ae-gyun, *Wŏnhyŏnggwa pyŏnyong*, 330–44.
48 Em, "Historians," 673–74.
49 Kyogwasŏ p'orŏm, "Ch'angnip sŏnŏnmun," in Chŏng In-hwan and Hwang Cha-hye, "Saeyŏngmoŭi kwagŏnŭn"; quoted in Chŏng Hae-gu, "Nyurait'ŭ undong," 223–24.
50 Lee, *Making of Minjung*, 127–42.
51 Yi Yŏng-hun, *Taehanmin'guk iyagi*, 6–7; Em, "Historians," 674.
52 Yoneyama, *Cold War Ruins*, 39.
53 Yun Hae-dong, "Nyurait'ŭ undong," 238–39; Pak T'ae-gyun, "Nyurait'ŭŭi tŭngjangg," 288–89.
54 See, among others, Yun Hae-dong, "Nyurait'ŭ undong."
55 Hong Sŏng-nyul, "Sasilgwa yŏksa sogŭi," 249.
56 Pak Myŏng-nim, "Yi Sŭngmanŭi Han'guk munje," 79.

57 Chŏng Pyŏng-jun, *Unam Yi Sŭngman yŏn'gu*, 5; quoted in Hong Sŏng-nyul, "Sasilgwa yŏksa sogŭi," 249-50.
58 Chŏn Sang-in, *Kogae sugin sujŏngjuŭi*, 429. Sociologist Yu Sŏk-ch'un [Seok-Choon Lew] sums up the New Right perspective: "The issue of how to assess President Rhee's life and activities, and the Republic of Korea that he established, is a key issue in the Korean intellectual community. Despite President Rhee's stellar [*kŏlch'ulhan*] achievement and the unique status he occupies in Korea's modern and contemporary history, some elements in the Korean intellectual community exaggerate his mistakes and denigrate or underrate his achievements." Yu Sŏk-ch'un, "Kanhaengsa," vi.
59 Ko Chŏng-hyu, "Uriyŏksa paroalja," 198.
60 Cumings, *Origins of the Korean War*; Lee, *Making of Minjung*, 61-64.
61 Cumings, *Origins of the Korean War*, 1:189-91; cited in Chŏn Sang-in, *Kogaesugin sujŏngjuŭi*, 428-29.
62 Song Kŏn-ho, "Uriyŏksa paroalja," 180-81.
63 Song Kŏn-ho, "Uriyŏksa paroalja," 181. This is also the view expressed in his chapter in the *Understanding*. Ch'inilp'a literally means "pro-Japanese clique."
64 Song Kŏn-ho, "Uriyŏksa paroalja," 181-86.
65 Kim Hak-chun, "Ch'oegŭn hwalbarhaejin," 449-50. Kim further argues that scholarly publications on Rhee until recently mostly highlighted his failures: his failure to detect and prevent the North Korean attack despite numerous indications of its imminence, his failure to protect the citizens of Seoul by fleeing the city by himself while telling them to remain in the city, his failure to prevent mass killings of civilians during the Korean War, and his causing both the political crisis in Pusan by forcefully revising the constitution in 1952 and again in 1954, and mayhem in the 1960 presidential election, which eventually led to the 1960 student uprising. Kim Hak-chun, "Ch'oegŭn hwalbarhaejin," 449-50.
66 See, among others, Lew, *Making of the First Korean President*; Kim Hyo-sŏn, *Urinara kŏn'guktaet'ongnyŏng Yi Sŭngman iyagi*.
67 Adding to this transformed intellectual climate is also the availability, since the 1990s, of formerly unavailable archival material from the Soviet Union.
68 Chŏn Sang-in, *Kogae sugin sujŏngjuŭi*, 429. I do not suggest that all of the research on Syngman Rhee during this period is hagiographic. A few monographs provide evenhanded analyses and critical reassessment, backed by extensive and meticulous research, such as Chŏng Pyŏng-jun's *Unam Yi Sŭngman yŏn'gu*.
69 Yi Yŏng-hun, "Kyojang insamalssŭm."
70 Yi Han-u, *Unam Yi Sŭngman*, 5-6.
71 Pae Chin-yŏng, "Hyŏndaesa parojapkie nasŏn Yi Sŭngman yŏn'guso."
72 Lew, *Making of the First Korean President*, xi-xii. IMKS was founded after Rhee's adopted son handed over to Yu large amounts of documents on Rhee that had been stored at Rhee's former home at Ihwa House. There are also other groups and organizations with various publication outlets and programs on Syngman Rhee to engage the public, although it is not clear that all of the individuals involved would claim or identify themselves as New Right. Some of these groups such as the Founding President Syngman Rhee Society are located in the United States. See,

among others, http://syngmanrheehawaii.org/bbs/content.php?co_id=company (accessed January 18, 2018).

73   Some major publications by IMKS include Young Ick Lew, *Syngman Rhee Correspondence in English*; Syngman Rhee, *Syngman Rhee Telegrams*; Yu Yŏng-ik et al., eds., *Yi Sŭngman tongmun sŏhanjip*.

74   See, among others, Lew, *Making of the First Korean President*; Yu Yŏng-ik, *Yi Sŭngmanŭi samgwa kkum*; Yu Yŏng-ik, *Chŏlmuŭn nal ŭi Yi Sŭng-man*; Yu Yŏng-ik, *Yi Sŭng-man Taet'ongnyŏng chaep'yŏngka*.

75   Yu Yŏng-ik, "Ihwajang munsŏ soge," 164–71.

76   Yu meticulously traces Rhee's life from birth to 1948 in this book, relying on sources such as Rhee's own correspondence, telegrams, speeches, interview records, essays, poems (many of which are in English or Classical Chinese), and interviews with Rhee's surviving friends and colleagues. The book also contains numerous photos of Rhee and the individuals and events discussed.

77   Yi Yŏng-hun, "Kyojang insamalssŭm." See also Yang Tong-an, "Kŭdŭrŭn Yi Sŭngmanŭl yŏksaesŏ chiuryŏ haetta," 39–44. On the Syngman Rhee School, see http://syngmanrhee.kr/.

78   Kwŏn Hŭi-yŏng, "Yi Sŭngmanŭi kungmin'gukka," 66.

79   Kwŏn Hŭi-yŏng, "Yi Sŭngmanŭi kungmin'gukka," 11.

80   Chŏn Sang-in, *Kogae sugin sujŏngjuŭi*, 429–30.

81   Lew, *Making of the First Korean President*, xii.

82   An Pyŏng-jik, "Mŏrimal," 6.

83   An Pyŏng-jik, "Mŏrimal," 7. See also Yang Tong-an, "Yi Sŭngman kwa pan'gong" [Syngman Rhee and anti-communism], in Yi Chu-yŏng et al., *Yi Sŭngman yŏn'guŭi hŭrŭmgwa chaengjŏm*, 111–38.

84   An Pyŏng-jik, "Mŏrimal," 7.

85   See, among others, Lee, *Making of Minjung*, 59–64. On the political and economic context of the land reform, see, among others, Sin Pyŏng-sik, "Cheɪkonghwaguk t'oji kaehyŏgŭi chŏngch'igyŏngje." On the disposal of Japanese-owned properties, see, among others, O Tu-hwan, "Haebanghu chŏksanch'ŏriŭi silt'aewa t'ŭkching." Nam Chae-hŭi, the former journalist and elder politician, attributes the land reform to the revolutionary political condition at the time that made it unavoidable, as well as to the work of Americans who were deeply influenced by the New Deal in the United States. Nam Chae-hŭi, "Wŏllo ŏllonin chŏngch'iin Nam Chae-hŭiga pon taet'ongnyŏngdŭl," pt. 2.

86   The *sa-sa o-ip* constitutional revision, also known as the February 4 crisis, refers to when Syngman Rhee received one vote short of the necessary two-thirds majority (135 instead of 136) to pass the amendment of the constitution; he enlisted a mathematics professor to suggest the *sa-sa, o-ip* formula (that two-thirds of 203 is 135.333, but 0.333 is below 0.5 and can be dropped; therefore, two-thirds of 203 is not 136 but 135) to promulgate the amendment.

87   Yi Chu-yŏng, "Yi sŭngman sidaeŭi posuseryŏk," 29, 34, 65.

88   Historian Serge Wolikow characterizes some of the scholarship on communism emphasizing only its crimes from the perspective of the Cold War concept of "totalitarianism," such as *The Black Book of Communism: Crimes, Terror, Repression* (Harvard

University Press, 1999), as a caricature of real history, that by "assimilating for example the Communist movement to a simple subversive enterprise, simplifies the phenomenon and prohibits one from understanding its impact and amplitude." Serge Wolikow, "Les interpretations du mouvement communiste international," in Dreyfus et al., *Le siècle des communismes*, 90; quoted in Aronson, "Communism's Posthumous Trial," 239.

89 An Pyŏng-jik, "Mŏrimal," 6.
90 *Zweckrationalität* is a term developed by Max Weber and denotes rationality in accordance with organizational demands instead of moral demands. See Max Weber, *Economy and Society: An Outline of Interpretive Sociology*, 2 vols. (Berkeley: University of California Press, 1978). An Pyŏng-jik writes, "Korea's economic development was akin to creating something out of nothing. . . . Furthermore, the people of South Korea at the time clamored for economic development that was not dependent on foreign powers [*chaju kyŏngje*]. It is truly revolutionary that Park achieved an autonomous economy in a roundabout way, even as he went about against the wishes of the people, with foreign capital and export-oriented industrialization. Therefore, we cannot judge Park's authoritarianism simply as a stepping-stone to long-term rule." An Pyŏng-jik, "Mŏrimal," 7.
91 An Pyŏng-jik, "Mŏrimal," 7.
92 Kim Se-jung, "Pak Chŏng-hŭi sidae sanŏphwa," 48–49.
93 Kim Se-jung, "Pak Chŏng-hŭi sidae sanŏphwa," 52.
94 Kim Se-jung, "Pak Chŏng-hŭi sidae sanŏphwa," 51–52. Park believed that South Korea's unique condition—a country divided and in a state of war with North Korea—required an alternative view of democracy different from the United States and Europe. He believed that universal values such as freedom, democracy, and civil rights could be curtailed or postponed in South Korea. His emphasis on Korean-style democracy intensified after he declared the Yusin Constitution in 1972. Lee and Kim, *South Korean Democratization Movement*, 342–43.
95 Kim Se-jung, "Pak Chŏng-hŭi sidae sanŏphwa," 56.
96 There are a number of such cases, but I will point out only three. In another chapter of his, Kim misrepresents Stephan Haggard's *Pathways from the Periphery* by saying "[Haggard also] acknowledges that authoritarianism is necessary to resolve the issue of collective action that lowers efficiency." See Haggard, *Pathways from the Periphery*, 361–70; cited in Kim Se-jung "Kwŏnwijuŭijŏk sanŏphwawa minjujuŭi," 90. Here is what Haggard actually says: "There are no theoretical reasons to think that authoritarian regimes are *uniquely* capable of solving the collective-action problems associated with development" (emphasis in original). Haggard, *Pathways from the Periphery*, 255–56. Kim also quotes a passage from Amsden's *Asia's Next Giant* but omits the part of the subsequent sentence (shown in italics below) that qualifies the quote: "It is unclear whether the strong economic measures taken by the Korean state could have been taken under political democracy, *although Japan, the etatist European countries, and recent events in Korea all suggest that such measures and political democracy are compatible*. What is clear is that, without a strong central authority, a necessary although not sufficient condition, little industrialization may be expected in 'backward' countries." Amsden, *Asia's Next Giant*, 18; quoted in "Kwŏnwijuŭijŏk sanŏphwawa minjujuŭi," 90. Also, Kim claims that Robert Wade argued that the

"lesson of the East Asian development model is to institutionalize an efficient authoritative political system before democratization and to subsume interest groups in a corporatist framework." Wade, *Governing the Market*, 29–30, cited in "Kwŏnwijuŭijŏk sanŏphwawa minjujuŭi," 90. Nowhere on these pages can one find the cited passages.

97   Ch'oe Hye-sŏng, "Kwayŏn urinarae kŏn'gukchŏri," 274. Liberation Day was designated a national holiday in South Korea in October 1949. North Korea designated September 9, 1948 as the day of founding of its state (*ch'anggŏnil*). Both South and North Korea observe National Foundational Day (*Kaech'ŏnjŏl*) on October 3, which celebrates the reputed beginning of the Korean people and the formation of the first Korean state of Kojosŏn in 2333 BC.

98   Even some conservatives expressed their opposition to the proposal to change Liberation Day to Foundation Day. According to a survey conducted by the Korea Society Opinion Institute (KSOI) from July 20 to 25, 2008, out of 114 academics and journalists, 83.3 percent opposed it. In another survey by the *Seoul Kyŏngje* (Seoul economic daily) conducted on August 17, 2008, 97 percent of the respondents said that the current name, Liberation Day, was proper. Cited in An Hyŏn-hyo, "*Haebang chŏnhusa ŭi chaeinsik*," 200n1.

99   Yi Yŏng-hun, "Urido kŏn'gukchŏrŭl mandŭlja." Actually, both former presidents Kim Dae-jung and Roh Moo-hyun emphasized the importance of the "foundation" of South Korea and in the case of Kim Dae-jung even set up the Pan-national Promotion Commission for Second National Foundation in December 1998. This commission was heavily criticized by the right as politically motivated and was dissolved in April 2003. Ch'oe Hye-sŏng, "Kwayŏn urinarae kŏn'gukchŏri," 275–76.

100 Lee, *Making of Minjung*, 1–69.

101 See, among others, Yi Wan-bŏm, "Kŏn'guk kijŏm nonjaeng."

102 Pak Myŏng-nim, "Yi Sŭngmanŭi Han'guk munje," 59. It is important to note that among those who actively participated in the debate on the side of the "division discourse" include historians, such as Pak Sŏng-su, who are extremely critical of "left-leaning" historians. See Pak Sŏng-su, "Taehanmin'guk Imsijŏngbu suripkwa kŏn'guk," 89–90.

103 Yi Wan-bŏm, "Kŏn'guk kijŏm nonjaeng," 72–73.

104 After World War I, "as national self-determination was proving to be panacea, placebo, and disorder all at once," English political scientist Ernest Barker outlined three material bases of the nation: "race, as a source of human identification; environment, as both a physical border and internal geography; and population, as a set of statistical forms." Barker, *National Character and the Factors in Its Formation*, 2–3; quoted in Miller and Lawrence, "Globalization and Culture," 496. The preamble of the constitution of the Republic of Korea states, "We, the people of Korea, proud of a resplendent history and traditions dating from time immemorial, uphold the cause of the Korean Provisional Republic of Korea Government born of the March First Independence Movement of 1919." *Constitution of the Republic of Korea*.

105 Yang Tong-an, "Taehanmin'guk kwa Imsijŏngbuŭi kwan'gye," 161–62; quoted in Yi Wan-bŏm, "Kŏn'guk kijŏm nonjaeng," 78–79.
106 *Constitution of the Republic of Korea.*
107 Kim Sŏng-uk, "Kŏn'guk 60chunyŏn kinyŏmsaŏp." Kim belongs to the Association of Those Who Love the Republic of Korea (*Taehanmin'guk saranghoe*), one of numerous grassroots organizations; it aims to promote Syngman Rhee as founder of the Republic of Korea and to establish August 15 as the day of the foundation of the republic. Its ongoing campaigns include erection of a statue of Syngman Rhee and putting him on the 100,000 won bill. See http://www.loverokorea.org/.
108 Yi Wan-bŏm, "Kŏn'guk kijŏm nonjaeng," 74.
109 Yi Wan-bŏm, "Kŏn'guk kijŏm nonjaeng," 79.
110 Ch'oe Hye-sŏng, "Kwayŏn urinarae kŏn'gukchŏri," 285.
111 Pak Sŏng-su, "Taehanmin'guk Imsijŏngbu suripkwa kŏn'guk"; quoted in Kim Yong-sam, "<Kim Yong-samŭi hyŏndaesa ch'ujŏk.>"
112 Yi Wan-bŏm, "Kŏn'guk kijŏm nonjaeng," 76. Pak also argues categorically that September 16, 1919—when all of the various provisional governments that had been set up in different places, such as the Assembly of the People of the Great Korea (*Taehan kungmin hoeŭi*) in Vladivostok (March 17) and the Hansŏng government (April 23), were merged with the Shanghai Provisional Government of the Republic of Korea (April 13)—is the day of the foundation of the republic. It was also the day when the sovereignty of Korea that Japan took away by force in 1910 was restored, according to Pak. Pak Sŏng-su, "Taehanmin'guk Imsijŏngbu suripkwa kŏn'guk," 90–91; cited in Yi Wan-bŏm, "Kŏn'guk kijŏm nonjaeng," 76.
113 Quoted in Kim Mi-yŏng and Hŏ Chae-hyŏn, "Nurikkun 'Kŏn'guk 60chunyŏn' kwangbok."
114 Kang Ch'ang-il, "(Sŏngmyŏngsŏ) 8.15nŭn kŏn'gukchŏri anira kwangbokchŏrida." On August 12, 2008, fourteen organizations and associations representing historians released a statement expressing the same concern as others who opposed the bill. Han'guk kŭnhyŏndae sahakhoe et al., "'Kŏn'gukchŏl' ch'ŏrhoerŭl ch'okkuhanŭn yŏksahagyeŭi sŏngmyŏngsŏ."
115 During the Park Geun-hye government (2013–2017), some in the ruling party again began to discuss submitting the bill to the National Assembly. In 2015, the Park government mandated schools to adopt government-issued history textbooks which used the phrase "establishment of the Republic of Korea" (*Taehanmin'guk surip*) in place of the previous "establishment of the government of the Republic of Korea" (*Taehanmin'guk chŏngbu surip*). The mandate was scrapped when Park was impeached in 2017. Ch'oe Hye-sŏng, "Kwayŏn urinarae kŏn'gukchŏri," 268–69.
116 Chi Su-gŏl, "Kŏn'gukchŏl nonjaeng," 16–17.
117 Benjamin, "Theses on the Philosophy of History," 255.
118 Duara, *Rescuing History.*
119 Duara, *Rescuing History*, 233.
120 Hegel, *Lectures on the Philosophy*, 139–49. On further elaboration of the Hegelian development of freedom for the individual and the state, see, among others, Lowe, *Intimacies of Four Continents*, 28–29, 57–58, 141–45.

EPILOGUE

1. Hobsbawm, "Social Function," 13-14.
2. Hobsbawm, "Social Function," 11; quoted in Olick, *Politics of Regret*, 178.
3. For some historians such as Reinhart Koselleck, the moment of crisis can be located much earlier, even as early as the upheaval between 1750 and 1850. For more details, see Koselleck, *Futures Past*.
4. Rüsen, "Historical Enlightenment," 110-12.
5. Michael Stürmer, *Dissonanzen des Fortschritts* (Munich: Piper 1986), 209; quoted in Rüsen, "Historical Enlightenment," 118.
6. Rüsen, "Historical Enlightenment," 118.
7. Rüsen, "Historical Enlightenment," 119.
8. Carlo Ginzburg, *The Cheese and the Worms: The Cosmos of a Sixteenth-Century Miller*, trans. John Tedeschi and Anne C. Tedeschi (Baltimore: Johns Hopkins University Press, 1987); cited in Rüsen, "Historical Enlightenment," 119-20.
9. Gallerano, "History and the Public Use," 97. Charles Maier, among others, has noted how this approach, an effort to capture the experiences of ordinary women and men, could serve a conservative cause of "normalization" in Germany. Maier, *Unmasterable Past*, 36-37.
10. Mercer, "Moral Rearmament of France," 113.
11. Hutchinson, *Reaganism, Thatcherism*, 19-20.
12. I thank my colleague Thu-Huong Nguyen-Vo for this insight.
13. Maier, *Unmasterable Past*, 169.
14. Naomi Klein, *The Shock Doctrines: The Rise of Disaster Capitalism* (New York: Picador, 2007), 3; quoted in Tassone, "Democracy at a Standstill," 78.
15. The resulting "provisional seizure" of labor union funds and salaries of union leaders and members have resulted in bankruptcies and a number of suicides of union members. See Jang, "Continuing Suicide among Laborers," 272-73.
16. Editorial, "APEC esŏ hwaginhan Taehanmin'gugi naagal kil" [The way forward for South Korea, confirmed at APEC], *Chosun Ilbo*, November 20, 2005, A19; quoted in Kim, "Discourse of *Sŏnjin'guk*," 177.
17. For example, many of the film directors who became internationally well known by the late 1990s and early 2000s, such as Park Chan-wook [Park Ch'an-uk] and Bong Joon-ho [Pong Chun-ho], were members of university film clubs, which, more often than not, were a part of, or sympathetic to, the democratization movement of the era.
18. Yi Yŏng-hun, *Taehanmin'guk yŏksa*, 18.
19. See Nietzsche, "On the Uses and Disadvantages of History"; Rüsen, "Historical Enlightenment," 120.
20. Rüsen, "Historical Enlightenment," 120.
21. On the case of the Japanese right, see, among others, Yoneyama, *Cold War Ruins*, 111-21; Gluck, "Operations of Memory," 47-77.
22. Maier, *Unmasterable Past*, 5-6; Hong Sŏng-nyul, "Naengjŏnjŏk yŏksasŏsul."
23. Adorno, "What Does Coming to Terms with the Past Mean?" For further discussion on Adorno's article and the historians' dispute, see, among others, Habermas, *Berlin Republic*, 17-40.

24 Habermas, *Berlin Republic*, 11. For further discussion of the historians' dispute, see, among others, Maier, *Unmasterable Past*.
25 Michael Stürmer, "Aus der Geschichte lernen?" *Sinn und Form* 2 (1994); quoted in Habermas, *Berlin Republic*, 5.
26 Maier, *Unmasterable Past*, 168.
27 As literary scholar Dominick LaCapra has suggested, Habermas's notion of enlightenment thinking should also include "commitment to the Enlightenment figure of the public intellectual who relies on the triad of rationality, ethical concern, and a dedication to public space as the only legitimate theater of political action." Cited in Gumbrecht, "On the Decent Uses," 119.
28 Habermas, *Berlin Republic*, 11.
29 Habermas, *Berlin Republic*, 44.
30 Habermas, *Berlin Republic*, 11–13.
31 Maier, *Unmasterable Past*, 137.
32 Habermas, *Berlin Republic*, 11.
33 Benjamin, "Theses on the Philosophy of History," 253. In fact, Habermas did not embrace Benjamin's theses on the concept of history, which he thought might be susceptible to conservative critique. Jürgen Habermas, "Walter Benjamin: Consciousness-Raising or Rescuing Critique," in *On Walter Benjamin: Critical Essays and Recollections*, ed. Gary Smith (Cambridge, MA: MIT Press, 1988), 99, 124; cited in Neocleous, "Let the Dead Bury," 29. My reading of both Habermas and Benjamin for the purpose of this chapter is in broad strokes and to find some possible connections with the philosophies of history, memory, and remembrance to further engage with the historiographical and ethical issues at hand.
34 Barglow, "Angel of History."
35 Benjamin, "Theses on the Philosophy of History," 257–58.
36 See, among others, Jessop, "Children, Redemption"; Wolin, *Walter Benjamin*.
37 Jessop, "Children, Redemption," 645.
38 Hartog, "End and a Beginning."
39 Neocleous, "Let the Dead Bury," 27.
40 Jessop, "Children, Redemption," 647. Benjamin wrote, "Whoever has emerged victorious participates to this day in the triumphal procession in which the present rulers step over those who are lying prostrate. . . . The spoils are carried along in the procession. They are called cultural treasures, and a historical materialist views them with cautious detachment. For without exception the cultural treasures he surveys have an origin which he cannot contemplate without horror. . . . There is no document of civilization which is not at the same time a document of barbarism." Benjamin, "Theses on the Philosophy of History," 258–59; quoted in Jessop, "Children, Redemption," 647.
41 Löwy, *Fire Alarm*, 47–48.
42 Löwy, *Fire Alarm*, 49.
43 Jessop, "Children, Redemption," 648; Neocleous, "Let the Dead Bury," 25.
44 Jessop, "Children, Redemption," 646.
45 Jessop, "Children, Redemption," 648.

46 Neocleous, "Let the Dead Bury," 28.
47 Jessop, "Children, Redemption," 648.
48 Hartog, "End and a Beginning."
49 *Arcades Project*, 462; quoted in Jessop, "Children, Redemption," 647.
50 Jessop, "Children, Redemption," 648. Again, what I present here is a simplified view of Benjamin's concept of historicism. For a more thorough discussion of Benjamin's concept of historicism and the complexity of the term, see, among others, Kittsteiner, "Walter Benjamin's Historicism." For the diversity of historicist thought and different meanings of the term *historicism* since the nineteenth century, see Iggers, "Historicism."
51 Jessop, "Children, Redemption," 648.
52 Jessop, "Children, Redemption," 647–48; Löwy, *Fire Alarm*, 32.
53 Lindroos, *Now-Time Image-Space*, 82. In *The Eighteenth Brumaire of Louis Bonaparte*, Marx writes, "Earlier revolutions required recollections of past world history in order to dull themselves to their own content. In order to arrive at its own content, the revolution of the nineteenth century must let the dead bury their dead." *The Eighteenth Brumaire of Louis Bonaparte* (1852), in Karl Marx and Frederick Engels, *Collected Works* (London: Lawrence & Wishart, 1979), 11:106; quoted in Neocleous, "Let the Dead Bury," 23.
54 Hartog, "End and a Beginning."
55 Neocleous, "Let the Dead Bury," 28. For a helpful discussion on the distinction between conservatives and reactionaries in terms of their view of tradition, see Ankersmit, "Sublime Dissociation."
56 Benjamin, "Theses on the Philosophy of History," 255 (emphasis in original).
57 Löwy, *Fire Alarm*, 44.
58 Yi Yŏng-hun, "Wae tasi Haebang chŏnhusain'ga," 63.
59 Appleby, Hunt, and Jacob, *Telling the Truth*, 65, 69.
60 In a 2013 publication, Yi Yŏng-hun discusses "freedom" as a concept developed in Western Europe during the sixteenth to eighteen centuries and spread to the rest of the world; as such, it "reflects most closely the human nature and natural order of society." Freedom is also "the most superior principle" for society's progress. Yi Yŏng-hun, *Taehanmin'guk yŏksa*, 34.
61 Yi Yŏng-hun et al., *Panil chongjokchuŭi*.
62 Jacoby, *Social Amnesia*, 1.
63 Yi Yŏng-hun, "P'ŭrollogŭ," 10–11.
64 Yi Yŏng-hun argues that the South Korean state also mobilized sex workers during the Korean War and that it also referred to those who worked around the U.S. military bases in post-1945 South Korea as "comfort women" (*wiwanbu*) until 1966. He also argues that the "comfort women" system during World War II was managed by civilians with the help of the military and, as such, it was essentially a continuation of existing state-regulated prostitution (*kongch'ang*)—hence his argument that "comfort women" were just a part of professional prostitutes. Yi Yŏng-hun, "Urian ui wianbu," 254–71; Yi Yŏng-hun, "Kongch'angje ŭi sŏngnip kwa munhwa," 272–86.

65 Yi U-yŏn, "Kangje tongwŏn ŭi sinhwa," 67–71; Yi U-yŏn, "Chosŏnin imgŭm ch'abyŏrŭi hŏgusŏng," 88–98.
66 Yi Yŏng-hun, *Taehanmin'guk yŏksa*, 20.
67 Lyotard, *Differend*, xi.
68 See also Jenkins, "Ethical Responsibility," 52–56.
69 See, among others, Abram and Torok, *Shell and the Kernel*; Aaron Hass, *In the Shadow of the Holocaust: The Second Generation* (New York: Cambridge University Press, 1996). As Antoon de Baets notes, transgenerational trauma has been recognized by the law and has been applied in adjudicating cases involving victims of the abuse of state power. De Baets, "Declarations of Responsibilities," 153–54.
70 Cho, *Haunting the Korean Diaspora*, 12. For more on the concept of "ethical memory" as it relates to representation of the traumatic experiences of the Korean War by second-generation Korean Americans, see Kim, "Suji Kwock Kim's 'Generation.'"
71 Benjamin, "Theses on the Philosophy of History," 256; quoted in Honnet, "Communicative Disclosure of the Past," 91.
72 Honnet, "Communicative Disclosure of the Past," 91.
73 Bevernage, "Past Is Evil." Bevernage here does not cite Benjamin, and my purpose here is not to explicate where his ideas come from but to bring together relevant theoretical and philosophical insights on the issue at hand.
74 Bevernage, "Past Is Evil," 334–35. For an illuminating discussion on how remembering the past and seeking the truth is not a responsibility but a right of individuals and society, not to mention historians, see De Baets, "Declaration of the Responsibilities," 151–53.
75 Bevernage, "Past Is Evil," 337.
76 This negative logic in Fukuyama's argument about the anachronism of political alternatives to liberalism was especially prominent in his original essay on the end of history thesis. Fukuyama, "End of History?"; cited in Bevernage, "Past Is Evil," 346. As Bevernage notes, Fukuyama resorts to negative logic when dealing with alternative ideologies and political systems, calling them, for example, "primitive," "stuck in history," "traditional," or "anachronistic." Fukuyama, *End of History*, 35–36. Fukuyama also dismisses any alternative visions that existed alongside the currently dominant form of capitalism and parliamentary democracy, famously declaring that "it matters very little what strange thoughts occur to people in Albania or Burkina Faso, for we are interested in what one could in some sense call the common ideological heritage of mankind." Fukuyama, "End of History?"; quoted in Bevernage, "Past Is Evil," 348.
77 Bevernage notes this kind of criticism is also directed to groups and organizations established to provide restorative justice to victims, such as the South African Truth and Reconciliation Commission. Bevernage, "Past Is Evil," 346n51.
78 Bevernage, "Past Is Evil," 337.
79 Bevernage, "Past Is Evil," 348.
80 Rancière, "In What Time Do We Live?"
81 Bevernage, "Past Is Evil," 351–52.

82 Khulumani Support Group, "Khulumani Case in New York's Second Circuit Court of Appeals from January 24, 2006" (November 15, 2007); quoted in Bevernage, "Past Is Evil," 351.
83 Bevernage, "Past Is Evil," 351.
84 Yi Yŏng-hun et al., *Panil chongjokchuŭi*, 254–68.
85 For academic works, see, among others, Yang, "Finding the 'Map of Memory'"; Soh, *Comfort Women*; Yi Na-yŏng, "Kŭl/rok'ŏl chendŏjilssŏwa Hanbando yŏsŏngŭi mom."
86 Chŏng Kyŏng-a tells in an interview how the 2003 Iraq War provided the initial impetus for working on her graphic novel, as she began to contemplate the relationship between war and violence against women. Another critical impetus was learning about the social stigma and isolation that the "comfort women" faced after they returned to their hometown. Chŏng Kyŏng-a, "'Wianbu' munjenŭn chigŭm."
87 Chu Ik-chong, "Haebang 40yŏnyŏn'gan," 340–51. Chŏngdaehyŏp (Han'guk chŏngsindae munje taech'aek hyŏbŭihoe), founded in 1990, and the Foundation for Justice and Remembrance (Ilbon'gun sŏngnoyeje munjehaegyŏrŭl wihan chŏngŭigiŏk chedan) merged in July 2018 as the Korean Council for Justice and Remembrance for the Issue of Military Sexual Slavery by Japan (Ilbon'gun sŏngnoyeje munjehaegyŏrŭl wihan chŏngŭigiŏk yŏndae, or Chŏngŭiyŏn).
88 See, among others, Bevernage, "Past Is Evil."
89 Yi Yŏng-hun, "Kongch'angje ŭi sŏngnip kwa munhwa," 272–92.
90 This is actually a critique Bevernage directs to those who work on behalf of victims of the past injustice, how they also share the epistemology "as analogous to that of the historian or the witness rather than of the morally more-problematic position of bystander, or worse, the beneficiary or accomplice." Bevernage, "Past Is Evil," 344.
91 There are ongoing cases of humiliating and tormenting victims and their families for their activities related to various redress movements. They range from the act of vandalism on, and the demands to get rid of, the "comfort women" statues, to the demand to reveal the names of recipients of compensation for victims of the Kwangju massacre, and more recently the case of a group of people gorging out on fried chicken and pizzas in front of fasting bereaved families of the Sewol Ferry tragedy who were waging a hunger strike to push for a bill to establish a fact-finding commission. See Ch'oe Chong-ho, "Sonyŏsang ch'imbaet'ŭn ch'ŏngnyŏndŭl"; Chŏng Sŏng-jo, "Posudanch'e 'Sonyŏsang sŏlch'i, suyojiphoe"; Lee, "Hunger Strike"; Pak Sun-jong, "5.18 yugongja myŏngdan chŏnmyŏn konggaehara."
92 Rancière, "In What Time Do We Live?"
93 Tassone, "Democracy at a Standstill," 92.
94 Tassone, "Democracy at a Standstill," 92.
95 See, among others, the Korean Council for Justice and Remembrance for the Issues of Military Sexual Slavery by Japan (Ilbon'gun sŏngnoyejemunje haegyŏrŭl wihan chŏngŭigiŏk yŏndae), http://womenandwar.net/kr/about-us/; Kwon, "The Sonyŏsang Phenomenon"; Yi Na-yŏng, "Ilbon'gun 'wianbu' undong tasi pogi."
96 Yoneyama, *Cold War Ruins*, 7. See also Ahn, "Together and Apart."
97 See, among others, Cho Han Hye-jŏng et al., *Nooryŏgŭi paesin*; Chun, "Contested Politics."

Bibliography

WORKS IN ENGLISH

Abram, Nicolas, and Maria Torok. *The Shell and the Kernel*, vol. 1. Edited and translated by Nicholas T. Rand. Chicago: University of Chicago Press, 1994.

Adorno, Theodor W. "What Does Coming to Terms with the Past Mean?" In *Bitburg in Moral and Political Perspective*, ed. Geoffrey Hartman, 114-29. Indianapolis: Indiana University Press, 1986.

Aguilar, Paloma. *Memory and Amnesia: The Road of the Spanish Civil War in the Transition to Democracy*. New York: Berghahn, 2002.

Ahn, Yonson. "Together and Apart: Transnational Women's Activism in the 'Comfort Women' Campaign in South Korea and Japan." *Comparative Korean Studies* 23, no. 1 (2015): 93-116.

Alexander, Jeffrey C. "Modern, Anti, Post, Neo." *New Left Review* 210 (March-April 1995): 63-101.

Amsden, Alice H. *Asia's Next Giant: South Korea and Late Industrialization*. Rev. ed. New York: Oxford University Press, 1992.

Ankersmit, F. R. "The Sublime Dissociation of the Past: Or How to Be(come) What One Is No Longer." *History and Theory* 40, no. 3 (October 2001): 295-323.

Appleby, Joyce, Lynn Hunt, and Margaret Jacob. *Telling the Truth about History*. New York: Norton, 1994.

Arblaster, Anthony. *The Rise and Decline of Western Liberalism*. Oxford: Blackwell, 1984.

Arendt, Hannah. *On Violence*. New York: Harcourt, Brace & Jovanovich, 1970.

Aronson, Ronald. "Communism's Posthumous Trial." *History and Theory* 42, no. 2 (May 2003): 222-45.

Badiou, Alain. *The Century*. Translated by Alberto Toscano. Malden, MA: Polity, 2007.

Barglow, Raymond. "The Angel of History: Walter Benjamin's Vision of Hope and Despair." *Tikkun Magazine*, November 1998. http://www.barglow.com/angel_of_history.htm.

Barker, Ernest. *National Character and the Factors in Its Formation*. London: Methuen, 1927.

Benjamin, Walter. *The Arcades Project*. Translated by Howard Eiland and Kevin McLaughlin. Cambridge, MA: Belknap Press of Harvard University Press, 1999.

——. "Left-Wing Melancholy." In *The Weimar Republic Sourcebook*, edited by Anton Kaes, Martin Jay, and Edward Dimendberg, 304–6. Berkeley: University of California Press, 1994.

——. *The Origin of German Tragic Drama*. Translated by John Osborne. New York: Verso, 2003.

——. "Theses on the Philosophy of History." In *Illuminations: Essays and Reflections by Walter Benjamin*, edited by Hannah Arendt and translated by Harry Zohn, 253–64. New York: Harcourt, Brace & World, 1968.

——. *Understanding Brecht*. Translated by Anna Bostock. New York: Verso, 1998.

Bernstein, David. "Some Dubious Claims in Nancy MacLean's 'Democracy in Chains.'" *Washington Post*, June 28, 2017.

Bevernage, Berber. "The Past Is Evil/Evil Is Past: On Retrospective Politics, Philosophy of History, and Temporal Manichaeism." *History and Theory* 54, no. 3 (October 2015): 333–52.

Bodnar, John. *Remaking America: Public Memory, Commemoration, and Patriotism in the Twentieth Century*. Princeton, NJ: Princeton University Press, 1992.

Bourdieu, Pierre. *Acts of Resistance: Against the Tyranny of the Market*. Translated by Richard Nice. New York: New Press, 1998.

Brown, Wendy. "Resisting Left Melancholy." *Boundary 2* 26, no. 3 (1999): 19–27.

——. *Undoing the Demos: Neoliberalism's Stealth Revolution*. Brooklyn, NY: Zone Books, 2015.

Buck-Morss, Susan. *Hegel, Haiti, and Universal History*. Pittsburgh, PA: University of Pittsburgh Press, 2009.

Chang, Paul Y. *Protest Dialectics: State Repression and South Korea's Democracy Movement, 1970–1979*. Stanford, CA: Stanford University Press, 2015.

Cho, Grace M. *Haunting the Korean Diaspora: Shame, Secrecy, and the Forgotten War*. Minneapolis: University of Minnesota Press, 2008.

Cho, Kuk. "Transitional Justice in Korea: Legally Coping with Past Wrongs after Democratization." *Pacific Rim Law & Policy Journal* 16, no. 3 (June 2007): 579–611.

Cho, Younghan. "Colonial Modernity Matters? Debates on Colonial Past in South Korea." *Cultural Studies* 26, no. 5 (2012): 645–69.

Choi, Cheong Rak, and Chul Moo Heo. "Economic Changes Resulting from Seoul 1988: Implications for London 2012 and Future Games." *International Journal of the History of Sport* 30, no. 15 (2013): 1854–66.

Choi, Jang-Jip [Ch'oe Chang-jip]. *Democracy after Democratization: The Korean Experience*. Translated by Kyung-hee Lee. Seoul: Humanitas, 2005.

——. "Democratization, Civil Society, and the Civil Social Movement in Korea: The Significance of the Citizens' Alliance for the 2000 General Election." *Korea Journal* 40, no. 4 (2000): 26–55.

Christofferson, Michael Scott. "An Antitotalitarian History of the French Revolution: François Furet's *Penser la révolution française*." *French Historical Studies* 22, no. 4 (1999): 557–611.

Chun, Jennifer Ji-hye. "The Contested Politics of Gender and Irregular Employment: The Revitalization of the South Korean Democratic Labour Movement." In *Labour and the Challenges of Globalisation: What Prospects for Transnational Solidarity?* edited by Andreas Bieler, Ingemar Lindberg, and Devan Pillay, 23–44. London: Pluto, 2008.

Cohen, Phil. "Finding Uncommon Ground: Working-Class Identity Politics after Labourism." *Soundings* 66 (Summer 2017): 113-28.
Connerton, Paul. *How Societies Remember*. Cambridge: Cambridge University Press, 1989.
Constitution of the Republic of Korea. July 12, 1948. http://english.ccourt.go.kr/cckhome/images/eng/main/Constitution_of_the_Republic_of_Korea.pdf.
Coronil, Fernando. "Towards a Critique of Globalcentrism: Speculations on Capitalism's Nature." *Public Culture* 12, no. 2 (Spring 2000): 351-74.
Crane, Susan A. "Memory, Distortion, and History in the Museum." *History & Theory* 36, no. 4 (1997): 44-63.
Cumings, Bruce. "The Asian Crisis, Democracy, and the End of 'Late' Development." In *The Politics of the Asian Economic Crisis*, edited by T. J. Pempel, 17-44. Ithaca, NY: Cornell University Press, 1999.
———. *Korea's Place in the Sun: A Modern History*. New York: Norton, 1997.
———. *The Origins of the Korean War*, 2 vols. Princeton, NJ: Princeton University Press, 1981, 1990.
Cushner, Ari. "Cold War Comrades: Left-Liberal Anticommunism and American Empire, 1941-1968." PhD diss., University of California, Santa Cruz, 2017.
de Baets, Antoon. "A Declaration of Responsibilities of Present Generations toward Past Generation." *History & Theory* 43, no. 4 (December 2004): 130-63.
de Ceuster, Koen. "The Nation Exorcised: The Historiography of Collaboration in South Korea." *Korean Studies* 25, no. 2 (2001): 207-42.
Dietz, Mary. "Context Is All: Feminism and Theories of Citizenship." In *Dimensions of Radical Democracy*, edited by Chantal Mouffe, 63-85. London: Verso, 1996.
Dirlik, Arif. *Postmodernity's Histories: The Past as Legacy and Project*. Lanham, MD: Rowman & Littlefield, 2000.
Donahue, William Collins. "Revising '68: Bernhard Schlink's *Der Vorleser*, Peter Schneider's *Vati*, and the Question of History." *Seminar* 40, no. 3 (September 2004): 293-311.
Doucette, Jamie, and Se-Woong Koo. "Distorting Democracy: Politics by Public Security in Contemporary South Korea." *Asia-Pacific Journal* 11, no. 4 (2013): 1-14.
Dreyfus, Michel et al., eds. *Le siècle des communismes*. Paris: Les Editions de l'atelier / Editions ouvrières, 2000.
Duara, Prasenjit. *Rescuing History from the Nation: Questioning Narratives of Modern China*. Chicago: University of Chicago Press, 1995.
Duggan, Lisa. *The Twilight of Equality? Neoliberalism, Cultural Politics, and the Attack on Democracy*. Boston: Beacon Press, 2003.
Eichengreen, Barry, Dwight H. Perkins, and Kwanho Shin. *From Miracle to Maturity: The Growth of the Korean Economy*. Cambridge, MA: Harvard University Asia Center, 2012.
Eley, Geoff. "History in a Moment of Danger? National Retrieval, Memory, and Everydayness." Paper delivered at the KCL/LSE Conference on "At the Crossroads of Past and Present: 'Contemporary History' and Historical Discipline." King's College London and London School of Economics, London, May 22-23, 2009.
———. "What Produces Democracy? Revolutionary Crises, Popular Politics and Democratic Gains in Twentieth-Century Europe." In *History and Revolution: Refuting Revisionism*, edited by Mike Haynes and Jim Wolfreys, 172-201. New York: Verso, 2007.

Em, Henry. "Historians and Historical Writing in Modern Korea." In *Oxford History of Historical Writing*, edited by Daniel Woolf and Axel Schneider, 659–77. Oxford: Oxford University Press, 2011.

Eperjesi, John R. "Communists Meet Gangnam Style: Alain Badiou and Slavoj Žižek in South Korea." *Huffington Post*, October 8, 2013. http://www.huffingtonpost.com/john-r-eperjesi/communists-meet-gangnam-style_b_4047098.html.

Feldman, Allen. "Political Terror and the Technologies of Memory: Excuse, Sacrifice, Commodification, and Actuarial Moralities." *Radical History Review* 85 (Winter 2003): 58–73.

Ferguson, Roderick A., and Grace Kyungwon Hong. "The Sexual and Racial Contradictions of Neoliberalism." *Journal of Homosexuality* 59 (2012): 1057–64.

Flatley, Jonathan. "Modernism and Melancholia." In *Affective Mapping: Melancholia and the Politics of Modernism*, 28–75. Cambridge, MA: Harvard University Press, 2008.

Foucault, Michael. *The Birth of Biopolitics: Lectures at the Collège de France, 1978–79*. Edited by Michel Senellart and translated by Graham Burchell. New York: Palgrave Macmillan, 2008.

———. *Discipline and Punish: The Birth of the Prison*. Translated by Alan Sheridan. New York: Vintage Books, 1979.

French, Howard W. "Despite Protests, Seoul to Send Troops to Iraq for Reconstruction." *New York Times*, April 2, 2003.

Friedman, Max Paul, and Padraic Kenney, eds. *Partisan Histories: The Past in Contemporary Global Politics*. New York: Palgrave Macmillan, 2005.

Fukuyama, Francis. "The End of History?" *The National Interest*, no. 16 (Summer 1989): 3–18.

———. *The End of History and the Last Man*. New York: Free Press, 1992.

Furet, François. *Interpreting the French Revolution*. Translated by Elborg Forster. Cambridge: Cambridge University Press, 1981.

Gallerano, Nicola. "History and the Public Use of History." *Diogenes* 42, no. 4 (Winter 1994): 85–102.

Gills, Barry K., and Dong-Sook S. Gills. "South Korea and Globalization: The Rise of Globalism?" *Asian Perspective* 23, no. 4 (1999): 199–228.

Gluck, Carol. "Operations of Memory: 'Comfort Women' and the World." In *Ruptured Histories: War, Memory, and the Post–Cold War in Asia*, edited by Sheila Miyoshi Jager and Rana Mitter, 47–77. Cambridge, MA: Harvard University Press, 2007.

Gramsci, Antonio. *Prison Notebooks*, vol. 3. Translated by J. A. Buttigieg. New York: Columbia University Press, 2007.

———. *Selections from the Prison Notebooks of Antonio Gramsci*. Edited and translated by Quintin Hoare and Geoffrey Nowell-Smith. London: Lawrence & Wishart, 1971.

Gumbrecht, Hans Ulrich. "On the Decent Uses of History." *History and Theory* 40, no. 1 (February 2001): 117–27.

Ha, Young Jun. "Mass Dictatorship and Transnational History." *Homo Migrans* 8 (June 2013): 48–69.

Habermas, Jürgen. *A Berlin Republic: Writings on Germany*. Translated by Steven Rendall. Lincoln: University of Nebraska Press, 1997.

Haggard, Stephan. *Pathways from the Periphery: The Politics of Growth in the Newly Industrializing Countries*. Ithaca, NY: Cornell University Press, 1990.

Halbwachs, Maurice. *On Collective Memory*. Edited and translated by Lewis A. Coser. Chicago: University of Chicago Press, 1992.

Han, In Sup. "Kwangju and Beyond: Coping with Past State Atrocities in South Korea." *Human Rights Quarterly* 27, no. 3 (2005): 998–1045.

Han, Sung-won [Han Sŭng-wŏn]. *Father and Son*. Translated by Young-nan Yu and Julie Pickering. Dumont, NJ: Homa and Sekey Books, 2002.

Hartog, François. "An End and a Beginning." *UNESCO Courier* 47, no. 5 (May 1994): 8–11.

Harvey, David. *A Brief History of Neoliberalism*. Oxford: Oxford University Press, 2005.

Hass, Aaron. *In the Shadow of the Holocaust: The Second Generation*. New York: Cambridge University Press, 1996.

Hayes, Peter, and Chung-in Moon. "Park Chung Hee, the CIA & the Bomb." NAPSNet Special Reports, September 23, 2011. https://nautilus.org/napsnet/napsnet-special-reports/park-chung-hee-the-cia-and-the-bomb/.

Hayes, Shannon. "The Historico-poetic Materialism of Benjamin and Celan." *Critical Horizons* 19, no. 2 (2018): 125–39.

Haynes, Mike, and Jim Wolfreys. Introduction to *History and Revolution: Refuting Revisionism*, edited by Mike Haynes and Jim Wolfreys, 1–24. New York: Verso, 2007.

Hegel, Georg Wilhelm Friedrich. *Lectures on the Philosophy of World History*. Translated by H. B. Nisbet. Cambridge: Cambridge University Press, 1981.

Heilbrunn, Jacob. "Germany's New Right." *Foreign Affairs* 75, no. 6 (1996): 80–98.

Heo, Uk, Houngcheul Jeon, Hayam Kim, and Okjin Kim. "The Political Economy of South Korea: Economic Growth, Democratization, and Financial Crisis." *Maryland Series in Contemporary Asian Studies* 2008, no. 2 (December 2008): 1–24.

Hobsbawm, E. J. "The Social Function of the Past: Some Questions." *Past and Present* 55, no. 1 (May 1972): 3–17.

Hong, Grace Kyungwon. *Death beyond Disavowal: The Impossible Politics of Difference*. Minneapolis: University of Minnesota Press, 2015.

Hong, Sung Gul. "The Search for Deterrence: Park's Nuclear Option." In *Park Chung Hee Era: The Transformation of South Korea*, edited by Byung-Kook Kim and Ezra F. Vogel, 483–510. Cambridge, MA: Harvard University Press, 2011.

Honneth, Axel. "A Communicative Disclosure of the Past: On the Relation between Anthropology and Philosophy of History in Walter Benjamin." *New Formations* 20 (1993): 83–96.

Hughes, Theodore H. *Literature and Film in Cold War South Korea: Freedom's Frontier*. New York: Columbia University Press, 2012.

Hutchinson, Colin. *Reaganism, Thatcherism, and the Social Novel*. New York: Palgrave Macmillan, 2008.

Huyssen, Andreas. *Present Pasts: Urban Palimpsests and the Politics of Memory*. Stanford, CA: Stanford University Press, 2003.

———. *Twilight Memories: Marking Time in a Culture of Amnesia*. New York: Routledge, 1994.

Hwang, Byeong-ju [Hwang Pyŏng-ju]. "The Ruling Discourse and Mass Politics and Mass Politics of the Park Chung Hee Regime." *Review of Korean Studies* 12, no. 3 (September 2009): 11–40.

Hwang, Jongyon [Hwang Chong-yŏn]. "After the Apocalypse of Literature: A Critique of Karatani Kojin's Thesis of the End of Modern Literature Korea." *Korea Journal* 47, no. 1 (Spring 2007): 102–25.

Iggers, Georg. "Historicism: The History and Meaning of the Term." *Journal of the History of Ideas* 56, no. 1 (1995): 129–52.

Jacoby, Russell. *Social Amnesia: A Critique of Conformist Psychology*. Boston: Beacon, 1975.

Jan, Ammar Ali. "'Beyond Good and Evil': Alain Badiou on Communist Politics in the 20th Century." spectre.cambridge, no. 1 (October 7, 2013). https://spectrecambridge.wordpress.com/2013/10/07/beyond-good-and-evil-alain-badiou-on-communist-politics-in-the-20th-century/.

Jang, Sang-Hwan [Chang Sang-hwan]. "Continuing Suicide among Laborers in Korea." *Labor History* 45, no. 3 (2004): 271–97.

Jenkins, Keith. "Ethical Responsibility and the Historian: On the Possible End of a History 'Of a Certain Kind.'" *History and Theory* 43, no. 4 (December 2004): 43–60.

Jenkins, Scott. "Nietzsche's Use of Monumental History." *Journal of Nietzsche Studies* 45, no. 2 (Summer 2014): 169–81.

Jessop, Sharon. "Children, Redemption and Remembrance in Water Benjamin." *Journal of Philosophy of Education* 47, no. 4 (2013): 642–57.

Kansteiner, Wulf. "Finding Meaning in Memory: A Methodological Critique of Collective Memory Studies." *History and Theory* 41, no. 2 (May 2002): 179–97.

Karatani, Kojin. *Origins of Modern Japanese Literature*. Translated by Brett de Bary. Durham, NC: Duke University Press, 1993.

Karl, Rebecca E. Foreword to *The End of the Revolution: China and the Limits of Modernity*, by Wang Hui, vii–x. New York: Verso, 2011.

Kim, Alice S. "Left Out: People's Solidarity for Social Progress and the Evolution of *Minjung* after Authoritarianism." In *South Korean Social Movements: From Democracy to Civil Society*, edited by Gi-Wook Shin and Paul Y. Chang, 245–69. New York: Routledge, 2011.

Kim, Byung-Kook, and Ezra F. Vogel, eds. *Park Chung Hee Era: The Transformation of South Korea*. Cambridge, MA: Harvard University Press, 2011.

Kim, Dong-Choon [Kim Tong-ch'un]. "The Long Road toward Truth and Reconciliation: Unwavering Attempts to Achieve Justice in South Korea." *Critical Asian Studies* 42, no. 4 (2010): 525–52.

———. *The Unending Korean War: A Social History*. Translated by Sung-ok Kim. Larkspur, CA: Tamal Vista Publications, 2009.

Kim, Hong Nack. "The 1988 Parliamentary Election in South Korea." *Asian Survey* 29, no. 5 (May 1989): 480–95.

Kim, Hyung-A, and Clark W. Sorensen, eds. *Reassessing the Park Chung Hee Era, 1961–1979*. Seattle: Center for Korean Studies, University of Washington Press, 2011.

Kim, Jin Kyoon [Kim Chin-gyun]. "Rethinking the New Beginning of the Democratic Union Movement in Korea: From the 1987 Great Workers' Struggle to the Construction of the Korean Trade Union Council (Chunnohyup) and the Korean Confederation of Trade Unions (KCTU)." *Inter-Asia Cultural Studies* 1, no. 3 (2000): 491–503.

Kim, Jongtae. "The Discourse of *Sŏnjin'guk*: South Korea's Eurocentric Modern Identities and Worldviews." PhD diss., University of Illinois at Urbana-Champaign, 2011.

Kim, Kihwan. "Kim Jae-Ik: His Life and Contributions." In *Liberalization in the Process of Economic Development*, edited by Lawrence B. Krause and Kim Kihwan, xi–xxiv. Berkeley: University of California Press, 1991.

Kim, Sandra So Hee Chi. "Suji Kwock Kim's 'Generation' and the Ethics of Diasporic Postmemory." *positions* 24, no. 3 (August 2016): 653–67.

Kim, Sookyung, and Paul Y. Chang. "Entry of Past Activists into the National Assembly and South Korea's Participation in the Iraq War." In *South Korean Social Movements: From Democracy to Civil Society*, edited by Gi-Wook Shin and Paul Y. Chang, 117–34. New York: Routledge, 2011.

Kim, Yun Tae. "DJnomics and the Transformation of the Developmental State." *Journal of Contemporary Asia* 35, no. 4 (2005): 471–82.

Kittsteiner, H. D. "Walter Benjamin's Historicism." *New German Critique* 39 (1986): 179–218.

Koo, Hagen. "The Dilemmas of Empowered Labor in Korea: Korean Workers in the Face of Global Capitalism." *Asian Survey* 40, no. 2 (2000): 227–250.

———. *Korean Workers: The Culture and Politics of Class Formation*. Ithaca, NY: Cornell University Press, 2001.

Koo, Se-Woong. "Korea, Thy Name Is Hell Joseon." *Korea Exposé*, September 22, 2015. https://www.koreaexpose.com/korea-thy-name-is-hell-joseon/.

Koschmann, J. Victor. *Revolution and Subjectivity in Postwar Japan*. Chicago: University of Chicago Press, 1996.

Koselleck, Reinhart. *Futures Past: On the Semantics of Historical Time*. Translated by Keith Tribe. New York: Columbia University Press, 2004.

Kotch, John Barry. "The *Chosun Ilbo* vs. *JoongAng Ilbo*: Historiographical Warfare in the Post–Cold War South Korean Press." *Korea Journal* 30, no. 3 (Fall 1994): 443–66.

Kwak, Ki-Sung. *Media and Democratic Transition in South Korea*. New York: Routledge, 2012.

Kwon, Heonik. *The Other Cold War*. New York: Columbia University Press, 2010.

Kwon, Vicki Sung-yeon. "The Sonyŏsang Phenomenon: Nationalism and Feminism Surrounding the 'Comfort Women' Statue." *Korean Studies* 43 (2019): 6–39.

Lasch, Christopher. *The Culture of Narcissism: American Life in an Age of Diminishing Expectations*. New York: W. W. Norton, 1979.

Lazarus, Neil. "'Third Worldism' and the Political Imaginary of Postcolonial Studies." In *The Oxford Handbook of Postcolonial Studies*, edited by Graham Huggan, 324–339. New York: Oxford University Press, 2013.

Lee, Byeong-Cheon, ed. *Developmental Dictatorship and the Park Chung-Hee Era: The Shaping of Modernity in the Republic of Korea*. Translated by Eungsoo Kim and Jaehun Cho. Paramus, NJ: Homa & Sekey, 2003.

Lee, Chang-sup. "Hunger Strike, Binge-Eating Strike." *Korea Times*, September 11, 2014. https://www.koreatimes.co.kr/www/nation/2020/05/298_164379.html.

Lee, Chung H. "Institutional Reform in Japan and Korea: Why the Difference?" Working Paper 204, Department of Economics, University of Hawai'i at Manoa, September 2014.

Lee, Hyunseon. "The South Korean Blockbuster and a Divided Nation." *International Journal of Korean History* 21, no. 1 (February 2016): 259–64.

Lee, Namhee. "From *Minjung* to *Simin*: The Discursive Shift in Korean Democratic Movements." In *South Korean Social Movements: From Democracy to Civil Society*, edited by Gi-Wook Shin and Paul Y. Chang, 51-57. New York: Routledge, 2011.

———. "'From the Streets to the National Assembly': Democratic Transition and the Demands for Truth about the Kwangju Massacre." In *State Violence in East Asia*, edited by Narayanan Ganesan and Sung Chull Kim, 47-73. Lexington: University of Kentucky Press, 2013.

———. *The Making of Minjung: Democracy and the Politics of Representation in South Korea*. Ithaca, NY: Cornell University Press, 2007.

———. "Public Intellectuals." In *The Oxford Handbook of South Korean Politics*, edited by JeongHun Han, Ramón Pacheco Pardo, and Youngho Cho, 423-438. New York: Oxford University Press, 2022.

———. "The South Korean Student Movement." In *Korean Society: Civil Society, Democracy and the State*, edited by Charles K. Armstrong, 95-120. 2nd ed. New York: Routledge, 2006.

Lee, Namhee, and Kim Won, eds. *The South Korean Democratization Movement: A Sourcebook*. Sŏngnam: Academy of Korean Studies Press, 2016.

Lee, Wonduck, and Joohee Lee. "Will the Model of Uncoordinated Decentralization Persist?" In *The New Structure of Labor Relations: Tripartism and Decentralization*, edited by Harry Charles Katz, Wonduck Lee, and Joohee Lee, 143-65. Ithaca, NY: ILR Press, 2004.

Lefebvre, Henri. *Critique of Everyday Life*, vol. 2. Translated by John Moore. London: Verso, 1991.

Lett, Denise P. *In Pursuit of Status: The Making of South Korea's "New" Urban Middle Class*. Cambridge, MA: Harvard University Asia Center, 1998.

Levy, Daniel. "The Future of the Past: Historiographical Disputes and Competing Memories in Germany and Israel." *History and Theory* 38, no. 1 (2002): 51-66.

Lew, Young Ick [Yu Yŏng-ik]. *The Making of the First Korean President: Syngman Rhee's Quest for Independence, 1875-1948*. Honolulu: University of Hawai'i Press, 2013.

———, ed. *Syngman Rhee Correspondence in English, 1904-1948*, 8 vols. Seoul: Institute for Modern Korean Studies (IMKS), Yonsei University, 2009.

Lew, Young Ick, Sangchul Cha, and Francesca Minah Song, comps. *The Syngman Rhee Presidential Papers, 1948-1960: A Catalog*. Seoul: Yonsei University Press, 2005.

Lim, Hyun-Chin, and Jin-Ho Jang. "Between Neoliberalism and Democracy: The Transformation of the Developmental State in South Korea." *Development and Society* 35, no. 1 (June 2006): 1-29.

Lindroos, Kia. *Now-Time Image-Space: Temporalization of Politics in Water Benjamin's Philosophy of History and Art*. Jyväskylä, Finland: Sophi Academic Press, 1998.

Lowe, Lisa. *Intimacies of Four Continents*. Durham, NC: Duke University Press, 2015.

Löwy, Michael. *Fire Alarm: Reading Walter Benjamin's "On the Concept of History."* Translated by Chris Turner. New York: Verso, 2005.

———. "On May '68: A Cocktail of Revolt." *Against the Current* (September/October 2008): 15-16.

Lyotard, Jean-François. *The Differend: Phrase in Dispute*. Manchester, UK: Manchester University Press, 1988.

MacLean, Nancy. *Democracy in Chains: The Deep History of the Radical Right's Stealth Plan for America*. New York: Viking, 2017.

Maier, Charles S. *The Unmasterable Past: History, Holocaust, and German National Identity*. Cambridge, MA: Harvard University Press, 1997.

Marlière, Philippe. "Sarkozysm as an Ideological Theme Park: Nicolas Sarkozy and Right-Wing Political Thought." *Modern & Contemporary France* 17, no. 4 (2009): 375–90.

Maxwell, Richard. "Political Economy within Cultural Studies." In *A Companion to Cultural Studies*, edited by Toby Miller, 116–38. Malden, MA: Wiley-Blackwell, 2001.

McClure, Kirstie. "On the Subject of Rights: Pluralism, Plurality, and Political Identity." In *Dimensions of Radical Democracy: Pluralism, Citizenship, Community*, edited by Chantal Mouffe, 108–27. London: Verso, 1996.

Mercer, Ben. "The Moral Rearmament of France: Nora, Memory, and the Crisis of Republicanism." *French Politics, Culture & Society* 31, no. 2 (Summer 2013): 102–16.

Miller, Owen. "The Idea of Stagnation in Korean Historiography: From Kukuda Tokuzo to the New Right." *Korean Histories* 2, no. 1 (2010): 1–12.

Miller, Toby, and Geoffrey Lawrence. "Globalization and Culture." In *A Companion to Cultural Studies*, edited by Toby Miller, 490–509. Malden, MA: Wiley-Blackwell, 2006.

Moon, Seungsook. "Cultural Politics of Remembering Park Chung Hee." *Harvard Asia Quarterly* 11 (Spring/Summer 2008): 26–44.

Neocleous, Mark. "Let the Dead Bury Their Dead: Marxism and the Politics of Redemption." *Radical Philosophy* 128 (November/December 2004): 23–32.

Nietzsche, Friedrich. "On the Uses and Disadvantages of History for Life." In *Untimely Meditations*, edited by Daniel Breazeale and translated by R. J. Hollingdale, 59–123. Cambridge: Cambridge University Press, 1997.

Nora, Pierre. "Between Memory and History: *Les lieux de mémoire*." *Representations* 26 (Spring 1989): 7–25.

Olick, Jeffrey K. *The Politics of Regret: On Collective Memory and Historical Responsibility*. New York: Routledge, 2007.

Orwell, George. "Why I Write." In *England Your England and Other Essays*, 7–16. London: Secker and Warburg, 1954.

Paik, Nak-chung. *Division System in Crisis: Essays on Contemporary Korea*. Translated by Kim Myung-hwan, Sol June-Kyu, Song Seung-cheol, and Ryu Young-joo. Berkeley: Global, Area, and International Archive, University of California Press, 2011.

Park, Hyun Ok. *The Capitalist Unconscious: From Korean Unification to Transnational Korea*. New York: Columbia University Press, 2015.

Park, Si-soo. "'A Taxi Driver' Attracts 10 Million Viewers: 15th Korean Film in History." *Korea Times*, April 20, 2017.

Park, Sunyoung. *The Proletarian Wave: Literature and Leftist Culture in Colonial Korea, 1910–1945*. Cambridge, MA: Harvard University Asia Center, 2015.

Parkes, Stuart. *Writers and Politics in Germany 1945–2008*. Rochester, NY: Camden House, 2009.

Pastreich, Emmanuel. "The Balancer: Roh Moo-hyun's Vision of Korean Politics and the Future of Northeast Asia." *Asia-Pacific Journal* 3, no. 8 (August 3, 2005): 1–14.

Pipes, Richard. *The Russian Revolution*. New York: Knopf, 1990.

Plass, Ulrich. "From Left-Wing to Communist Melancholy: Traverso's Wager." *History and Theory* 58, no. 1 (March 2019): 148–64.

Povinelli, Elizabeth A. *Economies of Abandonment: Social Belonging and Endurance in Late Liberalism*. Durham, NC: Duke University Press, 2011.

Rancière, Jacques. "In What Time Do We Live?" *Política común* 4 (2013). https://quod.lib.umich.edu/p/pc/12322227.0004.001?view=text;rgn=main.

Rhee, Syngman. *The Syngman Rhee Telegrams*. Edited by the Institute for Modern Korean Studies (IMKS). Seoul: IMKS, Yonsei University, 2000.

Ricoeur, Paul. *Time and Narrative*, vol. 3. Translated by Kathleen Blamey and David Pellauer. Chicago: University of Chicago Press, 1988.

Ross, Kristin. *May '68 and Its Afterlives*. Chicago: University of Chicago Press, 2002.

Rüsen, Jörn. "Historical Enlightenment in the Light of Postmodernism: History in the Age of the 'New Unintelligibility.'" Translated by Bill Templer. *History and Memory* 1, no. 2 (1989): 109–31.

Ryu, Youngju. *Writers of the Winter Republic: Literature and Resistance in Park Chung Hee's Korea*. Honolulu: University of Hawai'i Press, 2016.

Schwarz, Bill. "Memory, Temporality, Modernity: *Les lieux de mémoire*." In *Memory: Histories, Theories, Debates*, edited by Susannah Radstone and Bill Schwarz, 41–58. New York: Fordham University Press, 2010.

Shapiro, Ann-Louise. "Whose (Which) History Is It Anyway?" *History and Theory* 36, no. 4 (December 1997): 1–3.

Shaw, William, ed. *Human Rights in Korea: Historical and Policy Perspectives*. Cambridge, MA: Council on East Asian Studies, Harvard University, 1991.

Shin, Jang-Sup, and Ha-Joon Chang. *Restructuring Korea Inc*. London: RoutledgeCurzon, 2003.

Soh, Sarah. *The Comfort Women: Sexual Violence and Postcolonial Memory in Korea and Japan*. Chicago: University of Chicago Press, 2008.

Song, Ho-Keun. "Who Benefits from Industrial Restructuring?" *Korea Journal* 31, no. 3 (Autumn 1991): 69–84.

Song, Jesook. *South Koreans in the Debt Crisis: The Creation of a Neoliberal Welfare Society*. Durham, NC: Duke University Press, 2009.

Suh, Myung Sahm. "Generational Dynamics and the Consolidation of the Christian Right in Contemporary South Korea." PhD diss., University of Chicago, 2017.

Swedish Academy. "Dario Fo: The Nobel Prize for Literature 1997." October 9, 1997. https://www.nobelprize.org/prizes/literature/1997/press-release.

Tassone, Giuseppe. "Democracy at a Standstill: The Idea of Democracy as a Dialectic of Theory and Practice." *Critique* 41, no. 1 (2013): 77–92.

———. "It Is Not Over Yet: The Arab Revolution between Culture and Political Economy." *Arab Studies Quarterly* 37, no. 4 (Fall 2015): 334–50.

Thatcher, Margaret. "AIDS, Education, and the Year 2000!" *Woman's Own*, October 31, 1987, 8–10.

Therborn, Göran. "After Dialectics." *New Left Review* 43 (January–February 2007): 63–114.

———. "'New Masses?' Social Bases of Resistance." *New Left Review* 85 (January–February 2014): 7–16.

Thomas, Peter D. "Gramsci's Revolutions: Passive and Permanent." *Modern Intellectual History* 17, no. 1 (2010): 117–46.

Tikhonov, Vladimir. "The Rise and Fall of the New Right Movement and the Historical Wars in 2000s South Korea." *European Journal of Korean Studies* 18, no. 2 (2019): 5–36.

Tocqueville, Alexis de. *Democracy in America*. Translated by Arthur Goldhammer. New York: Library of America, 2004.

Traverso, Enzo. "Totalitarianism between History and Theory." *History and Theory* 56, no. 4 (December 2017): 97–118.

United States Institute of Peace. "Truth Commission: South Korea 2005." April 18, 2012. https://www.usip.org/publications/2012/04/truth-commission-south-korea-2005.

Varon, Jeremy, Michael S. Foley, and John McMillian. "Time Is an Ocean: The Past and Future of the Sixties." *The Sixties* 1, no. 1 (June 2008): 1–7.

Ventresca, Robert A. "Mussolini's Ghost: Italy's Duce in History and Memory." *History and Memory* 18, no. 1 (2006): 86–119.

Wade, Robert. *Governing the Market: Economic Theory and the Role of Government in East Asian Industrialization*. Princeton, NJ: Princeton University Press, 1990.

West, James M. "Martial Lawlessness: The Legal Aftermath of Kwangju." *Pacific Rim Law & Policy Journal* 6, no. 1 (1997): 85–168.

White, Hayden. *The Tropics of Discourse: Essays in Cultural Criticism*. Baltimore: Johns Hopkins University Press, 1978.

Wolin, Richard. *Walter Benjamin: An Aesthetic of Redemption*. Berkeley: University of California Press, 1994.

Woo-Cumings, Meredith, ed. *The Developmental State*. Ithaca, NY: Cornell University Press, 1999.

———. "The State, Democracy, and the Reform of the Corporate Sector in Korea." In *The Politics of the Asian Economic Crisis*, edited by T. J. Pempel, 116–42. Ithaca, NY: Cornell University Press, 1999.

Yang, Hyunah. "Finding the 'Map of Memory': Testimony of the Japanese Military Sexual Slavery Survivors." *positions* 16, no. 1 (Spring 2008): 79–107.

Yoneyama, Lisa. *Cold War Ruins: Transpacific Critique of American Justice and Japanese War Crimes*. Durham, NC: Duke University Press, 2016.

WORKS IN KOREAN

(Unless otherwise noted, works in Korean are published in Seoul, South Korea.)

An Hyŏn-hyo. "*Haebang chŏnhusa ŭi chaeinsik* e taehan chinghujŏk tokhae" [A symptomatic reading of *Reunderstanding Pre- and Post-liberation History*]. *Kyŏngjewa sahoe* 86 (2010): 199–232.

An Pyŏng-jik, ed. *Han'guk minjujuŭi ŭi kiwŏn kwa mirae: Posuga ikkŭlda* [The origin and future of South Korea's democracy: Conservatives have been leading the country's democracy]. Sidae chŏngsin, 2011.

———. Mŏrimal [Preface] to *Han'guk minjujuŭi ŭi kiwŏn kwa mirae: Posuga ikkŭlda*, edited by An Pyŏng-jik, 4–11. Sidae chŏngsin, 2011.

Böll, Heinrich. *Und sagte kein einziges Wort* [And never said a word]. Köln: Kiepenheuer & Witsch, 1953. Translated by Hong Sŏng-gwang as *Kŭrigo amumaldo haji anhatta*. Yŏllin ch'aektŭl, 2011.

Chang Ha-sŏng. *Han'guk chabonjuŭi: Kyŏngje minjuhwarŭl nŏmŏ chŏngŭiroun kyŏngjero* [South Korean capitalism: Beyond economic democracy to a just economy]. Sŏngnam: Hei puksŭ, 2014.

Chang Kang-myŏng. "Pyŏnmyŏng ŭl ch'ajasŏ—Pok Kŏ-il non" [Looking for excuses—on Pok Kŏ-il]. *alt.SF* (blog), February 1, 2011. https://altsf.wordpress.com/2011/02/01/sp04/.

Chayujuŭi yŏndae. "Chayujuŭi yŏndae ch'angnipsŏnŏnmun" [Inaugural statement of the Liberty Union]. Chogabje.com, November 22, 2004. http://www.chogabje.com/board/view.asp?C_IDX=5150&C_CC=AZ.

Chi Su-gŏl. "Kŏn'gukchŏl nonjaengŭi chihyŏng pakkugi" [To change the landscape of the debate regarding Foundation Day]. *Naeirŭl yŏnŭn yŏksa* 64 (Fall 2016): 15–25.

Chin Chung-gwŏn. "Chugŭn tokchaejaŭi sahoe: Pak Chŏng-hŭi sindŭromŭi chŏngsinbunsŏkhak" [Society of the dead dictator: Psychoanalysis of the Park Chung-hee syndrome]. In *Kaebal tokchaewa Pak Chŏng-hŭi sidae*, edited by Yi Pyŏng-ch'ŏn, 339–64. Ch'angjak kwa pip'yŏngsa, 1997.

———. "Pak Chŏng-hŭiwa angmajuŭi: Hogŭn 'sunggohan hŭigŭg'ŭi mihakchŏk kanŭngsŏnge kwanhan koch'al" [Park Chung-hee and diabolism: Or a study on the aesthetic possibility of "sublime comedy"]. *Munhak tongne* 4, no. 4 (Winter 1997): 569–95.

Chin Sŏng-ho. "Welk'ŏm t'u Kim Ilssŏng wangguk" [Welcome to the kingdom of Kim Il Sung]. *Premium Chosun*, August 24, 2005. http://premium.chosun.com/site/data/html_dir/2005/08/24/2005082467003.html.

Cho Han Hye-jŏng, Ŏm Ki-ho, Kang Chŏng-sŏk, Na Il-dŭng, Yi Ch'ung-han, Yi Yŏng-nong, Ch'oe Ŭn-ju, Ch'ŏn Chu-hŭi, Yi Kyu-ho, and Yang Ki-min. *Nooryŏgŭi paesin: Ch'ŏngnyŏnŭl kŏbuhanŭn kukka sahoerŭl kŏbuhanŭn ch'ŏngnyŏn* [Betrayal of effort: The state that refuses the youth and the youth that refuse society]. Ch'angjak kwa pip'yŏngsa, 2016.

Cho Hŭi-yŏn. "Minjung undong kwa 'simin sahoe,' 'simin undong'" [The *minjung* movement, "civil society," and "citizens' movement"]. In *Simin sahoewa simin undong* [Civil society and citizens' movement], edited by Yu P'al-mu and Kim Ho-gi, 298–336. Hanul, 1995.

Cho Kap-che. *Nae mudŏm e ch'im ŭl paet'ŏra: Cho Kap-che kija ka ssŭnŭn kŭndaehwa hyŏngmyŏngga Pak Chŏng-hŭi ŭi pijanghan saeng'ae* [Spit on my grave: The tragic life of Park Chung-hee, the revolutionary of modernization, written by reporter Cho Kap-che], 8 vols. Chosun Ilbosa, 1998–2001.

———. *Yugo! Pumasat'aeesŏ 10.26chŏngbyŏnkkaji Yusinjŏnggwŏnŭl punggoesik'in hamsŏnggwa ch'ongsŏngŭi hyŏnjang* [Posthumous work! At the sites of cries and gunfire from the Pusan-Masan incident to the October 26 incident], 2 vols. Han'gilsa, 1987.

Cho Kap-tong. "Aitie saemaŭrundong chiwŏnŭl" [We need to support the new village movement in Haiti]. *Chosun Ilbo*, April 14, 2010, A37.

Cho Myŏng-gi. "90nyŏndae taejung (wie kullimhanŭn) sosŏl" [Novels of the masses (and that also trample upon the masses)]. *Onŭrŭi munye pip'yŏng* (March 1997): 128–44.

Cho Ŭn-hŭi. "Pak Chŏng-hŭi hyungnaenaemyŏn taet'ongnyŏng toenda?" [Does one become a president by imitating Park Chung-hee?]. *Nyusŭmeik'ŏ*, April 24, 1997, 35.

Cho Yŏn-chŏng. "'Kwangju'rŭl' hyŏnjaehwa hanŭn il: Kwŏn Yŏ-sŏn ŭi *Regato* (2012) wa Han Kang ŭi *Sonyŏni onda* (2014) rŭl chungsimŭro" [To make "Kwangju" meaningful for today: Focusing on Kwŏn Yŏ-sŏn's *Legato* (2012) and Han Kang's *Human Acts* (2014)]. *Taejung sŏsa yŏn'gu* 20, no. 3 (2014): 101–38.

Cho Yong-hwan. "5.18 t'ŭkpyŏlbŏpkwa Chŏn-No chaep'anŭi munjejŏm" [The special act on the May 18 democratization movement and the problem with the trial of Chun Doo-hwan and Roh Tae-woo]. *Yŏksa pip'yŏng* 32 (Spring 1996): 61–79.

Cho Yŏng-il. "Mŏnamŏn segyemunhak: Siba Ryot'aro wa Yi Mun-yŏl" [A long way for world literature: Siba Ryot'aro and Yi Mun-yŏl]. *Onŭrŭi munye pip'yŏng* 79 (Winter 2010): 222–77.

Ch'oe Chin-sŏp. "6wŏrhangjaeng chuyŏktŭrŭi hyŏnjuso" [The current state of the leaders of the June uprising]. *Wŏlgan Mal* 60 (June 1991): 80–85.

Ch'oe Chong-ho. "Sonyŏsang ch'imbaet'ŭn ch'ŏngnyŏndŭl 'wianbu p'ihaejadŭl chorong haryŏgo kŭraetta'" [Youth who spat on the Statue of the Girl for Peace also made fun of the "comfort women"]. *Yonhapnews*, July 10, 2019. https://www.yna.co.kr/view/AKR20190710141700061.

Ch'oe Hong-jae, ed. *386 ŭi kkum, kŭ sŏngch'arŭi iyu* [The dream of the 386 generation and reasons for its self-reflection]. Nanam, 2005.

Ch'oe Hye-sŏng. "Kwayŏn urinarae kŏn'gukchŏri p'iryohan'ga?" [Is it really necessary to have a Foundation Day?]. *Ch'ŏrhakkwa hyŏnsil* 112 (2017): 268–92.

Ch'oe Kap-su. "Yŏksaesŏ pyŏnhyŏgiran muŏsin'ga" [What is a revolution in history]. *Ch'ŏrhakkwa hyŏnsil* 3 (2004): 32–44.

Ch'oe Sŭng-hŭi. *Chosŏn ch'ogi ŏn'gwan, ŏllon yŏn'gu* [A study of ŏn'gwa and journalism in early Chosŏn]. Sŏuldaehakkyo ch'ulp'anbu, 1984.

Ch'oe Wŏn-sik. "Munhak kwa chinbo" [Literature and progress]. *Onŭl ŭi munye pip'yŏng* 69 (Summer 2008): 144–58.

Ch'oe Yŏng-gi, Kim Chun, Cho Hyo-rae, and Yu Pŏm-sang. *1987nyŏn ihu Han'guk ŭi nodong undong* [The labor movement in post-1987 South Korea]. Sejong: Han'guk nodong yŏn'guwŏn, 2001.

Chŏn Chae-ho. "2000nyŏndae Han'guk posujuŭiŭi inyŏmjŏk t'ŭksŏnge kwanhan yŏn'gu: Nyurait'ŭrŭl chungsimŭro" [A study on the ideological characteristics of South Korean conservatism in the 2000s: Focusing on the New Right]. *Hyŏndae chŏngch'i yŏn'gu* 7, no. 1 (2014): 165–93.

———. "Pak Chŏng-hŭi robut'ŏ yŏksa rŭl kuch'ul haja" [Let's rescue history from Park Chung-hee]. *Chŏngch'i pip'yŏng* 7 (2000): 35–58.

———. *Pak Chŏng-hŭi tae Pak Chŏng-hŭi: Kaehyŏkkwa pandong sai Pak Chŏng-hŭi chejari ch'ajajugi*. [Park Chung-hee versus Park Chung-hee: To find a right place for Park Chung-hee between a reformer and a reactionary]. Imaejin, 2018.

Chŏn Chae-ho, Kim Wŏn, and Kim Chŏng-han. *91yŏn 5wŏl t'ujaengkwa Han'gukŭi minjujuŭi* [The May struggle of 1991 and South Korean democracy]. Minjuwha undong kinyŏm saŏphoe, 2004.

Chŏn Myŏng-hyŏk. "Han'gugesŏ kwagŏch'ŏngsanundongŭi yŏksa" [A history of the movement to cleanse the past in South Korea]. *Chŏnnamdaehakkyo Segyehansangmunhwayŏn'gudan kukchehaksurhoeŭi*, November 2005, 119-20.

Chŏn Sang-in. *Kogae sugin sujŏngjuŭi: Han'guk hyŏndaesaŭi yŏksasahoehak* [Demoralized revisionist history: A historical sociology of South Korean history]. Chŏnt'ong kwa hyŏndae, 2001.

———. "Singminji kŭndaehwarone taehan ihaewa ohae" [Colonial development thesis in Korea, revisited]. *Tongasia pip'yŏng* 1 (Winter 1998): 124-37.

Chŏng Chang-yŏl. "Pak Chŏng-hŭiwa Yi Pyŏng-ch'ŏrŭi mannami Taehanmin'gugŭi unmyŏngŭl pakkwŏtta" [South Korea's fate was changed with the meeting of Park Chung-hee and Yi Pyŏng-ch'ŏl]. *Chugan Chosun*, November 12, 2017. https://news.chosun.com/site/data/html_dir/2017/11/10/2017111002219.html.

Chŏng Chi-hwan. "Kim Yun-sik Sŏuldae kyosu, Ilbon p'yŏngnon'ga chŏsul p'yojŏrhaetta" [Kim Yun-sik, professor at Seoul National University, plagiarized a Japanese literary critic]. *Wŏlgan Mal* 172 (2000): 48-53.

Chŏng Hae-gu. "Nyurait'ŭ undong ŭi hyŏnsil insik e taehan pip'anjŏk kŏmt'o" [A critical review of historical consciousness in the New Right movement]. *Yŏksa pip'yŏng* 76 (Summer 2006): 215-37.

———. "Pak Chŏng-hŭi sindŭrŏm ŭi yangsang kwa sŏngkyŏk" [The appearance and characteristics of the Park Chung-hee syndrome]. In *Pak Chŏng-hŭi rŭl nŏmŏsŏ*, edited by Han'guk chŏngch'i yŏn'guhoe, 51-71. P'urŭn sup, 1998.

Chŏng Han-gu. *Soryŏn Tongyurŏp sahoejuŭiŭi punggoewa Pukhanŭi changnae: Ch'eje ihaengŭi pigyo* [The fall of the Soviet Union and Eastern Europe and the future of North Korea: A comparative study of system transition]. Sŏngnam: Sejong yŏn'guso, 1997.

Chŏng Hong-su. "Kohae ŭi chari: Kwŏn Yŏ-sŏn changp'yŏn sosŏl, *Regat'o* (Ch'angjak kwa pip'yŏngsa, 2012)" [A place of confession: Kwŏn Yŏ-sŏn's novel *Legato*]. *Munhakkwa sahoe* 25, no. 3 (2012): 346-49.

Chŏng In-hwan and Hwang Cha-hye. "Saeyŏngmoŭi kwagŏnŭn Nyurait'ŭŭi mirae" [The past of the new treason is the future of the New Right]. *Hankyoreh 21*, no. 723 (August 11, 2008). http://h21.hani.co.kr/arti/special/special_general/23125.html.

Chŏng Kyŏng-a. "'Wianbu' munjenŭn chigŭm uriŭi munjeyeyo" ["Comfort women" is now the issue for all of us]. In "Interview: 'Wiwanbu' rip'ot'ŭ ŭi chakka Chŏng Kyŏng-a," by Kang I-hyŏn and Chŏn-Hong Ki-hye. *Pressian*, August 21, 2006. https://m.pressian.com/m/pages/articles/81208?no=81208.

Chŏng Mun-sun. "T'ongsok kwa chagi yŏnmin, misŏngsukhan chaa: Chosukhan yŏjaai sujunŭi insik e mŏmurŭnŭn Taehanminguk yŏsŏng chakka" [Vulgarity and self-pity and the immature self: Women writers of South Korea with the cognitive level of a precocious girl]. *Hankyoreh 21*, no. 656 (April 19, 2007). http://legacy.h21.hani.co.kr/section-021150000/2007/04/021150000200704190656058.html.

Chŏng Pyŏng-jun. *Unam Yi Sŭngman yŏn'gu* [A study of Unam Syngman Rhee]. Yŏksa pip'yŏngsa, 2005.

Chŏng Sang-ho. "Pak Chŏng-hŭi sindŭrŏm ŭi chŏngch'ijŏk kiwŏn'gwa kŭ silssang" [The political origins and reality of the Park Chung-hee syndrome]. In *Pak Chŏng-hŭi rŭl nŏmŏsŏ*, edited by Han'guk chŏngch'i yŏn'guhoe, 72-105. P'urŭn sup, 1998.

Chŏng Sŏng-jo. "Posudanch'e 'Sonyŏsang sŏlch'i, suyojiphoe, ch'ŏngsonyŏn tŭng in'gwŏn ch'imhae'" [Conservative groups say, "It's a violation of human rights of 'comfort women' and youth to put up the Statue of the Girl for Peace and to continue with Wednesday protests"]. *Yonhapnews*, May 19, 2020. https://www.yna.co.kr/view/AKR20200519091800004.

Chŏng Un-hyŏn. "Pak Chŏng-hŭi sidaega kŭriun saramdŭl: Pak Chŏng-hŭi ŭi ch'umodanch'eŭi hwaldong gwa sŏnggyŏk" [People who long for the days of Park Chung-hee: Activities and characteristics of Park Chung-hee commemorative organizations]. *Yŏksa pip'yŏng* 21 (Summer 1993): 168–79.

Chŏng Yŏn-t'ae. "'Singminji kŭndaehwaron' nonjaengŭi pip'an'gwa sin'gŭndaesaronŭi mosaek" [Critique of the "colonial development thesis" and a search for a new modern historical framework]. *Ch'angjak kwa pip'yŏng* 27, no. 1 (1999): 352–76.

Chu Ik-chong. "Haebang 40yŏ nyŏn'gan wianbu munjenŭn ŏpsŏtta" [There was no issue of comfort women for 40 years since the liberation]. In *Panil chongjokchuŭi: Taehanmin'guk wigiŭi kŭnwŏn* [Anti-Japanese tribalism: The origin of South Korea's crisis], by Yi Yŏng-hun et al., 340–51. Miraesa, 2019.

Ha Chŏng-il. "*Haebang chŏnhusa ŭi chaeinsik* ŭi minjokkwa minjokchuŭi" [Nation and nationalism in *Reunderstanding Pre- and Post-liberation History*]. *Ch'angjak kwa pip'yŏng* 35, no. 1 (2007): 335–51.

———. "Minjok munhak, kungmin munhak, minjokchuŭi munhak" [National literature, *kungmin* literature, and nationalist literature]. *Yŏksa pip'yŏng* 74 (Spring 2006): 340–45.

———. "P'asijŭm ŭi sinhwa, tansŏnjŏk kŭndaegwan ŭi yŏksŏl—Kingŭp chindan 2. Sidaech'agojŏk kukka chisangjuŭija, Yi In-hwa" [The myth of fascism, an irony of the unilateral modern perspective—Emergency diagnosis 2. Yi In-hwa, the anachronistic worshipper of the state]. *Silch'ŏn munhak* 8 (1997): 65–77.

Ha Sang-bok. "Ŭijehyŏngsŏngŭi chŏngch'ihak: Ku Chosŏnch'ongdokpu kŏnmul ch'ŏlgŏgwajŏng ŭi punsŏk" [Politics of agenda setting: An analysis of the demolition of the former Government-General of Korea building]. *Hyŏndae chŏngch'i yŏn'gu* 4, no. 1 (April 2011): 153–78.

Ham Chae-bong, Kim Yŏng-jak, Chang Myŏng-guk, and Cho Kap-che. "Pak Chŏng-hŭirŭl ŏttŏk'e pol kŏsin'ga?" [How shall we assess Park Chung-hee?]. Roundtable discussion. *Chŏnt'onggwa hyŏndae* (Fall 1997): 160–92.

Han Chŏm-tol. "Han'guk e mich'in Togil chŏnhu sosŏl ŭi yŏnghyang—Heinrich Böll ŭi *Kŭrigo amumaldo haji anhatta* rŭl chungsimŭro" [Influence of postwar West German novels on South Korea: Focusing on Heinrich Böll's *And never said a word*]. *Han'guk munhak iron kwa pip'yŏng* 21 (2003): 250–82.

Han Hong-gu. *Taehanmin'guksa* [History of South Korea], 4 vols. Han'gyŏre ch'ulp'ansa, 2003–2006.

———. "Toesaranan ch'inil seryŏk kwa tokchaejaŭi mangnyŏng" [A revival of pro-Japanese force and the specter of dictatorship]. *Naeirŭl yŏnŭn yŏksa* 32 (Summer 2008): 14–24.

Han Ki-hong. "'Kakha, tangsini kŭripsŭmnida': Rŭp'o/saengga 96nyŏn hyŏnjŏngbu in'giharak ttaebut'ŏ pangmun'gaek kŭpchŭng" ["Your excellency, we miss you": A report on the rapid increase of visitors to the house where Park Chung-hee was born since the decrease in popularity of the current government in 1996]. *Nyusŭmeik'ŏ*, April 24, 1997, 32–34.

Han Man-su. "90yŏndae pesŭt'ŭsellŏ sosŏl, kŭ segyegwan kwa oraksŏng" [Best sellers of the 1990s, the old worldview, and its entertainment quality]. *Han'guk munhak yŏn'gu* 20, no. 3 (1998): 189–211.

Han Su-yŏng. *Sosŏl kwa ilsangsŏng* [Novel and everydayness]. Somyŏng ch'ulp'an, 2000.

Han Yun-hyŏng. *Ant'i Chosun undongsa: Taehanmin'guk hyŏndaesarŭl kwant'onghanŭn tto hanaŭi yŏksa* [A history of the anti-*Chosun Ilbo* movement: Another narrative that goes into the heart of contemporary history of South Korea]. T'eksŭt'ŭ, 2010.

Han'guk chŏngch'i yŏn'guhoe, ed. *Pak Chŏng-hŭi rŭl nŏmŏsŏ: Pak Chŏng-hŭi wa kŭ sidae e taehan pip'anjŏk yŏn'gu* [Overcoming Park Chung-hee: A critical study on Park Chung-hee and his era]. P'urŭn sup, 1998.

Han'guk kaebal yŏn'guwŏn, Chaejŏng kyŏngjebu. *Kungmin kwa hamkke naeil rŭl yŏnda: Kungmin ŭi chŏngbu kyŏngje ch'ŏngsajin* [To greet tomorrow with the people: A blueprint of the economy of the government of the people]. Taehan min'guk chŏngbu, 1998.

Han'guk kŭnhyŏndae sahakhoe et al. "'Kŏn'gukchŏl' ch'ŏrhoerŭl ch'okkuhanŭn yŏksahagyeŭi sŏngmyŏngsŏ" [A statement from the historical community calling for the withdrawal of the proposal to designate a Foundation Day]. Han'guk yŏksa yŏn'guhoe, August 12, 2008. http://www.koreanhistory.org/2471.

Han'guk minjok munhwa taebaekkwasajŏn [Encyclopedia of Korean culture]. Academy of Korean Studies. Accessed October 5, 2021. http://encykorea.aks.ac.kr/Contents/Item/E0068904.

Hong Chin-p'yo. "Han kolssu 386 chusap'a ch'ulssinŭi ch'ehŏmjŏk kobaek" [A confession of a hard-core *Chuch'e sasang* follower of the 386 generation]. BlueToday.net, May 16, 2012. http://www.bluetoday.net/news/articleView.html?idxno=883.

Hong Se-hwa. "Pak Chŏng-hŭi sindŭromŭn chiptanjŏgin 'chŏngŭiŭi p'ogi'" [The Park Chung-hee syndrome is a collective "renunciation of justice"]. *Wŏlgan Mal* 134 (August 1997): 44–47.

Hong Sŏng-nyul. "Naengjŏnjŏk yŏksasosulgwa sangch'ŏbadŭn chayujuŭi: Kyohaksa Han'guksa kyogwasŏ hyŏndaesa sŏsul pip'an" [The cold war historical narrative and injured liberalism: A critique of historical narratives of the textbook on Korean history published by Kyohaksa]. *Yŏksa pip'yŏng* 105 (Winter 2013): 82–103.

———. "Sasilgwa yŏksa sogŭi Yi Sŭng-man yŏn'gu" [A study of Syngman Rhee in reality and history]. Review of *Unam Yi Sŭngman yŏn'gu*, by Chŏng Pyŏng-jun. *Han'guksa yŏn'gu* 133 (2006): 249–59.

———. "Taehanmin'guk 60nyŏnŭi an'gwa pakk, kŭrigo chŏngch'esŏng" [The inside and outside of the sixty years of the Republic of Korea and its identity]. *Ch'angjak kwa pip'yŏng* 36, no. 1 (2008): 52–66.

Hong Yun-gi. "Tagŭkjŏk hyŏndaesŏng maeknaksok ŭi miwan ŭi p'asisŭm kwa misŏngsuk simin sahŏe" [Incomplete fascism and immature civil society in the context of multipolar modernity]. *Sahoe wa ch'ŏlhak* 2, no. 10 (2001): 57–103.

Hwang Chong-yŏn. "Chinchŏngsŏng ŭi inyŏm kwa sosŏl" [Ideology of honesty and the novel]. *Ch'angjak kwa pip'yŏng* 25, no. 4 (1997): 297–315.

Hwang Chŏng-yŏn, Chin Chŏng-sŏk, Kim Tong-sik, and Yi Kwang-ho. "90yŏndae munhak ŏttŏke polgŏsin'ga" [How shall we assess the literature of the 1990s]. Roundtable discussion. In 90-yŏndae munhak ŏttŏke polgŏsin'ga, by Kim Tong-sik, Kim Chin-su, U Ch'an-je, Yi Kwang-ho, Hwang Chŏng-yŏn, Kang Sang-hŭi, Ko Mi-suk, Paek Chi-yŏn, Sin Su-jŏng, Yang Chin-o, O Hyŏng-sŏp, and Chin Chŏng-sŏk, 1–24. Minŭmsa, 1999.

Hwang Kwang-su. "90-yŏndaeŭi chinghuwa tu sosŏljip" [Symptomatic of the 1990s and two novels]. Review of *Deep River Flows Far Away*, by Kim Yŏng-hyŏn (Silch'ŏn munhaksa, 1990) and *A House Made of Paper*, by Kim Hyang-suk (Munhak kwa pip'yŏngsa, 1989). *Ch'angjak kwa pip'yŏng* 18, no. 3 (1990): 412–20.

Hwang Pyŏng-ju. "Yusin, chabon'gwaŭi kongmo hogŭn taegyŏl" [Yusin, a conspiracy with capitalism or confrontation]. In *Pak Chŏng-hŭi modŏnijŭm: Yusinesŏ Sŏndeisŏulkkaji*, edited by Kwŏn Podŭrae et al., 31–44. Ch'ŏnnyŏnŭi sangsang, 2015.

Hwang Tong-il. "'Ŭngdang chon'gyŏngbadŭlmank'ŭm padŭlppun': Pak Chŏng-hui ch'umomoim Minjokchunghŭnghoe" ["He deserves all the respect he receives": The Association of National Restoration, a commemorative organization for Park Chung-hee]. *Hankook Ilbo*, July 16, 1997.

Hyŏndaesa charyoban, ed. *Pak Chŏng-hui p'yŏngga nonjaeng charyo moŭm* [A collection of resources related to the debates assessing Park Chung-hee]. January 15, 1998.

Im Chi-hyŏn [Lim Jie-Hyun] and Kim Yŏng-u, eds., *Taejung tokchae* [Mass dictatorship], 2 vols. Ch'aeksesang 2004, 2005.

Im Tae-sik. "*Haebang chŏnhusa ŭi chaeinsik* ŭl p'yŏlch'yŏbon kandanhan sohoe" [My brief impression upon opening the pages of *Reunderstanding Pre- and Post-liberation History*]. *Yŏksa pip'yŏng* 74 (Spring 2006): 10–18.

Kang Ch'ang-il. "<Sŏngmyŏngsŏ> 8.15nŭn kŏn'gukchŏri anira kwangbokchŏrida" [(A statement) August 15 is the day of liberation and not a day of foundation]. *Ŭiwŏnsil t'ongsin*, July 30, 2008.

Kang Chin-ho. "T'ŭmsaewa konggan saie nohin munhak: Kim Yŏng-hyŏnnon" [Literature between a crevice and space: On Kim Yŏng-hyŏn]. *Silch'ŏn munhak* 71 (August 2003): 70–88.

Kang Chŏng-gu. "Kim Yŏngsam chŏnggwŏnŭi minjoksajŏk p'yŏngga" [Assessment of the Kim Young Sam government from the perspective of national history]. *Han'guk sahoehak* 34 (Winter 2000): 833–65.

Kang Chun-man. "'Pak Chŏng-hŭi sindŭrŏm' kwa 'kongjŏngyŏngyŏk' ŭi somyŏl [The "Park Chung-hee syndrome" and the disappearance of "public space"]. *Wŏlgan Inmul kwa sasang* (December 2002): 24–37.

———. "Pok Kŏ-il ŭi sosŏl e sosŏl ro taphanda" [I respond with a novel to the novel of Pok Kŏ-il]. *Wŏlgan Inmul kwa sasang* (March 2002): 184–202.

———. "Wae Pak Chŏng-hŭi yuryŏngi ttŏdonŭn'ga" [Why is the ghost of Park Chung-hee wandering around]. *Inmul kwa sasang*, June 15, 1997, 15–37.

———. "Yi Mun-yŏl ŭl almyŏn Han'guk sahoe ŭi 'munbŏp' i poinda" [To figure out Yi Mun-yŏl is to figure out how Korean society operates]. *Wŏlgan Inmul kwa sasang* (March 2002): 130–54.

Kang Man-gil. *Pundan sidae ŭi yŏksa insik* [Historical consciousness in the era of the division]. Ch'angjak kwa pip'yŏngsa, 1978.

Kang Nae-hŭi. "Munhwa wa sijang: sinjayujuŭi sidaeŭi Han'guk munhwa" [Culture and market: South Korean culture in the era of neoliberalism]. *Marŭkŭsŭjuŭi yŏn'gu* 5, no. 2 (May 2008): 235–58.

———. "Sinjayujuŭi sidae munhwa chihyŏngŭi pyŏndonggwa munhwaundong" [Transformation of the topography of culture in the era of neoliberalism and cultural movements]. *Marŭkŭsŭjuŭi yŏn'gu* 4, no. 1 (May 2007): 278–303.

Kang Sang-hui. "Sosŏljŏk chinjŏngsŏng kwa hyŏndaesŏng ŭi mannam" [A meeting of novelistic honesty and modernness]. Review of *And Then There Was No Word*, by Kim Yŏng-hyŏn (Ch'angjak kwa pip'yŏngsa, 1995) and *Whispering, Whispering*, by Ch'oe Yun (Minŭmsa, 1995). *Ch'angjak kwa pip'yŏng* 23, no. 2 (1995): 423–31.

Kang Wŏn-t'aek, Pak Myŏng-nim, Pak T'ae-gyun, Ch'ŏn Chŏng-hwang, Han Chŏng-hun, and Yi Ki-hun. "6wŏl hangjaeng 30chunyŏn, '87nyŏn ch'ejerŭl p'yŏnggahanda" [On the thirtieth anniversary of the June uprising, to assess the '87 system]. Roundtable discussion. *Yŏksa pip'yŏng* 119 (Summer 2017): 69–114.

Kang Yŏng-hŭi. "*In'gan ui kil* ro Pak Chŏng-hŭi puhwal ŭi kitpal ŭl dŭn Yi In-hwa" [Yi In-hwa, with his novel *A Man's Road*, has raised high a banner to call for a revival of Park Chung-hee]. *Sahoe p'yongnon kil* 97 (1997): 78–87.

Karatani Kojin. *Kŭndaemunhagŭi chongŏn* [The end of modern literature]. Translated from the Japanese by Cho Yŏng-il. Tosŏch'ulp'an b, 2006.

Kim Chae-gyun. *5.18 kwa Han'guk chŏngch'i: Kwangju posangpŏp kwa 5.18 t'ŭkbyŏlpŏp kyŏlchŏng kwajŏng yŏn'gu* [May 18th and South Korean politics: A study on the process of the enactment of the Compensation Act for the Kwangju democratic movement and the Special Act on the May 18th democratization movement]. Hanul, 2000.

Kim Ch'ang-nam. "90nyŏndae sinsedae munhwaŭi aik'on, Sŏ T'aejiwa aidŭl" [A cultural icon of the 1990s generation: Seo Taiji and Boys]. *KB Rainbow Humanities* (May 2010). http://img2.kbstar.com/obj/money/rainbow-03-201005.pdf.

———. "Taejung munhwa 10nyŏn, pyŏnhwahan kŏtkwa pyŏnhwahaji anhŭn kŏt" [Ten years of mass culture: What has changed and what has not]. *Munhakkwa sahoe* 10, no. 4 (Winter 1997): 1379–94.

Kim Chi-ha. "Chŏlmŭn pŏttŭl, yŏksaesŏ muŏsŭl paeunŭn'ga, Chugŭmŭi kutp'an tangjang kŏdŏch'iwŏra [Young friends, what are you learning from history: Clear away the shamanic ritual of death]. *Chosun Ilbo*, May 5, 1991.

Kim Chin-myŏng. *Mugunghwa kkoti p'iŏtsŭmnida* [The rose of Sharon has blossomed], 2 vols. Saeum, 2016.

Kim Chŏng-hyŏn. *Abŏji* [Father]. Munidang, 1996.

Kim Chŏng-in. "Chongbukp'ŭreimgwa minjujuŭi wigi" [The framing of "leftists who follow the North Korean state ideology of self-reliance" and a crisis of democracy]. *Yŏksa wa hyŏnsil* 93 (September 2014): 209–32.

———. "*Sŏntaek* (Yi Mun-yŏl 1997) kwa na" [*Choice* (Yi Mun-yŏl 1997) and me]. *Han'guk yŏksa yŏn'guhŏe hŏebo* 31, no. 1 (1998): 31–34.

Kim Chŏng-nam. "Kŭndae munhak ŭi chongŏn kwa Han'guk munhak: Karat'ani Kojin ŭi kŭndae munhak chongŏllon tasi ilkki" [The end of modern literature and Korean literature: Rereading Karatani Kojin's thesis on the end of modern literature]. *Inmunhak yŏn'gu* 17 (December 2012): 109–33.

Kim Chŏng-nan. "Nuga yŏng'ungŭl ch'annŭn'ga" [Who is looking for a hero]. *Tangdae pip'yŏng* 6 (Spring 1999): 377–94.

Kim Chŏng-nan, Pang Min-ho, Kim Yŏng-ha, and Kim Sa-in. "90yŏndae munhak ŭl kyŏlsanhanda" [To settle the accounts of the 1990s literature]. *Ch'angjak kwa pip'yŏng* 26, no. 3 (1998): 6–52.

Kim Chŏng-nyŏm. *Ch'oebin'guk esŏ sŏnjin'guk munt'ŏk kkaji: Han'guk kyŏngje chŏngch'aek 30-yŏnsa* [From the poorest country to the threshold of an advanced country: A thirty-year history of South Korean economic planning]. Raendŏm hausŭ, 2006.

———. *Kim Chŏng-nyŏm chŏngch'i hoegorok: Ah Pak Chŏng-hŭi* [A political memoir of Kim Chŏng-nyŏm: *Ah, Park Chung-hee*]. Chung'ang M&B, 1997.

Kim Chong-wŏn. "Pyŏnsin mosaekhanŭn haksaengundongŭi hyŏnjuso" [The current status of the student movement seeking transformation]. *Wŏlgan Mal* 89 (November 1993): 210–15.

———. "Urinŭn moraesidae sedaeigirŭl kŏbuhanda" [We refused to be the generation of *Sandglass*]. *Wŏlgan Mal* 115 (January 1996): 132–37.

Kim Chong-yŏp. "87yŏn ch'ejeŭi kwejŏkgwa nonjaeng" [Trajectory and debates on the 1987 system]. *Ch'angjak kwa pip'yŏng* 35, no. 2 (2007): 358–79.

———. "Chagi kyebarŭl nŏmŏsŏn chayuŭi ŭijirŭl wihayŏ" [To will the freedom beyond self-development]. Review of *Will to Freedom, Will to Self-Development*, by Sŏ Tong-jin (Tolbegae, 2009). *Kyŏngje wa sahoe* 87 (Fall 2010): 292–99.

———. "P'osŭt'ŭmodŏn sahoeiron?" [Postmodern social theory?]. *Oeguk munhak* 34, no. 3 (1993): 264–80.

Kim Chu-wan. "Cho Tu-nam ch'inil nonjaeng kyŏnggwabogo: Masan Hŭimangyŏndae wa *Kyŏngnamdominilbo* ŭi 'yŏksa baro seugi' ssaum" [A report on the pro-Japanese Cho Tu-nam controversy: The Masan Alliance of Hope and *Kyŏngnam People's Daily*'s fight to correct history]. *Wŏgan Mal* 205 (July 2003): 112–15.

Kim Dae-jung [Kim Tae-jung]. *Kim Tae-jung chasŏjŏn* [Autobiography of Kim Dae-jung], 2 vols. Samin, 2010.

Kim Hak-chun. "Ch'oegŭn hwalbarhaejin Yi Sŭngman yŏn'gu" [Research on Syngman Rhee is very active recently]. *Han'guk chŏngch'i hakpo* 36, no. 2 (2002): 449–55.

Kim Ho-gi. "1987nyŏn ch'ejein'ga, 97nyŏn ch'ejein'ga: Minjuhwa sidaeesŏ segyehwa sidaero" [Is it the 1987 system or the 1997 system: From the era of democratization to the era of globalization]. *Sahoe pip'yŏng* 36 (2007): 12–26.

———. "Siminsahoe ŭi kujo wa pyŏndong, 1987–2000" [Structure and change of civil society, 1987–2000]. *Hang'uk sahoe* 3 (2000): 63–87.

Kim Ho-sŏp. "Nuga Pak Chŏnghŭirŭl purŭnŭn'ga" [Who is recalling Park Chung-hee]. *Chugan Han'guk* 1671 (May 22, 1997): 30–31.

Kim Hyo-sŏn. *Urinara kŏn'guktaet'ongnyŏng Yi Sŭngman iyagi* [The story of Syngman Rhee, the founding president of our country]. Taehanmin'guk saranghoe, 2010.

Kim In-suk. *'79–'80: Kyŏuresŏ pom sai* [1979–1980: Between the winter and spring], 2 vols. Segye, 1987.

———. *Hamkke kŏnnŭn'gil* [A path to walk together]. Segye, 1989.

———. "Sullaeege" [To a fellow hide-and-seek player]. In *Pŭrasŭ paendŭrŭl kidarimyŏ*. Munhak tongne, 2001.

———. "Yuri kudu" [Glass shoes]. In *Yuri kudu*. Ch'angjak kwa pip'yŏngsa, 1998.

Kim Kyu-hang. *B-kŭp chwap'a sebŏntchae iyagi* [The third story of a B-class leftist]. Ridŏsŭ hausŭ, 2010.

———. "Samsŏngŭn uriege muŏsin'ga" [What is Samsung to us]. *Kidokkyo sasang* 616 (April 2010): 22–26.

Kim Mi-yŏng and Hŏ Chae-hyŏn. "Nurikkun 'Kŏn'guk 60chunyŏn' kwangbok ijŏn yŏksa chŏngbuga ppaessatta" [Netizens, the government has taken away history with its celebration of August 15 as the "sixtieth anniversary of the foundation of the state"]. *Hankyoreh*, August 15, 2008. http://www.hani.co.kr/arti/PRINT/304494.html.

Kim Mun-su. *Ajikto nanŭn nekt'aiga ŏsaekhada* [Putting on a necktie is still awkward for me]. Paeksan sŏdang, 1995.

Kim Myŏng-hwan. "1987nyŏn 6wŏl hangjaeng: Kŭ ttaewa onŭl" [The June uprising of 1987: Then and now]. In *Han'guk hyŏndaesawa minjujuŭi* [Contemporary South Korean history and democracy], by Chŏng Yong-uk, Pak T'ae-gyun, Han In-sŏp, Pak Pae-gyun, Chŏng Kŭn-sik, and Kim Myŏng-hwan, 219–45. Kyŏngin munhwasa, 2015.

Kim Myŏng-in. *Hwanmyŏl ŭi munhak, paeban ŭi minjujuŭi* [Literature of disillusionment, democracy of betrayal]. Humanitas, 2006.

———. "Kamsangesŏ sŏngch'allo: Kong Chi-yŏng, *Chonjaenŭn nunmurŭl hŭllinda*" [From the sentimental to self-reflection: Kong Chi-yŏng's *Existence Has Tears*]. *Silch'ŏn munhak* 55 (Fall 1999): 538–41.

Kim Myŏng-u. "Hollo sidaerŭl kominhaettŏn Pak Hye-jŏng yŏlssarŭl kiŏkhada" [Remembering patriot Pak Hye-jŏng, who agonized alone about the era]. *Sŏuldaejŏnŏl*, March 11, 2016. http://www.snujn.com/news/19798?ckattempt=1.

Kim Nam-ok. "'386' sedae kyŏnghomŭi munhakjŏk hyŏngsanghwa: Kim In-suk, Kong chiyŏngŭl chungsimŭro" [Literary manifestation of the "386" generation: Focusing on Kim In-suk and Kong Chi-yŏng]. *Sahoe wa iron* 16 (Summer 2010): 271–303.

Kim Po-kyŏng. "Kiŏgŭn hegemoni ŭi yongmang e ŏttŏk'e hoch'uldoenŭn'ga: Huildam munhak kwa *Tokhakja* ŭi kwŏllyŏk yongmang" [How is memory interpolated to the desires of hegemony: *Huildam* literature and desire for power in *An autodidact*]. *Tangdae pip'yŏng* 28 (Winter 2004): 131–40.

Kim Pyŏng-ik. "Sinsedae wa saeroun salmŭi yangsik, kŭrigo munhak" [New generation, a new life style, and literature]. *Munhak kwa sahoe* 8, no. 2 (Summer 1995): 665–87.

Kim Pyŏng-ju. "Ch'ŏndanggwa chiongmank'ŭm kŭktanjŏk" [Extreme as heaven and hell]. *Chugan Han'guk* 1671 (May 22, 1997): 33.

Kim Sang-jo. "Samsung konghwaguk: Hwallani nahŭn chŏngbu wiŭi chŏngbu" [Samsung republic: A government above the government born out of the financial crisis]. *Hwanghae munhwa* 56, no. 9 (2007): 25–44.

Kim Se-gyun. "1987nyŏn ihu ŭi Han'guk nodong undong" [The post-1987 South Korean labor movement]. *Han'guk chŏngch'i yŏn'gu* 11, no. 1 (2002): 197–244.

Kim Se-jung. "Kwŏnwijuŭijŏk sanŏphwawa minjujuŭi" [Authoritarian industrialization and democracy]. In *Han'guk minjujuŭi ŭi kiwŏn kwa mirae: Posuga ikkŭlda*, edited by An Pyŏng-jik, 75–109. Sidae chŏngsin, 2011.

———. "Pak Chŏng-hŭi sidae sanŏphwa posujuŭiwa minjujuŭi" [Industrialization, conservatism and democracy during the Park Chung-hee era]. In *Han'guk minjujuŭi ŭi kiwŏn kwa mirae: Posuga ikkŭlda*, edited by An Pyŏng-jik, 41–74. Sidae chŏngsin, 2011.

Kim So-jŏng and Kim Kyu-t'ae. "Chisigindŭre taehan Pok Kŏ-il ŭi tangbu, *Yŏksa sogŭi nagŭne* wan'gan hŏnjŏngsik" [Pok Kŏ-il's appeal to intellectuals, at the ceremony of the publication of his novel *A Wayfarer of History*]. *Midiŏp'en*, July 21, 2015. http://www.mediapen.com/news/view/84617.

Kim Sŏng-dong. "Siryue panyŏkhanŭn chayujuŭi non'gaek—Pok Kŏ-il" [A liberal polemicist going against the current of the time—Pok Kŏ-il]. *Wŏlgan Chosun nyusŭrum*, July 2002. http://monthly.chosun.com/client/news/viw.asp?ctcd=&nNewsNumb=200207100011.

Kim Sŏng-nye. "P'ungsuwa singminji sigi" [Geomancy and the colonial period]. *Han'guk chonggyo yŏn'gu* 2 (2000): 123–57.

Kim Sŏng-uk. "Kŏn'guk 60chunyŏn kinyŏmsaŏp—Kongjisahang" [Commemorative projects for the sixtieth anniversary of the founding of the Republic of Korea—Official announcement]. *Taehanmin'guk saranghoe*, July 25, 2009. http://www.loverokorea.org/cafebbs/view.html?gid=main&bid=notice&pid=3738&page=4.

Kim Tong-ch'un [Dong-Choon Kim]. "Han'guk sahoe undong hyŏnjuso" [The current status of the Korean social movement]. *Hwanghae munhwa* 29 (Winter 2000): 10–25.

Kim Tong-gil, Pok Kŏ-il, and Yi Ch'un-gŭn. *Pukhan chayu sŏnŏn* [A declaration of free North Korea]. Rŭnesangsŭ, 2007.

Kim Tong-min. "Tasi Yi Mun-yŏl e taehayo" [Again on Yi Mun-yŏl]. *Hwanghae munhwa* 33 (Winter 2001): 390–96.

Kim Ŭn-ha. "386 sedae yŏsŏng huildam kwa chubyŏninŭrosŏ kŭlssŭgi" [386 generation women *huildam* and writing as the marginalized]. *Han'guk yŏsŏng ch'ŏrhakhoe haksuldaehoe palp'yojaryojip* (April 2010): 99–114.

Kim Wŏn. "80nyŏndaee taehan 'kiŏk'kwa 'changgi 80nyŏndae': Chisigindŭrŭi 80nyŏndae haesŏgŭl chungsimŭro" ["Memory" of the 1980s and the "Long 1980s": Focusing on the intellectuals' interpretation of the 1980s]. *Han'gukhak yŏn'gu* 36 (2015): 9–49.

———. *87nyŏn 6wŏl hangjaeng* [The 1987 June uprising]. Ch'aeksesang, 2017.

———. "Pumahangjaenggwa tosihach'ŭngmin" [The Pusan-Masan uprising and the urban lower class]. *Chŏngsin munhwa yŏn'gu* 29, no. 2 (2006): 419–53.

Kim Yong-gyu. "Sidaewaŭi hwahaerŭl kkumkkunŭn munhak t'oron" [Literary debates dreaming of the reconciliation with the era]. *Ch'angjak kwa pip'yŏng* 30, no. 1 (2002): 442–46.

Kim Yŏng-hwan. *Sidaejŏngsinŭl marhada* [Speaking zeitgeist]. Sidae Chŏngsin, 2013.

———. *Tasi Kangch'ŏllo sara: Kyŏkpyŏnŭi sidaerŭl saraon Kangch'ŏl Kim Yŏng-hwanŭi kobaek* [To live as Kangch'ŏl again: Confession of Kangch'ŏl Kim Yŏng-hwan, who has lived a life in turmoil]. Sidae chŏngsin, 2015.

Kim Yŏng-hyŏn. *Kipŭn kangŭn mŏlli hŭrŭnda* [Deep river flows far away]. Silch'ŏn munhaksa, 1990.

———. *Kŭrigo amumaldo haji anhatta* [And never said a word]. Ch'angjak kwa pip'yŏngsa, 1995.

———. *Naemaŭmŭi mangmyŏngjŏngbu* [A government in exile in my heart]. Kang ch'ulp'ansa, 1998.

———. *Namhae yŏpsŏ* [Postcards from Namhae]. Munhak tongne, 1994.

———. "'Riŏllijŭm munhak ŭi chŏngt'ongŭl sallyŏya hamnida': Sosŏlga Kim Yŏng-hyŏn, kŭ irŭmi kannŭn myohan ullim" ["We need to carry on the tradition of realism in literature": Novelist Kim Yŏng-hyŏn and a curious reverberation of his name]. Interview conducted by Chŏng Chi-yŏng. *Wŏgan Mal* 256 (October 2007): 144–47.

———. "Tasi 'Kim Yŏng-hyŏn nonjaeng'ŭl torabomyŏ" [Again, recalling the debates "on Kim Yŏng-hyŏn"]. *Onŭl ŭi munye pip'yŏng* 35 (Winter 1999): 53–60.

Kim Yŏng-min. "Yŏ Un-hyŏng, Yi Mun-yŏl, kŭrigo na.na.na (nŏ)" [Yŏ Un-hyŏng, Yi Mun-yŏl, and me, me, me (you)]. *Ch'ŏrhak kwa hyŏnsil* 34 (Fall 1997): 139–43.

Kim Yong-sam. "<Kim Yong-samŭi hyŏndaesa ch'ujŏk> 1919nyŏn Imsijŏngbu ch'ulbŏmŭl 'Taehanmin'guk kŏn'guk'irago uginŭn iyu" [<Kim Yong-sam's contemporary Korean history> Why do they insist that the establishment of the Provisional Government of Korea in 1919 was the "founding moment of South Korea"]. *P'enaendŭmaik'ŭ*, March 1, 2019. https://www.pennmike.com/news/articleView.html?idxno=16468.

Kim Yŏng-su. "Nosajŏngwiwŏnhoe ch'amyŏrŭl tullŏssan Minjunoch'ongŭi chŏllyakchŏk taeŭng" [The strategic response of the Korean Federation of Trade Unions on the issue of participating in the Korea Tripartite Commission]. *Sahoe kwahak yŏn'gu* 51, no. 1 (Summer 2012): 81–107.

Kim Yun-sik. "Han'guk kŭndaemunhaksaŭi sisŏnesŏ pon kungminmunhak: Ch'oe Chae-sŏwa Sato Kiyosi kyosu" [National literature from the perspective of Korean modern literary history: Ch'oe Chae-sŏ and Professor Sato Kiyosi]. *Sŏgang Inmunnonch'ong* 24 (2008): 5–28.

———. "Huildam munhakkwa sosŏlga sosŏrŭi nŏmŏsŏgiron" [*Huildam* literature and the thesis of moving beyond the novelist's novel]. *Munye chung'ang*, no. 2 (Summer 1993): 292–324.

"Kimdaet'ongnyŏng t'ŭkpyŏldamhwa ŭimi." [The meaning of the special announcement by President Kim]. *Maeil Kyŏngje*, May 13, 1993. https://www.mk.co.kr/news/home/view/1993/05/19407/.

"Kin'gŭpchindan: 'Nyurait'ŭ'ŭi yŏksainsikkwa hyŏnsirinsigŭl pip'anhanda" [Urgent diagnosis: Critiquing the "New Right" on its perspective on history and the present]. *Yŏksa pip'yŏng* 76 (Summer 2006): 180–237.

Ko Chŏng-hyu. "Uriyŏksa paroalja: Yi Sŭng-manŭn tongnibundongŭl haennŭn'ga" [Let us know our history correctly: Did Syngman Rhee really engage in the independence struggle]. *Yŏksa pip'yŏng* 14 (Winter 1991): 198–204.

Ko Chong-sŏk. *Ko Chong-sŏk ŭi nangman mirae* [Ko Chong-sŏk's romantic future]. Kom, 2013.

Kong Chi-yŏng. *Chonjaenŭn nunmurŭl hŭllinda* [Existence sheds tears]. Ch'angjak kwa pip'yŏngsa, 1999.

———. *In'gane taehan yeŭi* [Decency toward human beings]. Ch'angjak kwa pip'yŏngsa, 1994.

———. *Kodŭngŏ* [Mackerel]. Ungchin ch'ulp'an, 1994.

———. *Kŭrigo kŭdŭrŭi arŭmdaun sijak* [And then there is their splendid beginning], 2 vols. Tongnyŏk, 1991.

———. "Salmŭi pop'yŏnjŏk t'ongch'arŭl pogwŏnhanŭn changp'yŏn sosŏl" [The novel that restores life's general insight]. *Ch'angjak kwa pip'yŏng* 35, no. 2 (2007): 187–89.

———. *Tŏ isang arŭmdanun panghwang'ŭn ŏpta* [There is no more beautiful wandering]. 2nd ed. P'ulpit, 1994.

Ku Hyo-sŏ, Kim Yŏng-hyŏn, Sin Yong-mok, Ch'oe Yun, and Ch'oe In-sŏk. "Uri sidae ŭi chakkadŭrŭn muŏsŭl saengkakhanŭn'ga?—Sidae ŭi pyŏnhwa wa chakka ŭi komin"

[What are our contemporary era's writers thinking about? Transformation of the era and writers' dilemmas]. *Silch'ŏn munhak* 64 (Winter 2001): 285–323.

Ku Pon-gwŏn. "Yi Mun-yŏl sosŏrŭi 'pisu'rŭl majŭn kŏsŭn?" [What is the aim of the "dagger" of Yi Mun-yŏl's novel?]. *Onŭrŭi imeil*, October 11, 2001. http://legacy.www.hani.co.kr/section-001900005/2001/10/001900005200110111334001.html.

Kwŏn Hŭi-yŏng. "Yi Sŭngmanŭi kungmin'gukka kŏnsŏl chŏllyak" [The nation-state building strategy of Syngman Rhee]. In *Taehanmin'gugŭi kŏn'guk: Sisŏnŭi kyoch'a*, edited by Kwŏn Hŭi-yŏng et al., 11–67. Sŏngnam: Han'gukhak chungang yŏn'guwŏn ch'ulp'anbu, 2015.

Kwŏn Podŭrae, Kim Sŏng-hwan, Kim Wŏn, Ch'ŏn Chŏng-hwan, and Hwang Pyŏng-ju. *Pak Chŏng-hŭi modŏnijŭm: Yusinesŏ Sŏndeisŏulkkaji* [Park Chung-hee modernism: From Yusin to *Sunday Seoul*]. Ch'ŏnnyŏnŭi sangsang, 2015.

Kwŏn Sŏng-u. "Perŭllin, Chŏnnohyŏp, kŭriogo Kim Yŏng-hyŏn: 90yŏndae sahoe wa munhak" [Berlin, the National Council of Trade Unions and Kim Yŏng-hyŏn: Society and literature of the 1990s]. *Munhak kwa sahoe* 3, no. 1 (Spring 1990): 255–64.

Kwŏn Yŏ-sŏn. *Regat'o* [Legato]. Ch'angjak kwa pip'yŏngsa, 2012.

Kyogwasŏ p'orŏm. *Han'guk kŭn-hyŏndaesa: Taean kyogwasŏ* [The alternative textbook: Modern and contemporary Korean history]. Kip'arang, 2010.

Kyŏnghyang sinmun t'ŭkbyŏl chwijaeet'im. *Minjuhwa 20nyŏn ŭi yŏlmang kwa chŏlmang: Chinbo, kaehyŏk ui wigirul malhada* [Aspiration and despair after twenty years of democratization: The progressives speak of crisis of reform]. Humanitas, 2007.

MBC (Munhwa Broadcasting Corporation). "Sŭp'och'ŭro chibaehara! 5kong 3S chŏngch'aek" [Rule with sports! 3S policy of the Fifth Republic]. Ijenŭn marhalssu itta, 95-hoe, aired on May 22, 2005.

Mun Hŭng-sul. "Minjokchuŭi irŭm arae waegoktoen yŏksa wa chŏnmang: Kim Chin-myŏng ŭi minjokchuŭi sosŏre taehan pip'yŏng" [Distorted history and prospective under the name of nationalism: A critique of Kim Chin-myŏng's nationalist novel]. *Chakka segye* 11, no. 3 (Fall 1999): 119–36.

Nam Chae-hŭi. "Wŏllo ŏllonin chŏngch'iin Nam Chae-hŭiga pon taet'ongnyŏngdŭl" [A veteran journalist and elder politician Nam Chae-hui assesses presidents]. Interview conducted by Ku Hae-u and compiled by Song Hong-gŭn. *Sindong'a*, December 22, 2014. https://shindonga.donga.com/3/all/13/113607/3.

Nam Chong-sŏk. "87nyŏnch'ejewa nodong undong: Hoego, sŏngch'al, chŏnmang" [The '87 system and labor movement: Reflection, introspection, and prospectives]. *Redian*, September 21, 2017. http://www.redian.org/archive/115008.

No Chae-hyŏn. "'*Nae mudŏme ch'imŭl paet'ŏra*' Pak chŏn taet'ongnyŏng mal hubo Pak Kŭn-hye ŭi saenggagŭn" [What does Pak Geun-hye, the presidential candidate and Park's daughter, think of the former president Park's saying, "Spit on my grave"]. *JoongAng Ilbo*, September 11, 2012. https://news.joins.com/article/9289961.

No Chung-gi. "Minju nojo undong 20-nyŏn kwa sahoejŏk habŭijuŭi" [Twenty years of the democratic labor unionism and social corporatism]. *Tonghyang kwa chŏnmang* 71 (Fall 2007): 228–60.

———. "Wigi ŭi nodong undong, sin chayujuŭi e p'owidwen minju nojo undong" [Labor movement in crisis: The democratic labor movement beleaguered by neoliberalism]. *Chŏngch'i pip'yŏng* 14 (2005): 40–69.

No Tong-hyŏn. "Pak Chŏng-hŭiŭi Kwangbokkun naet'ongsŏrŭl kŏjit" [It is a lie that Park Chung-hee conspired with the Restoration Army]. *Sisat'op'ik*, October 18, 1990.

O Mi-hwan. "Pak Chŏng-hŭi tarun op'era 'Nunmulmanhŭn ch'oin'/Ŏngsŏnghan taebon . . . 'Ŭmak wansŏngdomajŏdo pitparae'" ["A superman with much tears," an opera about Park Chung-hee: Sloppy script . . . even the music is compromised]. *Hankook Ilbo*, August 9, 2002. https://www.hankookilbo.com/News/Read/200208090065405464.

O Pyŏng-hŏn. "Kunbu tokchae ŭi k'al: Kyeŏmnyŏng yŏn'gu" [Military dictatorship's knife: A study on martial law]. *Sindong'a* 36, no. 11 (November 1993): 494–505.

O Tu-hwan. "Haebanghu chŏksanch'ŏriŭi silt'aewa t'ŭkching" [Reality and characteristics of the Japanese-owned properties in post-liberation period]. *Hwanghae munhwa* 5 (Winter 1994): 111–29.

Pae Chin-yŏng. "Hyŏndaesa parojapkie nasŏn Yi Sŭngman yŏn'guso" [The Syngman Rhee Research Center to start correcting history of contemporary history]. *Wŏlgan Chosun Newsroom*, April 10, 2011. http://monthly.chosun.com/client/news/viw.asp?nNewsNumb=201104100006.

Pae Su-a. *Tokhakja* [An autodidact]. Yŏllimwŏn, 2004.

Pae Yŏng-dae. "Yi Mun-yŏl ege tŭnnŭnda: Segye ikkŭnŭn seryŏgŭn 'chinbo up'a'" [Listening to Yi Mun-yŏl: A "progressive rightist" is leading the world]. Interview. *JoongAng Ilbo*, September 21, 2006. http://blog.naver interview.com/bschun55/60028908228.

Paek Wŏn-dam. "Asiaesŏ 1960-70nyŏndae pidongmaeng/che3segye undong kwa minjok minjung kaenyŏm ŭi ch'angsin" [Innovation of concepts of nonalliance, the third world movement, and nationalist *minjung* concepts in 1960s and 1970s Asia]. *Chungguk hyŏndae munhak* 49 (2009): 127–90.

Pak Chi-hyang, Kim Ch'ŏl, Kim Iryŏng, and Yi Yŏng-hun. Mŏrimal [Preface] to *Haebang chŏnhusa ŭi chaeinsik*, edited by Pak Chi-hyang et al., 1:11–21. Ch'aeksesang, 2006.

———, eds. *Haebang chŏnhusa ŭi chaeinsik* [Reunderstanding Pre- and Post-liberation History], 2 vols. Ch'aeksesang, 2006.

Pak Chŏng-hŭi [Park Chung-hee]. *Minjok ŭi chŏryŏk* [The nation's potential strength]. Kwangmyŏng ch'ulp'ansa, 1971. Translated as *To Build a Nation* (Washington, DC: Acropolis Books, 1971).

Pak Kyŏng-su. *Chang Chun-ha: Minjokchuŭijaŭi kil* [Chang Chun-ha: The path of a nationalist]. Tolbegae, 2013.

Pak Myŏng-nim. "Yi Sŭngmanŭi Han'guk munje, Tong Asia kukche kwan'gye insikkwa kusang: Angmahwawa sinhwahwa, kŏn'guk tamnon'gwa pundan tamnonŭi taeribŭl nŏmŏ" [Syngman Rhee's Korea problem, his understanding and plan for international relationships in East Asia: Demonization, mythologization, and overcoming the confrontation between the discourse of foundation and the discourse of division]. *Yŏksa pip'yŏng* 83 (Summer 2008): 58–88.

Pak Sŏng-su. "Taehanmin'guk Imsijŏngbu suripkwa kŏn'guk" [The establishment of the Provisional Government of Korea and the founding of the Republic of Korea]. Paper presented at the public forum Taehanmin'guk kŏn'guk sijŏmgwa Imsijŏngbu sŏnggyŏge kwannan chaejomyŏng [Reinvestigating the relationship between the founding of the Republic of Korea and the characteristics of the Provisional Government of Korea], Seoul, South Korea, November 5, 2008, 87–120. Sŏngnam: Han'gukhak chungang yŏn'guwŏn.

Pak Sun-jong. "5.18 yugongja myŏngdan chŏnmyŏn konggaehara" [Make public the list of the recipients of the Compensation Act for the Kwangju democratic movement]. *P'enaendŭmaik'ŭ*, May 18, 2020. https://www.pennmike.com/news/articleView.html?idxno=31520.

Pak T'ae-gyun. "Haetpyŏt'chŏngch'aek: Taebuk kanggyŏngnonja 'p'ŏjugi' yŏkkong . . . Puk tobal ttaemada 'Namnamgaldŭng isyu'" [The Sunshine Policy: Hawks on North Korea blast the Sunshine Policy as "overgenerous." . . . Whenever North Korea provokes, conflict within South Korea arises]. *Kyunghyang shinmun*, November 10, 2015. https://news.khan.co.kr/kh_news/khan_art_view.html?artid=201511102044415&code=210100&s_code=af160.

——. "Nyurait'ŭŭi tŭngjanggwa yŏksainsik nonjaeng" [The emergence of the New Right and the debate on historical consciousness]. *Hwanghae munhwa* 56 (Fall 2007): 285–302.

——. *Wŏnhyŏnggwa pyŏnyong: Han'guk kyŏngje kaebal kyehwek ŭi kiwŏn* [An archetype and metamorphosis: The origins of South Korea's economic development plans]. Sŏuldaehakkyo ch'ulp'anbu, 2007.

Pak Wŏn-sun. "Paesangŭi ch'ŭngmyŏnesŏ pon kwangjuhangjaeng" [The Kwangju uprising from the perspective of compensation]. In *5.18 pŏpjŏk ch'aegim kwa yŏksajŏk ch'aegim* [Legal and historical responsibilities of the Kwangju uprising], edited by Pak Ŭn-chŏng and Han In-sŏp, 140–59. Ihwa yŏja taehakkyo ch'ulp'anbu, 1995.

Pak Yŏng-gyun. "Minjung undong kwa panchabonjŏk chuch'e" [The *minjung* movement and anticapitalistic capitalism]. *Ch'ŏlhak yŏn'gu* 102, no. 5 (2007): 13–36.

Pang Hyŏn-sŏk. *Chonjaeŭi hyŏngsik* [A form of existence]. Chung'ang M&B, 2003.

——. "Huildam munhak kwa 90-yŏndae in'gi sosŏl pip'an" [A critique on the *huildam* literature and popular novels of the 1990s]. *Wŏlgan Mal* 137 (November 1997): 144–50.

——. "Kyŏul mip'oman" [Winter Mip'oman]. *Ch'angjak kwa pip'yŏng* 25 no. 3 (1997): 72–142.

Pok Kŏ-il. "Chaengjŏm: Ch'inilmunjee taehan hamnijŏk chŏpkŭn" [At issue: A rational approach to the issue of collaboration with the Japanese]. *Ch'ŏrhak kwa hyŏnsil* 53 (Summer 2002): 134–60.

——. *Chindan kwa Ch'ŏbang: Han chayujuŭijaŭi sigak* [Diagnosis and prescription: A liberalist's point of view]. Munhak kwa chisongsa, 1994.

——. "Hondon'gwa chilssŏ saiesŏ" [Between confusion and order]. *Munhak kwa sahoe* 19, no. 2 (Summer 2006): 353–57.

——. *Hyŏnsil kwa Chihyang: Han chayujuŭijaŭi sigak* [Reality and future aims: A liberalist's point of view]. Munhak kwa chisongsa, 1990.

——. *Inyŏm ŭi him* [Power of ideology]. P'aju: Nanam, 2007.

——. "Kyŏngjejŏk chayujuŭijadŭrŭi kwaje" [The task of economic liberalists]. Paper presented at the public forum Wae tasi chayujuŭirŭl marhanŭnga, Seoul, South Korea, December 10, 2013, 3–15. Han'guk kyŏngje yŏn'guwŏn.

——. "Moksŏng chamŏnjip" [A collection of maxims from Jupiter]. *Munye chung'ang* 96 (Winter 2001): 226–79.

Pok To-hun. "Han'gugŭi SF, changnŭŭi palssaenggwa chŏngch'ijŏk muŭisik [Science fiction of South Korea: Origin of the genre and the political unconscious]. *Ch'angjak kwa pip'yŏng* 140, no. 2 (2008): 49–68.

Ryu Tong-min. "Kim Taejung ŭi kyŏngjesasang e kwanhan kŏmt'o" [Reflections on Kim Dae-jung's economic thought]. *Kiŏkkwa chŏnmang* 23 (Winter 2010): 142–71.

Sim Chin-kyŏng. "Kwŏn Yŏ-sŏn kwa hamkke *Regato* rŭl" [Reading *Legato* with Kwŏn Yŏ-sŏn]. *Ch'angjak kwa pip'yŏng* 156, no. 2 (2012): 352–68.

Sin Chi-ho. *Nyurait'ŭŭi sesangikki* [A New Right perspective on the world]. Kip'arang, 2006.

———. "Tangsinŭn ajikto 'hyŏngmyŏng'ŭl kkumkkunŭn'ga" [Are you still dreaming of "revolution"?] *Wŏlgan Kirŭl ch'annŭn saramdŭl* 92, no. 8 (1992): 158–62.

Sin Chun-bong. "Chingjingjingjing ulmyŏnsŏ magamhal ttae kajang sara ittago nŭkkyŏ" [Feeling most alive when meeting the deadline whining and crying]. *JoongAng Ilbo*, October 6, 2017. https://news.joins.com/article/21856106.

Sin Chun-yŏng. "Simch'ŭngch'ujŏk: Chŏn Tuhwan gwa Kukche insu 3saŭi kŏmŭn twitkŏrae" [Focused track: Chun Doo-hwan and the shadowy backdoor dealing in the acquisition of Kukje Group by three companies]. *Wŏlgan Mal* 88 (October 1993): 45–51.

Sin Hyŏn-jun. "Sahoe kwahak ŭi wigi?" [Crisis of social science?]. In *Chisigin rip'ot'ŭ 2: Han'guk chwap'a ŭi moksori*, edited by Hyŏndae sasang p'yŏnjipbu, 154–69. Minŭmsa, 1998.

Sin Pyŏng-sik. "Cheıkonghwaguk t'oji kaehyŏgŭi chŏngch'igyŏngje" [The political economy of the land reform of the First Republic]. *Han'guk chŏngch'ihak hoebo* 31, no. 3 (1997): 25–46.

Sin Sŭng-hŭi. "*Sŏntaek* kwa 'Ikmyŏng ui sŏm' e nat'anan Yi Mun-yŏl ŭi yŏsŏnggwan kyumyŏng" [Examining Yi Mun-yŏl's perspective on women in *Choice* and "Unnamed island"]. *Asia munhwa yŏn'gu* 40, no. 12 (2014): 55–85.

Sin Tong-ho. "Pak Chŏng-hŭi, kŭga torawatta" [Park Chung-hee, he has returned]. *Nyusŭmeik'ŏ*, April 24, 1997, 20–23.

Sŏ Chung-sŏk. *Sajin kwa kŭrim ŭro ponŭn Han'guk hyŏndaesa* [South Korea's contemporary history as seen through photos and drawings]. Yŏksa munje yŏn'guso, 2005.

Sŏ Kyŏng-sŏk. "Minjung sinhak ŭi wigi" [Crisis of *minjung* theology]. *Kidokkyo sasang* 417 (September 1993): 187–204.

Sŏ Sŏk-ku. "Ch'inundonggwŏn pyŏnhosaŭi kobaek: 'Narŭl posuhwhasik'in kŏn undonggwŏn'" [A pro-*undongkwŏn* lawyer's confession: "It was the *undongkwŏn* that turned me into a conservative"]. *Chogapchedatk'ŏm*, October 22, 2011. http://www.chogabje.com/board/column/view.asp?C_IDX=41019&C_CC=BC.

Sŏ Tong-jin. *Chayuŭi ŭiji, chagi kyebarŭl ŭiji* [Will to freedom, will to self-development]. P'aju: Tolbegae, 2009.

———. "Munhwa ŭi t'aja, chŏngchi: Minjuhwa ihuŭi munhwa kŭrigo munhwa wa chinbo rŭl saenggakhamyŏ" [Politics, the other of culture: Thinking about culture, and culture and progress since democratization]. *Munhak kwa sahoe* 20, no. 2 (2007): 267–82.

———. *Pyŏnjŭngpŏp ŭi natcham: Chŏktae wa chŏngch'i* [A nap of the dialectic: Antagonism and politics]. Kkurie buksŭ, 2014.

Sŏ Ŭn-kyŏng. "Kong Chi-yŏng non: Sŭrŏjin yŏksa ŭi kkum, kŭ sogesŏ p'iŏnan salmŭi chinsil" [On Kong Chi-yŏng: Bursting truth of life in the vanishing dream of history]. *Tonamŏ munhak* 13 (September 2000): 167–84.

Sohaengsŏng. "Abŏjirŭl chugyŏra" [Kill the fathers]. *Pwayahae pwayahae* (blog), March 10, 2007. https://m.blog.naver.com/PostView.nhn?blogId=sun2y&logNo=130015417440&proxyReferer=https%3A%2F%2Fwww.google.com%2F.

Sŏl Chun-kyu. "Somunnan chanch'i ŭi mŏgŭlgŏri: 'Segyegwan ŭi taerip'?" [Food at a talk of the town feast: "Confrontation of worldviews?"]. Review of *Everlasting Empire*, by Yi In-hwa (Segyesa, 1993). *Ch'angjak kwa pip'yŏng* 82, no. 4 (1993): 425–28.

Son Ho-ch'ŏl. "Pak Chŏng-hŭi chŏnggwŏnŭi chŏngch'ijŏk sŏnggyŏk" [Political characteristics of the Park Chung-hee regime]. *Yŏksa pip'yŏng* 23 (Winter 1993): 34–47.

———. *Sinjayujuŭi sidaeŭi Han'gukchŏngch'i* [Korean politics in the era of neoliberalism]. P'urŭnsup, 1999.

Song Kŏn-ho. "Uriyŏksa paroalja: Yi Ssŭngmanŭn kwayŏn aegukchain'ga" [Let us know our history correctly: Is Syngman Rhee a real patriot]. *Yŏksa pip'yŏng* 7 (Winter 1989): 181–86.

Song Kŏn-ho et al. *Haebang chŏnhusa ŭi insik* [*Understanding Pre- and Post-liberation History*], 6 vols. Han'gilsa, 1979–1989.

Yang Chin-o. "90 yŏndae munhak pipyŏng ŭi tu ŏlgul" [The two faces of literary criticism of the 1990s]. In *90-yŏndae munhak ŏttŏke polgŏsin'ga*, by Kim Tong-sik et al., 170–92. Minŭmsa, 1999.

———. "Mangmyŏngŭi yongmanggwa minjungŭi ch'osang" [Desire for exile and a portrait of minjung]. Review of *A Government in Exile in My Heart*, by Kim Yŏng-hyŏn (Kang ch'ulp'ansa, 1998). *Silch'ŏn munhak* 53 (Spring 1999): 366–68.

Yang Tong-an. "Kŭdŭrŭn Yi Sŭngmanŭl yŏksaesŏ chiuryŏ haetta" [They tried to erase Syngman Rhee from history]. In *Yi Sŭngman tasibogi: Uriga pŏrin kŏn'gugŭi abŏji* [Reassessing Syngman Rhee: The founding father whom we have abandoned], edited by In Po-gil, 39–44. Kip'arang, 2011.

———. "Taehanmin'guk kwa Imsijŏngbuŭi kwan'gye" [Relationship between the Republic of Korea and the Provisional Government of Korea]. In *Taehan Minguk kŏnguk ŭi chaeinsik*, edited by Yi In-ho, Kim yŏng-ho, and Kang Kyu-hyŏng, 139–63. Kip'arang, 2009.

Ye Tae-yŏl. "Nyurait'ŭwa t'algŭndaeronŭi mosunjŏk tonggŏŭi haech'erŭl wihan cheŏn: *Haebang chŏnhusa ŭi chaeinsik* ŭi panbungnolli pip'anŭl chungsimŭro" [A suggestion to dismantle the contradictory cohabitation of the New Right and postmodernism: Focusing on a critique of the anti–North Korea thesis of *Reunderstanding Pre- and Post-liberation History*]. *Han'guksa hakpo* 45 (November 2011): 207–46.

Yi Chae-hyŏn. "'Huildam hyŏnsang' e kwanhayŏ" [On "*huildam* phenomena"]. *Munhwa kwahak* 30 (Winter 2004): 180–89.

Yi Chin-hyŏng. "Minjok munhak, che3segye munhak, kŭrigo kuwŏnŭi munhak" [National literature, third world literature, and literature of salvation]. *Inmun kwahak yŏn'gu nonch'ong* 37, no. 1 (2016): 121–52.

Yi Ch'ŏl-hŭi. "Posunŭn wae Kim Dae-jungboda No Mu-hyŏnŭl tŏ sirhŏhanŭn'ga" [Why do conservatives hate Roh Moo-hyon more than Kim Dae-jung]. *Simin kwa segye* 24 (Spring 2014): 24–39.

Yi Chong-ch'ŏl and Yi Kwang-baek. *Naŭi kobaek: Chongbuk chusap'a haengwi chŭngŏnjip* [My confession: A collection of evidence by followers of North Korean *Chuch'e sasang*]. Sidae chŏngsin, 2012.

Yi Chŏng-hui. "Kŭnyŏŭi arŭmdaun sijak, kŭrigo naŭi Kong Chi-yŏngnon" [Her splendid beginning, and my thesis on Kong Chi-yŏng]. *Silch'ŏn munhak* 71 (Fall 2003): 129–46.

Yi Chu-ho, ed. "*Haebang chŏnhusa ŭi chaeinsik* e taehan ŏllonŭi panŭng" [Mass media's reaction to *Reunderstanding Pre- and Post-liberation History*]. KTUG, Korean TEX Users Group, March 2006.

Yi Chu-yŏng. "Yi sŭngman sidaeŭi posuseryŏkkwa minjujedo" [The conservative bloc of the Syngman Rhee period and the democratic system]. In *Han'guk minjujuŭi ŭi kiwŏn kwa mirae: Posuga ikkŭlda*, edited by An Pyŏng-jik, 15-40. Sidae Chŏngsin, 2011.

Yi Chun-sik. "Pak Chŏng-hŭiga Kwangbokkun? Pak Kŭn-hye yŏksagunsak'udet'aŭi chongch'agyŏk" [Park Chung-hee was in the Restoration Army? The final destination of Park Geun-hye's historical coup d'état]. *Minjungŭi sori*, October 30, 2016. http://www.vop.co.kr/A00001082911.html.

Yi Ch'ung-hun. "'Yŏngung' ŭi chŏngch'ihak—Pak Chŏng-hŭi kukkajuŭijŏk t'onghap tae minjujŏk sahoe t'onghap" [Politics of "heroes"—Park Chung-hee's state-oriented integration versus democratic social integration]. *Chŏngch'i pip'yŏng* 3 (1997): 251-61.

Yi Hae-nyŏn. "T'alssingminjuŭi wa taejungjŏk yŏngsanghwa" [Postcolonialism and mass-oriented filmic representation]. *Munhak kwa yŏngsang* 2, no. 2 (2001): 221-44.

Yi Han-u. *Unam Yi Sŭngman, Taehanmin'guk ŭl seuda* [Unam Syngman Rhee, the founder of the Republic of Korea]. Haenaem, 2008.

Yi Hye-wŏn. "Chich'igo pŏrimbadŭn abŏjidŭrŭi chahwasang: 1997-nyŏn ui hwajejak Kim Chŏng-hyŏn ŭi *Aboji*" [A self-portrait of the fathers who are weary and abandoned: The notable novel of the year 1997, Kim Chŏng-hyŏn's *Father*]. *Webzine Taesan Munhwa* (Fall 2006). http://daesan.or.kr/webzine_read.html?uid=1195&ho=18.

Yi In-hwa. *In'gan ŭi kil* [A man's road], 2 vols. Sallim, 1997-1998.

———. "*In'gan ŭi kil* e nat'anan kŭndaesŏng munje" [On the issue of modernity in *A Man's Road*]. *Sangsang* 5, no. 3 (1997): 258-76.

———. "Sŏnak ttwiŏnŏmŭn chinjŏnghan chidoja" [A true leader who overcomes good and evil]. *Hankyoreh*, May 13, 1997. https://newslibrary.naver.com/viewer/index.naver?articleId=1997051300289111003&editNo=5&printCount=1&publishDate=1997-05-13&officeId=00028&pageNo=11&printNo=2877&publishType=00010.

Yi In-yŏng. "Haksaengundong: Sŏndot'ujaengesŏ taejungsŏng kanghwaro" [The student movement: From a vanguard to the mass movement]. *Yŏksa pip'yŏng* 37 (Summer 1997): 64-86.

Yi Kwang-il. "Minjujuŭi ihaeng kwa simin undong ŭi chillo" [The democratic transition and direction of the citizens' movement]. *Simin kwa segye* 1, no. 2 (2002): 326-50.

———. *Pak Chŏng-hŭi ch'eje: Chayujuŭijŏk pip'an ttwiŏnŏmgi* [The Park Chung-hee system: Going beyond liberalist critique]. Meidei, 2011.

Yi Mun-yŏl. *Homo eksek'uttansŭ* [Homo executioner]. Minŭmsa, 2006.

———. *Sidaewaŭi purhwa* [Discord with one's time]. Chayu munhaksa, 1992.

———. *Sŏnt'aek* [Choice]. Minŭmsa, 1997.

———. *Sultanji wa chanŭl kkŭrŏdanggimyŏ* [Drawing near a wine jug and glass]. P'aju: Ach'im nara, 2001.

Yi Myŏng-wŏn. *Maŭm i sogŭm pat inde oraen mane tosŏgwan e katta* [My mind is a salt pit, and I went to the library for the first time in many days]. Saeum 2004.

———. "Yi Mun-yŏl nonjaeng: Kimanŭi susahakkwa sidaech'agojŏk ideollogi" [Yi Mun-yŏl controversy: Rhetoric in deception and anachronistic ideology]. In *P'amun: 2000nyŏn chŏnhu Han'guk munhak nonjaengŭi p'unggyŏng* [Scandal: The scene of Korean literary debates around 2000], 64-81. Saeum, 2003.

Yi Na-yŏng. "Ilbon'gun 'wianbu' undong tasi pogi: Munhwajŏk t'ŭrauma kŭkpokkwa konggamdoen ch'ŏngjungŭi hwaksan" [Reassessing the "comfort women" movement:

Overcoming cultural trauma and an expansion of empathetic audience]. *Sahoewa yŏksa* 115 (Fall 2017): 65-103.

———. "Kŭl/rok'ŏl chendŏjilssŏwa Hanbando yŏsŏngŭi mom: Ilbon'gun 'wianbu'wa Migun Kijich'on 'yanggongju'" [Global/local gender order and the body of Korean women: "Comfort women" and "Western princesses" in the camp town areas]. *Tongbang hakchi* 161 (March 2013): 3-38.

Yi Nam-ho, ed. *Yi Mun-yŏl: Chayurŭl wihan, ŏgabe taehan chinjihan t'amgu* [Yi Mun-yŏl: For liberty, a serious inquiry into oppression]. Ungjin ch'ulp'an, 1994.

Yi Sang-nok. "1980nyŏndae chungsanch'ŭng tamnon'gwa homo ek'onomik'usŭŭi hwaksan" [Expansion of the discourse on the middle class and *Homo economicus* in the 1980s]. *Sahak yŏn'gu* 130 (June 2018): 275-334.

———. "Sanŏphwa sigi 'ch'ulsse' 'sŏnggong' sŭt'oriwa paljŏnjuŭijŏk chuch'e mandŭlgi: Pak Chŏnghŭi ch'ejeesŏ t'ansaenghan 'homo ek'onomik'usŭ'rŭl chungsimŭro" [Creating "success stories" and developmental subjects during the 1960s-70s South Korea: Focusing on "Homo economicus" created during the Park Chung-hee system]. *Inmunhak yŏn'gu* 28 (Winter 2017): 43-93.

Yi Sŏng-uk. "Sosŏl munhak ŭi kyunhyŏng ŭl kidaehamyŏ" [Hoping for an equilibrium of novel]. Review of *An Old Well*, by O Chŏng-hŭi (Ch'ŏng'a ch'ulp'ansa, 1994), "And Never Said a Word" by Kim Yong-hyon (*Silch'ŏn munhak*, Summer 1994), and "An Encounter with a Younger Brother" by Yi Mun-yŏl (*Sangsang*, Summer 1994). *Silch'ŏn munhak* 35 (Fall 1994): 341-51.

Yi Sŭng-gu, Pak Myŏng-hun, Cho Pyŏng-ch'ŏl, and Chŏng In-hwa. "Chŏnggyŏngsanmaek: Han'guk kyŏngje kosoksŏngjang 20nyŏnŭi myŏngam <3> Kukche gŭrubŭi pigŭk" [Chains of politics and economy: The light and shade of the twenty years of the rapid economic development of South Korea <3> Tragedy of Kukje Group]. *Kyunghyang Shinmun*, June 29, 1991.

Yi U-yŏn. "Chosŏnin imgŭm ch'abyŏrŭi hŏgusŏng" [The fiction of wage discrimination against Koreans]. In *Panil chongjokchuŭi: Taehanmin'guk wigiŭi kŭnwŏn*, by Yi Yŏng-hun et al., 88-98. Miraesa, 2019.

———. "Kangje tongwŏn ŭi sinhwa" [The myth of forced conscription for labor]. In *Panil chongjokchuŭi: Taehanmin'guk wigiŭi kŭnwŏn*, by Yi Yŏng-hun et al., 67-76. Miraesa, 2019.

Yi Wan-bŏm. "Kŏn'guk kijŏm nonjaeng: 1919nyŏnsŏlgwa 1948nyŏnsŏrŭi yangnip" [Debates on when the Republic of Korea was founded: The coexistence of the thesis of 1919 and the thesis of 1948]. *Hyŏnsang kwa insik* 33, no. 4 (2009): 71-90.

Yi Yŏng-hun. "Kongch'angje ŭi sŏngnip kwa munhwa" [Establishment of the state-regulated prostitution and culture]. In *Panil chongjokchuŭi: Taehanmin'guk wigiŭi kŭnwŏn*, by Yi Yŏng-hun et al., 272-99. Miraesa, 2019.

———. "Kyojang insamalssŭm" [Principal's remarks]. Syngmanrhee.kr/42, n.d.

———. "P'ŭrollogŭ: Kŏjinmarŭi nara" [Prologue: A country of lies]. In *Panil chongjokchuŭi: Taehanmin'guk wigiŭi kŭnwŏn*, by Yi Yŏng-hun et al., 10-21. Miraesa, 2019.

———. *Taehanmin'guk iyagi: Haebang chŏnhusa ŭi chaeinsik ui kangŭi* [The story of the Republic of Korea: Lectures based on *Reunderstanding Pre- and Post-liberation History*]. Kip'arang, 2007.

———. *Taehanmin'guk yŏksa: Naramandŭlgi paljach'wi 1945-1987* [History of South Korea: The course of nation-making 1945-1987]. Kip'arang, 2013.

———. "Urian ui wianbu" [Comfort women within us]. In *Panil chongjokchuŭi: Taehanmin'guk wigiŭi kŭnwŏn*, by Yi Yŏng-hun et al., 254–71. Miraesa, 2019.

———. "Urido kŏn'gukchŏrŭl mandŭlja" [We, too, should have a Foundation Day]. *Dong-A Ilbo*, July 31, 2006.

———. "Wae tasi Haebang chŏnhusain'ga" [Why revisit *Understanding Pre- and Post-liberation History*]. In *Haebang chŏnhusa ŭi chaeinsik*, edited by Pak Chi-hyang et al., 1:25–63. Ch'aeksesang, 2006.

Yi Yŏng-hun, Kim Nak-nyŏn, Kim Yong-sam, Chu Ik-chong, Chŏng An-gi, and Yi U-yŏn. *Panil chongjokchuŭi: Taehanmin'guk wigiŭi kŭnwŏn* [Anti-Japanese tribalism: The origin of South Korea's crisis]. Miraesa, 2019.

Yu In-gyŏng. "Pan'golgijaesŏ kŭgunon'gaegŭro 'pip'anŭi p'en' Cho Kap-che" [From an uncompromising journalist to a far-right polemicist: Cho Kap-che, "the pen of criticism"]. *Kyunghyang Shinmun*, April 10, 2008. https://news.naver.com/main/read.nhn?mode=LSD&mid=sec&sid1=102&oid=032&aid=0001950222.

Yu In-hak. *Han'guk chaebŏrŭi haebu* [Dissecting South Korean capitalism]. P'ulbit, 1991.

Yu Kŭn-il and Hong Chin-p'yo. *Chisŏnggwa panjisŏng* [Intellect and anti-intellect]. Kip'arang, 2005.

Yu Pyŏng-mun. "Kim Se-gyun Min'gyohyŏp sangimgongdongdaep'yo: No Mu-hyŏn chŏngbunŭn sinjayujuŭijŏk kyŏngch'algukka, kidaehal kŏt ŏpta" [Kim Se-gyun, standing cochair of Min'gyohyŏp: Roh Moo-hyon government is a neoliberal police state, nothing to expect]. *Minjok 21* 66 (September 2006): 16–23.

Yu Sŏk-ch'un [Seok-Choon Lew]. "Kanhaengsa" [Preface] to *Yi Sŭngman yŏn'guŭi hŭrŭmgwa chaengjŏm*, edited by Yi Chu-yŏng et al., iii–vi. Yŏnse Taehakkyo taehakch'ulp'an munhwawŏn, 2012.

Yu Yŏng-ik [Young Ick Lew]. *Chŏlmuŭn nal ŭi Yi Sŭng-man: Hansŏng kamok saenghwal (1899–1904) kwa Okchung chapki yŏn'gu* [Syngman Rhee in his youth: A study of his life during his imprisonment in Seoul (1899–1904) and his prison writings]. Yŏnse Taehakkyo ch'ulp'anbu, 2002.

———. "Ihwajang munsŏ soge sumgyŏjin Yi Sŭngman ŭi ch'ammosŭbŭl ch'ajasŏ" [To discover the true image of Syngman Rhee buried in the documents of Ihwajang]. *Han'guksa simin'gangjwa* 35 (August 2004): 157–172.

———. *Yi Sŭng-man Taet'ongnyŏng chaep'yŏngka* [Reassessing President Syngman Rhee]. Hyŏndae Han'gukhak Yŏn'guso (IMKS), Yŏnse Taehakkyo ch'ulp'anbu, 2006.

———. *Yi Sŭngmanŭi samgwa kkum: taet'ongnyŏngi toegikkaji* [The life and dream of Syngman Rhee: Becoming president]. JoongAng Ilbosa, 1996.

Yu Yŏng-ik, Song Pyŏng-gi, Yi Myŏng-nae, O yŏng-sŏp, eds. *Yi Sŭngman tongmun sŏhanjip* [Ihwa House collection of Syngman Rhee materials in East Asian languages], 3 vols. Hyŏndae Han'gukhak Yŏn'guso (IMKS), Yŏnse Taehakkyo ch'ulp'anbu, 2009.

Yun Hae-dong. "Chedorosŏŭi yŏksahakkwa 'minjoksŏsa'ŭi mirae" [Institutional history and the future of "national history"]. *Yŏksa hakbo* 228 (Winter 2015): 151–74.

———. "Nyurait'ŭ undongkwa yŏksa insik—'piyŏksajŏk yŏksa'" [Ahistorical history: The New Right movement and its historical perspective]. *Minjok munhwa nonch'ong* 51, no. 8 (2012): 227–63.

Index

"actually existing socialism," 4, 16, 51, 102, 105, 110
Adorno, Theodor, 126
"advanced countries" (*sŏnjin'guk*), 77, 99, 100, 124, 165n17
"Aftereffect" (Kim Yŏng-hyŏn), 56
Ah Park Chung-hee (Kim Chŏng-nyŏm), 81
Alexander, Jeffrey, 16
Alternative Textbook: Korean Modern and Contemporary History, The (Textbook Forum), 97–98, 103–4, 119
An Pyŏng-jik, 113–15
And Never Said a Word (Heinrich Böll), 65
And Never Said a Word (Kim Yŏng-hyŏn), 58
"And Never Said a Word" (Kim Yŏng-hyŏn), 65
And Then There Is Their Splendid Beginning (Kong Chi-yŏng), 62
Angel of History. *See* Benjamin, Walter
Annales school, 18
anti-Americanism, 89
anti-communism, 104; Cold War, 114; of New Right, 108; scholarship, 105; of South Korean state, 96, 104; of Syngman Rhee, 110–13
Anti-Japanese Tribalism: The Origin of South Korea's Crisis (Yi Yŏng-hun et al.), 130
April 19, 1960 student uprising, 26, 108, 113
Asian Games (1986), 36
"Asiatic terror," 17

Badiou, Alain, 46, 148n6
Baudrillard, Jean, 20, 49

Benjamin, Walter, 3, 22, 119, 127, 135; Angel of History, 69, 127; on French revolutionaries, 129; Habermas and, 173n33; on "historical materialist," 128; on historicism, 128; "left-wing melancholy" and, 47; on "now-time," 127–28; on "remembrance," 21, 127, 131–33, 136; on "Thesis on the Philosophy of History," 3, 119
Bevernage, Berber, 132–33
Bolshevism, 17, 141n82
Bretton Woods Agreement, 10
Brown, Wendy, 4, 10, 148n9
Buchanan, James, 35, 145n69

Center for Free Enterprise, 35, 91–92, 162n121
chaebŏl: Center for Free Enterprise and, 35; changing attitudes toward, 146n70; conservative mass media and, 91, 163n131; as core power bloc of South Korea, 15; FKI and, 34, 145n69; *minjung* movement and, 39; as national capital (*minjok chabon*), 35; Pok Kŏ-il and, 91; state and, 7, 33–34, 35, 92, 123, 144n37; workers and, 28
Chang Ha-sŏng, 34–35
Chang Myon [Chang Myŏn], 114
Chi Su-gŏl, 119
ch'inilp'a (collaborators with Japanese colonial regime), 110, 118–19, 160n92. *See also* "pro-Japanese collaborators"
Cho, Grace M., 131
Cho Hŭi-yŏn, 36
Cho Kap-che, 81–83. *See also Posthumous Work, The*; *Spit on My Grave*; *Yugo!*

Ch'oe Chang-jip [Jang-jip Choi], 15, 26, 150n49
Ch'oe Kap-su, 18–19
Ch'oe Wŏn-sik, 27, 48
Ch'oe Yun, 53
Choice (Yi Mun-yŏl), 124, 162n112
Cho-Joong-Dong, 80, 92; literary complex, 88. *See also* conservative mass media
Chŏn Sang-in, 109, 111–12
Chŏng Hae-gu, 77
Chŏng Hong-su, 46, 68–69
Chŏng Kyŏng-a, 133–34
chongbuk chwap'a, 15, 140n68
Chŏngdaehyŏp (Korean Council for the Women Drafted for Military Sexual Slavery by Japan), 134, 176n87
Chŏnkyojo (Korean Teachers and Educational Workers Union), 60, 89, 161n105
Chŏnnohyŏp (Council of Trade Unions, NCTU), 24, 39, 41
chuch'e sasang, 101–2, 107, 140n68
Chun Doo-hwan, 8, 26, 76; economic development model of, 31; *Hanahoe* and, 155n22; indictment of, 12, 76; neoliberal measures of, 30–31; Park Chung-hee and, 74; Roh Tae-woo and, 24–25; social movement and, 36–37, 46; "society of justice" (*chŏngŭi kuhyŏn*) and, 74; survey of, 71
chusap'a (followers of *chuch'e sasang*), 101, 165nn20–21
citizen (*simin*), 11, 20–21, 24–25, 39–40, 44; paradigm shift from *minjung* to, 2, 4, 7, 9, 11, 20–21, 24–25, 44, 47–48, 57, 70
citizens' movement (*simin undong*), 20, 27–28, 36–40, 43
Citizens' Movement to Obtain a Democratic Constitution, 27
"civil war," 13, 21
"cleanse the past" (*kwagŏ ch'ŏngsan*), 88
Cold War, 14, 29, 124, 136; anti-communism, 6, 11, 90, 114, 164n12; continuing in Korea, 14–16, 20, 96, 101–2, 124; global end of, 24, 35, 52, 113; mentality, 104–5; security agenda, 136; and Syngman Rhee, 109; and United States, 87, 106. *See also* anti-communism
"Collection of Maxims from Jupiter, A" (Pok Kŏ-il), 91–92
"colonial modernization," 98

"comfort women" (*wiwanbu*), 130–31, 133–34, 136, 176n86; New Right and, 133, 174n64; statues of, 136, 176n91
"Comfort Women" Report (Chŏng Kyŏng-a), 133–34
Connerton, Paul, 80
conservative mass media, 5–6: as a core power bloc in South Korea, 15; intellectuals and, 90–91; during Kim Dae-jung and Roh Moo-hyun governments, 26, 90; during Kim Young-sam government, 75, 79; New Right and, 5, 15–16, 98–99, 103; Park Chung-hee syndrome and, 5–6, 72, 79, 80, 88, 94; *polifessor* and, 93; revisionist scholarship of Syngman Rhee and Park Chung-hee and, 111; during Yusin period, 79. *See also* Cho-Joong-Dong
"crisis of literature," 48–53
Cultural Revolution, 16, 89, 150n57
"culturedness" (*kyoyang*), 93
"culture war" 16, 21, 71. *See also* "civil war"
Cumings, Bruce, 76, 109

"Dawn Is Coming" (Kong Chi-yŏng), 62
"Decency toward Human Beings" (Kong Chi-yŏng), 64
Deep River Flows Far Away (Kim Yŏng-hyŏn), 58
"Deep River Flows Far Away" (Kim Yŏng-hyŏn), 57
democracy, 2, 4, 7, 8, 11, 13, 29, 31, 32, 42, 46, 74, 76, 80, 84, 105–6, 113, 115, 120, 134; authoritarianism versus, 73, 79, 94; crisis of, 35; "free market," 4, 10; Kim Dae-jung's participatory, 33; mass, 123; *minjung* (people)-oriented, 104; parliamentary, 6, 8, 24, 123–24; "procedural," 26; "substantial," 26; triumph of, 13; "whole" or "complete," 26. *See also* liberal democracy
Democratic Justice Party. *See* Roh Tae-woo
Democratic Liberal Party (DLP). *See* Kim Young-sam
Democratic Republican Party. *See* Park Chung-hee
"democratic union" (*minju nojo*), 42, 147n111
democratization, 8, 20, 98–99; from above, 37, 56; citizens' movement and, 37–38; discourse of de-democratization, 135; as neoliberalism, 31; Park Chung-hee and, 73–75, 78; Pok Kŏ-il and, 91; Yi Yŏng-hun and, 129

democratization movement, 2, 8–9, 23, 32, 42, 84, 87; evaluation of Korean history and, 79, 117; immediately after 1987, 25; Kim Dae-jung and, 32, 125; Kim Young-sam and, 23; literature and, 48; Roh Moo-hyun and, 125. *See also minjung* movement
Dietze, Mary, 39
Dirlik, Arif, 18, 44
"DJnomics," 33, 145n60
Duara, Prasenjit, 119

Eight-Person Political Conference, 27
election: 1956 presidential, 114; 1960 presidential, 167n65; 1963 presidential, 115; 1987 presidential, 7–8, 25–26, 28, 60; 1988 parliamentary, 23, 142n2; 1997 presidential, 33
Eley, Geoff, 17
emergency measures. *See* Park Chung-hee
Everlasting Empire (Yi In-hwa), 88

"Faraway Encounter, A" (Kim Yŏng-hyŏn), 59
Father (Kim Chŏng-hyŏn), 86–87, 94
Federation of Korean Industries (FKI), 34, 145n69
feminism, 87, 90
Fifth Republic. *See* Chun Doo-hwan
"forced labor," 130
"forced military conscription" (*kangje chingchip*), 57, 59
Form of Existence, A (Pang Hyŏn-sŏk), 56
Foucault, Michel, 4, 40, 49
four legislative reforms (*sadae ipbŏp*), 100, 164n15
French Revolution, 6–7, 16–18, 141n92. *See also* Furet, François
French revolutionaries, 129
"Frozen Republic," 95
Fukuyama, Francis, 7, 106, 132, 175n76
Furet, François, 16–17. *See also Interpreting the French Revolution*

garrison decrees, 73
Geist (*Sidae chŏngsin*, journal), 104, 165n20
Germany 51, 57, 78, 125–26, 159n83; Nazi, 89, 126; New Right in, 17; West, 55, 65, 122. *See also* historians' dispute (West Germany)
Ginzburg, Carlo, 122
"Glass Shoes" (Kim In-suk), 61

globalization, 4, 9, 15, 47; Kim Young-sam government's drive for, 25, 32; literature and, 49; New Right and, 99; as *segyehwa*, 15. *See also* neoliberalism
"Government in Exile in My Heart, A" (Kim Yŏng-hyŏn), 58
government-vested properties, 113
Gramsci, Antonio, 148n5
Grand National Party (Hannaradang), 118–19
Great Struggle of Workers (1987), 24, 28, 41

Habermas, Jürgen, 126, 157n50, 173n27, 173n33
han (long-accumulated suffering), 81
Hanahoe (Group of One), 25, 76, 155n22
Han'guk noch'ong (Federation of Korean Trade Unions, FKTU), 24, 41–42, 44
Han River, 62–63, 67
Hayek, Friedrich, 35, 145n69
historians' dispute (West Germany), 17, 125–26
"historiographical apparatus," 6, 16, 79–80
history of everyday life (*Alltagsgeschichte*), 123
Hobsbawm, Eric, 121
Holocaust, 18, 130
Homo Executans (Yi Mun-yŏl), 90, 162n109
Homo oeconomicus, 4–5, 130–31, 135
Hong, Grace Kyungwon, 10
Hong Yun-gi, 80, 82–84
Honnet, Axel, 131–32
hubae (one's junior in school or work), 65
huildam (literature of reminiscence), 21, 45–48, 55–56; Kim In-suk and, 59–61; Kim Yŏng-hyŏn and, 58–59, 65–66; Kong Chi-yŏng and, 61–64; Kwŏn Yŏ-sŏn and, 66–70; Pang Hyŏn-sŏk and, 45, 56–57; *undongkwŏn* and, 56–57
hujin'guk (backward country), 100
Huyssen, Andreas, 78, 83
Hwang Chang-yŏp, 102
Hwang Chong-yŏn [Hwang Jongyon], 49–50, 53, 149n35
Hwang Pyŏng-ju [Hwang Byeong-ju], 74
"Hwang Sŏk-yŏng Manifesto," 54

Im Tae-sik, 9
"IMF crisis," 4, 8, 32–35, 43, 100, 123–24, 138n21, 148n118
Independence Club, 108, 110
"industrial soldier," 86
"Insect" (Kim Yŏng-hyŏn), 59

Institute for Modern Korean Studies (IMKS).
  See Yu Yŏng-ik [Young Ick Lew]
International Monetary Fund (IMF), 30–32
Interpreting the French Revolution (Furet), 17
"irregular" (*pijŏnggyujik*) workers, 33, 136

Japan, 2, 7, 51, 89, 97, 125; Meiji, 84; modern literature of, 51; neoconservative ideologues of, 101; South Korea's normalization of relations with, 106
Japanese colonialism, 4, 13, 88–89, 108, 117; "comfort women" during, 133–34; as discussed in *Anti-Japanese Tribalism*, 130, 133; KAPF and, 55; legacies of, 89, 98; liberation from, 104, 111, 116; properties owned by Japanese during, 113; resistance to, 84–85, 107, 161n103; "unresolved issues" related to, 88–89, 99
Japanese governor-general building, demolition of, 12, 76
Japanese Manchurian Military School. *See* Park Chung-hee
June Uprising (1987), 26, 36, 38, 46; as middle-class revolution, 28–29, 143n21

Karatani, Kojin, 51
Khulumani Support Group (South Africa), 133
Kim Chi-ha, 93, 142n5
Kim Chin-myŏng. *See Rose of Sharon Has Blossomed, The*
Kim Chŏng-hyŏn. *See Father*
Kim Chŏng-nan, 50, 54, 158n67
Kim Chŏng-nyŏm. *See Ah Park Chung-hee; Thirty Years of Korean Economic Policy*
Kim Chong-yŏp, 26
Kim Dae-jung: *chaebŏl* and, 35; conservatives and, 15, 99–100, 103; Government of the People of, 8; labor and, 43, 123; mass media and, 26; merger of the party of, 28; neoliberal measures of, 8, 32–33; 1988 general election and, 142n2; NSL and, 15; Pan-national Promotion Commission for Second National Foundation and, 170n99; Park Chung-hee memorial building and, 154n3; Pok Kŏ-il and, 92, 163n127; rectification of history and, 13, 88–89; reform projects of, 105; Sunshine Policy of, 15; Truth and Reconciliation Commission and, 161n102; welfare policy of, 145n61; Yi Mun-yŏl and, 88, 90, 162n109

Kim Ho-gi, 38
Kim Il Sung, 85, 89, 102, 110, 150n49
Kim In-suk, 59–61, 65. *See also* "Glass Shoes"; "To a Fellow Hide-and-Seek Player"
Kim Jae Ik [Kim Chae-ik], 30
Kim Jong-pil, 23, 28, 75
Kim Myŏng-in, 49, 53, 62, 67
Kim Tong-ch'un (Dong-Choon Kim), 39
Kim Ŭn-ha, 61, 63–64
Kim Yŏng-hwan, 101–2
Kim Yŏng-hyŏn 56–57, 59. *See also* "Aftereffect"; *And Never Said a Word*; "And Never Said a Word"; *Deep River Flows Far Away*; "Deep River Flows Far Away"; "Faraway Encounter, A"; "Government in Exile in My Heart, A"; "Insect"; "Wisteria"
Kim Yŏng-min, 88
Kim Young-sam, 1, 12; Civilian Government of, 8; DLP and, 23; Eight-Person Political Conference and, 27; neoliberal measures of, 32, 43; Park Chung-hee syndrome and, 21, 71, 78, 80–81; rectification of history (*yŏksa parojapki*) and, 12, 76–77; reforms of, 79; Reunification Democratic Party and, 23; *segyehwa* and, 32; *sin Han'guk* (New Korea) and, 32
Kong Chi-yŏng, 48, 55–56, 60–62. See also *And Then There Is Their Splendid Beginning*; "Dawn Is Coming"; "Decency toward Human Beings"; *Mackerel*; *There Is No More Beautiful Wandering*; "What Is to Be Done"
kŏn'gukchŏl (day of founding of the Republic of Korea), 116–19
Korea Artista Proleta Federacio (KAPF), 55, 150n56, 158n71
Korea Central Intelligence Agency (KCIA), 72, 86, 155n22
Korea Democratic Party, 109
Korean Provisional Government (KPG), 108, 117–18, 171n112
"Korean-style democracy" (*Han'gukchŏk minjujuŭi*). *See* Park Chung-hee
Korean War, 59, 73, 88–89, 98, 109; revisionist scholarship of, 109–10; in *Tae Guk Gi: The Brotherhood of War* (film), 138n48; transgenerational trauma of, 131
"Korean wave" (*hallyu*), 11
Korea Tripartite Commission, 43, 148n120
Ku Hyo-sŏ, 50, 52

kwangbokchŏl (Day of Liberation), 116
Kwangju Uprising, 12, 67, 69, 76, 138n21, 139n52, 139n57; filmic representation of, 139n52, 143n21; literary representation of, 66–67, 69; television dramas of, 12, 139n52
Kwŏn Hŭi-yŏng, 112
Kwŏn Sŏng-u, 52, 58
Kwŏn Yŏ-sŏn, 66–67. See also *Legat'o*
Kyŏngsillyŏn (Citizens' Coalition for Economic Justice, CCEJ), 38

land reform, 112–13, 168n85
left-wing melancholy, 47, 148n9
Legat'o (Kwŏn Yŏ-sŏn), 66–69
Lepenies, Wolf, 16
Les lieux de mémoire, 123. See also Nora, Pierre
liberal democracy, 1, 7, 11, 17, 20–21, 25, 27, 164n12; Carl Schmitt and, 39; as Cold War anticommunism, 176n12; conservatives' principle of, 100; as founding principle of South Korea, 99, 106, 129, 135; Francis Fukuyama and, 132; middle class and, 40; North Korea and, 102; post-1987 as, 44; Syngman Rhee and, 108, 113–15
liberalists, 91, 162n114
Liberty Union (Chayujuŭi yŏndae), 99, 100, 103
literary field (*mundan*), 45, 48–49, 54–55
literary power (*munhak kwŏllyŏk*), 54–55, 88
literature of engagement. See *minjung*: literature
Löwy, Michael, 129
Lyotard, Jean-François, 16; *Différend*, 130

Mackerel (Kong Chi-yŏng), 62–63
Maier, Charles, 123, 126, 172n9
"Make America Great Again," 123
Man's Road, A (Yi In-hwa), 84
martial law, 73, 154n11
Marx, Karl, 49, 128–29, 174n53
Marxism, 51, 101, 140n75; and Leninism, 37, 102; political, 16
Marxist: historical narratives, 18; ideology, 91; revolutionary movements, 121; social theory, 16
mass consumption, 53
mass media, 1–2, 16, 32, 37. See also conservative mass media
"May 16 revolution," 74. See also military coup d'état: of Park Chung-hee
McClure, Kirstie, 40

memory, 5, 11–12, 21, 67–68, 69, 79; collective, 2, 6, 97–98, 123; construction of, 21, 72; contestation over, 5, 11, 21, 79; countermemory, 79, 84; "excess" of, 12; hypertrophy (Nietzsche) of, 78; of the 1980s, 60, 62, 67–68; of Park Chunghee and his regime, 72, 74, 80, 94; realms of, 6; reconstruction of, 21, 79, 98; social, 5–6, 21, 80; in Walter Benjamin, 119, 122, 136
middle class, 11, 36, 58, 63, 113, 138n44; ethnographical study of, 147n96; global discourse of 39–40; as leading June Uprising, 28, 143n21; *simin undong* and, 29, 38; *undongkwŏn* and, 58, 63–64. See also petit bourgeoisie (*sosimin*)
military coup d'état: of Chun Doo-hwan (1979), 25, 30, 74; of Park Chung-hee (1961), 74, 82
"military sexual slavery." See "comfort women"
minjok (nation), 8–9, 49; *chabon* (national capital) and *chaebŏl*, 35; history of, 82; literature, 48
Minju noch'ong (Korean Confederation of Trade Unions, KCTU), 39–43, 148n120
minjung (people), 2–3; historiography, 2, 96, 103, 106–7; in *huildam*, 63, 68, 70; literature, 48–54; minjung-ism, 51, 99; minjung-oriented democracy, 104; minjung-oriented scholars, 79; paradigm shift from, 2, 4, 7, 9, 11, 20–21, 24–25, 44; post-1987, 8, 9, 44; revolution, 61; theologians, 100
minjung discourse, 2, 19; *chaebŏl* and, 35; demise of, 24–25, 35–37
minjung movement, 7, 9, 21, 24, 26, 36, 42; citizens' movement and, 37–39; disavowal of, 3, 5, 22, 101; *huildam* and, 21, 46–48; in post-1987 era, 26–28, 32, 42
"Miracle on the Han River," 5
monumental history. See Nietzsche, Friedrich
Mothers of the Plaza de Mayo (Argentina), 133

National Security Law (NSL), 14, 102, 114, 140n64, 140n67, 164n15
"*nektie pudae*" (necktie corps), 28
neoliberalism, 4, 15, 20, 32, 44, 47, 101, 143n26; academic discussion of, 5; conflation with democratization, 31–32, 135; culture and, 5; democracy and, 4, 11, 21, 39, 44, 123; discourse of *sŏnjin'guk* and, 124; as economic policy before 1987, 29–31; former *undongkwŏn* and, 9, 102; as governing rationality, 4, 10, 137n12; labor and, 40; post–World War II social movements and, 4, 10

Index 211

neoliberal restructuring, 4, 5, 9–10, 20, 25, 79, 98, 135; *chaebŏl* and, 35; during Kim Dae-jung government, 32–33, 123; during Kim Young-sam government, 32; labor flexibility and, 40, 43; prior to 1987, 30
"New Christian Right," 100
New Daily, 111
New Democratic Republican Party (NDRP). *See* Kim Jong-pil
New Right: *Alternative Textbook* and, 97–98; Cold War and, 15; conservative mass media and, 15–16, 79, 98; debates on *kŏn'gukchŏl* and, 116–19; as elites, 100; historiography, 7, 94, 98–99, 103, 105, 107; Liberty Union and, 99, 100; neoliberalism and, 102; North Korea and, 101–3, 107; publications of, 104; scholarship, 2–3, 5, 13, 22, 108; studies of Park Chung-hee, 114–16; studies of Syngman Rhee, 108–14; Textbook Forum and, 106–8; textbook revisions by, 4, 13; as triumphalist discourse, 14, 21; *undongkwŏn* and, 93; in West Germany, 17; Yi In-hwa and, 84; Yi Yŏng-hun and, 96
Nietzsche, Friedrich, 78, 83, 125
1960s, 15–16, 122; in North America, 152n88
1968 generation, 52, 101
1987ch'eje (1987 system), 8, 25–29
1991 May struggle, 24
Nolte, Ernst, 17
Nora, Pierre, 6
"now-time" (*Jetztzeit*). *See* Benjamin, Walter

Olympic Games (1988), 36
Organisation for Economic Co-operation and Development (OECD), 32, 33
Orwell, George, 50

Paek Ki-wan, 26
Pak Myŏng-nim, 27, 117
Pak Sŏng-su, 118, 170n102
Pak Yŏng-gyun, 37, 42
Pang Hyŏn-sŏk, 45, 56–57. *See also Form of Existence, A*
Park, Hyun Ok, 11
Park Chung-hee, 1, 4–5, 13, 26, 36, 72–75; assassination of, 30, 73–74, 85, 159n82; assessment of, 73–74; biographies of, 81–83; commemoration of (pre-1997), 75, 156n17; defense of military coup, 82; development state of, 14, 29; Democratic Republican Party of, 74, 155n17; economic development plans, of, 30–31; emergency decrees of, 73, 154n11; garrison decrees, 73, 154n11; Japanese military academy and, 84; Kim Dae-jung and, 32–33, 154n3; Kim Jong-pil and, 28; Kim Young-sam and, 78; "Korean-style democracy" (*Han'gukchŏk minjujuŭi*) of, 115, 169n94; literary representation of, 83–87, 124; scholarship on, 95–98
Park Chung-hee syndrome, 2–3, 12, 15–16, 21, 71, 77; conservative mass media and, 79–81, 88, 93–94; New Right and, 102–4, 106, 108, 114–16, 119
Park Geun-hye, 75, 93, 171n115
passive revolution, 19, 42
patricide, 160n92
petite bourgeoisie (*sosimin*), 47, 56, 59
"phenomenon of polarization" (*yanggŭkhwa hyŏnsang*), 8
Pok Kŏ-il: conservative mass media and, 92–93; defense of *chaebŏl*, 91–92; as liberalist, 90–91; as public intellectual, 92; 162n114. *See also* "Collection of Maxims from Jupiter, A"; *Power of Ideology*; *Reality and Future Aim*
polifessor, 93
politics of confusion, 31, 123, 144n43
politics of time, 3–4, 6, 22, 123, 129, 133–35
popular culture, 4, 11, 21, 53; in *The Cheese and the Worms*, 122; mass consumption and, 53; "massification" of, 3; *minjung* movement in, 9
postcolonial: approach, 107; nationalism, 160n85; scholarship, 22; theories, 107, 166n34
Posthumous Work, The (Cho Kap-che), 81
postmodern, 9; theory, 16, 19; thinking, 16
postmodernism, 51; Korean literary field and, 54; Korean translations of texts of, 20
postmodernity, 16, 19–20
Power of Ideology (Pok Kŏ-il), 91
"pro-Japanese collaborators," 2, 13, 89, 109. *See also ch'inilp'a*
"pro-North Korea," 89–91. *See also chongbuk chwap'a*
public intellectuals, 92–93, 163n128
"purposive rationality" (*mokchŏk hamnisŏng* or *Zweckrationalität*), 114–15
Pusan-Masan uprising (1979), 30, 73

"radical noncontemporaneity," 133
Rancière, Jacques, 3, 133

Reagan, Ronald, 10, 34, 83, 91, 123, 165n28
Reaganomics, 31
Reality and Future Aim (Pok Kŏ-il), 91
realms of memory (*Les lieux de mémoire*). *See* Nora, Pierre
"rectification of history" (*yŏksa parojapki*), 12, 75–76
Red Terror, 17
regime of discontinuity, 7, 20, 25; function of, 20; *huildam* as, 21, 47, 49, 66; of New Right, 13; Park Chung-hee syndrome as, 21–22, 72, 80; Pierre Nora and, 6; politics of time and, 22, 135; as triumphalist discourse, 16
retrospective justice, 125, 132–33. *See also* transitional justice
Reunderstanding Pre- and Post-liberation History (Park Chi-hyang et al.), 95–96, 103–6
Rhee, Syngman, 7, 13, 96, 108–11; anticommunism of, 110; on *ch'inilp'a*, 110; in New Right scholarship, 13, 96, 104, 106, 108–9, 111–14, 119; *sa-sa o-ip* constitutional revision and, 141, 168n86; scholarly assessment of, 109–10; Syngman Rhee Society, 167n72
Ricoeur, Paul, 80
Roh Moo-hyun: *chaebŏl* and, 35; conservatives and, 15, 99–100, 103; "foundation" of South Korea and, 170n99; labor and, 43; mass media and, 26; neoliberal measures of, 8; Participatory Government of, 8; rectification of history and, 13, 88–89; reform projects of, 105; Yi Mun-yŏl and, 88–90, 162n109
Roh Tae-woo, 23–24; Chun Doo-hwan and, 24; Democratic Justice Party and, 23; election of, 25; *Hanahoe* and, 155n22; indicted, 76; Kwangju massacre and, 12; secret slush fund of, 77, 142n3
Rose of Sharon Has Blossomed, The (Kim Chinmyŏng), 86, 94, 124
Rüsen, Jörn, 122, 125
Ryōma Goes His Way (Shiba Ryōtarō), 84, 158n70

samsŏn kaehŏn ("revision of the constitution for a third term"), 115
Samsung Republic, 35
Sandglass (television drama), 12, 139n52
sa-sa o-ip constitutional revision. *See* Rhee, Syngman
Schmitt, Carl, 39, 157n50

segyehwa (internationalization). *See* Kim Young-sam
Shapiro, Ann-Louise, 78
simin (citizen). *See* citizen
Sin Chi-ho, 100, 165n18, 165n21
Sŏ Tong-jin, 26, 40, 54, 147n98
sŏnbae (one's senior in school or work), 63–65
Song, Jesook, 40
Song Kŏn-ho, 109–10
Soviet Union, 6, 17, 110, 167n67; breakdown of, 4, 16, 24, 51, 105
Spit on My Grave (Cho Kap-che), 81–83, 157n50
"Statue of a Girl for Peace" (*Sonyŏsang*), 136, 176n91. *See also* "comfort women"
Sunshine Policy, 15, 92

"temporal Manichaeism," 132
Thatcher, Margaret, 10, 34, 83, 91, 102, 123, 165n28
Therborn, Göran, 39
There Is No More Beautiful Wandering (Kong Chi-yŏng), 62
third world, 18–19, 156n44
Thirty Years of Korean Economic Policy (Kim Chŏng-nyŏm), 81
"386 generation," 9, 28, 56, 60, 61–63
"To a Fellow Hide-and-Seek Player" (Kim In-suk), 60–61
totalitarianism, 17, 91, 168n88
"transborder redress culture," 136
"transgenerational haunting," 131
transitional justice, 125, 134, 136. *See also* retrospective justice
Truth and Reconciliation Commission (TRC), 88–89, 161nn102–103

Understanding Pre- and Post-liberation History (Song Kŏn-ho et al.), 95–96, 103–5
undongkwŏn, 9, 21, 45–48, 55–65, 66–69, 93, 100–102, 107, 135, 151n64, 152n91, 152n94, 161n105
United States, 7, 63, 86, 114, 117, 118, 123; Cato Institute in, 35; Cold War and, 87, 106; Kim Daejung's exile in, 33; Korean PhDs in economics in, 31, 144n39; liberalization pressure from, 31; neoliberalism in, 10, 34; North Korea and, 102; Park Chung-hee and, 115, 159n81; South Korea's unequal relationship with, 39, 96; Syngman Rhee and, 109–10, 112–13; transgenerational trauma of Koreans in, 131; Yi Mun-yŏl on, 89

Index 213

US Military Government in Korea (1945–1948), 89, 112, 113–14

"Veritable Record, Park Chung-hee" (serialization in *JoongAng Ilbo*), 80
Vietnam War, 106

Wang Hui, 20
"war of position," 16
Washington Consensus, 30
Wednesday noon protest, 136
"What Is to Be Done" (Kong Chi-yŏng), 63–64
White, Hayden, 80
"Wisteria" (Kim Yŏng-hyŏn), 58
World War I, 17, 127, 170n104
World War II, 4 18, 65, 116, 174n64

Yang Tong-an, 117
"yellow unions" (company friendly, or *ŏyong*), 42
Yi In-hwa 84–85, 88. See also *Everlasting Empire*; *Man's Road, A*

Yi Mun-yŏl: conservative mass media and, 88–90, 92–93; on feminism, 90; Kim Daejung and Roh Moo-hyun governments and, 88–90; literary power and, 88; as public intellectual, 92. See also *Choice*; *Homo Executans*
Yi U-yŏn, 130
Yi Wan-bŏm, 118
Yi Yŏng-hun, 96, 104–7, 111–12, 116, 129–30, 133
Yoneyama, Lisa, 108, 136
yŏnjwaje (guilt by association), 89
yŏsoyadae (the ruling party as the minority in the National Assembly), 23
Yu Sŏk-ch'un, 111, 167n58
Yu Yŏng-ik (Young Ick Lew), 111–13, 167n72, 168n73
Yugo! (Cho Kap-che), 157n52
Yun Hae-dong, 104
Yusin, 72–73, 86, 79, 115, 155n17, 169n94

Zenkyoto, 101
Zola, Émile, 50

www.ingramcontent.com/pod-product-compliance
Lightning Source LLC
Chambersburg PA
CBHW050243170426
43202CB00015B/2896